DEVELOPING COMMUNICATION SKILLS

Second Edition

KRISHNA MOHAN

MEERA BANERJI

Birla Institute of Technology and Science
Pilani, Rajasthan

UNIVERSITY SCIENCE PRESS

(An Imprint of Laxmi Publications Pvt. Ltd.)

An ISO 9001:2015 Company

BENGALURU • CHENNAI • GUWAHATI • HYDERABAD • JALANDHAR
KOCHI • KOLKATA • LUCKNOW • MUMBAI • RANCHI
NEW DELHI

DEVELOPING COMMUNICATION SKILLS

Printed and bound in India

First Edition : 1990, *Reprinted* : 1994-2008 (*twenty-one times*), *Second Edition* : 2009

Reprinted : 2009, 2010, 2011, 2012, 2016, 2017, 2018, 2019, 2021, *Edition* : 2023

ISBN : 978-93-84872-89-2

Branches

Bengaluru	080-26 75 69 30
Chennai	044-24 34 47 26
Guwahati	0361-254 36 69
Hyderabad	040-27 55 53 83
Jalandhar	0181-222 12 72
Kochi	0484-405 13 03
Kolkata	033-40 04 77 79
Lucknow	0522-430 36 13
Ranchi	0651-224 24 64

PUBLISHED IN INDIA BY

UNIVERSITY SCIENCE PRESS

(An Imprint of Laxmi Publications Pvt. Ltd.)

An ISO 9001:2015 Company

113, GOLDEN HOUSE, GURUDWARA ROAD, DARYAGANJ,

NEW DELHI - 110002, INDIA

Telephone : 91-11-4353 2500, 4353 2501

www.laxmipublications.com

info@laxmipublications.com

C—00000/023/01

Printed at : Ajit Printing Press, Delhi.

Preface to the Second Edition

There has been a steady demand for this book since its publication in 1990 and to sustain the flow of supply it has been reprinted nineteen times so far. The feedback attained from the users of the book, our own experience in using it as a textbook for on-campus courses and those offered to professionals under the distance learning programmes, have prompted us to review its contents. While reviewing, we have also kept in mind the changes made in the syllabi of several universities. These changes have emanated from the realisation that communication is a multi-disciplinary subject and that proficiency in communication skills is a basic requirement for success and advancement in almost all professions. This exercise of reviewing has led us to update, revise and enlarge the present volume. The new chapters and appendices that have been added are as follows:

Chapters

- Memorandum Writing
- Words often Confused
- Common Errors
- Editing and Proofreading
- Communication through Technology
- Active Listening
- Public Speaking and Oral Presentation
- Reading Comprehension
- Precis Writing

Appendices

- Fundamentals of Speech
- Basics of Grammar

Besides making relevant changes in several chapters, samples of **brochure, technical report, research paper, technical article** and **correspondence** have been added at appropriate places. We hope that, with these changes, this edition would be better able to cater to the needs and requirements of a wider audience.

We express our profound gratitude to Professor L.K. Maheshwari, Vice-Chancellor, Birla Institute of Technology and Science, Pilani, who has been a source of inspiration in our academic pursuits. Our erstwhile colleagues, Professor Meenakshi Raman (Chief Publication and Media Relations Unit) Dr. Pushp Lata, and Dr. Sanjay Kumar, deserve our thanks for their support and encouragement. We are especially grateful to Dr. Sangeeta Sharma for her help in making available some of the references and materials we required for the revision. We are indebted to our students, Mr. Abhimanyu Gopalka and Mr. Gaurav Roongta, for providing us a sample technical report and Ms. Meeta Banerji and Sri Alok Srivastava for facilitating the task of revision. We also sincerely thank Sri Sita Ram Gopalka for word-processing the additional material promptly and efficiently.

We dedicate with affection this work to our dear readers and wish them success in acquiring the skills of oral and written communication. We also urge them to convey to us their suggestions for further improvement.

Krishna Mohan
Meera Banerji

PREFACE TO THE FIRST EDITION

With rapid industrialisation and economic growth in the country there has been an enormous increase in the number and size of professional organisations. As communication plays a vital role in the smooth functioning of an organisation, the need to impart communication skills has assumed greater importance. A realisation of this need by some universities has led to the introduction of courses such as, 'oral and written communication', 'executive communication', 'management communication', 'technical communication', etc. One can also observe a growing tendency to include 'communication skills' as part of the training schemes for young managers and the executive development programmes run by reputed institutions. It is however found that adequate and relevant instructional materials are not available for guidance and practice. This book has been designed to fill this gap.

The selection of materials is unique inasmuch as it is based on the observation of communication behaviour through field investigation and analysis of data collected from about 225 professionals belonging to different organisations. The data are fairly representative as these organisations are located in various parts of the country and are engaged in such diverse activities as management, production, consultancy, research, etc. A significant discovery of this study is that, whatever be the profession, the same skills are used in varying degrees for communication in different organisations.

Though the book is intended for use at an advanced level in Indian Universities, it is likely to prove to be of direct relevance to the professional in performing his communicative tasks. It would also prove equally useful to anyone who wishes to improve his communication skills. The coverage is comprehensive and self-contained and the approach is practical, making the book suitable both for classroom use and individual self-study.

The volume is divided into four parts. In Part One the theory of human communication has been briefly discussed. The aspects having a direct bearing on communication have been highlighted. The discussion includes the role of body language and proximity in oral interaction and the pattern of flow of communication in an organisation. The main focus of the book is on the elements and characteristics of major forms of oral and written communication. Their types, structure and style have been described in detail in Parts Two and Three respectively. Part Four has been added to provide useful material for ready reference by the reader. It is intended to help him take care of the mechanical details which enhance the effectiveness of written communication.

The book contains numerous specimens, vivid illustrations, and telling examples to elucidate the principles discussed and the ideas presented. The hints and guidelines have been selected for their utilitarian value. For practice, plenty of assignments are given at the end of each Chapter in Parts Two and Three. If done assiduously, they would enable the reader to acquire proficiency in speaking and writing skills for various professional purposes.

This book has been written under the University Grants Commission Scheme of Production of University Level Books by Indian Authors. We are grateful to the Commission for having sanctioned the project and for providing financial assistance for its completion. We express our sincere gratitude to Dr. S. Venkateswaran, Director, Birla Institute of Technology and Science, Pilani for his continuous encouragement and for making available necessary facilities for the completion of the project.

Our special thanks are due to Dr. S.N. Pathak, Reader in English, for going through the manuscript and making valuable suggestions for improvement and to Miss Sonia Chandhoke and Sri Aniruddh Kumar Srivastava for assistance in collecting material for illustrations. We acknowledge our debt to Sri K.C. Gupta, Assistant Librarian, for making the required books and journals readily available for reference, Sri H.S Kulhari for getting the typescript ready with speed and efficiency and Sri K.N. Sharma for preparing the figures at short notice.

We would like to thank Dr. R.K. Patnaik, Dean, Instruction Division and our friends and colleagues, Dr. P.D. Chaturvedi, Dr. S.D. Misra, Dr. G. Tripathi, Sri J.P. Varma, Dr. (Mrs.) S. Vasudeva, Mrs. K. Aruna and Mrs. Reeta Mukerjee for their encouragement in writing the book.

We would like to record our special debt to Late Sri N.N. Banerji, who was a source of constant inspiration for this project. He cheerfully sacrificed the time which rightfully belonged to him to facilitate the completion of this task.

We are also grateful to the following students who helped us in various ways to complete this project: Miss Seema Lall and Sarvasri Ramendra Singh Baoni, Rakesh Gcenka, S. Sridhar, R.J. Rao, Ambupad Thakur, Ani1 Bhatnagar, D. Radha Krishna Babu, Ashim Saraf and N. Siva Kumar.

Krishna Mohan
Meera Banerji

ACKNOWLEDGEMENTS

We are indebted to those officers of the following organisations who extended their help and cooperation in collecting data for the book:

Space Application Centre, Ahmedabad; Allahabad Mandal Nigam Ltd., Allahabad; Bharat Pumps and Compressors, Allahabad; National Aeronautical Lab., Visvesveraya Industrial and Technological Museum, Lower Jhelum Hydel Project, Baramulla; Bhilai Steel Plant, Bhilai; Bharat Heavy Electricals Ltd., Bhopal; Bhabha Atomic Research Centre, Mumbai; Central Bank of India, Mumbai; Century Spg. & Mfg. Co. Ltd., Mumbai; Indian Plastics Ltd., Mumbai; Life Insurance Corporation of India, Mumbai; National Institute of Bank Management, Mumbai; SSP Bank Training College, Mumbai; Wester Works Engineers Ltd., Mumbai; Development Consultants Pvt. Ltd., Kolkata; Chittaranjan Locomotive Works, Chittaranjan; Department of Science & Technology, Delhi; Delhi Financial Corporation, Delhi; The Hindustan Times, Delhi; National Council of Applied Economic Research, Delhi; National Physical Lab., Delhi; TSG Consultants Pvt. Ltd., Delhi; Bank of America, Delhi; Ministry of External Affairs, Govt. of India, Delhi; Publications and Information Directorate, CSIR, Delhi; Foundation to Aid Industrial Recovery (FAIR), Delhi; DCM Data Products, Delhi; Delhi Development Authority (DDA), Delhi; Delhi Cloth and General Mills Ltd., Delhi; Hindustan Fertilizer Corporation Ltd., Durgapur; Bharat Heavy Electricals Ltd., Hardwar; Defence Ministry Research Lab., Hyderabad; Defence Research Development Organization, Hyderabad; National Geophysical Research Institute, Hyderabad; Hukumchand Mills Ltd., Indore; Jaipur Metals and Electricals Ltd., Jaipur; National Engineering Industries Ltd., Jaipur; Rajasthan State Agro-Industries Corporation, Jaipur; Regional Research Lab., Jammu; Salal Hydro Electric Project, Jammu; Alcobex Metals Pvt. Ltd., Jodhpur, Laxmi Udyog, Jodhpur; National Hydro-Electric Power Corporation Ltd., Jyotipuram; The Sirpur Paper Mills Ltd., Kagaznagar, Century Rayon, Kalyan; Hindustan Aeronautics Ltd., Kanpur; Hindustan Copper Ltd., Khetrinagar; Instrumentation Ltd., Kota; JK Synthetics Ltd., Kota; Sri Ram Fertilizers and Chemicals, Kota; Central Drug Research Institute, Lucknow; Brakes India Ltd., Madras; Bharat Earth Movers Ltd., Mysore; Birla Research Institute, Nagda; Gwalior Rayon, Nagda; National Fertilizers Ltd., Naya Nangal; Thakur Vaidyanath Aiyar & Co., Patna; Central Electronics Engineering Research Institute, Pilani; United Commercial Bank, Pilani; Hindustan Aluminium Corporation, Renukoot; Indian Drugs & Pharmaceuticals Ltd., Rishikesh; Agricultural Research Institute, Srinagar; Century Rayon, Thane; Hindustan Motors, Trivallore; Hindustan Zinc Ltd., Udaipur; Gujarat Tractors Corporation Ltd., Vadodara; Diesel Locomotive Works, Varanasi; Indian Rayon Corporation, Veraval.

Contents

PART THREE: WRITTEN COMMUNICATION

PART FOUR: MECHANICS OF MANUSCRIPT PREPARATION

PART ONE

Aspects of Communication

Chapter 1

COMMUNICATION THROUGH WORDS

MAN has been using language as a tool of communication for centuries. It has enabled him to interact with the environment and to regulate his social behaviour. Though there are a number of means of communication, language is the most widely used instrument. Man communicates meaning through a sophisticated system of symbols. The sophistication that has been attained in devising this complex system of meaning-sharing activity has left the dance-of-the-honey-bee type of communication far behind.

Today, language is one of the most prized possessions of man. It acts as a repository of wisdom, a propeller for the advancement of knowledge and a telescope to view the vision of the future. Ever since the dawn of civilisation man has been trying to exploit the flexibility and dynamism of language for the conduct of his day-to-day affairs. But in this attempt he has been only partially successful. Though human society has progressed with remarkable speed, the use of language for communication is still not free from ignorance, prejudice and superstition.

1.1 PROCESS OF COMMUNICATION

Here we are concerned with linguistic communication. Let us now briefly discuss what it is and how it takes place. The word 'communication' is derived from the Latin term 'communicare' or 'communico', both of which mean 'to share'. But communication is not merely transmission of meaning from one person to another one through symbols. It implies that the system of communication is commonly owned, accepted and recognised by the members of a community. It enables them to acquire, exchange, store, retrieve and process information. Communication is thus essentially a social affair.

Looked at more closely, what is essential for communication to occur is the cooperation between two parties, one active or at the giving end and the other passive or at the receiving end.

The sender selects appropriate symbols to suit the situation and realises the meaning through speech or writing, depending upon the socially regulated requirements or self-perceived needs. At the receiving end, the symbols are identified and identification obviously implies recognition and realisation of meaning through the interpretive process.

Both these processes may be summarised as follows:

Parties	*Media*	*Mode*	*Function*
Sender	Spoken	Speaking	Selection Execution
	Written	Writing	Selection Execution
Receiver	Spoken	Listening	Identification Interpretation
	Written	Reading	Identification Interpretation

Communication is thus a network of interactions and naturally the sender and the receiver keep on changing their roles.

Another aspect of communication is the deployment of a code, consisting of arbitrarily evolved symbols and the determination of the appropriateness of their use in given situations, leading to the emergence of diverse communication patterns. In shaping these patterns, a number of factors come into play. Some of these are tangible (e.g. physical setting) and others intangible, such as intellectual, emotional and psychological. Communication cannot, therefore, always be regarded as a momentary event. In fact, it often is a momentary intensification of a continuing, cumulative process that starts before the actual communicative event takes place and continues even after it has occurred. The communicator, therefore, must acquire a true perspective of not only the present requirements of the situation but also its relationship with the past and its impact on the future.

For a clear understanding of the various components and their interrelationship see Fig. 1.1, indicating the process of communication.

It would be observed that the entire event takes place within a common frame of reference, also called communication environment. The source refers to the point of origin of a message which is encoded by the sender and transmitted through the channel to the receiver. The receipt of the message exercises an impact in communication environment leading to some result. The observance of the result by the sender is called 'feedback'. The message sent is not the same as the message received. For this a number of factors which we may collectively term as 'noise' are responsible. We shall look at it later. It is also to be noted that all the messages do not produce the intended result. Thus, the success of communication is measured in terms of not only the effective transmission of the message but also the achievement of the intended result. Figure 1.1 indicates the processes of initiation and reaction on the part of the sender and receiver respectively. The choice of channel is determined by socio-physical factors.

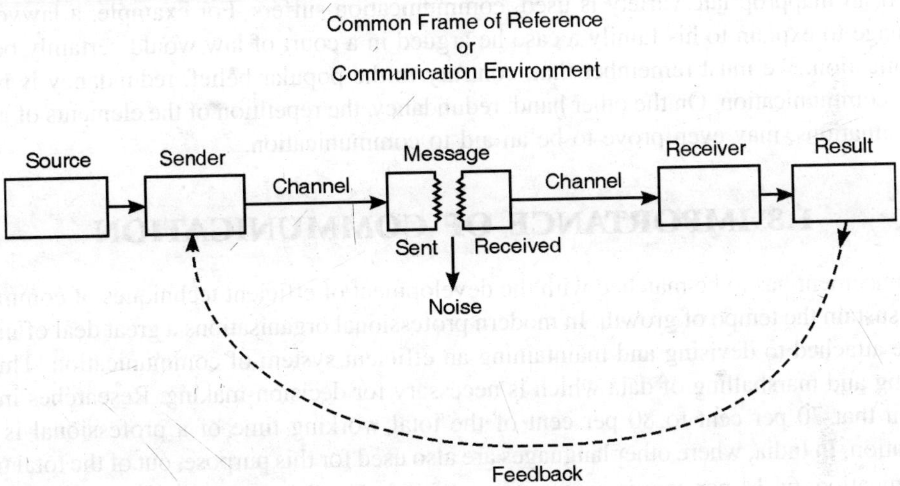

Fig. 1.1 Components of Communication

1.2 BARRIERS TO COMMUNICATION

There are a number of barriers which produce noise and prevent the achievement of the desired result. Some of these are: absence of a common frame of reference, badly encoded messages, disturbance in the transmission channel, poor retention (especially in face-to-face communication), inattention by the receiver, unclarified assumptions, mistrust between the sender and the receiver, premature evaluation of the message, different perceptions of reality, semantic difficulties, vagueness about the objectives, misinterpretation of the message, clash of attitudinal nuances, psycho-physical factors, and selection of a wrong variety of language.

Most of the barriers mentioned above are self-explanatory; a few however need clarification. The common frame of reference implies the social context in which communication takes place. Both the sender and the receiver would be able to focus their mind meaningfully on the message if the context is well-defined. The semantic difficulties arise when the sender uses ambiguous expressions or highly specialised vocabulary, inappropriate to the situation. Every sender superimposes his attitude on what he communicates. A message is therefore not just organised language but a verbal means of the realisation of an intention. Sometimes the attitude of the sender is at variance with that of the receiver and when this attitudinal clash occurs, communication suffers. Sometimes one is unable to communicate effectively because of mental or physical fatigue or when one is out of tune with oneself psychologically. Some persons, because of previous unpleasant experience in similar situations, may find it difficult to communicate effectively. In oral communication situations some persons may be reluctant to speak because they are afraid of being evaluated by their peers, superiors, etc. All such factors are termed as psycho-physical factors. Each language has a number of varieties determined on the basis of the place a person belongs to, the social status he enjoys, the profession he is engaged in or the activity he performs. If an inappropriate variety is used, communication suffers. For example, a lawyer's use of legal language to explain to his family a case he argued in a court of law would certainly be a barrier to communication. We must remember that, contrary to the popular belief, redundancy is not always a barrier to communication. On the other hand, redundancy, the repetition of the elements of a message, in certain situations, may even prove to be an aid to communication.

1.3 IMPORTANCE OF COMMUNICATION

Social advancement has to be matched with the development of efficient techniques of communication in order to sustain the tempo of growth. In modern professional organisations a great deal of importance is therefore attached to devising and maintaining an efficient system of communication. This enables the gathering and marshalling of data which is necessary for decision-making. Researches in this area have shown that 70 per cent to 80 per cent of the total working time of a professional is spent on communication. In India, where other languages are also used for this purpose, out of the total time spent on communication, 64.14 per cent is on communicating in English as against 27.22 per cent in Hindi and 8.64 per cent in regional languages. Thus the role of English in the professional world is still dominant and we have therefore focussed our attention on the conventions of communication in English followed in India.

1.4 CORPORATE COMMUNICATION

There are two aspects of communication in organisations: one, the development and maintenance of a communication pattern to ensure harmonious relationship among the employees and two, the use of technology to secure quicker and more effective flow of communication from one department or office to another or from one city or country to another. In this section we shall briefly discuss some of the ways of doing the first task and draw your attention to certain technological aids in Chapter 3.

An organisation is a body of persons working for a well-defined goal. To achieve the goal each member of this body has to be in constant touch with the others. There is both horizontal and vertical movement of information from one source to another. The horizontal flow keeps individuals of the same status and peer groups informed of what others are doing and what is expected of them. The commonality of interest towards the achievement of organisational goals sustains the flow. The vertical communication is both downward and upward. The top management keeps on sending information to the employees and also devises ways of eliciting information from them and thus the lines of communication are kept open. The two-way movement is essential to keep the organisation in a healthy state. Mere downward flow is like talking to a person continuously without giving him a chance to respond. In such a situation the pattern of communication will take the following form:

A instructs B

A speaks to B

A directs B to do something

A conveys to B a piece of information and so on.

This idea is vividly expressed in Fig. 1.2. Notice the expression on the receiver's face.

Fig. 1.2 One-way Communication

Enlightened managements however realise that communication is essentially interactive in nature, demanding the interchange of roles of the sender and the receiver and therefore, they lay equal emphasis on upward flow of communication. Any obstructions on the line are carefully looked into and quickly removed. The two-way flow then forms the following pattern:

A instructs B
B reports to A
A speaks to B
B responds to A
and so on.

The same idea is expressed in Fig. 1.3.

Communication performs a number of functions and plays a significant role in the running and growth of an organisation. We may classify these functions as follows:

(a) Internal, i.e. within the organisation:
 (i) to generate and disseminate information,
 (ii) to direct and instruct employees,
 (iii) to maintain and improve morale, and
 (iv) to cultivate a sense of belonging.

(b) External, i.e. outside the organisation:

(i) to sell and obtain goods and services,

(ii) to liaise with other organisations and

(iii) to create goodwill.

Usually within the organisation, members need the following types of information:

(i) Information of immediate concern, such as working procedure, skills required for the job, method of training available for advancement, etc.

(ii) Working environment-related information such as rules for safety, facilities for clubs, societies, unions, cafeteria, etc.

(iii) Information about personal benefits such as pay and allowances, health and insurance, holidays, etc.

(iv) Information about the organisation as a whole – work of other departments and sections, relationship of one's department with others, ultimate objective, etc.

It is obvious that conveying all the information to everybody would be a meaningless exercise. For proper functioning of a communication system, the following questions should be asked and the answers constantly reviewed on the basis of reliable feedback:

(i) What information is to be conveyed?

(ii) Who requires it?

(iii) What should be its form?

(iv) Which techniques of dissemination should be used?

(v) Which technological aids should be used?

There is a network of communication within every organisation. Such a network clearly indicates the lines of communication, viz., who is to speak to whom and for what. Generally there is no direct communication between the top management and the employee at the lowest rank of the, hierarchy. The *vice versa* is also true. The longer the distance, the greater are the chances of communication distortion or failure. Therefore, an efficient organisation often provides for an informal contact outside the usual channels of communication. It is difficult to specify the various methods of this kind of contact; each organisation keeps on evaluating and modifying these methods. Further, any information received through the grapevine must be rigorously filtered to ensure that mere gossip may not pass off as truth.

In recent years the importance of communication has greatly increased as a result of the growing complexity in organisational and individual behaviour under the impact of rapid industrialisation and modern technology. In the fast changing world of today it is clear that today's communication systems will not meet the demands of tomorrow. There is a need for constant review and modification.

Chapter 2

COMMUNICATION THROUGH BODY LANGUAGE

NON-verbal communication refers to 'all external stimuli other than spoken or written words, including body motion, characteristics of appearance, characteristics of voice and use of space and distancing.'* All these non-verbal clues taken together are also known as body language. In day-to-day oral communication we keep on interpreting non-verbal clues without being aware of them. It is only very recently that a systematic study has been made to analyse non-verbal communication and **Kinesics** is the name given to this branch of learning. Some scholars, however, prefer to call the use of space and distancing as **Proxemics** whereas some include the study of voice quality as part of the vocal aspect of oral communication.

Body language plays a significant role in oral communication. Sigmund Freud's observation may appear to be an exaggeration but it is the exaggeration of a vital truth: 'He that has eyes to see and ears to hear may convince himself that no mortal can keep a secret. If his lips are silent he chats with his fingertips; betrayal oozes out of him at every pore.** It is believed that a charming person has a pleasant voice, a dynamic person has a vibrant voice and a confident person an assured voice.

Recently an attempt has been made to carry out a systematic study of the elements, which are visually perceived, and their role in communication. That is why these elements are collectively termed as the 'visible code'. Though verbal and non-verbal means of communication are closely interlinked, certain studies have tried to separate their relative importance in terms of the impact of the message. According

---

* K.K. Sereno and E.M. Bodaken. *Trans-Per Understanding Human Communication*. Houghton Mifflin Company, 1975, p. 227.

** Cited in Knapp, Mark. *Non-verbal Communication in Human Interaction*. New York: Holt Rinehart Winston, 1972, p. 12.

to Birdwhistell*, 35 per cent of the message is carried verbally, while 65 per cent is conveyed non-verbally. Mehrabian** (1971) has analysed the impact of a message as follows: 7 per cent verbal, 38 per cent vocal and 55 per cent non-verbal. Though the studies in this are in their infancy, training in the proper use of the visible code is essential to acquire the skill of effective communication. In fact, efficiency in its use can, to some extent, make up for the deficiency in verbal communication. We can all recall situations in which the speaker's command over the language was deficient and yet he was able to drive the message home because of the proper use of his body language.

We may categorise the elements of the visible code as follows:

2.1 PERSONAL APPEARANCE

The first impact on the audience/listener is created by the personal appearance of the speaker. Even before the speaker utters the first syllable, we begin to form an opinion about him and visualise the way he is going to talk. One's appearance may put the audience into a resistant or even a hostile attitude or induce in them a receptive mood which is essential for the success of communication. It is partly because of this that uniforms have been prescribed by certain organisations as also the kind of dress that should be worn on certain specified occasions. A uniform may indicate the kind of work one does or instil a sense of oneness or be a marker of status. In fact, conventions have been established in regard to the use of dress and general physical appearance in respect of certain communication situations such as interviews, convocations, state banquets, etc. We are all accustomed to looking for clues about the personality of an individual in terms of his dress, hairstyle, make-up, etc. Always remember that you are never fully dressed *unless you wear a smile.*

2.2 POSTURE

Posture also conveys a wealth of meaning in an economical way. It is an important part of body language and generally refers to the way one stands, sits and walks. The movement of the body, the position of hands and legs and other parts of the body reveal an individual's personality: whether he is vibrant, alive and dynamic, nervous and jittery, confident and self-assured, etc. A good speaker stands tall, feet together with the weight directly over the instep, keeping his chin on a line parallel to the floor or at right angles to the backbone. Standing in this posture before a group is, in fact, one of the first essentials for success in speaking. A drooping shoulder and a protruding stomach indicate that the speaker is discouraged, tired and worn out. The posture of sitting may exude an air of optimism, or despondency, or be indicative of a sense of failure or of inattentiveness. To some extent a speaker can gauge the measure of success of his communication by observing the posture of the listener. The communication situation and the specific purpose which one has to achieve determine the way one sits. For example, a subordinate while selling an idea to his boss or explaining an important point would not recline in his chair. In a group

---

* Ibid.

** Albert, Mehrabian, *Silent Messages*, Wadsworth Publishing Company, Belmont, California, 1971.

discussion the person who takes a turn to speak changes his posture when he starts communicating. A prospective speaker on the dais is watched by the audience that tries to guess the kind of man he is from the way he sits. While different situations will demand different sitting postures, one should keep one's back straight from the waist up, both the feet should be on the floor, one slightly in front of the other. The abdominal muscles should be pulled in. The chest should come out in line. The ability to walk across the stage with ease and grace contributes a great deal to the first impression the speaker makes upon his audience. The walking posture may convey whether a speaker is confident, energetic and vital or withdrawn, diffident and nervous. To walk gracefully one should remember the following tips: move the legs freely from the hips; lift your feet from the floor; do not drag or shuffle them; walk in a straight line; avoid a stride or taking tiny steps.

While speaking, naturally, there would be shifts in the posture. These have to be cultivated. One must learn where to place one's hands and how to shift the weight of the body on the legs while speaking.

2.3 GESTURES

Gestures also play a significant role in making the communication effective. A well-timed gesture can drive a point home. Similarly, playing with a ring, twisting a key-chain, or clasping one's hand tightly rob a speaker of the effectiveness of his communication. Sometimes gestures do not accompany oral delivery and are used to communicate certain elementary and short messages such as 'yes', 'no', 'come here', 'go there', 'keep sitting', 'be silent', etc. However, all oral communications are accompanied by gestures such as shrugging of the shoulders, flourish of the hands, movement of the head, etc. In fact, without the accompanying gestures it would be difficult to speak. These gestures enhance the impact and add a greater value to what is being said besides exercising a more powerful impact upon the listener. To learn and to make appropriate gestures it would be useful to practise before a mirror, seeking guidance from friends and colleagues who are considered effective communicators. Thus through a process of self-evaluation in the use of gesture, one can certainly improve and achieve greater efficiency in the art of speaking.

2.4 FACIAL EXPRESSION

Of all the parts of the body the face is the most expressive. A smile (friendliness), a frown (discontent), raising the eyebrows (disbelief), or tightening the jaw muscles (antagonism) can add to the meaning being conveyed through verbal means. A wooden expression on the face may prejudice the listeners whereas brightness in the eyes may keep their interest sustained and also evoke an enthusiastic response. Exuding zeal when one is making a point or smiling while explaining an intricate problem makes the job of the speaker easy. We can recall occasions where what could have been effective communication turned out to be a failure because the speaker did not have proper facial expressions. Biting the lips, raising the eyebrows at regular intervals or blinking the eyes too often can certainly mar the smooth flow of communication.

2.5 EYE CONTACT

Eye contact with the listener is perhaps the most important aspect of body language. It has been rightly said that the eye is an extension of the brain and a window of the soul. Stress is laid on continuous eye contact between the speaker and the listener because it tells whether the speaker is sincere and also whether the listener is interested. Eye contact is a means of gaining feedback, enabling the communicator to alter, adjust and reframe his message while transmitting it. Very often this process is automatic and the interaction through the eyes of the speaker and the listener takes place unconsciously. Studies have shown that better eye-contact leads to more effective communication. A good speaker, therefore, looks at all sections of his audience and not on the ground, the ceiling or at the door. If a section of the audience is continuously ignored that section will lose interest in what is being communicated.

2.6 SPACE DISTANCING

Each communicator maintains a personal territory around himself. He normally does not allow it to be invaded at the time of communication unless the relationship between him and the listener is very friendly or intimate. In social intercourse, normally, a zone ranging from 4 to 12 feet is maintained, when the situation is formal. This is termed as *social distance*. This term also includes a reference to the *standing-seated position*. The person who is in the superior or commanding position, usually stands and the others remain seated. For example, it may be difficult to control the class (in fact, any group) if the teacher does not communicate in a standing position. Thus, in a large group discussion one can prove more effective if one stands while speaking. In public gatherings the distance between the audience and the communicator is much greater – it may range from 12 to 30 feet depending upon many other considerations (e.g. security).

Space distancing differs from culture to culture and it can cause embarrassment to a communicator in a foreign cultural setting. For example, in India two male adults may hug each other and walk hand in hand simply because they are friends, whereas in another country this same gesture may lead to a misconstruction of their relationship. An American may find an Indian too close (distance-wise) to him while talking and to avoid this he may lean back in his chair. However, in heightened emotional states of mind (e.g. anger, shock, danger), the normal distancing is ignored.

To conclude, two things clearly emerge out of this discussion: one, the visible code is as important as the verbal code and training in the use of the former is as essential as in the use of the latter; two, the visible code differs from culture to culture and care should be taken to use the appropriate symbols in cross-cultural contexts. In India the situation is more complex in as much as a foreign verbal code has to be accompanied by a native visible code.

Chapter 3

COMMUNICATION THROUGH TECHNOLOGY

ONE of the greatest concerns of an organisation is how to deal with the accumulation of information and at the same time keep its communication patterns strong and healthy enough to bear the burden of handling enormous data. Here technology has come in a big way to help organisations to keep their communication pattern vibrant and meaningful to meet the increasing demands. Now technological aids are available to store, process and disseminate information, so much so that professionals have started talking in terms of a paperless office, discarding the traditional ways of maintaining hundreds of paper files for the purpose of communication. The emphasis is on speed, efficiency and facility to recall the required information at a short notice.

If you go to a well-equipped office, you may find a number of technological aids such as Fax machine, photocopier, teleprinter, etc., buzzing with activity. Until recently the emphasis was on using electronic equipment for recording and preserving oral communication. Now there is an equal stress on using technology for what traditionally used to be recorded and transmitted on paper. Now we shall turn our attention to a few commonly used devices which have quickened the pace of communication and made it more convenient and efficient, especially if they are based on a computer system. To be specific, we shall deal with the following: Word Processor, Desk Top Publisher, Power Point Presentation, Electronic Mail, and the Voice Mail.

3.1 WORD PROCESSOR

In a modern office computers have slowly replaced the secretarial staff and as an executive or a professional, you may have to prepare documents like reports, financial estimates, proposals, etc., yourself. You would therefore have to develop new skills for reading print materials and writing with the help of word processors. Computers are not just typewriters with enhanced capabilities but they are much more powerful tools. It is the software which allows one to write the text and then customise and manipulate it according to the requirements, with the help of its in-built features. It enables one not only to create a document but also to store it electronically on a disk, display it on the screen, modify it by entering commands and characters from the keyboard and print it on a printer. One of the greatest advantages of word processing is that it allows you to revise and refine your text as much as you wish. You can also change the appearance of your document, its size, shape, colour and position on the page and adjust the space between individual letters, words, lines and paragraphs.

During the span of the last 400 years or so text processing has progressed from Gutenberg's press to Desktop Publishing with the help of electronic means of handling text. It was in the 1970s that word processing developed as specialised programs on mainframe computers as online computing with the use of personal terminal devices with keyboards and display screens. It is believed that such programs evolved from text-based editors, commonly used by programmers and computer professionals. Later, the advent of microprocessors and the placing of intelligent devices on the desks of professionals at a reasonable price, helped to make machines devoted entirely to word processing. With the passage of time cheaper and smaller printers followed to facilitate further the task of creating written texts.

Today offices are almost fully computerised. Most of the personal computers now come with a varied package of programs already installed in them. These are sometimes called 'bundled software' or 'software suites'. Two of the most popular packages are Microsoft Office and Microsoft Works. Microsoft Office is a package of mini-programs put together. It has an extremely powerful tool called Word Processor to help produce all kinds of written documents like letters, memos, reports and newsletters. It has Excel, a spreadsheet program that organises and calculates numerical data. It can also make a wide variety of charts and graphs for presenting a mass of data in a clear, alternative and comprehensive way. There is an information management program called Outlook to help you record contact details in the address book. Outlook also helps in sending and receiving e-mails through internet company network. Microsoft Office also has Power Point, most commonly used in business presentations, company meetings and conferences. Microsoft Works also has a Word Processor to help you create a vast range of word-based documents. It is not as sophisticated as Microsoft Word. Works also has an advanced feature called Communications to communicate with other computers through a network. Then it has Spreadsheet, a program which allows the monitoring and analysis of numerical data and Database for recording details and performing calculations. Both Office and Works have Task Wizards or pre-set documents which will help you with step-by-step guidance to customise documents according to your needs. Newer software packages with more advanced capabilities are being developed to perform more sophisticated and a variety of tasks. It is for these reasons that you have to develop proficiency in using styles and templates already present in many computer softwares. A style is any kind of formatting used in a document again and again and a template is a collection of styles that is applied to the same kind of document. These would enable you to produce written documents with ease and efficiency. You would also be able to create presentations for company meetings, seminars and projects. Further, these would help you structure information more efficiently and put your ideas across more effectively.

One of the greatest advantages of word processing is that you can introduce changes in the document without retyping the document all over again. All forms of corrections like adding or deleting words, rewriting sentences, making a different arrangement of paragraphs, etc., can be easily made. You can move parts of your text matter from one part of the document to another. Though there are a variety of word processing packages with different capabilities, most of them perform the following functions of a text editor in the production of a document:

- Adjust the structure of your document to make them easy to read.
- Move the text, insert the text from different files.
- Delete text or characters, words, lines or pages.
- Replace a word or a phrase anywhere in the text without disturbing the rest of the matter.
- Hyphenate long words occurring at the end of the line.
- Make duplicates of a section of a text or a whole document.
- Define page sizes and margins.
- Indent paragraphs to highlight them.
- Align paragraphs.
- Move automatically to the next line after you have finished typing a line.
- Add numbers and bullet points to highlight headings and sub-headings.
- Adjust spacing between words and sentences.
- Check spelling and grammatical mistakes.
- Mail merge (merging of routine form letter and the addresses)
- Sort information in alphabetical order.
- Store the text on magnetic tapes or on magnetic disks and get various combinations output of the texts so stored.
- Retrieve the text as and when required.
- Get some special formatting effects such as setting of margins, automatic indentation, etc.
- Display on the screen whatever is being typed, even the line breakups, paragraph setting, page break-ups, margins, etc.

Some of the more advanced word processing packages now have additional features that help you prepare your documents in a more sophisticated way. Some of these features are:

- Create, delete, move and search for files or folders.
- Change fonts according to your specifications.
- Insert graphs and illustrations in your text.
- Keep track of page numbers and put them correctly on every page.
- Enable you to customise headers and footers on the top and bottom of every page.
- Help you to have a proper layout of the document.
- Allow the merging of text from one file into another file so that you can generate many files with the same format but different matter.

- Make a table of contents and indices.
- Add and place footnotes and cross-references.
- Display on the screen the document exactly as it would look when printed.

Thus we see that word processing allows you to not only create a wide range of word-based documents but also have them in the desired format and style. There would be consistency in the styles you have chosen, thereby making your documents more presentable, readable and professional. Besides you can use Power Point to create presentations for your projects, company meetings and conferences. This program would help you to structure information efficiently in the slides and incorporate illustrations and graphics to optimise the impact of your presentation.

3.2 DESK TOP PUBLISHER (DTP)

DTP is another device, which can free you from tedious tasks like cutting, pasting, designing, and redesigning the presentation of material when you are assigned a printing job. It had made publishing easier and it is being increasingly used for bringing out reports, manuals, brochures, bulletins, etc. A unique feature of the device is its ability to combine the texts and graphics and to produce finished typeset quality printed material. Its production process is integrated and it enables the user to move directly from the author's design to camera-ready artwork. Thus when you use a DTP, you will have a greater control over the information structure. Briefly stated, the main functions of a DTP are as follows:

- Creating text and visuals on the PC with word processing and graphic software.
- Integrating text and visuals into a page using layout software.
- Printing with a laser printer, documents with typeset quality appearance.
- Designing, editing and producing high quality communication documents at a fraction of the time and expense required by conventional production techniques.

Usually a DTP has a laser printer which ensures quick and effective printouts. It is run by a computer system and uses software such as word processor, business graphics, picture designer, font designer, etc.

3.3 POWER POINT PRESENTATION

As mentioned earlier, most personal computers come with different software packages already installed in them. One of the most widely used packages is Power Point.

Power Point presentation enables you to create documents called presentations, commonly used for communicating ideas, messages and other information to a group. It is used in business, industry and academic world for making presentations for different purposes such as marketing projects, selling products to prospective buyer firms, interim and final reporting of research work undertaken for academic purposes. Power Point gives you the means to structure information efficiently, along with charts and graph, in your text. It also offers animation effects to maximise the impact of your presentation. Power Point can also help you to make notes for your own use in the presentation in addition to the handouts you may give to the audience. Besides, it provides ready-to-use sample presentations for consultations.

On the basis of Microsoft Power Point, you can use a feature called Autocontent Wizard, a tool within a program that would guide you through the process of customising a pre-designed document and help you with the arrangement of the content of presentation with an automated utility. Presentation graphics software provides formats with complementary colours for backgrounds and other items along with a variety of layouts for each individual slide. You could also make use of the Presentations Property page of the New Presentation Dialog box. It is a suite of dialog boxes that enables you to choose or specify essential features of a basic presentation. As these presentations are already formatted, you have to decide on the type of presentation you want, and what information you wish to display on each slide. You can also take the help of the Office Assistant, if necessary.

Though you have readymade slides, you can create your own presentations using blank slides. Prepare an outline of the subject matter you wish to present. Usually, the new matter that would form your text would have the title of the presentation, your name as presenter, the sub-titles of the main text or subject matter. Certain titles like Introduction and Conclusion form an essential part of all presentations and separate slides are used for them. Below each title of the slide, there is a list of bulleted items or sub-items. This is formatted. Let us take the example of the presentation slides of 'Elements of an Effective Oral Presentation.'

The slides that would follow may look like the following:

Slide: 1

Title: Elements of an Effective Oral Presentation

Presenter: Tarun Kumar Bose

Slide: 2

Introduction

- Oral Presentation
- Its Importance
- Its Effectiveness

Slide: 3

Organisation of Matter
- Introduction
- Ordering of Ideas (Body)
- Conclusion

Slide: 4

Delivery (Use of Voice)
- Proper Volume
- Rate
- Animation
- Vibrancy

Slide: 5

Use of Body Language
- Personal Appearance
- Posture
- Gestures
- Facial Expression
- Eye Contact
- Space Distancing

Slide: 6

Use of Audio-Visual Aids
- Blackboard
- Overhead Projector
- Power Point
- Tape Recorder

Slide: 7

Quality of Interaction
- Cool and Mature
- Brief, to the Point

Slide: 8

Conclusion

A presentation of a research paper on Women's Literacy Rate may have the following slides:

Slide: 1

Title: Female Literacy Rate in India

Presenter: Nirmala Arun

Slide: 2

Introduction

	Literacy Rates	
Census Years	Male (%)	Female (%)
1951	26.16	08.86
1961	40.40	15.35
1971	45.96	21.97
1981	56.38	29.76
1991	64.13	39.29
2001	75.85	54.16

Slide: 3

Factors Responsible

- Gender-based Inequality
- Social Discrimination
- Role Definition

Slide: 4

Factors Responsible (Continued.)

- Occupation of Girl-Child in Domestic Chores
- Low Enrolment of Girls in Schools
- High Dropout Rate of Girls

Slide: 5

Benefits of Increased Female Literacy

- Women's Empowerment
- Better Status for Women
- More Economic Independence
- Women Entrepreneur

Slide: 6

Other Benefits

- Better Education and Health
- Gender Equality
- Progress and Development of Women

Slide: 7

Conclusion

A campaign against smoking and use of tobacco organised in colleges and universities could have a presentation with the following slides:

Slide: 1

Title: How Tobacco Hits You

Presenter: Nitin Kumar

Slide: 2

Brain

- Strokes
- Altered Chemistry

Mouth and Throat

- Cancer of Lips, Mouth, Throat and Larynx

Heart

- Weakness of Arteries
- Increased Risk of Heart Attack

Slide: 3

Chest

- Cancer of Oesophagus

Lungs

- Cancer
- Emphysema
- Asthma
- Chronic Obstructive Pulmonary Disease

Liver

- Cancer

Slide: 4

Abdomen
- Stomach Ulcers
- Cancer of Stomach, Pancreas and Colon
- Aortic Swelling

Kidney and Bladder
- Cancer

Slide: 5

Male Reproduction
- Sperm Deformities
- Impotence

Female Reproduction
- Cancer of Cervix
- Infertility

Slide: 6

Legs and Feet
- Gangrene Caused by Blood Clots

Slide: 7

Conclusion

Some of the biggest advantages of a Power Point presentation are that you can view the slides after you have made them, change the contents of the slides, edit the matter, introduce different sizes of fonts, use different backgrounds for different slides or make any other changes you like, without retyping or making new slides all over again. You can take off a few slides and add new ones in their place. The matter given in the slides should also be in the form of Note Cards, so that while speaking there would be no need for you to look at the screen for dealing with the points under discussion. Take care that the numbering of the Note Cards corresponds to the numbering of the slides. During the presentation, you would be free to follow the strategies of effective oral presentation discussed in Chapter 5.

3.4 ELECTRONIC MAIL

Before the advent of the internet, professionals felt a strong need to share information among IBM users spread far apart and a unique way developed for multiple users of time-sharing mainframe computer for the purpose of communication. Now the Internet, which is made up of a network of millions of computers throughout the world, allows people to access a wide range of information and services. Apart from helping users find information on almost all subjects, the Internet allows them to send messages in the form of electronic mail (e-mail). The e-mail is one of the most useful features of the Internet. e-mail functions at a staggering speed. Messages are typed into the computer and then sent to other e-mail users thousands of miles away, all at the cost of a local phone call. Besides being cheap, it is very convenient in comparison to transmission by post. e-mail has now emerged as the most acceptable form of written communication, replacing typed memos and letters in business and industry. In some cases, e-mails replace telephonic conversations, saving time of the users.

3.4.1 Advantages

There are many advantages of sending messages through e-mail. It is an efficient and quick means of communication. It is easy to understand and it overcomes the problems of inconvenience in face-to-face meetings and expenses of travelling from one place to another. Its speed, almost instantaneous, is a boon in this fast modern age.

3.4.2 Disadvantages

However, e-mails have their drawbacks too. There is no privacy as e-mails can be easily intercepted and read by others. Like letters written on emotionally-charged issues, e-mails can cause harm besides communicating message or information. They also cause loss of context as information is often communicated in fragments. Then there are junk e-mails or spams which lead to an information overload. Sometimes such spams come with attached files containing viruses.

Whatever be the drawbacks of e-mail, there is no denying the fact that it continues to be the favourite communicating medium in business and industry both within the organisation and outside the organisation.

Structure and Form of e-mails

e-mail messages consist of two major sections: Header and Body. A Header includes names of the receiver to whom the message is directed and that of the sender who sends the message, e-mail address, subject, giving the contents of the message to provide context and date. Sometimes the local time of writing the message is also written. The e-mail address of both the sender and receiver are also a part of the Header. If needed, a carbon copy (CC) can also be added. Body has the actual content of the message. An e-mail may or may not have a complimentary close of a formal letter. As e-mails contain informal messages they are commonly used for conveying information, placing orders or asking questions to ascertain the status of an on-going project or investigation. The tone depends upon the terms and relationship between the receiver and the sender of the mail. Official e-mails are informative, well-organised, short and their tone is formal.

Keep the following guidelines and principles in mind when you want to send e-mails:

- Decide whether an e-mail would be a better medium than a letter, a telephone call or a face-to-face meeting.
- Keep your sentences short, avoiding too many adjective clauses, noun clauses and adverb clauses, to enhance readability.
- Organise the message by stating the main points first and details in the middle.
- Give sufficient reference for the receiver to respond to your e-mail.
- Keep paragraphs short to provide eye-relief.
- Don't convey information which is confidential and personal.
- Avoid sending e-mails when you are angry or emotionally upset.
- Be friendly and courteous. Poorly written e-mail would do more harm than good.
- Write grammatically correct sentences and avoid making spelling mistakes.
- Be brief. Let your e-mail not be longer then 200 words. If it is more than screen long, use headings to break up the text of your message.
- Ascertain that your e-mail is addressed to the correct receiver.
- Note that the e-mail header comprises 'To: the e-mail address(es) and name(s) of the receiver(s) of the message; From: the e-mail address and name of the sender of the message; Subject: a brief summary of the contents of the message to provide the context and date: the local time when the message was written.' The Header may also include 'CC' (Carbon Copy).
- Send attachments, if necessary, separately but remember to mention this below the subject so that the receiver is aware that the attachment sent to him is genuine and not a junk-mail.
- Safeguard your e-mail address. Give your e-mail address only to individuals of your choice. Omit writing your e-mail address in forms to avoid getting junk e-mail.
- Beware of computer viruses. The best way to avoid getting a virus from the internet or any other source is to use an anti-virus utility software.
- For added security when downloading files, ensure that the 'Always ask before opening' box is ticked on your virus scanner.
- Remember, there is a risk of infection from 'macro viruses' that enter your PC via e-mail attachments.
- Do not use only uppercase letters. These are hard to read and amount to shouting. Similarly, avoid using only lowercase letters.
- Be wary of opening a file attached to an e-mail as the file itself may carry a virus. As a general rule, do not open files attached to unsolicited e-mails.

A few examples of e-mails follow:

(i) **Date** : Monday 10 September, 2007
To : Deven Prasad Varma dpv@rediffimail. com
From : Hiren Singh cblcomputers@mega.com
Subject : Installation of Personal Computers in Girls'PG Hostel

Dear Mr. Varma

We had assured Prof Anita Mehra that all the fifteen XYZ personal computers would be installed in the postgraduate students' rooms by 12 September 2007.

I didn't get your report on this. Do keep me posted on the progress.

Regards

Hiren Singh

(ii) **Date** : Tuesday, 11 September, 07
To : Hiren Singh cblcomputers@mega.com
From : Deven Prasad Varma dpv@rediffmail.com
Subject : Report on Installation of Computers in PG Girls Hostel.

Dear Mr. Singh,

Sorry for not sending a report earlier. All the fifteen XYZ personal computers have now been installed. One of the computers had to be replaced as it had a manufacturing defect. Our technician was down with viral fever, and was on leave for two days. But now the work is complete and in time too. Sorry once again.

Regards

Deven Varma

Note that this is an e-mail within the firm. The language is informal and the enquiry about installation of personal computers was made by the Manager of the CBL Computers. The reply too is informal in tone and gives the report on installation without any additional information of designations, complementary close of a formal letter. Such a mode of communication is very common in business and industry. Another example follows:

(iii) **Date** : 15 October, 2007
To : Amit Kumar ak@swedn.com
From : Om Pratap Gupta opg@swedn.com
CC : xyz@swedn.com
Subject : Regarding Ph.D. Research in Progress

Dear Mr. Kumar

I find that there are many students registered for Ph.D. programme for more than five years and they have still not made sufficient progress yet. Some of the registered students have gone and left their programmes incomplete. Further, the bulk of the Ph.D. students are still from Humanities and Science streams.

Please let me know what the Research Advisory Committee has done in this respect.

Om Pratap Gupta

(iv) **Date** : 18 October, 2007

To : Om Pratap Gupta opg@swedn.com

From : Amit Kumar ak@swedn.com

CC : xyz@swedn.com

Subject : Ph.D. Research in Progress

The Research Advisory Committee (RAC) carried out a survey and noted that there is a drop in the number of Ph.D. students who registered in Engineering, Humanities and Sciences in the years 2004-06 and not completed their thesis requirements. RAC met several times and brought in several flexibilities in the interpretation of 'pure' and 'applied' research and enabled students to have a wider choice of themes and areas of research. RAC has put stress on research being relevant to social and environmental needs in the wider national context. Some success has already been achieved in research areas like solar energy, renewable energy, planning and management of water resources and interdisciplinary and multi-disciplinary approaches to research in Engineering, Sciences and Humanities. The increase in the number of Ph. D. students in all three major disciplines is an indication that this trend is popular among students. Regarding Ph.D. students leaving their research work, RAC strongly feels that it is the outstanding and evolutionary progress made by the IT sector that attracts students. They do not hesitate to give up academic work and join IT sectors for high salaries and perks offered to them. Even fresh graduates do not opt for higher studies but prefer to go to different IT firms.

We would carry out another survey next year to ascertain the trends in research and make appropriate changes in our policy accordingly.

Regards,

Amit Kumar

You would have noticed that both the above e-mails have 'CC' and this indicates that the copies of the e-mail from Om Pratap Gupta are to be sent to all the members of the Research Advisory Committee. The recipient is the Secretary, Amit Kumar, who is responsible for monitoring and guiding research work.

Sometimes, a reply thanking the person who has conducted the survey and sent the report is also sent. It is believed that politeness pays dividends and paves the way for smooth, hassle-free business relations.

3.5 VOICE MAIL

There arose a need for an alternative mode of communication in the early nineteen seventies and eighties. Secretaries were scarce and labour costs had shot up. Telephone costs had come down so the telephone lines were busier. Still the bulk of the official communication was carried out by telephones. Unfortunately telephone calls were hampered as many officials were not present in their offices because they were busy attending meetings elsewhere or were out on business trips. As a consequence, prime time was wasted, business activity suffered and important issues could not be sorted out. It was then that many organisations set up Private Branch Exchanges (PBXs) in their office telephone systems. Later, answering machines with message centres were added to the offices to record telephone messages. These were operated manually and manned by a few employees in the office. As the volume of official work increased, the number of calls increased too, making it difficult for the operators to take messages accurately or direct them to the concerned official's extension number. A lot of delay was inevitable in delivering these messages, which were noted down on slips of paper and distributed through the internal transit system. This process was time-consuming but the correct interpretation of the messages was also difficult. Usually incorrect names and contact numbers were noted and sent to the extension numbers. Even the tape-based answering machines did not bring in a visible improvement in this mode of communication.

With the enhanced capabilities of the computers, Voice Mail, abbreviated as vmail or VMS, became a popular mode of communication. A vmail resembles an answering machine but it is much more sophisticated. vmail uses a standard telephone handset for a user interface along with a centralised computer system instead of separate telephones. This system had successfully overcome the shortcomings of the older technology of answering machines. Some of the unique features of vmail include its ability to answer many phones simultaneously and store voice messages received in the user's mailbox associated with his phone number. A user can forward messages received to other voice mail boxes. A few more advanced vmail systems offer an automated attendant facility which help callers in accessing directory service through a main business number. Thus the earlier problem of retrieval of messages and recording them correctly was successfully overcome.

You would notice that this new technology ushered in a new and more effective way of professional communication. vmail made it possible for a user to leave lengthy and detailed messages working in perfect harmony with telephone systems. A user needs to become a subscriber and have a mailbox number to send voice messages to other subscribers. If an organization has an vmail system, the PBX there is programmed to forward messages to the vmail system and subscriber.

Voice messages in vmail are sent in the user's natural voice. Its use has increased the flow of communication, saving time and money. The twin modes of vmail operation, namely, telephone answering and voice messaging use natural voice. Therefore, clarity in speech is of utmost importance. In order to derive maximum advantage from vmail, you have to train yourself in the art of clear speaking. Your voice in the vmail is often the first impression a person receives of you and the organisation you belong to.

The following tips would help you convey your message effectively.

- Enunciate each syllable contained in the words of the message clearly.
- Let your voice communicate that you are interested in the message.
- Give your full name, the name of your organisation and the date and the time of sending this Vmail at the very beginning.

- Get to the point quickly.
- Make your message more effective by speaking small sentences, with only one or two clauses.
- Pause at the end of each sentence.
- Be brief and to the point.
- Give your own subscriber number at the end of the message.
- End your mail with a courteous phrase such as 'good bye' or 'thank you.'

There are many more devices other than those we have mentioned above. With the computer as the hub, communication technology has made spectacular advancements. As you are aware, the International Network (Internet) of computers is being widely used for a number of activities requiring contact between individual and organisations. In addition to what we have discussed earlier, some such activities are video conferencing, distance education, accounting, ticketing, transacting business, consulting experts for various purposes, etc. Further, Internet itself acts as a consultant, providing as it does, a staggering amount of information on a large variety of subjects through thousands of websites. No wonder, for advanced study and research, the use of internet has become almost inevitable. We may also, in this context, mention two more storage devices, namely, micro computers and microfilms. The former is used for storing documents of all kinds in large databases. The information contained in these documents can be recalled quickly, modified or revised or completely erased. The latter can also store a mass of written or printed material which can be magnified and read, whenever required. But do remember that, whatever methods and devices you use, the human factor is the most important. The proper exchange and transmission of information depends upon you and us. The sophisticated technology available for the purpose is of no consequence if the communication is distorted or misunderstood.

PART TWO
ORAL COMMUNICATION

Chapter 4

DYADIC COMMUNICATION

THE term 'dyadic communication', in general, refers to an interaction between two persons. Even if more than two persons are present in a situation, it is only two communicators who play a fundamental role. Basically, this a person-to-person transaction and one of the commonest forms of speech communication. It provides ideal conditions for close-range continuous feedback. The meaning exchanged between the sender and the receiver is marked by high fidelity. There is frequent change in the role of the participants and body language acquires a greater significance. This is so because the minutest reactions are mutually observable.

The formal dyadic communication, with which we are concerned, demands artistry that can be acquired through practice. Dyadic communication may take a number of forms but we shall discuss only the following five: face-to-face conversation, telephonic conversation, interview, instruction and dictation.

4.1 FACE-TO-FACE CONVERSATION

Conversation is the most common form of dyadic communication. It links people together, be it in social or professional life. Conversation may be defined as oral and usually informal or friendly exchange of views, ideas, etc. In a conversation the participant has to play the role of a speaker or a listener interchangeably. Very often we form an impression about an individual from the way he talks and the topic(s) on which he converses.

Most of us find it easy to converse with our friends, relatives and colleagues whom we like and trust. That is why conversation rarely finds a place in a programme of formal instruction. Since every professional is required to participate in this form of dyadic communication, let us briefly look at some of the important points to be borne in mind. However, the rule that 'the best practice for conversation is conversation itself' still holds true.

It is useful to first analyse your own conversation habits and then try to change them for greater effectiveness. For self-analysis ask yourself questions such as the following:

(i) Do I find it difficult to start a conversation?
(ii) Am I unable to pick a topic?
(iii) Am I unable to keep the conversation flowing smoothly?
(iv) Do I always agree with what others say or disagree with them all the time?
(v) Do I frequently talk about myself, my family and my interests?
(vi) Have I a tendency to dominate every conversation situation?
(vii) Do I give the other participants a chance to speak?
(viii) Have I any mannerisms that are likely to annoy people?
(ix) Do I respect other people's time and interests?
(x) Am I self-conscious about the language I use – grammar, pronunciation, articulation, etc.?

The answers that you get would prove useful for both formal as well as informal conversation. Now we give below a few helpful hints.

Helpful Hints

- The conversation should be of interest to the participant and may begin with a topic of common interest. As it flows into new channels, adjust yourself to the comments and new points of view. Occasionally there would be spells of silence. These need not bother you because often during these spells new thoughts are often generated.
- Be alert to the attitudes that others may have and don't be surprised when you realise that the attitudes are likely to change.
- Occasionally, call the person by name and look at him while speaking. If you speak the name aloud you would be generating a more friendly feeling. To cap it all, take care of your language and oral demeanour.
- Always be courteous and cheerful. Feel interested in what is being said.
- Being dogmatic and argumentative may spoil your conversation, but it is useful to have a point of view.
- Avoid pet and superfluous words and phrases. We often develop a fancy for a particular expression. An analysis of your own speech may reveal that you have a fad for certain words or phrases (e.g. 'time frame', 'allergic', etc.). Avoid using them frequently in conversation. Similarly, expressions that smack of affectation and exaggeration should be shunned. The smooth flow of conversation is likely to be hampered if you deliberately use foreign words or use high-flown vocabulary to impress the listener. An overuse of words such as 'very lovely', 'wonderful', 'excellent' may also mar the pleasant informal atmosphere in which the conversation ought to take place.

A few additional hints, specially useful in difficult situations at a workplace, are given below:

- Control your emotions while conversing.
- Concentrate on the issue, not the person.

- Make conversation collaborative, including the listener in addressing the issue.
- Repair the damage rather than lament the loss, if any.

4.2 TELEPHONIC CONVERSATION

One form of dyadic conversation is interaction between two persons on the telephone. In this form the advantage of using body language and eye-contact is lost. But it is one of the commonest and fastest ways of contacting people. It is simple, handy, and in the long run economical. It has therefore been termed as 'a priceless means of communication'.

Here are a few guidelines for telephonic conversation:

- Cultivate a cheerful and friendly tone.
- Modulate your voice.
- Never sound hurried, flustered or impatient.
- Enunciate your words clearly.
- Do not use slang.
- Speak distinctly. If you use a word which is likely to be misunderstood, spell it out.
- Listen attentively to the caller. If the message is long, keep reassuring that you are listening by speaking words such as 'Yes', 'Okay', etc.
- Be courteous in all circumstances.
- Don't engage your telephone longer than necessary.

Bear the following points in mind when you receive or make a call.

4.2.1 Receiving Calls

- Lift the receiver or press the call button promptly.
- Reveal your identity, e.g. Ram Gopal, Chief Accountant.
- Hold the mouthpiece properly.
- If you do not know who the caller is, obtain his name and designation.
- Even if the caller is annoyed, keep yourself cool.
- Give the required information accurately. If it is not readily available promise to ring back and of course, keep your promise.
- If a wrong number call comes to you, do not abuse the caller or slam down the receiver.
- Keep a jot pad and a pencil handy to note down messages.
- Keep the telephone on your left hand side so that the right hand is free to write.
- Take down the message fully and correctly; a suggested form is given below:

TELEPHONE MESSAGE		
________________ Department/Section		
Message from:		
Telephone No.:		
Message for:		
Received	at (time)	on (date)
MESSAGE		
Message taken by:		

4.2.2 Making Calls

- Have a personal telephone directory listing the telephone numbers which you use often.
- If you are making a call for somebody else, follow his instructions.
- Have all the material ready before you dial the number. It is bad manners to keep somebody on the line while you rummage through the files.
- If you have to say a number of things, alert the listener by saying something like this: 'I want your opinion on two points. One...., two....'
- If you wish to leave a message say so and give a few seconds to the receiver to get ready. Let your message be clear and accurate. If it is important, you may repeat it.

However amiable you may be, there are likely to be persons in your organisation with whom you may not like to have any face-to-face interaction. Unless circumstances force you, you can use the telephone as a tool of contact. Similarly, if you find that an officer is busy interacting with others very often or for long periods and you have an urgent business to transact with him, telephone is the answer. Of course you would have to decide in individual cases and situations when to use the telephone and when not to use it.

4.3 INTERVIEW

The word 'interview' is derived from *intrevue* meaning 'sight between'. It is a meeting between two persons with a specific purpose. It may be defined as any purposeful inter-personal communication between two individuals or parties. In terms of structure and format interviewing is therefore a more formal form of dyadic communication. However, an interview situation may consist of one interviewee and several interviewers and vice versa. Here we shall discuss dyadic interviews but many of the points will be applicable to all interview situations.

An interview demands direct and dynamic interaction. By its very nature the process involves an assessment of one participant by another. Sometimes one of the participants represents an organisation or a group whereas the other participates in his individual capacity. One of the purposes of an interview is to elicit information which is not otherwise available from the written records or other sources.

4.3.1 Types of Interview

There are various types of interviews ranging from the one conducted by a journalist for newspaper reporting to that by a psychiatrist with a patient. The purpose defines the type of interviews. The interview broadcast and telecast on the radio and television is generally to seek an expert's opinion on issues of current interest to people or to educate the public on a matter of general importance. Such interviews have the semblance of privacy but we all know that they are meant for public consumption. Similar is the case with a journalistic interview, except that it is made public after a time-lag. Then there are situations where interview takes the form of a series of probing questions with a view to discovering the truth, for example, the kind of interrogation that is done by the police. Another type of interview termed counselling interview is conducted to provide guidance and psychological support to the interviewee. This may be done by an educational psychologist or a trained counsellor, the purpose being to bring the mind of the interviewee back to a state of normalcy or to help him steer through a period of emotional crisis. In large professional organisations and educational institutions provision may exist for the conduct of such interviews.

Here we are interested in the following two types of interview: (i) *employment interview* and (ii) *data collection interview*. These are the types of interview in which you will have to participate in your professional life. Closely related with the first type of interview are promotion interview and annual interview. The term 'employment interview' refers to the interview of a candidate for a job in a particular organisation. Promotion interview and annual interview are conducted in respect of the employees who are already in service. The former is arranged when a proposal for promotion of an employee is under consideration. The latter is a routine annual feature; its purpose is to assess, through personal interaction, the contribution and progress made by an employee during the year under review. But in India, these types of interviews are not common. We shall therefore discuss only the employment interview in some detail. It is clear that several fundamental points in this discussion are relevant for not only promotion and annual interviews but also for data collection interview. Obviously the discussion of any employment interview is from the viewpoint of the interviewee, whereas that of data collection interview is from the viewpoint of the interviewer. Nonetheless, in both cases the other participants would find sufficient valuable information.

4.3.2 Employment Interview

The main purpose of the prospective employer is to judge the suitability of the applicant to the job and that of the applicant, to find out whether the needs and requirements of the job would suit him and also whether the environment in the organisation would be conducive to his professional growth. Clearly, this form of dyadic communication provides an opportunity to both the participants for intense interaction and close observation of each other's personality traits, as reflected in their verbal behaviour and body language. As we are aware, the employment interview takes place when on the face of it there is a case for the acceptance of the applicant's services. The employer knows fully well the basic details about the career of the applicant – his educational background, his other interests, his experience, social status, etc. In the case of experienced employees he also knows the assessment of the applicant's earlier employer(s). What then is the interview for?

A prospective employer's main aim is to judge your sense of values, and your attitude towards work. He wants to get a feel of your respect for fair play and sense of justice and honesty in the discharge of duties. In fact, while conducting the interview, he looks for signs of these traits in your personality. Every employer, no wonder, wants people around who possess positive personal qualities and are dependable. The qualifications and the kind of educational background the interviewee has do not give an adequate idea of these important requirements.

Planning the interview, whatever be its type, demands adequate and careful prior preparation. How should one plan to appear in an interview of this sort? Surely each applicant wants to be successful, to be offered the job, even if he may ultimately decide not to accept it. Failure in an interview certainly injures the ego of a person temporarily. You should therefore pay close attention to the following, if you wish to achieve success.

It has been rightly said that the apparel oft proclaims the man; certainly so in the case of an interview. Physical appearance creates the first impression and tells something about the personality of the individual. Cleanliness and neatness are the first requirements for a smart turn out. While going for an interview spend a few minutes and take a critical look at your appearance: the clothes that you wear, the hairstyle and the footwear. Harmony and sobriety should mark your attire. You should never put on something in which you feel uncomfortable because it may lead to inconvenience and oddities in your behaviour while you are being assessed for the job. Loud colours, and other such ornamentations are likely to distract the attention of the interviewer from your countenance, which plays a definite role in an interaction of this kind. Your aim should be to use your physical appearance to create the first right impression on the interviewer.

A pleasing physical appearance should be accompanied by proper deportment and the right poise. How you carry yourself, how you walk and sit, how you make an exit – all these are important. Good deportment and good manners together generate a proper atmosphere and puts you at ease. Be observant and try to imbibe these qualities from the people who possess a high degree of social charm and poise. Nothing should appear to be artificial, imitative and odd in your demeanour. You should appear to be your natural self. These qualities will help you in making a mark not only at the employment interview but also throughout your career.

Take care that you do not indulge in certain mannerisms in your speech or behaviour. Expressions like 'err', 'you know', 'Oh my God', 'Well', etc., should be avoided. Similarly, do not use slang and highly colloquial language or uncommon abbreviations. The tone should be friendly but not intimate. Make sure that you are not in the habit of making odd gestures while talking. Playing with the hair or with the buttons of your bushshirt, or the keys in your hand creates a bad impression. Similarly, fixing your gaze on the interviewer or a painting or other objects in the room is also considered as bad manners.

Listening is an art that helps as much at the interview as in social situations. If you maintain a stony silence when the interviewer is speaking, he may feel uneasy. It is therefore necessary to give signals that you are listening to him. Your response may take the form of a nod or a smile or even sometimes whispering approvals, such as 'mm', 'yes', etc. You should not interrupt the interviewer. Wait till he has finished, howsoever impatient you may be to react to what he is saying. Detailed guidelines for improving the power of listening are given in Chapter 6.

Cultivate your speech. The best way to do so is to tape-record it and listen to it critically. Analyse your speech to find out whether you speak clearly, or you eat your syllables and slur your words. Does your speech sound dull and monotonous or lively and animated? Is the pitch of your voice too high or too low? Do you stress the right syllable and use the appropriate intonation? Satisfy yourself that your speech is clear, has proper rhythm and sounds pleasant. Practicing daily can certainly enhance the quality of your speech. Shakespeare's remark, 'Mend your speech a little, lest it should mar your fortune' holds good even today. Proper speech will help you not merely in getting the job but also in moving up on the ladder of your career.

More important than all these is what you say. Are you clear in your thoughts? Can you express them in simple language? Do you understand your own point of view on current issues in unmistakable terms? Do you have a philosophy of your own (a set of opinions) which you can put before others with conviction supported by valid arguments? Have you acquired the habit of coolly arguing your case? Do you feel crestfallen when your point of view is not accepted? These are some of the questions whose answers are obvious and you must have been made, aware of them in the course of your education. What is required is that at the time of interview you refresh your memory.

Always avoid giving uncomplimentary references to your former employers or other associates and making uncharitable remarks about them.

Types of Interview Questions

There is a great diversity in the types of questions that may be asked at an interview. You should try to anticipate the type of questions likely to be asked. Partly, this will be determined by the situation and the specific purpose that the interviewer has in mind. In general, the questions will be based on what you have stated in your biodata and your reaction to the organisation's visualisation of your role in it. We may classify the questions into the following categories: direct questions, open-ended questions, closed questions, bipolar questions and loaded questions.

Direct questions, generally used at the initial stage, are explicit, demanding specific information: What's your name? How old are you? In which company did you work last? etc.

Open-ended questions are not so straight, only the topic on which information is required is specified and the interviewee is asked to elaborate: What is your educational background? How did you find your experience of working on this plant in ABC company? etc.

Closed questions demand responses from a limited and narrow area. Often these questions provide alternatives from which the response is selected. An extreme form of the closed question is the one which demands only a 'Yes' or 'No' response. This is also called a bipolar question. A few examples are as follows: If selected, would you be able to join next month? Would you like to be posted in Mumbai or Kolkata? We are prepared to offer this job to you on a contract of three years; is it acceptable to you?

Loaded questions generally demand a response which the interviewer expects. They are suggestive in nature and encourage the interviewee to agree with the interviewer. Sometimes these may be used as a trap to discover whether the interviewee is clear in his mind about what he is in for. Ideally, as a general rule, loaded questions should not be used by the interviewer. However, as an interviewee, you should be prepared to face any type of questions.

The core of the body of the interview is the set of various types of questions discussed above. In a structured interview, apart from these, there are preliminary questions which set the tone for the interview and establish rapport between the interviewer and the interviewee. Similarly, at the end there are a few questions to signal the end of the interview. The interviewer aims at helping the interviewee to complete the expression of his thoughts and to clarify his stand before the interview ends.

It is difficult to visualise the questions that may be asked at an interview. However, we give below a sample of questions that could be asked at an employment interview.

A. Educational Background
- (i) Give a brief resume of your educational career.
- (ii) Why did you decide to offer Economics in your MA?
- (iii) Have you studied some books in this field other than those prescribed?
- (iv) Could you name a few such books and describe their themes?
- (v) Apart from Economics which field of knowledge interests you?
- (vi) Could you name some of the books you have read in this area of your interest?

B. Co-curricular Activities
- (i) You have produced a number of plays during your educational career. Tell us how you got interested in drama.
- (ii) Do you think your interest in drama affected your studies?
- (iii) What work did you do as a member of the editorial board of your college newsletter?
- (iv) Do you think this kind of work has added something to your academic experience?
- (v) What difficulties, in your opinion, does an editor face in producing a newsletter of this type?

C. Extra-curricular Activities
- (i) How is it that, although you played badminton throughout your college career, you never participated in any worthwhile tournament?
- (ii) Apart from physical exercise, does this game impart any other qualities to the player?
- (iii) What is the size of the badminton court?
- (iv) Do you play any other games?

D. Experience
- (i) Describe the specific work that you were doing in the production department.
- (ii) What new things have you learnt?

(iii) What are the ways of maximising production?
(iv) Did you introduce any new technique or procedure to increase production?
(v) In what way will your experience help our organisation?

E. General Knowledge

(i) What is your opinion about the new industrial policy announced by the Government of India?
(ii) What are the main causes of inflation in India?
(iii) Do you think deficit financing should be stopped? Why?
(iv) Give your comments on the Seventh Five-Year Plan.
(v) Do you think the Government of India's 20-point programme will usher in a new era? How?
(vi) What further steps should be taken to attract investment from Indians living abroad?
(vii) How should the pace of technology transfer be accelerated?
(viii) Comment on the current economic climate in the country.

F. Miscellaneous

(i) What do you understand by team-spirit?
(ii) Do you think it can be cultivated? If yes, how?
(iii) What are the qualities of an efficient manager?
(iv) Do you think you possess these qualities?
(v) How can the conflicts between the management and labour be resolved?

Employer's Expectations

We may classify the information which an employer seeks while considering a person for a job, into the following sub-headings:

(i) State of health: Every organisation desires its employees to be in a healthy state. Apart from judging at the interview, the organisation requires a new entrant to undergo a medical examination, the standards of which differ from profession to profession.
(ii) Attainments: A probe is made through searching questions to verify what is written by the candidate in the biodata and to assess the nature and quality of his achievements.
(iii) Intelligence: A close observation is made of the reflexes and responses of the interviewee to discover the extent of his grasp and confidence.
(iv) Aptitude: Certain questions are directed merely to find out the candidate's aptitude for the job he has applied for.
(v) Interests: An attempt is made to understand the other dimensions of the personality of the candidate by encouraging him to speak about his intellectual or social pursuits.
(vi) Disposition: A vital piece of information that all employers would like to have is whether the candidate has the ability to work with others,
(vii) Circumstances: A peep into the interviewee's previous environment and family circumstances may give some clue to the candidate's capacity to work.

Some employers use an assessment record sheet to judge the suitability of interviewees. An example is given as follows.

ASSESSMENT RECORD SHEET

Assessment → Items ↓	A (Excellent)	B (Good)	C (Average)	D (Below Average)	E (Poor)
I. Physical Make-Up and Manners: Appearance					
Poise					
Speech					
II. Qualifications: Education					
Training					
Experience					
III. Personality: Self-reliance					
Initiative					
Team-spirit					
Leadership					
IV. Intellectual Ability: Intelligence					
Memory					
Potential for Development					
V. Motivation: Objective Interests					
Consistency					
Aptitude					

4.3.3 DATA COLLECTION INTERVIEW

Very often you would be called upon to collect data for a specific purpose and present it in the form of a letter, memo, report, etc. This information may either be available with the officers in your own organisation or other organisations. Many of the points we have already discussed are also relevant for conducting this type of interview. However, since the nature of this interview differs both in respect of nterviewer-interviewee relationship and in the purpose for which it is conducted, certain additional points need to be borne in mind in the conduct of data collection interview. One, be clear in your own mind about the type and the amount of information you are seeking. Two, frame the questions which will elicit the required information. Three, be ready with a strategy of bringing the interviewee back to the point, if he goes off the track. Four, be as unobtrusive as possible in note-taking. Accuracy in recording data is essential and so you may decide to use certain abbreviations to be translated later. Five, do not enter into a discussion or argument with the interviewee. Six, always assume a subordinate position, leaving the dominant role to the interviewee. Seven, occasionally you may seek clarification, but too many interruptions can prove annoying. Eight, be an attentive listener, giving clues to your interest in whatever is being conveyed. Nine, if your questions embarrass the interviewee and he hesitates to answer them, do not insist on a response.

Planning for Data Collection Interview

Professionals are busy persons and you must therefore seek an appointment for the interview. Also indicate the amount of time it is likely to take. Go prepared with a notebook to record the points. Carefully visualise how you are going to open the dialogue and how you propose to end the interview. You may, in fact, write a few questions that you would use to begin the interview and also the remarks that you would make to conclude the interview.

Whatever be the type of interview, be courteous and tactful. Take maximum advantage of the immediate feedback that is available to you. Maintain a pleasant atmosphere throughout, controlling the environment by selecting appropriate verbal and non-verbal symbols. As far as possible introduce diversity in interaction. For example, if a number of questions have elicited 'no' response, manipulate your enquiry in such a way that it elicits an affirmative answer. A climate of mutual trust can result in a successful interview.

You may sometimes decide to write all the main questions that you wish to ask for eliciting the relevant information. To record, the answers you should carry a handy notebook with you. You can also use the answer sheet itself for writing the answers. But then you should ensure that enough space is available on the sheet for responses both to the main and to the supplementary questions.

A specimen copy of the interview sheet used to collect data for this book is given below:

UGC Book Writing Project on Professional Communication

[Authors: Prof Krishna Mohan & Dr (Mrs) Meera Banerji]

INTERVIEW SHEET

(i) Name:
(ii) Designation:
(iii) Organisation:
(iv) Total experience:
(v) Main function:

(*Continued*)

(*Continued*)

(vi) (a) How important are written and oral communications to your particular job?
(b) Which one do you think is more important from the point of view of the main function that you perform?
(c) Name some of the written communications that you send or receive.
(i) You write (ii) You receive
(d) Specify the modes of oral communication (telephone, interview, face-to-face discussion etc.),

(vii) (a) Do communication misunderstandings sometimes interfere with the efficiency of your Department?
(b) If yes, kindly explain briefly how this happens.
(c) How can barriers to communication be removed?

(viii) What kind of problems, if any, do you face while communicating
(a) with superiors?
(b) with peers?
(c) with subordinates?

(ix) (a) Do you feel that there is a need for training the employees of your organisation in English communication skills?
(b) If yes, what kind of training should they be imparted?
(c) Can you give us some idea about the kind of materials to be used and techniques to be employed for their training?

(x) What kind of reference material (mechanics of writing, words often confused, words often misspelt, pronunciation of words generally used in your profession, etc.) do you think can prove useful to a professional in doing his job?

(xi) Any other remarks that you would like to make in this context.

4.4 INSTRUCTION

Directing others to perform a particular act is one of the functions of a professional. Contrary to the general belief, it is not an easy task to tell others what one expects them to do without causing any psychological or emotional resistance. In fact, giving instruction is an art which can be cultivated. For the purpose of this discussion, we shall treat all that is said to achieve a single task as one instruction. For example, if you ask your secretary to make arrangements for a meeting, you may instruct her to supervise the seating arrangement, supply of stationery, serving of coffee, etc. Here the task is the arrangements for the meeting and all that you have asked your secretary to do is related to that task and is therefore one instruction.

Most often you will be required to give instruction to subordinates and junior officers. While doing so, keep in mind:

(i) the background knowledge of the recipient;
(ii) his psychological make-up;
(iii) his capacity to grasp; and
(iv) his ability to act upon your instructions.

Further, make sure that you restrict yourself to one task which you want to be performed. If a situation requires you to give more than one instruction, separate each by a time-gap or a clear signal for the end of one instruction and the beginning of the other. The language you use should be plain, direct and polite and the sentence short. Generally, the response to an instruction is an action and its success is measured by the extent to which it has been performed, according to your visualisation.

The main difference between the instruction on the one hand and conversation and interview on the other is in terms of response. In the latter two, the response is verbal whereas in the former it is action. The verbal response to it is only to indicate that the recipient has understood the message or to affirm his ability to act upon it.

4.5 DICTATION

Dictation is another type of dyadic communication, which is very frequently used in professional organisations. It is an art which every professional has to learn in order to transact his day-to-day business efficiently. It is wrong to suppose that one automatically acquires the ability to dictate as soon as one joins an organisation. In fact, it requires lively imagination and constructive mentality to practise this art successfully. Some of the hints given below would prove to be helpful for you in learning the art of dictation:

(i) Tell the steno the form of communication you are going to use and the situation prompting it. For example, one may begin by saying the following to put the steno in a receptive mood: 'This is a letter in response to the enquiry we have received from Bharat Steel Corporation ... .' 'Now we shall write a circular inviting quotations from registered firms ....' 'This is a memo to all heads of sections asking them to implement resolution No. 48 recently passed by the Board of Directors.'

(ii) Picture the entire composition, i.e. the total matter to be dictated, in verbal terms. The sequencing of ideas and the structure should be clear in your mind before you start dictating.

(iii) Develop the capacity of one sentence buffer memory into which you should be able to cast each sentence as it takes shape and is uttered. Remember that in dictation the initial editing and rewriting is done before the sentence is recorded in the notebook of the steno. This is the most flexible stage and requires deft handling of the process of converting meaning into linguistic material.

(iv) Speak every syllable with equal emphasis, deviating from the normal stress pattern. Take extra care in dictating homonyms, e.g. pale, pail; ascent, assent; compliment, complement; stationery, stationary etc. Similarly, words which have homonymic relationship are likely to confuse the steno; so special care should be taken in dictating them. A few examples of this category are: later, latter; proceed, precede; eligible, illegible; accede, exceed; accept, except, etc.

(v) Dictate all the punctuation marks. It may be too much to expect the steno to punctuate at the time of transcription. The beginning of a new paragraph should also be signalled.

(vi) Dictate in phrases, with appropriate pauses between them. The steno notes down your words in phrases. In shorthand transcriptions long words do not necessarily take more time than short words. Generally special abbreviations are provided for commonly used long words. But if you have to dictate an unfamiliar or uncommon long word, give more time to the stenographer. Unusual proper names and technical words may have to be written in long hand. You should therefore spell them and pause long enough for them to be written. Spelling more words than necessary is not a bad practice because it will save your time later when you go through the transcription.

(vii) Match the speed of your dictation to the speed of your steno.

(viii) Do not change the construction of your sentences too often.

(ix) When you receive the transcription and find in it words or phrases or sentences which do not exactly fit into the context, do not attempt to interpret meaning out of them. Instead, read them aloud, listening to the sounds carefully to see whether another group of words emerges, which is either what you originally said or is more appropriate in the context.

(x) If you dictate into a machine, listen to the material recorded before asking your steno to type it. This should be done also with a steno new to the job.

Acquisition of the ability to dictate has great professional significance. It prompts a professional to transmit his meaning without delay, adding not only to his own efficiency but also to the healthy functioning of the organisation to which he belongs. An incidental gain is that the development of effective dictating techniques can inculcate the capacity to speak extemporaneously.

ASSIGNMENTS

1. As a special correspondent of the *Bharat Times*, you have been deputed to interview the survivors of an air crash. A report based on this interview is slated for publication in your newspaper. Draft the list of questions that you would use for interviewing the passengers.
2. As a special correspondent of the *Employment News*, you have been asked to interview the Bank Managers of the nationalised banks in your town. The purpose is to elicit the latest information on the facilities available to the educated unemployed youth and the procedures for availing of them. Prepare a list of questions for interviewing the Bank Managers.
3. As Personnel Manager of a Public Limited Company, you have to interview fresh graduates for recruitment to the junior management cadre. Prepare a list of questions which you are likely to use for interviewing the candidates.

4. Assume that you are the Production Manager of a manufacturing plant, which has gone out of order. The maintenance engineer of the company which installed the machine has been deputed for repairing it. Inventing the necessary details, prepare a set of instructions that you would give to your Deputy Manager. You yourself would be away on tour on the day the maintenance engineer is to come.
5. Prepare a set of instructions for the newly recruited stenographers in your organisation on the technique of listening and recording dictation.
6. For the benefit of your junior colleagues, write a detailed guidance note on how to dictate replies to letters. You may use one of the letters given in Chapter 16 for this purpose.

Chapter 5

PUBLIC SPEAKING AND ORAL PRESENTATION

SPEECH is a gift of Nature; it distinguishes man from other living beings. Pericles has rightly said, 'the thinking human being not able to express himself stands at the same level as those who cannot think'. If put to proper use this faculty can work wonders. It can instil new zeal, uplift sagging confidence, and soothe injured feeling. There is truth in what Adolf Hitler once remarked, 'All epoch-making revolutionary events have been produced not by the written word but by the spoken word'. However, if it is misused, speech can tear asunder even well-established, harmonious relationships and engender dissension, strife and destruction. Though war begins in mind, it is first fought with spoken words and then with weapons. You may have observed that, often, a heated verbal exchange precedes violence.

In this Chapter, we shall focus attention on public speaking, which means speaking to a group of persons (audience) on a subject that is academic or professional in nature and not on a matter which is private or personal. Some speaking situations in which you will have to speak publicly at your workplace are: lecture on a given subject, paper presentation in a seminar, briefing employees, putting forward a proposal in a meeting, oral reporting to co-workers, addressing a general body meeting, inaugurating an official event, bidding farewell to a colleague, etc. In fact, the higher the position you hold, the greater would be the number of occasions for public speaking. In the discussion that follows, we have used the word 'speech' for all kinds of public speaking such as 'lecture', 'talk', 'address', or 'oral presentation'. We have also used these words interchangeably.

In this context the first thing that we need to understand is that public speaking is not an inborn talent, it is a set of skills that is acquired by persistent efforts.

The phrase oral presentation is generally used for a speech containing specialised or technical information on a specific topic for a relatively smaller but knowledgeable audience.

Even eminent orators like Abraham Lincoln and Winston Churchill had to work hard to attain excellence in public speaking. What should then be done to attain proficiency in speaking? It is obvious that all speakers cannot become great orators. But certainly, by keeping in mind a few points and acting on the suggestions given in this chapter, you can acquire adequate ability to meet all the common requirements of your work situation. Incidentally, the ability imbibed for this purpose would serve you well in other speaking situations. It would add value to your performance and quality to your life. In fact, effective speaking is an important trait and a person's personality is fully revealed when he speaks, as well as by what he speaks and how he speaks. If you ponder for a while, you would realise that you do not like some persons simply because they are not able to speak properly.

You might have already attained the required level of proficiency, even then, you need to sustain it. And maintaining the level of performance in speech is like maintaining a state of good health: constant awareness of basics and regular practice.

Always remember 'Dissemination of knowledge is no less important than the acquisition of knowledge.' And speech is a powerful instrument for achieving this purpose.

Now we would like to discuss a few suggestions which can improve your ability for public speaking.

5.1 PREPARATORY STEPS

Preparation is perhaps the surest and shortest path towards success in public speaking. A well-known author, Dale Carnegie, has rightly remarked, 'A talk is a voyage with a purpose and must be charted. The person who starts out going nowhere generally gets there'. Undoubtedly, it takes time to make a thorough preparation. But the time spent in getting ready to speak is time well-spent. If you take the following steps, you would normally be well-prepared for the event.

- Gather the relevant material.
- Structure the material
- Prepare the material for display and distribution.
- Inspect the venue for physical arrangements
- Size up the audience.
- Decide on audio-visual aids to be used by you.

The last two steps would be discussed a little later under the sub-heading 'Audience Awareness' in this chapter and 'Audio-Visual Aids' in Chapter 10; the rest are being briefly touched upon in this section.

The first step that you should take is to gather the relevant material from sources such as newspapers, journals, books, Internet websites, etc., and note it down in an organised way in Note Cards or thick Note Sheets. But if you have already got the material, go through it carefully to ensure that it is appropriate for the audience you are going to address. In some cases a rearrangement of points may be necessary. You should also visualise whether you would need any support material (e.g. a handout) or would like to exhibit some matter visually, e.g. through overhead projector or slides. If yes, then you must prepare such material well in time. The best preparation for tomorrow is doing your best today.

Most speakers prefer to prepare an outline of speech and the main points, sub-points and key words and phrases. These help a speaker recall the particular matter that is to be presented. You may also follow this practice. First, prepare the outline and then Note Cards, writing the points, sub-points, etc., in the same sequence as noted in the outline. The cards should also show where you have to display the support material. When you go to speak, keep with you both the outline and the cards. Use the latter while speaking, and keep the former for reference. The matter should be written neatly in bold letters only on one side of the cards. Do not forget to number the cards and the exhibits that you are going to use for support. A preparation of this kind will enable you to find time to observe the reaction of the audience and help you fine-tune your delivery and in some cases even to reorganise or to omit some matter. If you ponder, you would realise that the material for presentation can, in general, be divided into three parts:

- One, that must be presented because it is crucial to the understanding of the topic;
- Two, that should be presented because without it the audience would not be able to fully understand the matter in part one;
- Three, that might be presented if time permits or the occasion demands.

Now let us take an example. Suppose you have been asked to give an overview of 'Advertising: Its Function and Strategy' to students of Marketing Management. One way of organising the matter for this talk could be as shown in the following outline:

1. Introduction
   - 1.1 Historical Perspective
   - 1.2 Purposes
2. Mediums used
   - 2.1 Radio
   - 2.2 Television and films
   - 2.3 Newspapers and periodicals
   - 2.4 Hoardings, banners and neon signs
3. Techniques employed
   - 3.1 Syntactic dislocations
   - 3.2 Cartoons and graphic devices
   - 3.3 Slogans and rhymes
   - 3.4 Pictures and photographs
   - 3.5 Statements by celebrities
4. Legal aspects
   - 4.1 Existing provisions
   - 4.2 Suggestions for change

5. Moral aspects
   - 5.1 Impact on consumers
   - 5.2 Public awareness
6. Conclusion
   - 6.1 Summary
   - 6.2 Vision of the future

The note card to discuss the 'Purposes of Advertising' may be prepared as follows:

Sample Note Card

PURPOSES

- TO INFORM ABOUT NEW PRODUCTS
  (e.g. maggi, sunfeast biscuits)
- TO WIDEN SALES BASE
  (e.g. nirma washing powder, TV, water pumps in rural areas)
- TO SUSTAIN REPUTATION
  (e.g. bournvita, bajaj auto)
- TO EDUCATE POTENTIAL CONSUMERS
  (e.g. saving habits by LIC and banking companies; health care consciousness by processed food, soap, toothpaste industries)

The purposes are NOT MUTUALLY EXCLUSIVE

Another preparatory step to which attention is seldom paid is the inspection of the venue of speech before hand. If feasible, do find out whether:

- The venue is well-ventilated;
- The seats are properly arranged;
- There is a podium with steps;
- There is a screen for display;
- There is a lectern on the podium;
- A mike (fixed or lapel) is provided;
- The required equipment is available, and
- A technician would be available to assist you.

This information would put you in a proper frame of mind and help you perform better. At times, the arrangement may not be satisfactory and you may have to make minor changes in your strategy. For example, if the venue is not well-ventilated, you many compress your thoughts and reduce the duration of your speech. Or if the mike is not provided and there are about 50 persons in the gathering, you may ask for a glass of water to be kept within your easy reach. It is true that sometimes you would not get an opportunity to inspect the physical arrangements before hand. In such situations you can quickly gather the relevant information by interacting with the organisers of the event. Moreover, when you arrive at the venue, you are likely to get a breathing time of a minute or two before being asked to speak. Utilise this time gap to look around to take in the details of the physical setting.

5.2 STRUCTURING THE CONTENTS

For spectacular success in public speaking it is necessary to organise the material meticulously, keeping the following factors in mind:

- Key idea.
- Supporting ideas.
- Time available.
- Expectations of the audience.

The outline and the Note Cards would help you visualise what you are going to say to elaborate the points and sub-points. It is customary to divide the contents into three main parts, namely,

- Introduction,
- Main Body,
- Conclusion.

Let us adhere to the beaten path and see how each part should be handled.

5.2.1 Introduction

'The first impression is the lasting impression' You should therefore go all-out to win the audience right from the beginning. You may be aware that their attention level is very high at this stage. There is an air of expectancy and curiosity among them. As a speaker, you too are likely to be full of gusto and in a state of excitement. So the first few minutes are crucial. You need to establish a rapport with the audience and exercise a favourable impact upon their minds. In a way, at the initial stage, speaking in public is like riding a horse. Once you manage to settle firmly in the saddle, it would go galloping to the goal. A good start besides enhancing your confidence level, would set the tone for the rest of the speech.

There are a number of ways to motivate the audience to listen to you and to look forward with interest to what is to follow. Given below are a few elements that you could include in the Introduction to achieve this purpose:

- Spell out the objective of the talk clearly.
- Provide a context for the speech in brief.
- Give a preview of what you are going to say.
- Relate the topic to the need or interest of the audience.

- Establish your credibility.
- Lead the audience seamlessly to the main body of the speech.

To gain immediate attention, start your speech with a punch. Construct beforehand a few sentences with which you would like to open your speech. To help you do this, here are a few suggestions:

(a) ***Enkindle the curiosity.***

A speech on 'Advertising as a Profession' may begin with the question: 'Do you know that in India alone, five lakh persons are directly or indirectly engaged in the advertising industry?'

(b) ***Make a dramatic statement.***

In a lecture on 'Salesmanship', the speaker began with the following remark: 'Salesmanship is picking the pocket of the consumer after telling him that you are doing so'. Take another example. In a talk on 'The Menace of Growing Population' the speaker opened his speech thus: 'By the time I finish my talk, five thousand new mouths would have arrived in this world requiring food, care and attention.'

(c) ***Quote an eminent person or an apt statement.***

A learned speaker opened his speech on 'The Secret of Gaining Power' by quoting Margaret Thatcher: 'Being powerful is like being a lady. If you have to tell people you are, you aren't.' On another occasion a speaker invited to give a talk on 'Aging is a Blessing' remarked: 'Young age comes and goes; old age comes and stays, which one is better?'

(d) ***Narrate an anecdote or tell a story.***

In a lecture on 'The Cultural Aspect of Communication' a learned speaker used the following two stories to introduce his topic: (a) A newly arrived English man went for shopping to a posh shopping complex in Delhi. There, a sales girl approached him and said, 'Sir, can I help you?' Non-plussed, after a pause, the English man responded: 'Well ... you should know better.' (b) A young man from an Arab country was invited to a party in London. He enjoyed the food as well as phatic communion with the guests. When the party was over, a small group of girls went up to him and said 'Bye. See you later' and disappeared in the crowd. After a few days, on observing the sullen face of my friend, I asked 'What's the matter?' He replied, 'The girls here don't mean what they say. Not a single girl has yet come to see me.'

(e) ***Pay compliments to the audience.***

For example, one may open one's speech thus: 'I am delighted to be here this afternoon and to share my thoughts with you. I always love to interact with young and intelligent persons like you.' Let there be a ring of sincerity in your voice when you make such statements. Once the ego of the audience is boosted they are likely to develop a positive attitude towards you and the topic on which you are going to speak. In any case, the remarks would certainly induce a receptive mood which you can cash on as you proceed.

5.2.2 Main Body

This part forms the bulk of a speech because at this stage the central thought or the key idea is presented in detail. The presentation of the idea together with explanatory and supporting material takes about

90 per cent of the allotted time. The discussion may contain complex abstractions, exposition of subtle thoughts, explanation of complicated processes, or reference to fine points related to the issue. All these require close attention from the audience. Further, your introduction might have raised the expectations of the audience. So you need to make extra efforts to handle the contents of the main body. A few suggestions are given below to assist you in performing this task.

Presentation Patterns

The material relating to the points you have already identified should be divided into small modules. Each module should have a clear beginning, middle, and an end. Usually the attention span of an adult is about 60 minutes. But there are a few who cannot pay sustained attention for more than 15 minutes or so. Since you have to cater to the needs all members of the audience, try to provide relief by sprinkling your presentation with personal references, quotations, questions and audio-visual material. But do ensure that there is a variety in the use of these attention-getting strategies.

Follow a particular pattern or order in arranging the modules of the contents. A few examples are described below.

(a) The most commonly used pattern is the arrangement of sub-topics and modules constituting them, into an order of their importance.
(b) If the topic is predominantly informative, the modules may be arranged in a chronological order and each module should be related to a period or point of time or an event.
(c) Occasionally your speech may centre round a problem. Here the contents would have mainly two divisions: the first, describing or explaining the problem and its causes; and the second, offering a solution and its impact. If the situation so requires, you may split each division into sub-topics and each sub-topic into modules and then deal with them in the manner discussed earlier.
(d) In a speech to explain why something happened or happens you have to describe the causes or factors responsible for the happening and then explain the effects. For example, in a lecture on 'The Menace of Recurring Floods in the Northern Region', you have to state natural causes and man-made causes and then highlight the effects in terms of loss of animal and human lives, loss of property, impact on the economy of the region, and so on.

Development of Points

A speech is an oral composition. In developing the points you have included in a speech you have to follow, more or less, the same strategy as in developing the points in written communication, the detailed guidance for which is provided in the chapter on Style. However, you have to bear in mind that in a speech the audience would be present in front of you and so you will have to talk to them, using the principles of I-you communication. In the section on Qualities in the Chapter on Business Correspondence, we have discussed the basic principles. Consult and use them in composing your speech after necessary changes.

Try to recall the various devices used by eminent writers and effective speakers for unfolding their thoughts. You will find a great variety in their approach to the development of points they wish to make.

Here we shall discuss a few common devices used for this purpose.

(i) ***Example***: The most commonly used device is the example. Its function is to clarify, illustrate or fortify the assertion previously made. A telling example can remove the cobwebs, if any, from the mind of listeners and assist them in perceiving your thoughts in a clear light. It may also arrest the attention of the wandering minds and cajole them to focus it on you speech. While discussing the ways of making introduction effective, earlier in this chapter, we have given a number of examples. Go through them again, analyse them and try to understand their role in driving the point home. In other chapters too we have frequently used this device to achieve our purpose.

(ii) ***Comparison and Contrast***: Occasionally you may find yourself apparently at a dead end. You may get stuck and see no way to proceed. In such a situation this device would become handy. Assume that you have to talk about the points to be kept in mind for article writing. You may compare and contrast it with essay writing with which the audience is likely to be familiar. First, draw their attention to the similarities in terms of structure and style and then to dissimilarities in terms of objective and approach.

(iii) ***Statistics***: To develop support to a viewpoint or to convince the listeners, quoting statistics is helpful. But its use would depend upon the topic of your speech. For example, if you have to speak on 'Combating Cancer', you may give statistics culled from a reliable source to show the magnitude of the problem. However, remember that, if you use this device too frequently the audience may withdraw their attention and interest and switch off their receivers! So use this device where you must and that too in different forms such as graph, chart, etc.

(iv) ***Testimony***: The use of views expressed by others to support your viewpoint is called testimony. You may either quote the exact words or paraphrase them. In either case, mentioning the source is advisable. For instance, in a lecture on the importance of spoken language, you may quote, Thomas Carlyle: 'the art of speech is noble, even divine ...' The testimony from experienced experts or authorities in the field carries more weight than any lay testimony. The latter is usually taken from newspaper reports or articles in periodicals.

(v) ***Definition***: A definition usually leads a listener to the unknown or the unfamiliar from the known and the familiar. It sets the boundary of the semantic area of a concept or idea under discussion and thus helps the listener concentrate on the central thought. You can use this device by selecting or constructing an apt definition and making it a base for developing the various elements of the main body. After the definition, you may spend some time in explaining the key words and phrases to highlight the full import of the definition and its relevance to your speech. You may have observed that definition is widely used in all communications, oral or written, where conveying exact meaning is crucial and imperative, e.g. the constitution of a country, law books, technical and reference documents such as a dictionary or an encyclopedia. In a speech on a topic which is abstract or theoretical in nature, the use of this device is equally essential. Thus while speaking on 'The Secret of Happiness', it would be advisable to define 'happiness' and distinguish it from 'pleasure', 'delight', 'bliss', etc. The audience would need to know the exact nature of the feeling you are going to talk about.

5.2.3 Conclusion

If you have successfully handled the first two parts of your speech, namely, Introduction and Main Body, the audience would expect you to end it with an interesting and powerful punch. Their attention level is likely to be high at this stage. Even those who were not attentive during the presentation of the earlier parts, may become alert when they sense that you are about to complete your talk. What Michael Faraday said a long time ago is worth remembering: 'A flame should be lighted at the commencement and kept alive with unremitting splendour to the end'.

Like preparing the earlier parts, there is a need to map out clearly how you would conclude your speech. Do not leave it for decision till the moment comes. A lacklustre conclusion can leave a bitter taste in the mouth and erase the good impression that you had made. In fact, the composition of conclusion should be done beforehand with skill and uncanny insight of the whole situation. According to the noted author, H.W. Longfellow, 'Great is the art of beginning but greater is the art of ending'.

If you keep in focus the function of the conclusion, it would not at all be difficult to end your speech effectively. Usually a good conclusion repeats, concisely but powerfully, the central idea besides giving a signal that you are approaching the end. Some of the expressions used to signal the end are:

- In conclusion
- Before I close
- The last point I wish to make
- To summarize
- In the end I would like

and so on.

You can also, by the pace of delivery, volume of voice, and intonation, indicate that you are moving towards the end. At the same time you may also show to the audience how you have done what you promised in the beginning. But while doing so, try to avoid the language used earlier. Instead, couch the conclusion in new expressions, using telling phrases and diverse syntactical patterns. There are some speakers who quote an eminent person or make a dramatic statement to induce the desired impact. For example, a speech on 'Modern Warfare' ended with the following statement: 'Today winning a war is not an act of unsullied glory, for the victory is that of the dying over the dead.' Look at another example. Addressing a rally in Burma in August 1994, Subhash Chandra Bose ended his speech with the following words: 'Friends! My comrades in the War of Liberation! Today I demand of you one thing, above all. I demand of you blood. It is blood alone that can avenge the blood that the enemy has split. It is blood alone that can pay the price of freedom. Give me blood and I promise you freedom.'

In the end, we are tempted to quote an interesting statement made by Lord Mancroft: ***A good speech is like a love affair; any fool can start one but to end it requires considerable skill***. We do not agree with the view expressed in the first part, though we are certainly in full agreement with what is stated in the second part. But we are not sure whether you would agree with us or not.

5.3 AUDIENCE AWARENESS

The human mind is the most wonderful thing – it starts working the moment one is born and never stops until one gets up to speak to an audience. Has this ever happened to you? If not, you are an exceptionally gifted person. Most of us sometimes have had to face the embarrassment of becoming speechless or of being able to mumble a few words in front of an audience. The ability to get going and then to maintain the speech flow depends upon a number of factors. The first is through preparation, which we have already discussed. Another is audience awareness, which we are going to discuss. We shall draw your attention later to other factors as well.

For every speech it is necessary to gather information about the audience before hand – their number, their gender, age group, educational level, social status, professional status, extent of knowledge about the topic and their attitude towards it. If circumstances do not permit you to do so, size up the audience when you reach the venue of your talk and make a quick assessment by looking at the entire audience before you begin to speak.

While speaking, keep a close watch on the listener's reactions. Is there a glimmer of joy in their eyes? Do their faces wear a cheerful expression? Does their posture indicate that they have a positive attitude? If the answer to these questions is Yes, continue with the strategy you have chosen and at the pace you have decided. But if you notice a sign of boredom, dejection or disappointment among the listeners, modify your strategy by varying pace and volume and introducing more attention-getters such as narrating anecdotes, quoting eminent persons, reciting lines of poetry, dramatising certain statements, asking rhetorical questions, etc. You may also give an internal summary of what you had spoken, up to a point of time, and restate very briefly the relevance of the topic to the needs of the audience.

In most cases the audience would be a heterogeneous group in terms of attitude, tolerance, background, etc. It would consist of persons with diverse personality traits. Broadly speaking your audience is likely to consist of the following types of persons.

- *The inverted reticent*: Such a person is not slow in grasping what you say. He simply does not give evidence of having understood the message and is rather reluctant to speak in interactive situations. To draw an active response from such a person you may ask him a question directly and appreciate his response. You may also, through your nods and smiles, give him the impression that you greatly value his presence and participation.
- *The intelligent aggressor*: Such a person has a large ego and rejoices in converting a useful talk into a controversial, trivial conversation. Usually you would find him sitting in the last row in a corner in an aggressive posture. Intelligent as he is, he makes an all-out effort to steal the show. He cannot tolerate the slightest threat or challenge to his mind-set and to the views on matters of concern to him. The worst thing that can happen is that the audience begin to look towards him for approval of the points you have made. One way to deal with such a participant is to seek his assistance in making your talk successful. For example, you could request him to distribute the hand outs or other material among the audience or help you analyse the visual material displayed by you or add matter to a point you have made or give an example to illustrate the viewpoint expressed by you, etc. Another thing you could do is to acknowledge his contribution in the area. But do not

give him too long a rope. To cut him short, encourage and prompt other members of the audience to come out with their views. Not much time should be devoted to these activities otherwise the flow of your presentation would be adversely affected. Let there be two or three such interludes in a talk of about one hour.

- *The submissive recipient*: Such a person would accept everything you say without a thought or question. He waits for words of wisdom to fall from the lips of a speaker and laps them up with relish. To activate his mind you may, during the course of your talk, ask opinion-based questions requiring an application of the concepts you have discussed. Try to stimulate such participants into independent thinking and reacting maturely. Your growth as a speaker partly depends upon the kind of audience you have to deal with. It is rightly said: 'Effective teaching begets effective learning and effective learning begets effective teaching.' And this circle is considered to be happy and desirable and not vicious.
- *The gloomy pessimist*: A listener of this type has a negative attitude. He always tries to pick a hole, howsoever well-framed and tightly-structured a speech may be. He habitually looks at the dark side of things. Remember, such a person can infect others with his 'gloom' and create an atmosphere of despondency and hopelessness. If you notice such a person, do not ignore him. Instead, try to involve him in the process of communication by making more frequent eye contact with him and occasionally asking fact-based questions, requiring 'yes or no' type or 'right or wrong' type answers.
- *The eager cooperator*: Unless you are especially unlucky, the audience will have a majority of eager cooperators. A listener belonging to this category usually has an open mind and is eager to learn, to gather information, to acquire new knowledge and to imbibe new skills. He would make a sincere effort to understand what you say and cooperate with you by giving signals such as a nod, a smile, an appropriate receptive gesture and so on. During the interaction at question time also he would help you keep the discussion on the track and support you if distractors try to negate your speech. You must therefore quickly win the cooperation of such listeners by employing strategies of effective speaking discussed elsewhere in this chapter.

5.4 MODES OF DELIVERY

Once a well-known speaker, on being asked the secret of his success, said; 'Elementary my dear. Have something to say and say it well.' The subject matter referred to in the first part of this statement has been briefly touched upon earlier in the Section on 'Structure of Speech.' Here, the latter part shall be the focus of our attention in the discussion that follows.

Let us first clearly understand and realise that no less important than the contents is the manner in which it is delivered to the audience. It has been estimated that words (which convey the contents) contribute only 7 per cent, vocal aspects 38 per cent and non-verbal aspects, the balance of 55 per cent to the communication of meaning in public speech. No wonder then, sometimes a well-prepared speech, rich in contents, fails to exercise a positive impact on the audience merely because of poor delivery. You may have had the occasion of sitting through a dull, drab or the so-called 'smooth' presentation that had lulled you to sleep. This generally happens when there is no variation in the speaker's pace of delivery, volume of voice and accompanying body movements. In fact, effective delivery depends upon a set of skills that have to be acquired through repeated practice. Before going into details of how to deliver your talk, we would like to draw your attention to the following two basic requirements for success in public speaking. One, speak with a vibrant voice, animated gestures and pleasant facial expression. Two, mix judiciously the elements of an informal conversation and those of a formal communication. You can achieve these objectives in several ways. Here we shall discuss the following four modes of delivery which are used by speakers:

- Reading the Text
- Memorising the Text
- Speaking Extemporaneously
- Speaking Impromptu

Do remember that, whatever be the mode, a speech delivered through the standing position exercises greater impact than that delivered through the sitting position.

5.4.1 Reading the Text

This mode of delivery is generally used in highly formal situations which require strict adherence to a time limit and the use of appropriate-to-the-occasion phraseology. Political leaders often use this mode so that they are reported correctly by the media persons. A single mistake in the use of language can add to their problems. The speeches of high dignitaries (such as President, Prime Minister, etc.) broadcast on the radio or telecast on the television are read by them with the help of a tele-prompter. Since, in this mode, the entire speech is written and then read aloud, it requires the deployment of three language skills, namely, writing, reading and speaking. If you also wish to use this mode on certain occasions, you should be aware that a text meant to be read before a gathering of listeners is different in certain respects from the text meant for silent reading. The former ought to have an oral flavour, i.e. elements of I-You face to face communication. While reading the text, give the impression that you are talking to the audience. Otherwise they would lose interest in your presentation. Do not let it become a barrier between you and the audience. For using this mode effectively, you need to take the following steps:

(a) Write the text carefully, keeping in mind that it is to be read aloud.

(b) Familiarise yourself with the text by reading it several times before the actual presentation. You should be able to recall quickly the location of points included in the speech.

(c) Rehearse reading the speech before your friends, colleagues or even before a mirror with appropriate pauses, voice control and body language. Change the contents and delivery, if necessary, in the light of comments by others or your own observation.

(d) Mark in the text the places where you have to pause longer, where you have to speak with emphasis, where you have to raise your voice, where you have to speak at a low pitch, and where you have to speak at a greater or less than the normal speed.

This mode of delivery has certain advantages; the main ones are mentioned below:

- You can enrich the content and improve the style of the text by going through it several times before presentation.
- You would feel fully confident because the entire speech in written form would be with you.
- You can pay extra attention to the nuances of delivery because you do not have to think and organise your thoughts as you speak.
- The text of your speech would be available for future use. In fact, in some situations, you may distribute copies of the text after delivering it.

Despite these advantages, this mode should be used only in special circumstances, i.e. in situations where you must. In using it you may face certain problems/difficulties. We would like to draw your attention to these so that you may prepare yourself well in time.

- It is not easy to combine the features of oral communication with those of written communication.
- There is little room for addition or modification of an approach or idea which may flash upon your mind while speaking. Moreover, the expression of frozen thoughts may lack the sparkle and liveliness.
- The frequency of eye contact with the audience may become less than desirable.
- The body movement is also likely to get restricted because you have to remain closely tied with the text throughout your speech.

5.4.2 Memorising the Text

In this mode also, the entire speech is written. It is memorised and delivered word for word. What we said to the writing of the text for the first mode is equally true of the text for this mode. This mode is generally used by a novice or by a person who, owing to utter lack of confidence, suffers from stage fright. Experienced speakers use this mode with consummate skill for short speeches such as introducting a presenter to the audience, welcoming an important guest, proposing a vote of thanks, etc. Some of the advantages that this mode has are stated below:

- The speaker feels confident because the entire speech is stored in his memory.
- Since it is prepared beforehand, the text is likely to have a proper structure and an effective style.
- It would be easy to concentrate on suitable use of body movement, body language and vocal elements.
- The length of the speech can be tailored according to the time available. The delivery too can be well managed within this limit.

We may hasten to add that these advantages are not unique to this mode. Further, the disadvantages outweigh them. Look at the following critically:

- It is difficult to memorise lengthy texts. Even if the text is short, learning it by heart can be very time-consuming and sometimes even irritating.

- While speaking, you would not be able to alter the tenor of your presentation in the light of feedback from the audience.
- If perchance you are not able to recall a word, phrase or sentence, you are likely to feel flustered or even to become speechless for a while. Some among the audience may feel amused at your embarrassment, adding fuel to the fire. Your credibility would be lost and the audience may pay little attention to what you say subsequently.
- A memorised speech, howsoever well-written, is likely to lose its animation and vitality unless it is delivered with great care, zeal and ease in a natural style – a style that does not show that the speech is memorised. Remember, generally persons think poorly of a presenter who delivers a memorised speech. In the mind of some, there could be a vehement denouncement of memorisation as a method of education. We still remember an oft-repeated statement that used to be made in our school days to condemn this method: 'In rote learning the information passes from the notebook of the teacher to the notebook of the student without passing through the mind of either.'

5.4.3 Speaking Extemporaneously

This mode is rightly considered to be the most effective mode of delivery. A vast majority of speakers use it and the audience too expect the speakers to use this mode. For using it, you have to prepare well, as for the other modes. But the nature of preparation is slightly different. After deciding the quantity of matter to be presented on a given occasion, organise it into a well-knit logical structure. As we have discussed in the section on Preparatory Steps, prepare an outline of the entire speech and Note Cards for each point you propose to discuss, May we remind you that in these Cards you should indicate.

- The key words and phrases;
- The points you would like to emphasise;
- The places where you would use audio-visual aids;
- The places where you wish to give an internal summary;
- The places where you wish to quote; and
- The places where you propose to narrate an anecdote.

As part of their preparation, some speakers, in addition, write the full text of the speech and after reading it several times discard it. It is not advisable to do so because one may be tempted to memorise certain portions and deliver them at appropriate places. The mixing of the two modes may land you in difficulty. A better course would be to look at the outline and Note Cards and examine the thoughts that these generate in your mind. You can then modify them if they are unsuitable or discard them, if they are trite or entirely irrelevant. After doing this exercise several times you would become clear about how to develop each point. In fact, you will have a clear picture of the semantic structure of the entire presentation. At the time of delivery all you will have to do is to give a linguistic form to this structure. You may, however, at the most memorise one or two opening remarks, quotations that you wish to use, and a few closing statements.

From the discussion so far you can easily deduce the advantages that this mode has. Let us draw your attention to the main ones in specific terms:

- The presentation of ideas is direct and spontaneous and so fresh and attention-arresting.
- There is a greater room for the accommodation of new ideas that may occur to you while speaking.
- The linguistic material can be maneuvered to generate the desired effect or impact. For example, a complex thought can be explained in different words twice or thrice.
- It is easy to change the tenor of speech in the light of feedback from the audience. For example, you may take more time or less time in explaining a point, pose rhetorical questions, give additional examples, etc.
- This mode permits an effective use of all means of non-verbal communication such as body language, body movements, voice manipulation, etc.
- As they are not frozen with the text, the supporting materials such as charts graphs, maps, etc. can be used with greater ease and effect.
- It is not difficult to adjust to the unexpected situations such as reduction in the allotted time, modification in the composition of the audience, change in the physical setting, non-availability of technical aid, etc.

5.4.4 Speaking Impromptu

There would be several occasions when you would be called upon to speak impromptu, i.e. without a prior and specific preparation. If you ponder for a while, you would realise that you have been doing this daily. When we interact with persons for personal or professional work, we speak spontaneously a number of times during the course of the day. In fact, a person is said to have acquired competence in speaking a language, if he is able to transact his daily business with fluency and accuracy in natural social settings, requiring oral communication. His responses are automatically generated by the store of knowledge he possesses and his ability to convert it into words. But here we are concerned with speaking before a gathering of listeners on an informal or formal occasion. If you are asked to 'say a few words' on any such occasion (formal dinner, farewell function or seminar), do not get panicky. Walk gently and confidently to the podium, collecting your thoughts on the subject, as you go. On reaching the podium settle yourself before the mike, pause for a while and make eye contact with the entire audience. If you are not able to speak to the point immediately, repeat or summarise one or two points made by earlier speakers. This would give you time and strength to proceed further. Remember, nobody would expect a perfect speech from you in such a situation. So also, if your speech is a little disorganised, nobody would mind. Since your response would be natural and spontaneous, you are likely to be heard with attention and appreciation, you can do one thing more.

Before going to participate in the event, refresh your memory and collect your thoughts on the subject of the talk if it belongs to or is related to your experience or area of specialisation. You can, in many cases, easily anticipate that you could be asked to speak. Being mentally prepared to meet this eventuality would enable you to benefit more from mere participation as well.

If you develop the ability to use this mode effectively and earn a reputation as a good impromptu speaker, your upward mobility in the organisation would become easier. All forward-looking managements wish to have persons who can communicate without preparation and make important points or put forward their view point on a subject or issue convincingly.

5.5 VOCAL ASPECTS

As we have shown in Chapter 2, non-verbal communication is that part of communication which takes place without the use of words. The studies in this field have established that approximately 55 per cent of face-to-face oral communication takes place through non-verbal means. Out of the three elements, namely,

- body language (kinesics)
- space distancing (proxemics) and
- vocal aspects (paraphonetics)

that constitute non-verbal communication, we have already discussed the first two. Here we shall briefly look at the third, vocal aspects. The vocal aspects of communication are: pitch, volume, rate, quality, animation and pause. **Pitch** is the tone of sounds depending upon the rate of vibration of the vocal chords. You must have observed that when you speak, there is a continual variation in the levels at which your voice is pitched. The variation ranges from the soprano level to the bass level. **Volume** refers to the power of the sound and it ranges from very loud to very soft. **Rate** is the degree of speed at which you speak words. The characteristic tone of a voice is its **quality**. Sometimes a voice may be termed as creaky or jarring to the ears or it may be labeled as pleasant. The liveliness of speech is known as **animation**.

Pause refers to junctures in speech. Except the quality of the voice you can control and regulate all vocal elements by careful perception and repeated practice. A well-prepared presentation can be lost if you speak in a monotone, i.e. when you use a constant pitch, volume and rate. Similarly, lack of animation and inappropriate pauses can cause communication breakdown. If you want to be a successful speaker you should fully exploit the potential of all the six vocal elements. Your speech will then have the variations and effects to suit the material you are presenting. For self-improvement you may tape-record your speech and critically examine it. In the subsequent efforts, try to suitably amend your delivery in the light of your self-analysis. You should also test your oral presentation among friends and observe their reactions. Through systematic and persistent efforts, you can certainly become a good speaker.

There are two more things to which we would like to draw your attention:

- Vocal noise
- Voice training

5.5.1 Vocal Noise

Some speakers have certain speech mannerisms. While speaking, they mutter em..., mmm....., er...., eh......, etc. Some use certain words, phrases, or even sentences as time fillers after short intervals. *Right? Understand?, Well..., Isn't it?,* I mean....., etc. Such expressions are semantically hollow in the context and the audience may get irritated. Avoid all types of speech mannerisms as their continual use may make your presentation less effective.

5.5.2 Voice Training

Voice is nature's blessing to human being. It conveys their involvement and conviction and reveals to some extent their personality. That is why the quality of voice differs from person to person. Ponder for a while and you would be able to recall different kinds of voice you have heard. If you examine them critically, you may come to the following conclusion. Some people nasalise their voice and some have harsh or hoarse voice. A few exhale more air than necessary and this makes their voice breathy. Those who do not move their jaw, tongue and lips properly have a muffled voice. A small number of speakers suffer from throatiness. Their voice has a guttural quality caused by deep resonance in their throat. Does your voice belong to any of these categories? Even if it does not, you can certainly improve the quality of your voice by exercise. It requires very little time but the effort has to be sustained. That the gain is worth the effort you would soon realise and feel happy to experience the generation of new self-confidence within your inner self.

In the cultivation of voice three factors play a key role. A set of exercises related to each are suggested below. They are likely to help you attain power and richness in you speech:

- Activating tongue
- Relaxing facial muscles
- Breathing properly

Activating Tongue

The correct placing of the tongue is essential for clear and distinct delivery. Pronounce the individual sounds of English and you would feel the movement of the various parts of the tongue at different places in the mouth. To keep your tongue agile, do the following exercises:

- Fill air in your mouth and close it. Roll your tongue clockwise arid then anti-clockwise, without letting the air escape.
- Touch the teeth ridge and the centre of the mouth with the tip of your tongue in quick succession.
- Energise your tongue by flapping and fluttering it.

Relaxing Facial Muscles

Tense muscles may muffle or even choke your voice. To keep them relaxed you may try the following exercises.

- Open your mouth wide and move your lower jaw from side to side.
- Close your mouth and do what is stated above.
- Spread your lips as much as you can and then round them.
- Pretend to chew or munch something.
- Make funny faces before a mirror.
- Massage gently your cheeks, jaw and throat.

Breathing Properly

Breath is the stuff of which sound is made. When we produce sound, it travels through air waves. For proper breathing, which is essential for clear production of sounds, you may do the following exercises:

- Inhale the air, hold it for some time and then exhale it.
- Inhale and exhale the puffs of air in quick succession.
- Hold your breath and speak as many words as you can.

These exercises are elementary but sufficient for our purposes. If you desire advanced training in breath control, you should consult an authoritative book on yoga or a yoga guru.

5.6 TIME MANAGEMENT

You know that time is precious, but do you also know that time is an instrument of communication? The value you attach to time tends to reveal certain traits of your personality. For example, if you arrive late at the venue of your talk, you may be considered to be lazy, indisciplined or even lacking in professional etiquette. And if you reach there much before time, people may think you are nervous, overcautious or immature. These first impressions can generate a negative attitude among the listeners and you will have to put in extra efforts to win their attention. To avoid this, you must reach the venue on time so that the proceedings can start immediately after your arrival.

Normally you would be informed of the time allotted for your talk but merely hearing this information is not enough. You should also know whether there are other speakers and how much time has been allotted to each. Keep in mind the total amount of time made available for the event so that, should the need arise, you may take slightly less or more time for your talk.

At the planning stage, while organising the contents, structure the time as well, i.e. determine time slot for each sub-topic or point. In the Note Cards you may indicate the time limits also. While speaking, adhere to these time limits. Keep a check on time without making it too evident to the audience. If you look at your wrist watch at regular intervals, the audience may think that you lack interest in the topic or want to complete your talk quickly. To obviate obtrusion you may, therefore, place the writs watch on the lectern near the Note Cards so that you may look at both while speaking.

Despite your efforts, sometimes you may find that your talk is likely to finish too early or too late. To meet the first situation you may summarise your speech, explain a point already, made in greater detail, or fall back upon the 'reserve points' – the points which were to be discussed, if time permitted. In the second situation, omit discussing not-so-important points or compress the remaining matter. But never end your talk abruptly: 'I have nothing more to say. Thank you' or 'Oh! Time is up. I must stop. Thank you.'

5.7 HANDLING QUESTIONS

'Questions are magic – they have the power to turn confusion into clarity, resistance into acceptance, division into consensus and the frustration of not knowing what to say into the satisfaction of having said it.' This statement by Sam Deep and Lyle Stutsman emphatically sums up the importance of questions in formal speech situations. You should therefore welcome questions from the audience. The questions are critical indicators of the success of your talk. They would also help you re-establish your credibility by giving you an opportunity to amend your original observations or to fill in the gaps, if any, in your presentation. You can also deal with a point in greater depth. Thus they are good instruments of enhancing one's image in the eyes of the audience. As you know, spoken language, by its very nature is interactive and so a speech event would appear to be truncated if it does not include a question-answer session.

The questions asked by the audience are likely to be of two types: one, direct questions to seek clarification or additional information; two, indirect questions in the form of observations or comments. The speaker is expected to respond to each question, whatever be its purpose, keeping in view the time available. The allotment of time for the question-answer session depends upon the nature of speech event. For example, the time allotted for a seminar is likely to be more than that for a lecture on the same topic.

To handle questions effectively, you should not only be knowledgeable but also tactful, besides having a good understanding of the body language. A few helpful hints are given below:

- Listen to the question attentively and understand what the question wants. If it is not clear, you can do two things: one, ask the questioner to repeat or rephrase the question; two, you yourself repeat or rephrase the question and ask the questioner to confirm before answering it.
- Answer the question for the benefit of the whole group; do not address it merely to the questioner.
- Let your answer be brief and to the point. Long answers at this stage tend to be boring and the audience is likely to lose interest in the ongoing interaction.
- Listen patiently; do not interrupt questioner and jump to conclusions. Some people start with a negative statement in order to draw focused attention to the positive aspect of an idea or view.
- If you are not in a position to answer a question, admit your inability. You may, however repeat the question and invite the audience to answer it.
- Develop an insight for distinguishing a relevant question from an irrelevant question and a sincere question from a flippant one. You need not try to answer the questions of the latter category in each case. However, your refusal should tickle the ego of the questioner and at the same time evoke a nod of approval from the other members of the group. For example, you may say: 'That is a very good question but I am afraid it goes beyond the scope of my talk.' Alternatively, you may repeat the question and ask the audience to respond. If there is no response from any body, continue the proceedings by inviting new questions.

5.8 MEETING UNEXPECTED SITUATIONS

Michael Pritchard once observed: '*Fear is that little darkroom where negatives are developed.*' And now look at the following punch line used by a presenter: '*Confidence flows from the barrel of preparation.*'

Taken together, these two statements point to the fact that preparation is the base on which success is built. Thorough preparation engenders confidence and if you have confidence what is there to fear? Fearlessness is the mother of hope, optimism, and positive attitude. Armed with confidence you can be effective in presentation as well as in handling unexpected situations. Remember, howsoever well-prepared you may be, sometimes things go wrong. In a speech event, every aspect cannot be under control.

It is difficult to anticipate all kinds of unexpected situations that may develop. A few which we faced and the way we met the challenges are described below. These are merely indicative; ultimately you have to find your own solutions to the problems as and when may arise.

Situation A – Hostile audience: The audience do not want to listen to you and express their resentment by not looking at you, pretending to write with their heads bowed or by grinning and flashing unfriendly smiles.

Solution: You should not retaliate by becoming hostile. Keep your cool and exude confidence and determination. Try to find a common ground by asking questions and engaging some members in discussion. Appreciate the contributions they make. This may have a multiplier effect and once the ball gets rolling, start your speech. If there is no response, try to tell a relevant joke or anecdote or story to enlist their cooperation. You can also pick a visual aid and display it and then making it a base start or resume your talk.

Situation B – Change in the compositions of the audience: You have prepared your presentation for persons knowledgeable in your area of specialisation or advanced study. But you discover just before starting your presentation that among the audience are specialists from other related fields as well.

Solution: Welcome the presence of other specialists and appeal for their indulgence if they find that the presentation is not directly related to their areas of interest. At the same time, try to reduce the use of technical jargon to explain your ideas. Since other specialists would be professionals like you, in all probability they would appreciate your concern and extend their full cooperation.

Situation C – Forgetting the opening lines: Finding among the audience, strangers or persons who seemingly have come to assess you, you may forget the opening lines of your speech – those remarks which you had planned to make in the beginning.

Solution: Since it is a passing phase, with a little effort, you can get your nerves together soon. To put yourself at ease, engage the audience by asking them to state their expectations from your speech, to narrate their experience or work done in their fields and its relationship to your topic, etc. But ensure that the time devoted to this initial interaction is very short and you must return to your talk on the announced topic quickly.

Situation D – Reduction in allotted time: You are asked to complete your presentation, say, within 15 minutes instead of 50 minutes originally allotted.

Solution: There are two ways to meet this situation. One, give a summary of the whole speech, highlighting and explaining the most important points, Two, omit altogether the discussion of certain points. In either case, you should adhere to the original organizational structure of your speech.

Situation E – Answer not known: You do not know the answer to a relevant question asked by the audience.

Solution: Neither get panicky nor nervous. Frankly admit your inability to answer that question. Never try to give a wrong answer knowingly. If however, you have an inkling of the answer, make a judicious guess. Do tell the audience that you have done so and what you have stated needs to be verified. You can also request the audience to answer. If nobody responds, write down the questions and promise to deal with it in the next lecture. If you are not likely to meet the same audience in the near future, invite the questioner for a discussion after the talk is over. If you have to depart immediately after the talk, promise to e-mail the answer. Of course, in all cases keep your words.

Situation F – Failure of technical aid: The instrument for technical support has stopped working or does not work at all, from the start.

Solution: Do not get involved with the technical personnel who are likely to be called upon to tackle the problem. Also, do not quietly stand, watch and wait for the instrument to become operational again. Instead, keep talking to the audience and if possible, engage them in some intellectual activity even if it is not directly related to the topic. You may ask them to recall the points you have already discussed or anticipate what you are going to say. To act on these suggestions you would require extra effort, energy and ingenuity. And that is why speakers are advised to always be overprepared for a speech.

5.9 DO'S AND DON'TS

In the earlier sections of this chapter we have discussed how to speak to an audience effectively. For quick recall we shall now list the fundamentals in the form of Do's and Don'ts.

DO'S

- Have a clear objective.
- Prepare thoroughly.
- Start on time with a punch.
- End with a bang within the time limit.
- Articulate clearly.
- Keep supporting material handy.
- Talk to the whole group.
- Keep eye contact with the entire audience
- Maintain cheerful expression throughout.
- Be vibrant and animated.

DON'TS

- Ramble.
- Repeat yourself.
- Tell stories.

- Emphasise every point.
- Make vocal noises.
- Use shortened forms.
- Use acronyms.
- Read from slides.
- Use too many visuals.
- Interrupt the questioner.

5.10 SPEECHES FOR SPECIAL OCCASIONS

These are speeches given on certain ceremonial occasions or for special purposes such as welcoming a guest at a function, introducing a speaker or chief guest to the audience, inaugurating an event, felicitating an important person, bidding farewell to some body, proposing a vote of thanks, etc. Such speeches are generally short and business-like. The basic principles of preparation and delivery for them are the same as those discussed earlier. However, remember that reference to individuals and their contributions and achievements dominate the contents. Utmost courtesy in the use of language and flawless accuracy in the presentation of information should therefore characterise your speech. Further, generally the purpose of the address is mentioned in the very beginning. A few examples are given below.

- I am delighted to welcome Mr. Lalit Agarwal, Chairman, Innovative Technologies Limited, Bangalore to the inaugural session of the seminar...,
- It gives me great pleasure to introduce Prof. P.T. Verghese to this learned a Nudience...,
- I consider it to be a privilege to have been invited to inaugurate the National Seminar on Professional Communication...,
- It is indeed a memorable occasion for us to have gathered here to felicitate Dr. T.N. Bhatnagar, the well-known economist, who has been selected for the International Award for Economic Studies.,
- As you know, we have assembled here to bid farewell to our colleague, Mr. A. Hussain, who would be retiring next week after rendering thirty-one years of distinguished service to this Company...,
- It is my pleasant duty to propose a vote of thanks. First of all, I would like to....

Like-wise you can construct sentences to begin your speech on other similar occasions. And you would find it easy to handle the body and conclusion if you also bear in mind the additional points mentioned in this section.

5.11 EVALUATING SPEECH AND ORAL PRESENTATION

You may occasionally be asked to evaluate the quality of speech or presentation made by another student or officer. You have then to keep in mind the various factors that make a presentation effective and also to quantify your judgment for record or comparison. There could be many ways to perform this task. We suggest below an evaluation plan which we have tried out in various situations and found satisfactory and workable.

EVALUATION SHEET

Name of the Presenter

Date of Presentation

Note: The qualitative meaning of the numerals is as follows:

1. = Poor; 2 = Average; 3 = Good; 4 = Very Good; 5 = Excellent.

(a)	Introduction to the topic	1	2	3	4	5
(b)	Clarity of presentation	1	2	3	4	5
(c)	Sequence and continuity	1	2	3	4	5
(d)	Voice, pitch and delivery	1	2	3	4	5
(e)	Use of audio-visual aids	1	2	3	4	5
(f)	Eye contact & audience awareness	1	2	3	4	5
(g)	Interaction with audience	1	2	3	4	5
(h)	General poise and bearing	1	2	3	4	5
(i)	Knowledge of the subject	1	2	3	4	5
(j)	Style of concluding the presentation	1	2	3	4	5

Total

Remarks (if any)

Date: Signature of the Evaluator

ASSIGNMENTS

1. 'Begin your speech with a punch and end it with a bang'. Explain this statement, giving examples to illustrate your answer.
2. Distinguish clearly between
   (i) Kinesics and proxemics; and
   (ii) Speaking extemporaneously and speaking impromptu.
3. Describe different types of participants and ways of dealing with them. Also describe any other type you know or may have come across.
4. Mention any three (unexpected) situations that may arise in public speaking and state how you would handle them.
5. In what respects does a public lecture by a political leader differ from an oral presentation by a professional in terms of organisational structure, choice of language and nuances of delivery?
6. What precautions should be taken in preparing and using visual aids for an oral presentation?

7. As Sales Manager of New Horizons Publishing Co. Ltd, New Delhi you have to give a speech to bid farewell to Mr. Arun Halwani, Assistant Manager, Marketing, who is retiring next week. Write the full text of your speech in about 200 words. Invent the details you think necessary.
8. Under the Public Health Awareness Programme, you as Chief Medical Officer of the District Civil Hospital of your town, have been invited to speak to students of a college on 'Cancer The Giant Killer.' Write the Introduction and Conclusion of your speech.
9. Assume that a reputed Institute of Management has invited you to deliver the key C note address at a National Seminar on 'Ethical Aspects of Professional Communication.' Prepare (a) an outline of your speech and (b) the matter to be exhibited on individual slides for PowerPoint presentation. Invent the necessary details.
10. Select a speech given by a well-known public leader on an important occasion. Analyse its structure, stating how far it is on the lines of organization suggested by us in this chapter. Enclose the text of the speech along with your assignment.

Chapter 6

ACTIVE LISTENING

DO you love to listen to the sound of your own voice? If you do, there is nothing to feel embarrassed about it. Most people are like you. But here we wish to draw your attention to another closely related fact, i.e. most people also like those who listen to them. They are pleased to observe the relish, interest, and appreciation transmitted by listeners through vocal and physical responses. The feedback they thus get often acts as a stimulus and inspires them to put in more efforts to make the speech effective. In interactive social situations one may come across boastful babblers or garrulous socialites. Such persons have a one-track mind and they do not give listeners a chance to respond. Instead, they drown them in the deluge of words. If you meet such people, would you be able to like them? The answer is obvious.

For being accepted, liked and respected in one's profession, the cultivation of the skill of active listening is essential. It has been estimated that a professional spends 45 per cent of his time in listening.

Unfortunately, some people consider listening as a natural ability and think that nothing can be done to improve it. Because of this attitude, listening as a skill often does not find an important place in communication skills development programmes designed by professionals for enhancing the efficiency level of organisations. One of the reasons for this could be the inability to perceive the distinctions between hearing and listening. Let us, therefore, first remove the cobweb surrounding this notion.

6.1 HEARING AND LISTENING

Hearing is a physiological process in which the sounds emanating from a source within a certain range strike the eardrums and cause vibrations. These are transmitted to the central auditory system of the brain, generating a neutral, pleasant, or unpleasant sensation. The process of hearing is, in fact, as natural as breathing. Like nostrils, ears remain open whether we are wide awake or fast asleep, though in the latter state, we cease hearing whereas breathing continues. To prevent the entry of unwanted air or sound we have to close both with external objects. Throughout our waking hour, we continue to hear the sounds coming from different sources, without any conscious effort. In hearing thus no physical effort is required as in speaking. The latter, as you know, requires the movement of the jaw, tongue and lips.

Nature has given us 'one small mouth to speak and two big ears to hear.' But listening is hearing plus something more. It is hearing with a purposeful, meaningful understanding and demands intellectual effort. When we begin to pay close attention to what we hear and interpret the contents in the context of our background, experience and expectations, we step into the domain of listening. Not that hearing ends where listening begins. Listening is both a physiological as well as a cognitive process, a sort of qualitative add-on to hearing.

There are many speech situations in which we listen from the very beginning. Sometimes we slide back to hearing. We then alert our mind, bring it back to track and start listening again. It is difficult to realise at what point of time in the continuum of this sensory experience, hearing transforms itself into listening and vice versa. There is no clear line of demarcation between hearing and listening. One probable reason for this phenomenon is that listening consumes more energy and so tires us sooner than hearing does. So we revert from listening to hearing.

There are situations in which some people listen and the rest merely hear. For example, a knowledgeable person listens to classical music, appreciating its subtle nuances and deft improvisations by the performer but a non-initiated person merely hears it, at best terming it as sweet or unpleasant on the basis of his rudimentary sensations.

6.2 IMPORTANCE OF LISTENING

Listening plays an important role in our social as well as professional life. If you ponder for a while, you would realise that sometimes we act or react wrongly, simply because our listening was not effective. As an experiment, a teacher in a class of forty students whispered into the ears of a student a phrase and asked him to pass it on orally to his neighbour in a similar manner till it reached the last student. The original phrase was 'Buy now, pay later scheme'. When the last student was asked what the phrase was, pat came the response: 'Pay now, buy later scheme'. For full understanding many a time we seek clarification, further explanations or ask even a good speaker to repeat the message.

In certain professions the role of listening is crucial. For example, if a judge is not an effective listener, he may arrive at a wrong conclusion. Similarly, if a psychiatrist is not a good listener, he would not be able to provide proper advice to his patients. Successful businessmen and the apex management of reputed companies consider listening as important as other communication skills. All successful industrialists, advocates, teachers, doctors, etc., are good listeners. It would not be an exaggeration to say that effective listening is the hallmark of a successful professional.

6.3 LISTENING SITUATIONS

During the course of the day we hear so many sounds, but there are only a few specific situations which demand careful listening. Some situations are personal such as conversation with members of the family, relatives and friends, interactions with professionals such as traders, shopkeepers, doctors, bank officials and government servants, public announcements, news and programmes on radio and televisions, etc. Among the professional situations are meetings, seminars, briefings, oral presentations, group discussions, lectures, talks, and interaction (both formal and informal) with fellow professionals. In each organisation generally written guidelines to regulate work and behaviour are available in the form of manuals, regulations, etc., but an employee learns a lot from colleagues by listening to them carefully. Listening also helps the cultivation of smooth interpersonal relationships with fellow workers, which is essential for efficient functioning of the organisation. For proper decision-making, too, one has to be a good listener to the ideas and views of others. Obviously the response to a situation can not be relevant or to the point unless one has this ability.

6.4 BARRIERS TO LISTENING

There are certain factors which impede effective listening. Be aware of them. The important ones are briefly discussed below.

(i) *Adverse physical atmosphere*

Proper physical environment induces good listening. For example, if you have a comfortable seat in a quiet, well-ventilated room, you are likely to be a better listener than you would be in a room full of noisy children running about all around you or in a room where loud music is being played.

(ii) *Lack of motivation.*

The lack of a strong desire to understand, to learn, to acquire skills, or to gain knowledge hinders effective listening. It has been found that the expectation of a tangible or an intangible benefit promotes proper listening. In formal teaching, listening, comprehension and dictocomposition exercises are designed to achieve this purpose.

(iii) *Improper perception*

A distorted or truncated perception of the relevance and usefulness of the topic affects listening adversely. It creates a mental block and reception dips to a low level. Often the initial inertia to understand the scope of the topic affects the grasp of even a significant piece of information or an important message that follows the introduction.

(iv) *Negative personality traits*

Studies on the relationship between listening and personality traits show that, in general, those persons who are self-centered, boastful and domineering are poor listeners as compared to those persons who are methodical, analytical and thoughtful by nature. In course of time, the former category of persons develops within themselves a negative attitude towards the speaker. If he is smart, lively and effective, their ego is hurt and a feeling of resentment is generated, preventing them from making a sincere effort to understand what is being said.

6.5 DEVELOPING LISTENING SKILLS

From the discussion so far, you can deduce what should be done to improve the listening skill. What follows now is an attempt to put together the implied suggestions in specific terms.

Familiarise Yourself with the Sound System of English

The sound system of every language is unique. So listening sometimes suffers because the sound system of one's mother tongue interferes with the sound system of English. When a medical officer on a routine visit to a school for check-up asked a student with rural background to show his teeth, he promptly turned round and raised his shirt to show his peeth (back). There are certain sounds in English which we Indians find difficult to speak and to understand when spoken to. For example, some of us fail to distinguish 'last' from 'lost', 'zest' from, 'jest', 'same' from 'shame', 'voice' from 'vice', 'vent' from 'went', 'worthy' from 'wordy', etc. Apart from individual sounds, there are other important features which play a significant role in conveying meaning. To comprehend fully, it is essential to recognise the difference between a stressed word and an unstressed word, falling intonation and rising intonation, short pause and long pause. Further information in this regard is given in Appendix-A.

Focus on Your Purpose

Listening serves a number of purposes. As a student, when you attend lectures and seminars, your purpose is to gather information, to gain knowledge, to understand concepts, and to learn the procedure or process of doing things. And your purpose is the same when at the workplace. You attend an orientation of programme, a briefing session, or a meeting called to give a set of instructions or directions. These situations require full attention and complete understanding. Sometimes your listening has to be critical as well. For example, when a proposal is put forward or a plan of action is suggested, you have to be critical in your approach while examining their suitability or feasibility. The two purposes just mentioned demand a rapid grasp and quick interpretation of the matter presented by the speaker. Yet another purpose of listening is to relax and to derive aesthetic pleasure. You do this when you listen to your favourite music or watch a TV serial or a movie. Occasionally, you listen to your friends and relatives to share their grief and to support them in their moments of sorrow. In such situation, you have to listen with utmost patience and sympathy, encouraging the speaker to pour out his heart. As you know, the burden of stress lessens when shared by patient listeners.

Have a Positive Attitude Towards the Speaker and the Topic

Prevent yourself from paying attention to the dress and physical features of the speaker and musing over the phraseology of the topic. Instead, concentrate on what the speaker says on the topic, its thought-content. Keep your mind open and ready to receive. Try to understand the matter being presented with all the sincerity at your command. Do not entertain thoughts such as the following: 'How is this topic related to my studies or work ?' Mr. X (the speaker) looks so dull and shabby', 'What can he contribute' 'I think I know more than he does,' etc. These are negative thoughts; they hinder the process of listening and the time spent on it may be an utter waste.

Listen with Your Eyes as Well as Ears

You must carefully pay attention not only to the spoken words but also on how they are being uttered and the accompanying body language. The non-verbal clues such as the twinkle in the eyes, the flourish of hands, shrugging of shoulders, the movement on podium, the facial expression, etc., also convey meaning besides reflecting the speaker's attitude towards the topic and the audience. The vocal clues such as raising or lowering the pitch of the voice, the variations in the rate of delivery, dramatic pauses at certain places communicate the subtle nuances of different units of thought. These devices are also used to emphasise certain points and to draw focussed attention on certain aspects of the topic. They are also helpful in waking up the sleeping minds and in bringing back to the track the wandering thoughts.

Avoid Premature Evaluation

Some listeners start evaluating just after one or two points have been made by the speakers. To say the least, it is unfair to do so. Sometimes the points discussed at the initial stage appear to be irrelevant but later they are connected with the theme or the central thought. It could also be a strategy consciously deployed by the speaker to keep the listeners wondering and guessing what is to follow, in a bid to enlist their concentrated attention. So let the speaker unfold his thoughts and complete the presentation. Once this process is over, by all means go ahead and tear the presentation into pieces, if you can!

Resist Distractions

One of the reasons for distraction is the time gap between the capacity to speak and the capacity to listen. The average speed of speaking is about 150 words per minute and that of listening about 650 words per minute. The listener's mind therefore begins to wander unless he engages himself in recalling the points made earlier and anticipating what is to follow and establishing a relationship with what he is listening at the moment.

There are two main sources of distraction. One, the speaker himself may distract the listeners by his odd body movements, peculiar speech mannerisms, unpleasant facial expressions or improper physical appearance. Two, distraction may be caused by an external source. For example, the gaudy dress of a foppish gentleman, the loud perfume used by a dainty lady, the murmurous comments by a Mr. Know-all present among the audience or a creaky sound, an unusual movement of men and things near the speech event – all these tend to distract the listeners. You have, therefore, to discipline your mind and ignore the disturbances. If you express your attentiveness through nods, smiles, proper postures, pleasant facial expressions and sparkle in your eyes, the speaker would feel encouraged. He would put in more effort to make his presentation animated and lively. Ultimately, as a listener, you would be a beneficiary.

Take Notes

Good listeners generally take notes in all speech situations related to their work. But, if the purpose of listening is to gather specific information or to acquire knowledge for future use, you must take notes. In a lecture, seminar, presentation or a briefing session, a speaker usually makes a few (say five or six) basic points. While listening to him, identify these points and note them down systematically, along with a gist of supporting ideas, evidence or illustrative material. Some speakers give a signal when they move from one point to another. Some, in addition, summarise what they had said up to a point of time. Your task would be easier in such cases. But if this does not happen, you yourself will have to identify and record the points using key words and phrases used by the speaker. Paraphrasing the contents presented up to a point of time would prove helpful in performing this task. To save time, you may use accepted abbreviations. You may also invent your personal abbreviations or short forms to take notes. However, whatever you jot down should be easily decipherable.

6.6 DO'S

To help you develop this skill we now give below the main points discussed earlier in the form of DO's:

- Gather information about the setting, the topic and the speaker.
- Visualise the contents of the topic.
- Have a positive attitude.
- Discipline your mind and concentrate on the contents.
- Observe non-verbal signals, both physical and vocal.
- Give evidence of your attentiveness.
- Rephrase the contents from time to time.
- Take easily decipherable notes.

Remember

The improvement in listening skill would enhance your intellectual ability to gather accurate information and help you establish harmonious, interactive relationship with your relatives, friends and co-workers.

ASSIGNMENTS

1. Describe the role of listening in the communication process.
2. Discuss the difference between listening for personal purposes and that for professional purposes. Give illustrative examples.
3. Examine the following statements critically and give arguments in support of your viewpoint.

   (a) Listening is to speaking as reading is to writing.

   (b) All listening is hearing but all hearing is not listening.

   (c) We listen not only with our ears but also with our eyes.
4. Describe the ways of improving listening as a skill.
5. List the benefits that would accrue to you if you improve your listening skill.
6. Listen to the following pairs of sentences which will be read out to you and then point out the semantic difference between the two.

   (a) (i) Wait here for a while; I'm coming.

   (ii) Do you mind waiting here?; I'll be back in a minute.

   (b) (i) Has Simi already submitted the assignment?

   (ii) Simi has already submitted the assignment?

   (c) (i) All old men and women, may please leave the hall.

   (ii) All old men, and women may please leave the hall.

(d) (i) Mr. Patkey's conduct is worthy of emulation.
(ii) Conduct Mr. Patkey round the factory.

(e) (i) I CAN SEE a great deal from here.
(ii) I can see a great deal from HERE.

7. Go through the following extracts from different conversations. In each extract one question (Q) is asked but two responses (R) are given. Point out the difference between the two responses.

(a) Q. A husband asks his wife 'Did Simi come home late, last night?'
R1. Yes, she did, so what?
R2. Yes, the party continued till 11 pm but her friends, Meena and Sheena, were good enough to drop her home.

(b) Q. In a restaurant, the waiter asks a lady: 'May I take your order, Madam?'
R1. Can't you wait for a while?
R2. I'll call you a minute later.

(c) Q. A student asks his friend: 'I haven't seen you for a long time. Where have you been?'
R1. On the campus only. Where have you been?
R2. On the campus only. Just a chance we didn't meet.

(d) The receptionist of an office asks a visitor: 'Good morning, Sir. Can I help you?'
R1. Yes, I have an appointment with Ms Khokhale at 11 am.
R2. Yes, I have come to see Ms Khokhale. I was asked to report at 11 am.

(e) Q. An Office Manager speaks to a mechanic on phone: 'Can you come quickly, please? Everyone is in a dreadful panic.'
R1. What's wrong, Sir?
R2. I'd be there in a moment, Sir.

8. Listen carefully to the following extracts from different poems. They would be read aloud twice at normal speed. You have to reproduce them with proper punctuation for which you have to use your imagination. However, to help you there will be a pause after each line.

(a) Between the idea
And the reality
Between the motion
And the act
Falls the shadow.

(b) Faster than fairies, faster than witches,
Bridges and houses, hedges and ditches;
And charging along like troops in a battle,
All through the meadows, the houses and cattle.

(c) We can pull and haul and push and lift and drive,
We can print and plough and weave and heat and light,
We can run and race and swing and fly and dive,
We can see and hear and count and read and write.

(d) A piping poet,
A twittering bird;
It's all that we need
To be happy on earth.
The eye of a poet,
A bird on the wing,
It's all that we need
To feel like a king.

(e) For oft, when on my couch I lie
In vacant or in pensive mood,
They flash upon that inward eye
Which is bliss of solitude;
And then my heart with pleasure fills,
And dances with the daffodils.

(f) Twinkle, twinkle, little bat!
How I wonder what you're at!
Up above the world you fly,
Like a tea-tray in the sky.

(g) Oh, the brave old Duke of York,
He had ten thousand men,
He marched them up to the top of a hill
And he marched them down again.
And when they were up, they were up,
And when they were down, they were down
And when they were only half-way up,
They were neither up nor down.

(h) The lapse of time and rivers is the same;
Both speed their journey with a restless stream;
The silent pace with which they steal away;
No wealth and bribe, no prayers persuade to stay;
Alike irrevocable both when past,
And a wide ocean swallows both at last.

9. Given below are a few passages and questions based on them. First, the questions will be read out to help you focus your attention to the key points while listening to the passage. After the passage has been read, the questions will be read out again, this time one by one. A gap of one minute will be provided after each question to enable you to answer it.

PASSAGE 1

Questions:

(i) What is common among all living things?

(ii) How is the structural organisation of the human body related to its functionality?

(iii) In what way can 'a human body' be defined from a layman's point of view?

(iv) What is the difference between a cell and an organism?

Every living being is a complex of matter and energy, both continuously interacting and changing forms. Further, every living organism, in order to perform certain functions, is structurally organised. The human body too has a structure. From a layman's point of view it can be described as a structure of bones plastered with flesh and having a casing of skin. But if we were to go into its minutest details, we would be baffled at the excellent blueprint and design of our bodies. The structure of the human body is much more complex than any other structure known so far.

The human body consists of a mass which has to be supported against gravity. The various bones in the system provide the beam work, protecting and supporting the rest of the body mass and giving the organism its shape and rigidity.

This body mass is a collection of innumerable cells working together towards a common purpose. But all of them do not perform the same function. Hence cells are organised into aggregations known as tissues, which are further differentiated into organs. A number of organs constitute the organism. Functionally, the human body consists of several departments or divisions.

PASSAGE 2

Questions:

(i) What are the causes of insomnia?

(ii) How does auto-suggestion help a man to go to sleep?

(iii) What is contra-suggestion?

(iv) What is the best cure for a headache?

Insomnia or sleeplessness is a very complicated phenomenon, and its causes are numerous. It may be caused by an undigested supper, a strain of music, or a secret şorrow; and its relief may be found in a drug, a bath or the sound of a dear voice. Nevertheless, sleep and lack of sleep can be controlled.

The facts revealed and analysed by modern hypnotism support the common experience. Suggestion is important in sleep as in many other matters.

If you are confident that you can do something, more often than not, you will do it. This self-confidence of yours is called auto-suggestion. On the contrary, if you believe that you can never sleep in a strange room the first night, chances are that you will not. This belief or lack of confidence is called contra-suggestion. Auto-suggestion and contra-suggestion greatly control our lives.

Contra-suggestion is the main cause of insomnia. People may modify their diet and get the digestion right, take exercise and massage to relax their bodies, avoid excitement and stimulants like coffee, and yet they may fail to get any sleep, if everything they have done during the day in order to sleep has but induced contra-suggestion.

Sleeplessness is the major cause of headache, while sleep is its best cure. The mere going to bed is treatment enough for a headache. This treatment is rational and scientific because it removes the cause itself. It means complete rest for overstrained eyes, it means a more even distribution of blood within the body, and it means rest for the brain.

Passage 3

Questions:

(i) What are the main ingredients of milk?

(ii) Why do children need milk?

(iii) Why is it not advisable for adults to take an exclusive milk diet?

(iv) Which minerals required by the human body are not found in the milk?

Milk ordinarily sold for household use, varies in composition. On the average, it contains 87 per cent water and 13 per cent solids, consisting of proteins, fat, sugar and a variety of mineral substances.

Milk is an extremely valuable food because it contains: firstly, materials that children need for growth; secondly, materials that young and old alike need for the repair of their body machinery; and thirdly, materials that everyone needs as fuel to provide the necessary heat and energy for work. This, however, does not mean that milk has these ingredients in such proportions that it can serve satisfactorily as the only food of a grown-up person or even that of a child. Since milk contains such a high percentage of water, five or six quarts of it would be required each day to meet the energy needs of an adult, if it were his only food. Also, grown-up persons and children past the normal nursing period need iron in greater quantities than is found in milk. In fact, milk is a very poor source of iron as proved by feeding experiments. Many investigators have found that they can produce very definite nutritional anemia in healthy young rats by feeding them an exclusively whole milk diet. It is the iron already stored in the body of a newborn child that enables the infant to live for a few months on the small amount of iron available in milk. Older children and adults need much more generous supplies, such as can be obtained from egg yolk, meat, whole grain, cereals, and some fruits and vegetables. At present evidence is accumulating to indicate that copper is essential for the utilisation of iron. Not only is milk poor in iron, but it is also relatively poorer in copper. Another mineral constituent that is required by the body in minute amounts is iodine, and milk is deficient in this also.

Passage 4

Questions:

(i) What is the main condition for a country to become great?

(ii) How can a country's freedom be preserved?

(iii) In what way does self-control help a man to feel free?

(iv) What can endanger the freedom of a country?

What do you want your country to be in order that she may be ranked among the great nations of the world? Clearly, one condition of progress, one condition of any development, one condition of greatness is – Freedom. Hence your first wish for the country should be that she should remain free. One condition of freedom is that you yourself be free and you are not free as long as you are under the domination of the lower side of your nature. You cannot preserve the freedom of your country without making yourself free and no man is free who is not the master of his own mind and of his own body. No man can safely enjoy extrinsic freedom until he has gained that inner freedom which we call self-control. Freedom may become dangerous in the hands of men who are not worthy of it.

Passage 5

Questions:

(i) Who is a well-educated man, according to the author?

(ii) What is the chief intention of a soldier?

(iii) What should a good doctor not do?

(iv) What is something better than making money?

It is improbable for a well-educated intellectual, or a brave man to make money the chief object of his thoughts just as it is for him to make his dinner the principal object of his life. All healthy people like their dinner but their dinner is not the main object of their lives. So all healthy-minded people like making money, ought to like it and enjoy the sensation of winning it; there is something better than money. A good soldier, for instance, mainly wishes to do his fighting well. He is glad of his pay, very properly so, and justly grumbles when you keep him ten years without a raise. Still, his main notion of life is to win battle, not to be paid for winning them. So also of doctors. They like fees no doubt, ought to like them, yet if they are well-motivated, the entire object of their life is not fees. They, on the whole desire to cure the sick; if they are good doctors, and if a choice were fairly put to them, would rather cure their patient and lose their fee than kill him and gain it. And so with all the other brave and rightly trained men; their work is first, their fee second – very important always, but still second.

PASSAGE 6

Questions:

(i) Why is air travel not considered safe by some people?

(ii) What does the pilot do when engines fail in midair?

(iii) What is likely to happen if the engines fail when the aircraft is taking off?

(iv) Why does the pilot race the engine before taking off?

Air travel has now become very common. Even school boys and school girls travel thousands of miles alone to distant places to spend their holidays with their parents. Accidents do occur, but they are infrequent. We read of the accidents in our daily papers and perhaps get a false idea of their number. We do not hear of the hundreds of safe flights made every day, because they have no news value. Nevertheless, there is still some slight danger in traveling by air, as there is in any form of travel. If the engines fail, the only way in which the pilot can keep the air rushing under the wings to support the machine is to point the nose slightly downwards, and let the gravity do the work usually done by the engines. If he is at a good height when this happens, he may have the time and the luck to find a suitable place to land, and so avoid any serious consequences. But if the engines fail when the aircraft is taking off, a crash can rarely be avoided; there is no time to do anything about it. Therefore the engines are kept in the best possible order, and tested again and again. If you have travelled by air, you may have noticed that the pilot races his engines for a considerable time before taking off, to warm it up and to be sure that there is nothing wrong with it.

Chapter 7

MEETINGS

VERY often you will be required to participate in group discussions which may be small, consisting of three or four persons, or large, consisting of several hundred members. A group may be assigned a specific time-bound task or meet at periodic intervals when there is a need, or may share common experience, concerns or interests. This coming together of persons is labelled by different names on the basis of one or more of the following criteria; the purpose for which the group meets, the types of participants, and communicative pattern. The following are some of the more common labels used to name different types of discussion groups: meeting, seminar, conference, symposium, panel discussion, and convention. In this chapter we shall have a closer look at the meeting.

The word *meeting* is used in two senses; one, to refer to a small group meeting, committee meeting, meeting of Board of Directors, cabinet meeting, meeting of sectional heads, etc., and two, to refer to any coming together of two or more persons, whatever be the label applicable to such a group.

Meeting is perhaps the most commonly used form of discussion in a professional organisation. The person who chairs the meeting acts as the leader of the group and usually has a higher status or enjoys authority over the other members. Every meeting is result-oriented and therefore the discussion is directed towards a specific end. Let us now turn our attention to certain important aspects of conducting and participating in meetings.

7.1 PURPOSE

There are a number of purposes for which meetings are held. It is difficult to prepare an exhaustive list but some of the following are typical of most situations:

- To save time on communication.
- To convey information to a group at one time.
- To instruct a group.

- To brief members on plans already made or work already done.
- To give and get new ideas.
- To get immediate reactions to new ideas, proposals and plans.
- To exchange ideas and experiences.
- To discuss and solve problems.
- To resolve conflicts, confusions and disagreements.
- To arrive at widely acceptable decisions or to advise persons in power to take decisions.
- To generate enthusiasm and a positive attitude.

Many of these purposes cannot be achieved through a person-to-person interaction mainly because of the nature of the business to be transacted and every organisation's desire to enlist the support and to draw on the expertise of as large a number of persons as possible. The group activity that a meeting generates leads not merely to the achievement of the objective for which if is called but also to the development of a correct perspective. Thus the test of the success of a meeting lies not so much in what happens at the meeting but in what happens when the members have returned to their jobs. If afterwards nothing positive comes out of it, howsoever efficiently the meeting might have been conducted, it has in fact failed. Similarly, if the participants feel at the end of the meeting that they have gained nothing; the meeting has failed. Remember that the meeting raises an expectation among the members – an expectation to get something out of it. Failure to fulfil the expectation may exercise a negative impact, besides causing loss of precious man-hours which could otherwise have been devoted to productive work. So to obtain results the organisation of a meeting needs expertise, careful planning and prompt follow-up action.

7.2 PROCEDURE

A meeting of the members of a committee or any other constituted body is generally convened by the chairman or a member authorised by him. In other cases it is called by an authorised official who wishes to use it for any of the purposes mentioned earlier. In this case he acts as the chairman and he may name a member of the group to act as the secretary of a particular meeting. In practice most organisations develop a convention as to who will act as secretary and who as chairman and in what situation. For example, if the meeting is called by the personnel manager, the assistant personnel manager may be asked to act as secretary or when a vice-chancellor calls a meeting of the heads of departments, the assistant registrar (academic) may be called upon to act as secretary. However, in well-defined organisational groups such as the Board of Directors, the Executive Committee, etc., a person is designated as secretary and another as convener or chairman. The following points should be borne in mind by the person who calls the meeting:

- The announcement for every meeting must be made in writing, at least a week before the fixed date.
- The notice should be sent to all members, even if it is known that some of them would not attend.
- The notice should clearly state the agenda, i.e. the programme of business to be transacted.

We shall return to the detailed discussion of notices, agenda and minutes in Chapter 18.

7.3 CHAIRMANSHIP

Chairing a meeting requires tact, patience, a sense of humour and sound knowledge of the technique of making people discuss a subject intelligently and arrive at well-reasoned conclusions. When you are called upon to conduct a meeting, read through the agenda carefully and prepare a discussion plan. Before the meeting begins, ensure that proper physical arrangements have been made and aids and materials to be used are available at the venue.

A discussion plan is nothing but a guideline prepared by you, reflecting your own thinking on the subject to be discussed, a logical sequence of the ideas expected to be presented, the questions likely to be raised, by the members and the conclusions that might be reached. You should also estimate the time you would like to devote to each item in the agenda.

In every meeting, the beginning is crucial. Don't wait for those who are not present; think of those who are present. The latter should not get the feeling that they are less important than the absentees. Moreover, if you start on time, you would end on time. Members begin to get restive if the meeting starts late or continues long after the scheduled time of conclusion. If the majority of the meetings do not begin punctually, the members are likely to develop a casual attitude to what is discussed. This would decidedly defeat the very purpose for which the meeting is called.

Though the agenda is circulated beforehand, a restatement of the objective of the meeting is essential. Your presentation should focus on the attention on the subject, besides removing any confusion that might have arisen from the agenda. However, your initial statement should be short, crisp and vivid and should reflect a positive attitude, clearly emphasising the worthwhileness of the meeting. Lengthy opening remarks may jeopardise the smooth running of the meeting.

After you have set the discussion in motion, invite responses but don't get unnerved if there is silence for some time. Some members take time to open up and some are reluctant to be the first to speak. After the discussion gets going, you may, in fact, find it difficult to control and to keep it on the track. Here your tact and ingenuity must come into play. Without injuring a member's feelings or hurting his ego, you should be able to bring him back to the point. If the spell of silence is too long and the discussion does not develop on a particular item, you may frame questions and direct them to the entire group or sometimes to the individuals who, in your judgement, would be able to give the best response. Another strategy which might be adopted could be to invite comments or opinions on an already expressed view. Do not rush the group to arrive at a decision. Let the meeting be problem-centred and discussion-oriented. Give a fair chance to every member to speak and do not take sides. Even if you do not like a particular idea, do not immediately express your disagreement. You should in all circumstances remain cool and impartial. Occasionally there would be clash of personalities and emotional flare-ups. These need to be handled with utmost care. Sometimes giving background information on a point which has become a bone of contention might prove helpful. It is a good practice to summarise the discussion at appropriate intervals and certainly at the end. When you do so emphasise the areas of agreement.

Be specially alert about problem-participants: the commentator, the monopoliser, and the reticent. The whispered side-conversations in which the commentator indulges can distract and split the group. An effective way to deal with such a situation would be to bring about silence by abrupt interruption of the general discussion. This would make the commentator's misbehaviour obvious and single him out for disapproval by the entire group. The monopoliser who talks too often and often too long, is generally the one who cannot express his point of view precisely and clearly. He is therefore likely to confuse the discussion and annoy the group. You should not hesitate to politely interrupt him by asking a question or rewording the point yourself. Your aim should be to silence him for the time being and to encourage the others to take over the thread of discussion. The group may have participants who sit sphinx-like and are too reticent to utter even a single word. Remember that their presence may have an adverse effect on the entire group. They should therefore not be ignored by you; instead, you should try to draw them out of their self-imposed silence.

During the course of discussion, questions may be directed to you. If you do not wish to answer a question immediately, direct it to another member of the group, asking him to respond. If the question is loaded or provocative, you may tactfully postpone any response to it by making remarks such as the following: 'That's a good question, but shall we first consider the earlier comment made by Mr. X?' or 'It's an important question and needs careful thought. May I urge you all to ponder over it and express your views after a while?' Another way may be to restate the question, removing the sting from it and then invite discussion.

The conclusion of the meeting puts special responsibility on the chairman. As chairman, it is now your duty to take a position of authority and to state clearly and firmly the results of the discussion, namely, the decisions reached, and the future course of action. Any major disagreement should also be stated by you before concluding the meeting. Apart from the minutes* which in any case would be prepared, follow up every meeting with a written note containing the decisions taken and the steps to be taken to implement them. To obtain the maximum benefits the summarising and closing of the meeting are of equal importance. It is the duty of the chairman to bring various points of view into proper perspective skilfully and to set forth how the conclusions reached would affect the members or would lead to a specific course of action.

To sum up, the chairman performs the following functions:

(i) He draws preliminary plans and makes arrangements for the meeting.

(ii) He initiates, directs and controls the discussion.

(iii) He facilitates the reaching of conclusions.

(iv) He formulates or directs the plan of action for implementing the conclusions.

7.4 PARTICIPATION

The role of a participant is an equally important aspect of a meeting, which very much depends upon the kind and quality of contributions made by the participants. When you are asked to attend a meeting, acquaint yourself with the problems and topics to be discussed by going through the agenda carefully. Collect any information which may prove useful in the discussion. Though you should develop a

* This is the official record of discussion held and the decisions taken (see Chapter 18)

tentative point of view on each issue, keep an open mind. Remember others' points of view are as important as yours and therefore deserve your consideration and respect.

Be a good listener and try to read the thoughts behind the expressions. Do not miss anything that is being said; it may be a significant link in the chain of ideas. Even if you do not like the person who is speaking or feel that what the person is saying is irrelevant, listen to him attentively. Examine every opinion or suggestion on merits, irrespective of the source. Do not hesitate to volunteer any relevant information you may have on the topic under discussion and do speak up when you have something to say on it. Sometimes what you consider of little importance may be found by the group as significant.

Help the chairman maintain order. Do not engage in side conversation or shuffle papers in too obtrusive a manner so as to distract others' attention. Raise your hand to draw the attention of the chairman when you want to speak. When your turn comes express your views clearly and with confidence. Do not take any direct issue with any speaker by making personal references or belittling or ridiculing his ideas. Nothing is gained through a controversy of this type. You may well find that your views are criticised or your suggestions rejected. This should not dismay you. Wisdom often emerges when there is a clash of opinions. Sincere participation should be your main goal.

Do jot down important points at the meeting. Date and file them for future reference. Note-taking serves two purposes; it helps you keep your attention focussed throughout the meeting and fix the important points in your mind. Before you file the notes do mention the name of the chairman and the subject of the meeting. Keep the following points in mind while taking notes:

- Write rapidly and legibly. Write in block letters if you can.
- Let the entries be like the newspaper headlines – just adequate to trigger off the thought later.
- Do not falter over terms. Using your judgement make changes when necessary.
- Do not record any irrelevant information. However, rather than miss any important point, record more than what ultimately may be found essential. It is easier to eliminate than to recall.
- Be tactful in selecting pertinent material, exercising your editorial judgement.

7.5 PHYSICAL ARRANGEMENTS

There is no ideal room for holding a meeting. If a room can accommodate sixty persons, it won't be considered suitable for six. One has to be realistic enough to make the best use of the existing environment and the facilities available. In practice, most meetings are held in an executive's office. There are certain physical conditions which you should ensure, wherever the meetings are held. A good physical arrangement contributes to the success of the meeting.

The most favourable seating arrangement for a meeting is around a large round table. Ideally, every member should be able to look directly at others without turning his chair. However, the round table is not commonly available and often the members have to sit at a rectangular table. In this arrangement at least the chairman should seat himself at a position from where he can face everyone directly as shown in Fig. 7.1.

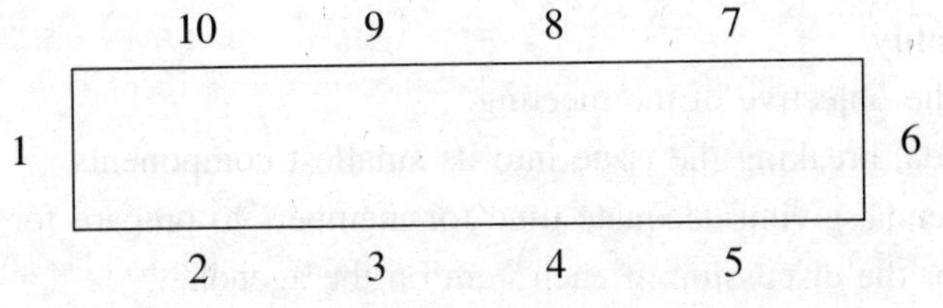

Fig. 7.1 Seating Arrangement for a Small Group

In Fig. 7.1 the chairman should occupy the position at (1) or (6). If the group is larger the seating arrangement may be as follows:

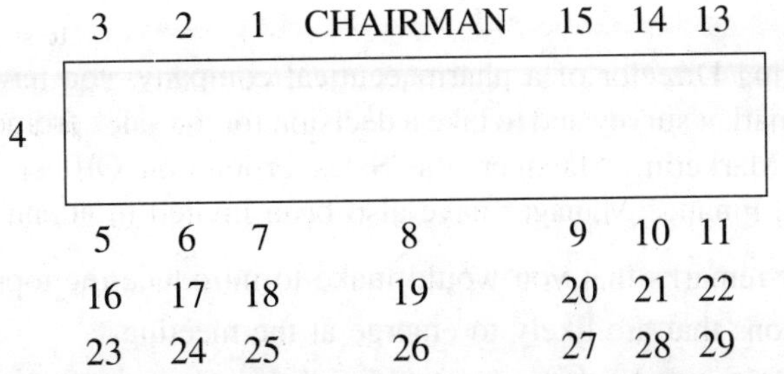

Fig. 7.2 Seating Arrangement for a Large Group

Another consideration in the seating arrangement is the power structure within the group, i.e. the question of placing members in relation to each other and the chairman. Since the chairman plays an influential role, the most powerful persons should not be placed next to him. A concentration of persons of higher status (for example at positions 1, 2, 3, 13, 14, 15 in Fig. 7.2) is likely to make it difficult for persons of lower status to speak up or disagree. Yet another consideration should be the placing of participants who are highly vocal vis-a-vis the shy and reluctant communicators. The former should be placed in the least comfortable physical locations. (For example, at positions 5 and 7 in Fig. 7.1 and positions 23 and 29 in Fig. 7.2).

Sitting sufficiently close together develops the necessary feeling of camaraderie and the interaction becomes easy. It should however, be ensured that every member is given easy accessibility to the supply of water, tea, etc.

The room where the meeting takes place should have privacy. Some people are unable to discuss problems properly, openly and meaningfully in the presence of prying eyes. The room should also be free from distractions and noise. It should be well-ventilated and have arrangements for lights and provision of facilities such as an overhead projector, etc.

Ten Rules for a Successful Meeting

(i) Convene a meeting when it is essential to consult others for taking action/decision.

(ii) Hold a meeting when consultations on telephone would not yield the desired result.

(iii) Invite only those who are essential to the meeting.

(iv) Insist on punctuality.
(v) Be clear about the objective of the meeting.
(vi) Prepare an agenda, breaking the issue into its smallest components.
(vii) Circulate the agenda, giving adequate time for members to prepare for the meeting.
(viii) Set time-limit for the discussion of each item on the agenda.
(ix) Summarise the conclusions briefly.
(x) Close the meeting on a pleasant note, indicating the future course of action.

ASSIGNMENTS

1. Assume that as Managing Director of a pharmaceutical company, you have called a meeting to discuss the results of a market survey and to take a decision for the sales promotion of your products. Note that besides the Marketing Manager, the Sales Promotion Officer, Production Manager, Personnel Manager and Finance Manager have also been invited to attend the meeting.
   (a) Write introductory remarks that you would make to introduce the topic of the meeting.
   (b) Write the suggestions that are likely to emerge at the meeting.
   (c) Write the concluding remarks that you would make as chairman.
2. The Management Association of a university has decided to organise an All-India Management Convention from 16 July to 19 July 2008. The theme of the Convention is *Indian Management: Challenge and Response* and the overall objective is to help bridge the gap between management theory and its application. As Convener you have called a meeting of the members of the Executive Committee to chalk out a detailed plan for the organisation of the Convention.
   (a) Write preliminary remarks that you would make to introduce the business of the meeting.
   (b) Draft a detailed plan that you would prepare for the conduct of the meeting. This plan should include your own tentative thoughts on the physical arrangements, schedule of lectures and discussions, assignment of tasks to various members, etc.

Chapter 8

SEMINARS AND CONFERENCES

THE academic world has a long tradition of organising seminars and conferences but now these have also become common in the professional world. The ever-increasing need for optimum utilisation of men and material demands deep thinking and the realisation that this can be best done by a group and not by an individual.

8.1 TYPES OF DISCUSSION GROUPS

The terms **seminar** and **conference** are sometimes confused with other discussion groups. We shall therefore first try to describe what we mean by seminar, symposium, panel discussion, conference and convention. Most of the characteristic features of seminar and conference are applicable to others also and hence they have not been taken up for detailed treatment.

A **seminar** refers to the discussion in a small group in which the result of original research or advanced study is presented through oral or written reports. It may also be organised for cross-fertilisation of ideas. Generally one person presents a lead paper, incorporating his findings and then there is an in-depth discussion on the material presented.

The other members are knowledgeable and take active part in the discussion. They closely interact with the lead speaker by expressing their views as seen from their individual angles. The doubts, if any, are sought to be clarified by putting specific questions. The main purpose of a seminar is to share knowledge and to get the viewpoints of equally well-informed persons.

In the university context the seminar refers to the discussion by a group of advanced level students under the supervision of a tutor.

In a **symposium** a small group of experts or well-informed persons discuss different aspects of a problem for the benefit of an audience. Each speaker is allotted a certain amount of time for making his presentation.

Speakers follow each other in turn until all have been heard. A discussion then ensues in which the audience may also participate. Though the symposium is formal, an element of spontaneity is introduced through audience participation. Generally, it is suited to programmes presented to a relatively large audience.

In a **panel discussion** instead of a series of speeches on different aspects of a problem, each member speaks on the announced topic which is generally worded as a question. The number of panelists is small and they are usually the people who have a lot of experience in the problem area selected for discussion. There is a direct conversational interchange of ideas. Thus a panel discussion may be termed as a process of cooperative thinking. A panel discussion may be followed by a session in which questions are put to the panel members by the listeners. The panel discussion is perhaps best suited to public discussion programmes on radio and TV.

Another type of meeting is called **conference**. The purpose of the conference is, as the name indicates, to confer – to confer with persons having similar interests and also to pool their experiences and opinions. The discussion usually results in a set of suggestions or recommendations on the central theme of the conference. The participant and subject matter spectrums are wider than those of a seminar or a symposium. It is not uncommon to hold small group discussions on different aspects of the conference theme, the delegates choosing among several discussion sessions going on simultaneously at the venue. Formal lectures, audio-visual presentations and exhibitions are also generally organised on the occasion. Thus a wide range of activities take place under the omnibus label – conference.

The conference is a closed group discussion. The participants have to register for attending it. Any other person present at the conference is either permitted observer or an invited guest.

A **convention** is generally a fellowship meeting of a closely linked fraternal group. It is usually more rigorously structured than a conference and only matters of professional interest are discussed. Thus the term is applied to professional gatherings held by companies, societies, associations, etc., and also to the assembly of the delegates of a political party.

Thus we see that there are a number of terms applied to group discussion activities. Although in each case individuals meet and discuss a topic, an issue, a problem or merely exchange views and share information, it would not be proper to use all these labels interchangeably. At the same time it is true that despite differences between one discussion group and another it is possible to abstract certain generalised rules applicable to all oral communication situations.

8.2 CONDUCTING SEMINARS

When a seminar has to be organised by you*, it is advisable to draw a detailed plan. Each seminar has an objective, a lead speaker and a number of participants. First, formulate the theme, determine the lead speaker and identify the participants. Next, select the venue and fix the time and date of the seminar. If you visualise more than one session, identify a chairman for each.

---

* Usually the person who organises the seminar is given a label such as seminar director or seminar coordinator.

As the seminar coordinator it would be your duty to send the above mentioned information to all participants well in time either through a circular letter, an e-mail or through a brochure with a covering note. This communication should be properly structured and should clearly state the objective of the seminar and the arrangements that have been made for conducting it and also those for board and lodging if you are inviting participants from other towns and cities.

For example, if you are organising a seminar on vocational education, you may send a circular such as the following:

NATIONAL INSTITUTE OF VOCATIONAL EDUCATION
Vivekanand Marg, New Delhi 110011

12 May, 2007

Dear ______________

You will be pleased to know that we are organising a one-day seminar on Vocational Education on Saturday, 7 July 2007.

The objective of the seminar is to discuss the necessity of more effective linkage between vocational education and employment, the identification of strategies for implementation, and determination of the directions for the future. Dr. S.K. Das, Professor and Head, Department of Education, Jamia Millia Islamia, New Delhi has kindly agreed to be the lead speaker. Other details of the Seminar are given below:

VENUE : National Institute of Vocational Education, Vivekanand Marg, New Delhi 110011
TELEGRAM : Education, New Delhi
PHONES : 426378, 429652

0900-1030
SESSION I : Necessity of More Effective Linkage between Vocational Education and Employment
CHAIRMAN : Mr. Ramgopal Sharma
Secretary
Ministry of Human Resource Development Government of India

1100-1230
SESSION II : Identification of Strategies for Implementation
CHAIRMAN : Dr. Abdul Hussain
Director
National Institute for Educational Planning Kasturba Gandhi Marg

1530-1700
SESSION III : Directions for the Future
CHAIRMAN : Mr. R.S. Krishnan
Personnel Manager
Bharat Heavy Electricals Ltd.
Bhopal

I hope you would be able to attend the seminar. Your participation, I am sure, would make the discussion meaningful and fruitful. For your perusal, I am enclosing a background paper incorporating the results of a study on vocational education carried out by the Department of Education, Jamia Millia Islamia.

Please return the enclosed form giving the required information, so as to reach us latest by 16 June 2007, to enable us to make suitable arrangements for transport, board and lodging.

We look forward to your participating in the seminar.

With kind regards,

Yours sincerely

(S. Bhagat)
Seminar Coordinator
Enclosures: Two

REPLY FORM

Seminar on Vocational Education to be held at the National Institute of Vocational Eduction, New Delhi, on 7 July, 2007

(a) I am glad to inform you that I would be able to attend the Seminar. I would be arriving by bus/train/ air at ____________, on ____________ . Please arrange transport, board and lodging for me and inform me of the same.

(b) I am sorry I would not be able to attend the seminar. I would however be grateful to receive a copy of the Proceedings of the Seminar.

Name:

Address:

Date: ____________

You should expect the replies from the intending participants to arrive around the last date given by you. When a sizeable number of replies have been received, you should get the information tabulated for further action. You would need to make arrangements for the following:

(i) Transport
(ii) Allotment of rooms in the booked guest houses, hotels, etc.
(iii) Menu, timing and place for different meals, snacks, tea and coffee, cold drinks, etc.
(iv) Seating; audio-visual aids; photocopying/cyclostyling facilities; stationery, OHP, whiteboard and markers or blackboard, chalk – both white and coloured, and pointer; public address system; facilities for recording and note-taking.
(v) Rapporteuring.
(vi) Deployment of manpower for the various tasks/allocation of duties.

Before the first session begins, as the coordinator you should welcome the participants, introduce the topic of the seminar, the lead speaker and the chairmen of the sessions. Also briefly mention the arrangements that have been made for the conduct of the discussion. You may then hand over the floor to the Chairman of the first session. He would be expected to make introductory remarks, delineating the scope of the topic of the session and then invite the lead speaker to begin his presentation.

The lead speaker generally gives the background of the study he has made, the methods or procedures of investigation he has followed and the results or conclusions he has reached. The emphasis is obviously on the conclusions. After his presentation is over, the chairmen invites discussion. The duties of the Chairman are similar in nature to what we have discussed in Chapter 7, but since the character of discussion, in a seminar is different, the Chairman should ensure that the results of the study are clearly presented and fully understood. It should become clear from the discussion, in what way the study has furthered the advancement of knowledge and added, howsoever humbly, to the body of knowledge in the particular field. We are often stimulated in our thinking in the presence of others. The discussion should take advantage of this aspect of human nature and exploit it for shedding new light on the topic under examination. In this the role of the lead speaker is crucial. The Chairman, however, has to ensure that each member plays his expected role and this he can do only if he is clear about his own role.

In the last session the coordinator sums up the conclusions reached in individual sessions and states their significance. He also proposes a ***vote of thanks***. The least you can do is to acknowledge publicly your gratitude to people who have helped to make the seminar a success. You may, in your appreciation, very briefly emphasise the facts of the presentation and contributions rather than embarrass the speakers by eulogising them. The overriding consideration is courtesy. Whenever possible you may introduce a light touch without resorting to flippancy.

It is also a good idea to construct, beforehand, at least the opening and the closing sentences to avoid any embarrassing situation. You may begin and close as follows:

Opening Sentence

Mr. Chairman, I have great pleasure in proposing a vote of thanks ...

Closing Sentence

In the end I would like to thank you all for having accepted our invitation and for making the discussion lively and purposeful.

The order in which you would like to refer to persons should be clear in your mind. If you do not feel confident you may write all you wish to say and memorise it. A vote of thanks should never be read out as it is the last face-to-face contact between you and the members of the seminar group. If you read it, the impact of oral interaction, which a seminar essentially is, would be lost.

After the seminar is over you may have to get the proceedings/ conclusions printed for circulation to participants. For doing this task with speed you should plan well in advance so that the impact of the discussion is not lost.

You may send this document along with a thank you letter, such as the following:

Dear ____________

I am enclosing a copy of the Proceedings of the Seminar on Vocational Education held on 7 July 2007. If you have any comments or suggestions to make, please let us know.

It was a real pleasure to have you with us on this occasion. Your presence enhanced the value of the seminar and we are really grateful to you for having made significant contributions in the discussion.

With kind regards

Yours sincerely

Enclosure: One

What we have discussed above is applicable to the seminar that would be attended by a large number of participants from other organisations and towns. In actual practice you may often be required to organise seminars on a much smaller scale – one session seminars with participants drawn from your own organisation. And then obviously all the elaborate arrangements discussed above may not have to be made. What is intended here is a broad guideline; you will have to formulate in each case your own strategy in implementation, keeping in view the specific requirements of the situation.

8.3 ORGANISING CONFERENCES

Most of the steps that have to be taken for preparation, presentation and conclusion of the seminar are broadly relevant for the organisation of a conference also. As we have stated earlier, a conference is usually a large gathering of persons who meet to confer on a particular theme or to exchange experience or information.

Since the information to be sent to the potential delegates is substantial, it is better to prepare a brochure containing all the details. It should be mailed to the expected participants well in advance. You may structure your brochure as follows:

Page 1 : Theme of the conference, name of the sponsors, dates, name of the organisers.

Page 2 : A short note on the theme of the conference.

Page 3 : Names of the Conference President and Secretary; names of rapporteurs; venue; time, date and place of plenary and valedictory sessions and also those of small group discussions.

Page 4 : Details of invited lectures – name of the speaker, topic, time, date and place; exhibitions – nature, timings and venue; audio-visual aids available for use during the Conference.

Page 5 : Reception, transport, board and lodging arrangements; postal and telegraphic address of the conference Secretary and his phone number, delegate fee.

Usually the size of the brochure is 12 cm by 21 cm and it is sent along with a covering letter and proforma for reply from the intending participants. The samples of letter and proforma, given earlier can be suitably amended and used by you for the conference and other discussion groups also. A **sample brochure** announcing a national convention is given at the end of this chapter.

After the replies are received, prepare a list of delegates and go ahead with the arrangements for 'their reception, transport, board and lodging. At the same time send a short note acknowledging the receipt of the acceptance form and informing them of the arrangements you have made. An example is given as follows:

> Dear ______________
>
> We are glad to know that you would be attending the Conference.
>
> We note that you would be arriving at ______________, on ____________, by bus/train/air. We have set up Reception Desks near the main exits at the bus stand, the railway station and the airport. The reception desks would work round the clock from 4 am ____________ (date) to 10 pm ____________ (date).
>
> You have been allotted a room in Atithi Bhavan, Mahatma Gandhi Road (Telephone Number 629274).
>
> Further details will be given to you at the Reception Desk. Just in case you are not able to contact the Reception for some reason, please report directly to the Bhavan at the counter marked 'arrivals.'
>
> A receipt for Rs. ____________, the delegate fee sent by you, is enclosed.
>
> We look forward to meeting you soon.
>
> With kind regards
>
> Yours sincerely
>
> Name
>
> Conference Secretary
>
> Enclosure: One

At the plenary session there is usually a Welcome Address by the Secretary, Keynote Address by the Conference President and a Vote of Thanks. Sometimes a conference is inaugurated by a dignitary and in this case the inaugural address is scheduled between the Welcome Address and the Keynote Address. Often the important addresses are printed and distributed to the audience before they are read out. The practice of doing so takes away the impact of the face-to-face oral communication as most of the people keep their eyes glued on the distributed written material and miss the nuances of oral delivery and body language. We would therefore advise you to distribute the text of the speeches after they have been delivered.

Some organisations wish to find out the extent to which the conference objectives were achieved. Such an evaluation is helpful in determining more effective follow-up action and suggesting how future programmes can be made more successful. The most convenient way to do so is through a conference questionnaire which should be filled in by the participants. The basic principles of preparing a questionnaire have been discussed in Chapter 9. Following are some questions, which you may find useful when you are asked to draft a questionnaire.

(i) To guide us in interpreting your reactions please give the name of your organisation ______________ production or services of your organisation ____________ , your department ______________ , your position _____________ , and description of your work ______________.

(ii) Have the conference topics been fairly pertinent to your field of interest? Yes ____________ No ______________ .

(iii) Was the general level of information exchanged at formal sessions too elementary? Yes _______ No_______ Too theoretical? Yes _______ No _______ . Just about right? Yes _______ No _______ .

(iv) What topics would you like to be included in a future conference? ______________.

(v) What benefits did you hope to derive from attending this conference? ______________

(vi) In view of the benefits derived from this conference, do you, recommend that we organise another such conference? Yes _______ No _______ .

(vii) Were you satisfied with the board and lodging arrangements? Yes _______ No _______

(viii) Would you like any exhibitions to be held in conjunction with a future conference? Yes _______ No _______ . Give specific suggestions.

(ix) Please write further criticisms, observations, or suggestions on the blank sheets attached: Thanks for your help.

Name (optional): ______________________________

Date: __________

Place: __________

SECOND NATIONAL CONVENTION ON ENERGISING ENTEREPRENEURSHIP THROUGH INNOVATION

2-3 November 2007

Incubate... Illuminate... Innovate

Entrepreneurship Development & IPR Unit &
Technology Business Incubator

Birla Institute of Technology & Science
Pilani-333031 Rajasthan

Background

India has emerged as a promising global economic hub in the last two decades. To carry forward this economic upsurge, it is imperative to promote entrepreneurship and develop technology incubators. The need of the hour is to create an ecosystem consisting of the corporate world, the university system, the government as well as other support systems. This would promote entrepreneurship, particularly in high technology and high growth areas.

The emergence of new potential areas presents exciting challenges and opportunities to young and budding entrepreneurs. Financial institutions are keen to support well-established entrepreneurs; however, search for new and innovative enterprises is inevitable. Currently, the Venture Capitalists (VCs) are scouting for high-tech and knowledge-based enterprises. The focus of the convention is to introduce young scientists and innovators to different aspects and dimensions of entrepreneurship to realize their dreams.

Purpose

The convention is primarily meant for introducing the youth and young professionals in technical fields to entrepreneurship. Keeping pace with the current scenario of entrepreneurship development, a convention was organized last year on 'Energizing Entrepreneurship in Academia through Innovation'. The outcomes of the convention were visible in the form of taking concrete steps for patenting high technology innovations and launching ventures. This not only bolstered the confidence of the young entrepreneurs but also gave them the right direction for start-up ventures. This year, the convention aims to carry forward the efforts initiated last time. It proposes to provide a platform for developing domain expertise in different aspects and dimensions of entrepreneurship so that the new ventures can attain success.

Objectives

- To showcase the innovative ideas and prototypes developed by creative students, scientists and technologists, providing an opportunity to have such **ideas objectively evaluated** by various interest groups involved in the process of promoting entrepreneurship.
- To enable students, faculty and scientists to asses whether the ideas and concepts can be transformed into **workable commercial prepositions.**
- To provide a platform for building channels and networks for availing effective **mentoring, support, and incubation facilities.**
- To explore the possibilities of **financial support** from bankers, venture capitalists and angel investors.
- To impart knowledge and skills for the preparation of a **Business Plan**.
- To create awareness about the importance of **Intellectual Property Rights (IPR)** in the present context as well as procedures for patenting.

PROGRAMME DETAILS

The Tech Bazaar will provide space for showcasing innovative products in the following technical domains:

- Information and Communication Technology
- Electronic System Design and Embedded Systems
- Auto Ancillary Products
- Technologies for Rural Applications
- Pharma, Bio-technology, Bio-metrics and Bio medical areas
- Entertainment, Animation and Education
- Others

The Technology Clinic and Boutique will offer individual guidance, presentations and interactive sessions on the following topics:

- Entrepreneurship Skills
- Developing Business Plans
- Venturing and Financing Process
- Government Policies and Perspectives on Enterprise Development
- Patenting Processes and IPR issues

RESOURCE PERSONS

- Successful entrepreneurs
- Bankers
- Venture Capitalists
- Academicians
- R&D Professionals

REGISTRATION

Students, professionals and scientists interested in participating are requested to fill in the Registration Form. Those interested in showcasing their products have to send an executive summary (a brief outline about the idea, uniqueness, market potential, competitive edge, technical feasibility and cost effectiveness) along with 2 copies of a personal photographs and resume to one of the conveners. The last date for registration is 8 October 2007. The entries will be evaluated by an expert panel and an intimation of acceptance will be sent by 15 October 2007.

Fees: (to be sent by DD favouring BITS, Pilani.)

Corporate Executives/Entrepreneurs	Rs. 3500
Academicians	Rs. 1500
Students	Rs. 750

Registration fee includes board, lodging and delegate kit. Corporate executives and academics would be housed in the VFAST Hostel (Guest House) of the Institute Campus while students would be accommodated in hostels. No Registration Fee will be charged from the invited participants.

Route to Pilani

Pilani is 220 kms from Delhi and 240 kms from Jaipur. The nearest railway stations are Loharu on Northern Railways and Chirawa on Western Railway about 26 kms and 16 kms away respectively. Buses are available from ISBT, Delhi and Sundhi Camp, Jaipur at frequent intervals.

Organisers

Entrepreneurship Development and IPR Unit at BITS is focusing its efforts on promotion of entrepreneurship development programmes – educational, executive development and research. It also facilitates faculty and students to take necessary steps to protect their intellectual property.

Center for Entrepreneurial Leadership (CEL) at BITS is one of the co-founding partners of National Entrepreneurship Network (NEN). CEL is actively involved in the promotion of students' related entrepreneurial activities. Participants of the Convention can benefit from the multifarious activities of CEL in the area of networking, mentoring, research and education and also participate in its Business Plan Competition 'Conquest'.

Technology Business Incubator (TBD) at BITS has been established in association with DST, Govt. of India and aims at new technology-based enterprises. Highly innovative projects can be developed further at TBI. Facilities provided by TBI include independent office facilities with round the clock internet access and Analytical Lab equipped with sophisticated instruments.

Conveners

Dr. Usha Manjunath	Dr. Sangeeta Sharma
Management Group	Languages Group
usham.bits@gmail.com	sang@bits-pilani.ac.in

Entrepreneurship Development & IPR Unit
Visit: www.celbits.org

- *Reproduced with the permission of conveners*

ASSIGNMENTS

1. (a) Assume that you acted as the Chairman of the first session of the Seminar on Vocational Education. Inventing the necessary details, write the concluding remarks, summarising the main points and highlighting the significant aspects of the discussion.

   (b) As a participant at the third session of the above Seminar, you spoke immediately after the lead speaker. Write your observations (i) expressing your disagreement with his approach, and (ii) supporting his point of view.

2. A national conference on Technology Forecasting Techniques is being organised in Delhi under the auspices of Department of Science and Technology, Government of India. About 200 scientists, engineers, technocrats from academic, research and industrial organisations, both government and private are expected to attend. The topics such as frontiers in biotechnology, energy prospects, telecommunication, appropriate technology, education for 21st century, etc., are likely to come up for discussion.

   (i) Write welcome remarks that you would make as the Conference Secretary at the inaugural session and also the vote of thanks that you would propose at the concluding session.

   (ii) Write the address that you would deliver as the Chairman of the first session.

Chapter 9

GROUP DISCUSSION

9.1 GROUP DYNAMICS

THE term **group discussion** is used to refer to a situation in which a small number of persons meet face-to-face and, through free oral interaction among themselves, exchange information or attempt to reach a decision on shared problems. It is difficult to specify the number of participants that would make the group discussion useful. It has been found that the character of interaction undergoes a change when one or two persons are added to a dyadic communication situation. Similarly, if the number of persons in a group is ten or more, some tend to avoid participation and remain just passive listeners. Thus, the significance of group discussion is lost because in it each member is expected to participate actively. Researches indicate that if the number is kept between five to nine, fruitful discussion can take place. If the number is less than five, the discussion suffers from a lack of diversity of opinion, knowledge and skill. It has also been observed that groups of even numbers of participants tend to be less stable and rewarding than groups of odd numbers.

There is no named leader of the group. As the discussion proceeds, one of the participants may emerge as a leader. The expectation is that as responsible professionals the members of the group would ensure the smooth flow of interaction and ultimately arrive at an agreed solution or a strategy of action to achieve the specific purpose for which the discussion was organised. Effective communication in a small group requires sensitivity to the dynamics of the group process. Each participant should give a fair chance to others to speak and express their opinion. This would ensure crystallisation of thought and bring to light different aspects of the topic under discussion. Emotional outburst and display of excitement have, therefore, no place in this type of discussion.

One advantage of this type of discussion is that there is a self-imposed discipline on the discussion and greater responsibility on participants for making it useful. If the group finds that a particular member is reticent, it is the duty of the others to elicit his opinion on the issue. Since the number of participants is small, it should not be difficult to involve every member in the debate. If a member tries to dominate the discussion or to go on speaking continuously for a long time, it is the duty of others to curb his ebullience and to interrupt him politely so that others are also able to make their contributions. To keep the discussion on the track it may be worthwhile for a participant to summarise the points made till that time and then to present his viewpoint.

Occasionally when the group discussion takes place some persons may be invited as observers. This may be done for two purposes:

(i) to let the observers learn the process of group discussion and

(ii) to evaluate the contributions by members.

9.2 PURPOSES

Very often group discussion is used in addition to written test/ interview for employment. Obviously therefore a representative of the prospective employer sits through the group discussion and observes the group performance. He judges each individual's personality traits such as intellectual ability, creativity, approach to solving problems; qualities of leadership, tolerance and group behaviour. It is clear that in this process he would also note the clarity of thought and felicity of expression of each member.

Sometimes a group discussion is also an instrument of education to develop and judge the student's personality traits mentioned above. It trains the student to function in the professional world efficiently. Several qualities can be inculcated by a proper use of this tool, for example, conceptual clarity, discernment of subtle nuances of a problem, mature reaction to others' views, effective communication of one's own ideas, ability to persuade, sagacity to see reason, etc. – highly valued qualities in a professional. This method of self-education meets the increasing desire for a clearer understanding of day-to-day problems, so essential to counter the isolation of individual thought which can lead to biased judgement and prejudiced action. Howsoever competent an individual professional may be, the modern democratic society expects collective, mutually agreed, harmonious decisions for nurturing and developing the capability of an organisation.

9.3 ORGANISATION

There are two ways of organising a group discussion. One, the topic is announced beforehand and the participants are expected to have done their homework before coming to the discussion table. Two, the topic is announced after the members have assembled and they are given five to ten minutes for collecting their thoughts. In both the cases, formality is avoided and the rules are kept to the minimum.

The room is to be chosen with care; it should have proper ventilation and sufficient light. The chairs should be arranged in a circle so that a member's expression can be seen by all the others.

Hints for Self-improvement

Often you would be called upon to participate in a group discussion in your organisation to find a solution to a problem. Each time after participation, you should analyse your performance so that there is continuous improvement. While doing so you should bear in mind the following:

(i) Whether you articulated your words clearly and distinctly and put the required stress on appropriate syllables.

(ii) Whether you regulated the speed of your speech and paused wherever necessary to make your presentation clear and effective.

(iii) Whether in your judgement, what you said was grasped by other participants and reflected in their responses.

(iv) Whether your intervention, if any, annoyed the concerned speaker.

(v) Whether you could keep your mind focused all the time on what was being said.

If you find yourself deficient in any of the areas mentioned above, you should try to attain the required levels of these skills. You may go in for self-training or seek the help of experts. Do not hesitate to take the latter path as it is never too late to learn.

ASSIGNMENTS

A few controversial statements are listed below for practice in group discussion.

(i) Television exercises a baneful influence on all sections of society.

(ii) Democracy has failed in India, what the country needs is dictatorship.

(iii) To make it socially relevant higher education should be nationalised.

(iv) The only solution to Kashmir issue is to divide it on the basis of line of control.

(v) To accelerate the advancement of the country a more meaningful participation of women in all areas of socio-economic activities is essential.

(vi) Indian cinema today is neither a source of healthy entertainment nor an agent of social change.

(vii) It is necessary to control unbridled growth of technology if man wants to survive on this planet.

(viii) Management, to be effective, depends more on experience than on educational qualifications.

Chapter 10

AUDIO-VISUAL AIDS

THERE are many occasions when a professional has to make an oral presentation. The use of audio-visual aids can greatly enhance the presentation's value. The impact of what we see and hear lasts longer than what we only see or merely hear.

The term **audio-visual aids** refers to the equipment available to us for amplifying or supplementing our message. An aid thus makes the communication lucid, vivid, stimulating and interesting. It helps the speaker arrest the attention of the audience and enables him to enliven even a dull topic. The technology of communication is rapidly becoming more advanced and sophisticated. The immense possibilities of exploiting it sometime fascinate the speaker so much that he permits technology to take over. Remember, too many aids or the overuse of an aid may cripple the impact of your presentation. Let an aid complement and not dominate, reinforce and not distract, illustrate and not exaggerate. An aid is not merely a help to the audience but also to the speaker. If he has planned well and prepared his aid material properly, he can sustain the interest of the audience and thus drive home the meaning he wants to convey. The aids also serve as prompts to the points the speaker wants to make and give him time for smooth transition.

In specific terms, we are concerned with the following audio-visual aids: white board/blackboard, overhead projector, filmstrip and slide projector, movie film projector, video tape recorder, audio tape recorder and models. Sometimes the graphic aids such as charts, diagrams, maps, etc., are also referred to as visual aids. We have however discussed them separately in Cnapter 17 as they constitute a significant part of written communication.

10.1 BASIC PRINCIPLES AND GUIDELINES

Keep the following principles and guidelines in mind when you decide to use an audio- or a visual-aid:

(i) Decide the content you wish to support with aid.

(ii) Choose the appropriate medium.

(iii) Integrate the aid with the presentation.

(iv) Choose a suitable place for the equipment to be kept. Whatever you present through the aid should be capable of being heard or seen by everyone in the audience.

(v) Ensure that you have a basic non-technical knowledge of how to operate the equipment. If you hate machines (as some people do), have somebody to help you. Fumbling may prove counter-productive.

(vi) When not in use, keep the equipment away or at least covered. If it is left in view throughout the presentation, it may distract the audience.

(vii) Inspect the venue of presentation if possible, to check the physical arrangements such as switches, power supply, size of the room, lectern, pointer, etc.

(viii) Prepare the audio-visual material with great care emphasising those aspects which you consider significant. Do not clutter it with irrelevant or excessive information. Use devices such as underlining, arrows, heavy lettering, colour, etc., for emphasis, wherever possible. But in no circumstances should the display material become the centre of attraction.

(ix) When you use several items of visual material, number them. Ensure that their appearance and exit are properly timed.

10.2 TYPES OF AUDIO-VISUAL AIDS AND THEIR USE

Let us now briefly discuss the various audio-visual aids that are used in oral presentation, be it a meeting, panel discussion, seminar, or a conference.

10.2.1 Whiteboard/Blackboard

The Whiteboard/Blackboard are the most easily available visual aid equipment. They are the cheapest and the most useful aid, requiring minimum expertise. But you will be ill-advised to use them without planning and practice Some of the obvious advantages in the use of the these boards are the following:

- A board offers plenty of space to the user to present simple drawings, diagrams, maps, graphs and of course words and phrases.
- You can give the audience a feeling of spontaneity. Further, if some new idea occurs to you at the time of presentation, you can modify what you have presented on the board. You can also modify the material in the light of comments and suggestions received from the audience.
- You can involve the listeners by demanding inputs from them for incorporation on the board.
- The board permits the progressive development of a design, process or idea. This sustains the audience interest.
- You can vary the pace of writing to suit the speed of the listener's comprehension.
- To a nervous speaker the board acts as a pressure reliever.

Now here are a few tips

- Plan carefully how you will use your board and what you will write on it. Decide what you would like to stay permanently on the board and what temporarily. In your lecture notes let there be a clear indication of this intention.
- Write legibly and neatly. Separate your letters and let them be larger than usual. Ensure that your writing is not cursive.
- Hold the marker or the chalk at approximately 45° angle. Use good quality chalk/marker and press it hard against the board. If the chalk squeaks, break it into two pieces or replace it by another.
- Write fast but not at the expense of clarity.
- Divide the board into several portions using one or two for the material that is going to stay throughout your presentation. You may use one portion for writing the main points of your presentation or technical words, key words and phrases and definitions.
- Maintain the flow of talk as you write but avoid speaking to the board. Look frequently at the audience for eye contact.
- While writing, ensure that the material is not completely hidden by your body.
- After you have written the material, stand clear of the board so that all listeners can see it.
- Allow sufficient time for the audience to copy or absorb the material.
- Use standard abbreviations and be consistent throughout.
- If you have put on the board something ahead of time, keep it covered, if possible, until you need it.
- Underline, write in capitals or use coloured chalk for drawing special attention to important points or significant portions of drawings, diagrams, etc.

10.2.2 Overhead Projector

An overhead, projector is a clean, often superior substitute for the blackboard. Since it is a versatile and relatively inexpensive aid to the speaker, it is becoming increasingly popular. You can use it to project clear images of prepared transparencies of many kinds, on the screen or even on a light coloured wall. Written material, diagrams, charts, maps, etc., can be transferred to transparencies for projection.

The projector is placed on a table approximately nine feet away from the screen but this distance is adjustable. No blackout is required but if the room is brightly lit, the images may lose their sharpness. Display material is put on transparencies (specially treated sheets of acetate) by several methods. You can simply write or draw on a transparency by a special pen, in colour if required. Or you may photocopy on a transparency the printed material you wish to display. A little practice will teach you how to write on a transparency; no special skills are required. You may prepare the transparencies beforehand or you may build up the information you wish to project while speaking. You can also mask some information in an already prepared transparency until you reach the relevant point. Another great advantage is that you can continue to face the audience and maintain eye-contact while using an overhead projector. Further, you can put it on or off as many times as you like.

10.2.3 Filmstrip and Slide Projector

Projectors which can show both filmstrips and slides are now easily available in the market. Filmstrips are a sequence of transparencies on 8 or 16 mm films. They are commercially produced but can also be prepared by professionals to meet the special needs of your organisation. The sequence of projection cannot be changed but the advantage is that they can be handled easily. The sequence of projection of slides can be varied. These too are available in the market but can be easily prepared.

When you use a projector of this kind, the lights would have to be switched off. However, certain improved projectors now available, obviate this requirement. If you use a projector which can be operated by remote control, you can place it anywhere in the room and use it as and when required.

10.2.4 Movie Film Projector

We are all familiar with the tremendous impact that a film exercises on us. This medium is now being used not only for entertainment but also for teaching, training and advertising.

Film is available in four sizes – 8 mm, 16 mm, 35 mm and 70 mm with sound. The last two are used for commercial cinema projection as they have the largest image potential. The films which are professionally produced for teaching and training purposes are usually in 16 mm format. Very few are produced in 8mm size because these can be projected on a 4 sq ft small screen, and thus are fit for small audiences only. When you have to use this medium, first find out whether films on suitable subjects to meet your needs are available in the market with authorised agencies on hire basis. As you may be aware, films on technical and educational subjects (such as science, technology, business, management, culture, etc.) are produced mostly by government departments and agencies and foreign embassies. They are available either free of cost or on easy terms. Certain forward looking companies have also produced films which deal with matters which you may find of interest. For example, Philips India Ltd. have produced a very good film on basic concepts of electronics and electrical engineering. Usually each film producing organisation maintains a catalogue which you can scan to identify the films you need.

Sometimes you may be required to produce your own films. However, its production requires time, money, skill and experience. This job can be handled by film-producing agencies which can do exactly what you want. Your job then will be to specify the requirements of your subject and to ensure that these are met.

Before showing a film prepare your audience by a short introduction and after the show is over, conduct a meaningful discussion, ending the session with a summary. Don't let the film take over your entire responsibility. It is of utmost importance that the film is of sufficient merit to justify its inclusion in your plan. And it must be previewed so that it can be properly integrated with your presentation.

Some practical hints are given below for the use of a film projector. Before you start to do the following things:

- Check the film-strip manually to ensure that there are no cracks, cuts and perforations in it.
- Check for proper threading, run the projector to set focus and position.

- Check and set the sound level to suit the size of the audience.
- Keep spare lamps, fuses and a set of belts within easy reach, to avoid inconvenience and failure.

To start a film follow the procedure given below:

- Switch on the machine and the projection lamp.
- Darken the room.
- Adjust sound and focus, if necessary.
- Start showing the film.
- Turn off the sound and lamp simultaneously after THE END.
- Switch off the machine.
- Turn on the room lights thereafter.

10.2.5 VCD and DVD Players

The use of video equipment is now becoming commonplace. Any display material requiring visual motion and sound can be recorded or downloaded from a reliable source on a compact disc (CD) and used for presentation on VCD or DVD players. It is easy to handle a player and to monitor a television set. No blackout is required and without almost any technical knowledge you can operate them. The material recorded can be displayed instantly. Further, the equipment is easily portable. Thus for reaching a small audience you can choose this medium as an aid to your presentation.

To meet your needs you may well find professionally produced material in the market. There is an increasing trend to make available on the Internet recorded lectures by eminent technocrats, scientists, management specialists, etc. for easy accessibility by a large population spread over a wide area. It is because of this reason that Internet and close circuit television are becoming a powerful tool of formal instruction.

10.2.6 Models

A model is a miniature representation of something. It is the closest alternative to a real object such as a bridge, car, plane, etc. When, in your presentation, you wish to refer in some detail to a particular object, you can do so by using a model of that object. A model would evoke considerable interest and attract close attention of the audience, making your explanation more meaningful and easily assimilable.

When you decide to use a model you can get it made by an expert but simple models can be made by you also. Keep the following two points in mind for preparing a model:

(i) The size of the audience should determine the size of the model.

(ii) Make it sufficiently strong so that it is capable of being handled repeatedly.

Apart from conventional materials you can use cardboard, balsa wood, soap, string, polystyrene, etc., for making simple models.

While using the model, ensure that it is kept at a place where it can be viewed by every member of the audience. Display it long enough to make an impact but do remove it from view when not required.

10.3 CONCLUSIONS

As you would have observed, we-have discussed in greater detail the use of two aids, namely whiteboard/ blackboard and film. The former are still the most widely used whereas the latter is at the same time most complex and most effective – nearest to real-life situations. In recent years there has been spectacular advancement in Information Technology. The main developments which have revolutionised the use of audio-visual aids are discussed separately in Chapter 3. Before we conclude we would like to emphasise the following two points. One, an aid is just an aid and not a replacement for any portion of the message. Two, every audio-visual aid is helpful for both the speaker and the listener; both aspects of communication, production and reception, become vibrant and absorbing when an aid is properly used.

ASSIGNMENTS

1. Assume that you are the Financial Manager of a Public Limited Company, which has recently computerised its accounting procedure. What visual aids would be useful, if you were asked to give a talk to the sectional heads and other senior officers of your company to explain the procedure adopted, the problems faced and the advantages accrued from computerisation. Describe clearly what material you would present through the aids selected by you.
2. You have to give an introductory lecture on Principles and Process of Communication as Training Manager to a group of sixteen management trainees of your company. Indicate the points and other matter that you would like to write on the whiteboard/blackboard during the course of your presentation. Describe also how you would organise your board work and give an illustration by means of a diagram.
3. If you were to tape record the above mentioned lecture, to be played in your absence, what precautions would you take to compensate for the absence of whiteboard\blackboard work? What precautions would you make before recording and what points would you keep in mind at the time of recording? Describe the entire procedure step by step in detail.
4. As the Public Relations Officer of a company, you have been asked to prepare a video film showing glimpses of the various facets of the pioneering work done by your organisation.
   (a) List the sequence of scenes that you would like to present.
   (b) Write the script to accompany the scenes.
   (c) Indicate the places where you would like to use background music.

PART THREE

WRITTEN COMMUNICATION

Chapter 11

READING COMPREHENSION

THERE would be many occasions in your life when you would have to use your ability to read written or printed word as quickly and efficiently as possible to gather information for writing a paper or a report or for gathering knowledge. We may define reading as an act of taking in or comprehending written or printed words. Reading effectively is an important skill which can be acquired only through practice. As a student you have to read and answer questions on comprehension passages in competitive examinations. As a professional you would have to read various printed materials like books, research journals, articles, word processed or typed materials to collect information for writing a paper, giving a seminar, submitting a proposal, and writing a project. You would have to do some or all of the above tasks. In addition, you may have to read official reports, files, correspondence (letters, memos, e-mails, etc.) and write your comments in the margin of files and send replies. Besides, you read news paper, magazines, and books for keeping abreast of the times, to know the latest ideas, events, etc. You may read for entertainment too.

11.1 READING TECHNIQUES

In fact, in order to read various kinds of printed material, you would have to use various reading techniques. It is the purpose for which you read that would decide the technique of reading. For example, at a book stall, you may read the title of a book, go through the pages quickly *surveying* or *skimming* to know what the book is all about. Reading every word or every line is not necessary then. Sometimes, the back cover of a book gives enough information about the contents or theme of the book. But whenever you need specific information or details on a topic you would have to *scan* through the body of the text so that you can rapidly take in the gist of what is written there. Here too, not every printed word is read. On different occasions there is no escape from reading the whole text carefully, that is studying the text with close attention and concentration for in-depth understanding of the material and getting the relevant data. For example, when you have to write a paper or an assignment, you have to collect a lot of points, facts and information related to the theme of the paper. You have then to read the text, understand its meaning; infer the meaning of unfamiliar words. For interpreting the material too, you would sometimes have to go back to the previous lines or words for the sake of clarity. Another academic reading exercise comes in the form of writing a 'precis' of a given passage apart from comprehension passages. Both need effective reading skills. A discussion on precis writing is given in Chapter 12.

Guidelines for Effective Reading:

- Read actively, using your judgement to pay attention to what the author is trying to convey through the printed text.
- Use 'eye-span' to read a group of words at one attempt instead of focusing on each individual word.
- Avoid vocalising, i.e. uttering the individual words either loudly or saying them to yourself. This hampers the speed of reading and slows down the rate of reading.
- Do not use a pencil or your finger to keep track of the words or lines you are reading.
- Practice 'silent' reading to increase your reading speed.
- Remember, every kind of reading does not require the same fast reading rate. Some texts need slow in-depth and intensive reading while others require a faster rate or skimming.
- Develop the habit of reading everyday to increase your reading rate.
- Note down the unfamiliar words you find in the reading material in a notebook.
- Consult a good dictionary to find the meaning and usage of new words you have come across while reading. This will help you increase your vocabulary, too.

Many universities conduct tests for admission to their programme of studies and these tests include reading comprehension passages. Similarly, many competitive examinations set reading comprehension exercises for testing the candidate's ability of understanding the printed text. Therefore, acquisition of effective reading skills is very important for comprehending the implicit or explicit meaning of words in the given passage and answering the questions based on it.

11.2 HELPFUL HINTS FOR COMPREHENSION EXERCISES

1. Read the passage slowly, paying close attention to the ideas and the theme discussed in it.
2. Identify the theme or the subject of the passage.
3. Read the passage once again, and note down the main points this time.
4. Do not be discouraged if you come across unfamiliar words. Try to interpret their meaning from the context in which they have been used.
5. Read the passage once again and try to find the answer of the questions given at the end of the passage.
6. Note the tense of the question and write the answer in the same tense.
7. Write the answers in your own words.
8. Ensure that your answers are in the third person.

9. Do not add any additional information or facts, and your own opinion or views.
10. Revise your answers.

11.3 ILLUSTRATIVE EXAMPLES

***Illustrative Example* 1**

Floods, earthquakes, droughts, cyclones, tsunamis, etc. are natural disasters. There is no fixed time for these disasters. Thousands of lives are lost and property worth several thousand crores of rupees is destroyed on account of these natural disasters every year. Natural disasters are caused by the forces of nature and are unpredictable. Man has no control over these disasters. Over the years technological development has enabled man to check some of the natural disasters. Man has created dams to store excess water during rains and thus, check the floods. The excess water collected in the dams can be utilised during the times of no rain or drought. Cyclones today can be predicted beforehand. But there is no reliable method of predicting the earthquakes.

When disaster strikes it does not discriminate between rich and poor, classes and masses, and men and women. Everyone is prone to lose everything he or she has. Thousands of people turn destitute within a matter of few minutes. Natural disaster, therefore, is a human problem. People affected by it need all kinds of help from the rest of the humanity. But before we can understand how to manage a natural disaster we must know the nature of disaster and the extent of destruction it can cause.

Questions

1. What is the central idea of the passage?
2. What damages are caused by natural disasters?
3. What causes natural disasters?
4. Name the step that man has taken to lessen the effect of some of the natural disasters.
5. What are the advantages of building dams?
6. Write in one sentence how disasters do not differentiate among people.
7. Give the antonyms (opposite words) of the following:

   (i) natural (ii) lost (iii) utilised
   (iv) valuable (v) predictable (vi) problem
8. Tick the meaning nearest to the words given below:

   (a) draught
      (i) continuous dry weather (ii) lack of moisture (iii) scantiness

   (b) disaster
      (i) scourge (ii) mishap (iii) calamity

   (c) control
      (i) authority (ii) power (iii) regulation

   (d) excess
      (i) residue (ii) surplus (iii) redundance

(e) discriminate

(i) distinguish (ii) different (iii) distinct

(f) destitute

(i) poverty (ii) in want (iii) without resources

Answers

1. The central idea of the passage is how natural calamities cause loss of lives and property and what steps man has taken to minimise their impact.
2. The damages caused by natural disasters are loss of human and animal lives and destruction of property worth crores of rupees.
3. Natural disasters are caused by the unpredictable forces of nature.
4. With the help of technology man has checked some of the natural disasters by building dams to store excess water during rainy seasons.
5. The extra water stored in the dams can be used during dry seasons. Building dams can lessen the impact of floods.
6. Disasters do not distinguish between rich and poor people or between low class and higher class people and ruin everyone.
7. *Words* — *Antonyms*

	Words		Antonyms
(i)	natural	-	unnatural
(ii)	lost	-	found
(iii)	utilised	-	unutilized
(iv)	valuable	-	invaluable
(v)	predictable	-	unpredictable
(vi)	problem	-	solution

8. *Words* — *Meaning*

	Words		Meaning
(a)	drought	-	(i) continuous dry weather
(b)	disaster	-	(iii) calamity
(c)	control	-	(ii) power
(d)	excess	-	(ii) surplus
(e)	discriminate	-	(i) distinguish
(f)	destitute		(iii) without resources

***Illustrative Example* 2**

Among the many who have enforced the duty of giving, I am surprised there are none to inculcate the ignominy of receiving; to show that by every favour we accept, we, in some measure, forfeit our native freedom; and that a state of continual dependence on the generosity of others is a life of gradual debasement.

Were men taught to despise this receiving of obligations with the same force of reasoning and declamation that they are instructed to confer them? We might then see every person in society filling up the requisite duties of his station with cheerful industry, neither relaxed by hope, nor sullen from disappointment.

Every favour a man receives, in some measure, sinks him below his dignity and in proportion to the value of the benefit, or the frequency of its acceptance, he gives up so much of his natural independence. He, therefore, who thrives upon the unmerited bounty of another, if he has any sensibility, suffers the worst of servitude; the shackled slave may murmur without reproach but he, humble dependents, taxed with ingratitude upon every symptom of discount; the one may rave round the walls of his cell, but the other lingers in all the silence of mental confinement. To increase his distress, every new obligation adds to the former load, which kept the vigorous mind from rising; till at last, elastic no longer, it shapes itself to constraint and puts on habitual servility.

Questions

1. Write the theme of the above passage.
2. What harm does generosity cause in man?
3. Why is the writer critical of a generous act?
4. What might have happened if men were taught to despise servility?
5. Explain briefly how accepting favours lowers man's dignity.
6. How is dependence encouraged?
7. What might happen if the habit of giving alms is discouraged?
8. Choose the most appropriate synonym or each of the following words:

(i) inculcate:
(a) instruct (b) guide (c) enlighten (d) develop

(ii) ignominy:
(a) disgrace (b) dishonour (c) shame (d) degradation

(iii) forfeit:
(a) lose (b) dispossess (c) forego (d) rid

(iv) debasement:
(a) deterioration (b) degeneration (c) degeneracy (d) depreciation

(v) bounty:
(a) gift (b) benevolence (c) alms-giving (d) charity

(vi) shackled:
(a) hindered (b) restrained (c) fettered (d) confined

(vii) reproach:
(a) blame (b) shame (c) disapproval (d) disesteem

(viii) confinement:
(a) limitation (b) indisposition (c) malady (d) imprisonment

(ix) servility:

(a) obsequiousness (b) flattery (c) slavishness (d) fawning

(x) dignity:

(a) glory (b) self-respect (c) nobleness (d) renown

Answers

1. The passage deals with the great harm that alms-giving does to man; people praise generosity but rarely think how slavish attitude, loss of self-respect and initiative are promoted as a result of accepting gifts and favours.
2. Generosity takes away the freedom of the receiver of gifts, making him wholly dependent on the kindness of others.
3. The writer is critical of a generous act because this makes a man lose his freedom and he leads a life of a degenerated man.
4. If men were taught to hate receiving alms with the same vigour as they were taught to give generously they would have been responsible people, doing their duties cheerfully without disappointment.
5. Accepting favours without working for them makes a man a slave; lose his self-respect and glory. He becomes a slave to the generosity of others and has no dignity left in him.
6. Giving alms and making the receiver dependent on such gifts encourages dependence.
7. If the habit of giving alms is discouraged there would be initiative, self-confidence and dignity in man, and he would happily do his duties without expecting someone to support him with gifts.
8. (i) (d) (ii) (c) (iii) (c) (iv) (b) (v) (d)
   (vi) (c) (vii) (b) (viii) (d) (ix) (c) (x) (b)

ASSIGNMENTS

Read the following passages carefully and then answer the questions and do the exercise given at the end of each passage.

PASSAGE 1

There are people who will tell you that they have no fear of jungle, that they know it as well as the streets of their own town. Such people are either liars or boasters or they are fools, without understanding or feeling for things as they actually are. I knew such a man once, a hunter, a little man with cunning little eyes and a small dark face. He spent his life looking through the undergrowth and the trees. He was more silent than the leopard and more cunning than the jackal; he knew the tracks better than the doe who leads the herd. He would boast that he could see a buck down wind before it could see him. 'Why should I fear the jungle' he would say. 'If know it better than my own compound.' Some foolish beasts a few trees and bushes and leaves. There is nothing to fear there. One day he took his axe in his hand, and the sandals of deer-hide to sell to traders from the towns. He never returned to the village again, and months afterwards in the thick jungle I found his bones scattered upon the group, beneath some thorn bushes bitten by wild pig and jackal and crushed and broken by the elephants. And among his bones lay a bunch of peacocks feathers that he had collected and tied together with a piece of creeper and his betel case and the key of his house and the torn pieces of his red cloth. In the fork of one of the thorn bushes hung his axe: the huge wooden handle had been cut in two. I do not know how he died, but I know that he had boasted that there was no fear in the jungle and in the end the jungle took him.

1. What is the central idea of the passage?
2. Who are liars and boasters according to the writer?
3. What was the false claim of the hunter?
4. What things did the hunter take along with him?
5. How did the author know that the dead man was the same hunter?
6. In what way did the hunter die?
7. What is the moral conveyed by the writer through the given passage?
8. Give the synonyms of the following words, choosing one from the ones given in the brackets:
   (i) liar (deceiver, hypocrite, taleteller)
   (ii) cunning (artful, shrewd, duplicity)
   (iii) boaster (braggart, vaunt, flourish)
   (iv) beneath (lowness, debased, under)
   (v) huge (large, vast, enormous)

PASSAGE II

Though television first made its appearance in the country in 1959, it plodded along unimpressively for 23 years coming to life only with the release of colour TV sets in the market in 1982. In fact the government's desire to realise the full potential of television as a means of communication took concrete shape and gained momentum only with the successful coverage of the Asiad. And after this event, it was found that a large percentage of consumers had become TV owners, and were open to persuasion and through the medium a vast new market had simply opened up. It was observed, noting the beginning of the advertising race right in earnest.

A further fillip was given to this race when the advertising costs were allowed as deductible expenditure from taxable income and companies were allowed to advertise on television in four different ways: they could sponsor programmes produced or routinely telecast by Doordarshan, e.g. Phool Khilen Hain Gulshan Gulshan, Chitrahaar, the weekly Hindi film and the trailblaising soap serial, Hum Log; they could produce and sponsor their own programmes, the script being subject to Doordarshan's approval and lastly, they could sponsor programmes imported from abroad, this being by far the most expensive proposition.

So armed with Government encouragement in the form of budgetary incentives for advertising and the opening up of Doordarshan to commercial use, manufacturers jumped into the fray. And as grandpa, grandson, master, servant, mother-in-law, daughter-in-law, husband and wife sat in glassy-eyed togetherness, gulping assorted slices of other's fictional lives during prime, time, beginning to wonder whether the new brand of detergent could indeed lend greater brightness to clothes at less cost, the demand for sponsored serials began to outstrip supply. The result: an episode of a sponsored serial which cost Rs.1,50,000 in early 1985 now bears a price tag of Rs. 3,00,000.

This does not bother advertisers, as television is still the most cost-effective medium of advertising, the cost per thousand consumers reached being less, compared to press, periodical, radio and cinema. The arithmetic is simple: there are an estimated 60 million set owners now (7-10 million sets being added every year) and an average viewership of 5-6 people per set. So a 30-second spot ad on prime time, costing around Rs.1,50,000 has a viewership of over 300 million, a degree of exposure it could never hope to have gained through any other medium at the same price.

1. What is the central idea of the passage?
2. How did TV become a common medium of communication?
3. What role did advertising play in developing TV?
4. Name the additional factor which helped TV to be more popular.
5. List the ways in which companies could advertise on television.
6. Why are advertisers not unhappy with the rising cost of advertising?
7. Choose the word closest to the contextual meaning from the choices given below each word:
   (i) plodded
      (a) trudged (b) wearily along lingered on
      (c) continued working slowly without resting
   (ii) potential
      (a) possibility (b) power (c) validity
   (iii) deductible
      (a) deprive (b) that can be taken away (c) that can be inferred
   (iv) trailblasing
      (a) pioneering (b) successor (c) sequel
   (v) fray
      (a) struggle (b) rivalry (c) competition
   (vi) fictional
      (a) imaginary (b) untruthful (c) fanciful

8. Give the antonyms of the following words:

(i) appearance	(ii) concrete	(iii) taxable
(iv) different	(v) expensive	(vi) demand

PASSAGE III

More people are looking for jobs than ever before. The result is that for every job advertised, there is a large number of candidates offering to do it. Getting jobs is, therefore, becoming more and more difficult. This is an age of competition. If you want to compete for a job, it is necessary for you to go on improving your qualifications. In a competitive market only the best qualified person has a chance of being successful. For this, one must learn how to get more done.

Do you remember the old saying, 'Well begun is half done'? The first and the most difficult step is to begin. How often do we hear people complain that they are not in the mood to work! It is, however, easy to control one's actions. That is why, very often, just getting into the position for work can put us in the mood.

Another very useful way of getting more done is to have a living source of inspiration, someone who symbolies an idea to be worked for. Most of us do not mind doing things which others say are good. But we will do our best to achieve something we ourselves like and admire. If we want to be rated high, it is necessary for us to choose the best model.

Yet another prescription for getting more work done is making conscious efforts to save time. We should set a time limit for every task so that we may prevent any wastage of time. Overspending time is more harmful than overspending money. Make every effort to finish a task within the prescribed time limit. If necessary, sit for an extra hour or two. The pleasure of finishing a job on time will more than compensate for the additional expenditure of time. Proper budgeting of time will open up new ways of making life richer and more rewarding.

Lastly, to get more work done, one must have gift for effective speech. Nothing distinguishes you from others more sharply than the power and manner of your speaking. Good speech is acquired. There are professional courses on the subject available at some places in India. Most schools and colleges have Debating Clubs and Dramatic Societies. Much can be learned under the guidance of able teachers in charge of these clubs and societies. Make the best of these opportunities and you will find no job beyond your reach.

1. What is the central idea of the passage?
2. Why, according to the author, it is important to get more work done?
3. What should one do if one is not in the mood to work 'l?
4. Why does the author suggest having a living source of inspiration?
5. How can one save time?
6. Why should one save time?
7. In what way can one learn to make effective speeches?

8. Compete the table by writing down the correct forms of these words:

Noun	Verb	Adjective
	Compete	
		Successful
	Symbolizes	
	Admire	
Excellence		
	Compensate	
		Debatable

Passage IV

To be meaningful, a conversation should have an orientation or direction. It need not be strategically planted but there should be a general drift of ideas in it. It has been said by the wise that speech is silver and silence is golden. Surely silence is preferable to inconsequential chitchat. No good conversation is possible unless two or more individuals sit together feeling fully relaxed. Congeniality and understanding are the salient features of a good conversation.

I have often observed that strangers meeting for the first time look very uncomfortable. They are like two islands of experience and there is little sharing of ideas and notions between them. Two ladies meeting at the bus-stand while waiting for the bus would talk about the bus timings or about the weather by way of phatic conversation. But once they are on the bus and are together for half an hour, they would be as intimate as real sisters. Let us remember that conversation with friends is a mode of relaxation. Intimate friends could be, at times, very witty and satirical in tone. When a teacher establishes a rapport with his senior students, his conversation becomes very homely and endering. Conversation need not be a pontifical sermon but an exchange of amicable and pleasant ideas.

A good conversation is fragile enough to be arbitrarily interrupted when a friend says, 'Let's have coffee now,' wish to encourage something amusing, something agreeable, and something buoyant in conversation. Let us be prompt without being stubborn, refuse without argument, and clothe, if possible, weighty matters in a motley garb. Conversation is an art but it must come artlessly, spontaneously and genuinely. It must develop organically.

1. Write in one line the main idea of this passage.
2. What are the salient features of good conversation?
3. Why do the strangers meeting for the first time look very uncomfortable?
4. Explain: 'Conversation is an art but must come artlessly.'

5. What condition has to be fulfilled for good conversation?
6. The synonyms of the following words are given below. Choose the ones used in this context:

(a) Strategically
(i) Planned (ii) tactically (iii) thoughtfully

(b) Inconsequential
(i) Importantly (ii) unimportant (iii) negligently

(c) Congeniality
(i) Agreeability (ii) friendliness (iii) consequential

(d) Rapport
(i) Communication (ii) harmonious relations (iii) friendship

(e) Stubborn
(i) Willful (ii) self-will (iii) obstinate

(f) Fragile
(i) Brittle (ii) crumble (iii) punishable

(g) Spontaneously
(i) Instinctively (ii) automatically (iii) voluntarily

(h) Genuine
(i) Original (ii) pure (iii) real

Passage V

The world is full of different organisms, all fighting for survival. At one end of the scale are men; at the other, a very simple form of life-bacteria. These tiny organisms which can only be studied through a microscope, consist only one cell. A cell is the tiniest structure which can exist on its own, each one having a 'brain' inside it which contains programmed information. Using information as a guideline the cell can carry out all the functions that are necessary to life. Because bacteria are very small and composed of one cell only, they can easily squeeze through gaps into the complex tissues of a large animal such as man, where they may in some circumstances, cause disease. But such a resting place is by no means safe. The human body makes every attempt to get rid of the troublesome stranger and in about 99 times out of every 100 the larger body succeeds admirably: that is to say, disease is the exception rather than the rule.

Bacteria vary tremendously and have a great ability which enables them to develop resistance to some antibiotics, like penicillin, and so defeat our attempt to overcome them. Fortunately our own system is able to absorb. Whatever drugs are given, it is always the body's own recourses that beat the enemy at the end.

Man's skill in evading infection is very often not to his credit at all, for many bacteria much prefer to keep well out of harm's way and remain free living in the open air. Others live in complete harmony inside the body tissues, taking care not to disturb their 'protector' so that the body which shelters them is never provoked sufficiently to retaliate and expel them.

Bacteria are universally distributed throughout the animal world also. Despite their microscopic dimension (about 1/250000 of an inch) there are no living things that do not come under their influence. They play an essential part in making soil fertile and cause the decay of dead animals and plants, ensuring the completion of the chemical cycle that allow life to continue. Bacteria are used in industry, for the manufacture of milk products, especially butter and cheese; for fermentation products like vinegar; and for the disposal of sewage material.

Both because of the variety of their conditions for growth and because of the rapid rate of reproduction, bacteria are almost everywhere. The rapidity of bacterial reproduction is astounding. When conditions of temperature and nutrition are favourable, bacteria can successfully divide every 20 to 30 minutes. In the space of 15 hours, 1 bacterium can give rise to 1,00,000 descendants. If this phenomenal rate of reproduction were allowed to proceed unhindered, the entire surface of the earth would soon be covered by the microscopic offering of a single cell. But the growth conditions for bacteria never remain favourable for long periods, therefore many bacteria die without reproducing themselves and the general rate of multiplication slowly ceases.

1. Write the theme of the above passage.
2. Name the two organisms which are at extreme points on the scale of life.
3. Point out who wins more often in a struggle between the human body and the bacteria.
4. Why is it possible for bacteria to enter the human body without much difficulty?
5. State why bacteria develop resistance to some antibiotics?
6. Give two reasons why bacteria are almost everywhere.
7. Why have bacteria not been able to cover the entire face of the world?
8. Write the antonyms of the following words:

(i) different	(ii) simple	(iii) tiniest	(iv) safe
(v) necessary	(vi) stranger	(vii) succeed	(viii) defeat
(ix) overcome	(x) harmony	(xi) expel	(xii) fertile
(xiii) favourable	(xiv) unhindered		

PASSAGE VI

After knowledge there is no other passion which has done so much good to mankind as the love of money. It is to the love of money that we owe all trade and commerce, in other words, the possession of every comfort and luxury which our own country is unable to supply. Trade and commerce have made us familiar with productions of many lands, have awakened curiosity, and have widened our ideas by bringing us in contact with nations of various manners, speech and thought. They have supplied an outlet for energies, which would otherwise have been wasted, have accustomed men to habits of enterprise, forethought and calculation, have communicated to us many arts of great utility and have put us in possession of some of the most valuable remedies with which we are acquainted either to live or to lessen pain. These things we owe to the love of money. If the theologians could succeed in their desire to destroy that love, all these things would cease, and should relapse into barbarism.

1. What is the central idea of the above passage?
2. Name the two things which have done great good to mankind.
3. Enumerate the advantages trade and commerce have brought about.
4. What have the above accustomed men to practise?
5. Which is the most valuable possession mentioned in this passage?
6. How would the people return to the state of barbarism?
7. Explain: The theologians could succeed in their desire to destroy that love.
8. Give the appropriate forms of the words given below:

Verb	Noun	Adjective
	Possession	
	Comfort	
	Productions	
Calculate		
Destroy		

PASSAGE VII

The greatest reason for dissatisfaction against educational developments in the post-independence period is the failure, by and large, to re-orientate the educational system to the requirements of the new social order which the country has decided to create. India has deliberately chosen the democratic way of life and the socialistic pattern of society. If such a social order is to be ushered in and stabilised, citizens imbued with several important values are needed. These would include: a love of the motherland combined with a deep insight into its 'unity in diversity'; a catholic and tolerant attitude towards others; respect and understanding of a democratic way of life; a love of discipline and a capacity for self-restraint; an interest in science and the development of a scientific outlook; a faith in the dignity of labour and a basic humanism that will scorn all privileges based on caste, race, colour, sex or religion. The relevant questions, in this context, therefore, are:

What should be the content of education and the methods of teaching in order to build up these values? How far does the existing system help to promote them? To what extent do our administrators and teachers show an awareness of these problems and what measures should be adopted to make them realize the significance of these values and to train them in the methods of building them up through school programmes? To what extent do pupils coming out of the schools and colleges imbibe these values? What type of a machinery for evaluation should be built into the educational system to find out the extent to which the students imbibe these values and to reform the contents and techniques of education in the light of the findings from time to time? Any attempt to answer questions of this type is a little disturbing.

1. Write in brief the main idea of the above passage.
2. Why are the educational developments in the post-independent period dissatisfactory?
3. What has to be done to establish the new social order?
4. Explain: 'Unity in diversity'.
5. What values are to be developed in the citizens?
6. What is the role of education in this scenario?
7. Why does the author say that answering these questions 'is a little disturbing'?
8. Give the antonyms of the following words:

(i) Dissatisfaction	(ii) Deliberately	(iii) Stabilised
(iv) Tolerant	(v) Scorn	(vi) Relevant

PASSAGE VIII

As material civilisation advances and the supply of available goods and services increases, man's needs correspondingly multiply. Advertising plays a key role in this never-ending process of stimulating the public's desire for certain products and thereby promoting the sales thereof, until it has, in effect created new needs, real or supposed, where there were none before. A familiar example is the motor car, once a rare and costly novelty, now an ubiquitous and relatively inexpensive necessity. More recently, the television set has undergone the same transformation. While some people would deny that television is a necessity, the fact that TV sets are found in a majority of Western homes shows that it answers to a greater or lesser degree, the need felt by millions of people for entertainment and information.

A product, service or commodity that the public needs, and knows it needs, tends, of course to 'sell itself'. We might therefore assume that in such cases, advertising would be of minor importance. To some extent this is true: meat packers, vegetable and fruit growers, and dairy operators spend less on advertising, for instance, than manufacturers of cigarettes, liquors, cosmetics and other items of this type. On the other hand, the competition that exists between rival brands means that the suppliers of such basic necessities as food, clothing, and housing must advertise their wares to stay in business.

Significantly, the industry that spends most on advertising turns out a product which almost everyone considers a necessity.

1. Write the central idea of the passage.
2. How does a man's needs increase?
3. What role does advertising play in creating a desire?
4. Explain: '...... the motor car once a rare and costly novelty (is) now an ubiquitous and relatively inexpensive necessity.'
5. What according to some people is the need for a television?
6. How does a product 'sell itself'?
7. Why do manufacturers of cigarettes, liquors, cosmetics and other items like these spend more on advertisements?
8. Write TRUE or FALSE against the following statements:
   (i) Advertisements create new needs.
   (ii) The motor car is a rare and costly novelty.
   (iii) The author of this passage gives two examples from India.
   (iv) People like to keep television sets for information.
   (v) If the public needs a product, there is little need for advertising.
   (vi) Vegetable and fruit growers spend a huge amount of money on advertising.
   (vii) Brands do not require any advertising.
   (viii) Everyone needs a product on which industry spends a great deal of money.

PASSAGE IX

What is the place of religion in education? Good values and moral caliber are indispensable for social security and progress. One major aim of education is to help to the individual realise his true self. Ours is a democratic society in which we try to practice equality, liberty and fraternity. Respect for others and their way of life, tolerance of different religions and their practice of it, cooperation, participation and moral integrity are the forces that add strength to the social structure. Individual excellence and group progress are to be the goals. It is well-known that religion as a strengthening and unifying force can help to achieve these laudable goals. School is the place where religion and education should go together to make youth help develop positively and in the best way possible.

India's society and culture and every aspect of life are inextricably interwoven with religion. Religion and education cannot be separated here. The day begins with morning prayer and it ends with another prayer. But history slows that where other countries invaded India and brought her under their political suzerainty, education and religion were the casualties. The policy of divide and rule was followed by the British to keep the Indians under their control. The term 'religion' was used for creating intolerance and hatred among the several communities in India, who were already divided by language, caste and class. The result of such a policy was the division of India into separate nations when ultimately it became free in 1947. A legacy of mistrust and rejection of all that is good in religion was another consequence. The reaction of religion has been so strong that any effort to give proper recognition to religion in education is looked at with doubt and mistrust. Advocates of the anti-religious group expressed that moral and spiritual values could be taught to youth without advocating any religion. But in practice, we find that education without religions is soulless and utterly materialistic. Throughout her history India had been strengthened by its culture and religion. But today even the great nation of ours is on the verge of a culture crisis as a result of education which is merely utilitarian.

1. What is the central idea of the passage?
2. What is the role of religion in education?
3. What are the benefits of linking religion with education?
4. Mention the disadvantages of making religion apart of education.
5. Comment on the vision of the author.
6. Why is any effort to given proper recognition in education looked at with doubt and mistrust?
7. Explain: the 'laudable goals'.
8. Write the antonyms of the following words:

(i) liberty	(ii) tolerance	(iii) moral
(iv) unifying	(v) best	(vi) separate
(vii) suzerainty	(viii) hatred	(ix) mistrust
(x) anti-religious	(xi) materialistic	(xii) strengthened

PASSAGE X

Who are really the happiest people? It is odd that we have no answer ready; for with most of us happiness is our being's end and aim.' We are sometimes in doubt whether our own balance is on the right side or the wrong. Looking back, I think I can separate the years when I was happy and those when I was unhappy. But perhaps at the time I should have judged differently. We are never either so happy or so miserable as we suppose ourselves to be.

The successful man generally tells us that he was happiest while he was still struggling for his success, or sometimes before he discovered that an ambitious career was open to him. As a rule, the game of life is worth playing, but struggle is the prize.

It is generally supposed that, the young are happier than the old. This seems to me very doubtful. Young people are often very unhappy, torn by conflicting elements in their characters, which, after a time, come to some kind of a mutual understanding. Robert Browning boldly claims that old age is 'the best of life' and some old people agree with him.

The married are supposed to be happier than the single. They are certainly less prone to commit suicide; but suicide is not a very good test, and it has been pointed out that married people with no children are not much less suicidally inclined than bachelors and spinsters. Still, as a rule, marriage is probably the happiest state. It all depends on whether the pairs are well-matched and very bad choices are, I think, the exception.

On the whole, the happiest people seem to be those who have a particular cause for being happy. And yet I should not choose a naturally contented temperament as my first request from a fairy godmother. It would be unfortunate if I said, 'I wish to be the happiest man in India and promptly found myself locked in an asylum,' a cheerful lunatic who believed himself to be the Emperor of China. For all we know to the contrary, the happiest man in India may be a mad man and none of us would wish to change places with him. And even if the always cheerful person is perfectly sane, he is without the 'splendid spur' which most men need if they are to do much with their lives.

The busy are happier than the idle, and the man who has found his work is much happier than the man who has not found it. Recognition by others is essential to all but the strongest and the proudest. I think I should put it third among the gifts which I should ask from the fairy godmother. I should wish first for wisdom, like King Solomon, and by wisdom I mean a just estimate of the relative values of things. My second wish would be for domestic happiness, and my third for the approval of my fellowmen.

1. What is the central idea of the above passage?
2. Why is it difficult to define true happiness?
3 At what stage of life is a successful man happy?
4. Who in your opinion are happier – the young people or the old?
5. What makes married people unhappy?
6. Explain: 'a naturally contented temperament'.
7. What does the author want the godmother to grant him?
8. Give the antonyms of the following words:

(i) miserable	(ii) separate	(iii) conflict
(iv) balance	(v) inclined	(vi) contented
(vii) unfortunate	(viii) cheerful	(ix) perfect
(x) recognise	(xi) strongest	(xii) approval

Chapter 12

Precis Writing

THE ability of quickly and accurately understanding the essentials of written matter and then to reduce it to a simple, orderly precis is certainly of utmost importance for every educated person. The word 'Precis' is derived from French and it means 'precise'. Writing precis is an excellent exercise in careful reading and accurate writing. Precis is not just a paraphrase of the original writing. It is a condensed version of the essential thoughts of the original passage. A good precis is a straight-forward condensed statement of the salient features, ideas or information contained in the original passage and it is written in a clear and concise way in the writer's own words. As a precis writer you must posses, the power of judgement to be able to evaluate the important ideas. You must have a sense of balance to identify the important points and know how to separate them from the unimportant ones.

12.1 FORMS OF CONDENSATION

A precis is sometimes used interchangeably or synonymously with **summary** and **abstract**. Other forms of condensation include **outline**, **synonsis**, **abridgement**, and **digest**. But these forms of condensations are for different purposes. These forms are different from each other in many respects. **Summary** is the most general form of condensation and implies any effort to present briefly an all encompassing and comprehensive account of the passage. It is more of a pithy paraphrase of the main ideas of the passage. **Abstract** on the other hand, gives the gist of the important points or important results of the report or paper. More specifically, an abstract refers to a scholarly citation which gives the main points of a piece of research or study. It is a brief, qualitative presentation of the more complex ideas contained in the passage. **Precis** on the other hand, is lengthier than the abstract and follows the exact order of points of the original passage. It is a clear statement of bare facts without any unnecessary frills. In fact, precis writing requires writing of the essential facts/ideas in a clear, exact and concise way. In this sense, precis is more like original piece of writing. As a precis writer you use your own words to write the gist of the passage. A good precis is terse and succinct; it incorporates the rules of unity and coherence. (Also see Chapter 13: Formal Reports).

Outline and synopsis, like precis, follow the order of points of the original passage. **Outline** covers a wider range than synopsis. Outline numbers the salient or principal features of the document or project work. It uses the key words or phrases of the given material to give its extended paraphrase in prose. **Synopsis** is a shortened or condensed form of a great mass of material. It sometimes refers to a summary of the plot of a novel or a piece of fiction. Many a time an author submits a chapter of a proposed book along with the synopses of the unwritten or planned chapters to the publisher for his perusal. The outline also may sometimes state in a short and compact form points mentioned in the material.

Other important forms of condensation are **abridgement** and **digest**. These are expanded forms of condensation of the original writing without changing the words and style of the original written material. **Abridgement** retains the general sense and unity of the original. It shortens the length by omission of words without sacrificing the sense. In **abridgement** least changes are made, thereby retaining the flavour of the original, like for example, a one-volume abridgement of Edward Gibbon's great and voluminous work 'The Decline and Fall of the Roman Empire. However a systematic condensation of essential points into a convenient form of the original is called a **digest** like, for example, a digest of weekly news. It can be a condensed compilation of legal rules, statutes or decisions for easy reference, it may or may not retain the flavour and style of the original piece of writing. Sometimes, passages of the original document are rewritten as 'digest' to bring in brevity and clarity. It can also refer to the collection of condensed technical and scholarly papers like a quarterly digest of articles on alternate sources of fuel or space research.

12.2 SKILLS REQUIRED

When you read the passage given for precis writing, you would observe that the writer has used a more words than are necessary to express his ideas. It is difficult to express one's ideas comprehensively in a few words and this is why precis writing is an ardous task. The aim of precis is to present to a busy reader, the main ideas of the original passage as concisely and clearly as possible, in a readable form. In this sense a precis is like an original piece of writing.

Precis writing demands power of judgement and evaluation, as the passage usually contains important ideas and a number of unnecessary words. So you have to read the passage carefully, paying close attention in order to identify the important ideas and discard those which are not required. You would need to develop a sense of balance. For the purpose of reduction of the original passage, you have to train yourself to express ideas concisely. Vocabulary extension is extremely helpful because you would have to substitute one single word for a clause or even a sentence.As you go on practicing precis wiring you would be training yourself to think logically and present the author's ideas in a way which is clearly understood. The final precis that you write should be in your own words and have the same tone as the original. It must be a good piece of writing. The art of precis writing develops in the student a proper reading habit, forcing him to read attentively and carefully. It helps in vocabulary extension and it also inculcates in the precis writer the power of judgement to discriminate between essential ideas, and facts and not so essential ones given in the passage. It trains the precis writer to think logically and present the author's ideas in a way which is clearly understood. You would have to train yourself to shorten the sentences for conciseness, select important ideas and discard unimportant ones and generalise.

12.3 GUIDELINES

1. Read the passage at least two times to familiarise yourself with the theme and the main ideas contained in the passage.
2. Give the passage a title; a suitable title would help you to identify the theme of the passage.
3. Write down important points, and arrange them in the same sequence as the original passage.
4. Make a rough draft. A precis should not be more than 1/3 of the original, unless otherwise directed.
5. Write the precis in the indirect form of narration, using only the third person.
6. Scrupulously avoid all examples, figures of speech, illustrations and comments.
7. Retain all those facts and ideas which are related to the main idea; reject those which have minor importance.
8. Drop all redundant words and expressions and circumlocutions.

12.4 PRACTICAL HINTS

- Find one word which means the same as several.
  1. His excuse was such that it could not be believed.

     Reduced – His excuse was unbelievable.
  2. Suhana is one who never commits a mistake.

     Reduced – Suhana is infallible.
  3. She was caught in the act of listening through the keyhole.

     Reduced – She was caught eaves-dropping.
- Identify and delete redundant words.
  4. The little child was found sitting all alone with no one with her.

     Reduced – The little child was sitting alone.
  5. There came to his recollection the words of a great poet that when sorrows come, they come not in single spies but in battalions.

     Reduced – He remembered that sorrows never come alone.
  6. He gained universal esteem of all men everywhere.

     Reduced – He gained universal recognition.
- Replace a clause by a phrase or a phrase by word.
  7. Mr. Ramakrishna came across his friend in the vicinity of the college.

     Reduced – Mr. Ramakrishna met his friend near the college.
  8. When she enquired into the matter, she found the accused was innocent.

     Reduced – On enquiry she found the accused to be innocent.

9. In case of a dispute they wanted a direct vote of the electorate of the state.

   Reduced – In case of a dispute they wanted a plebiscite.

- Reframe sentences by changing sentences and clauses into phrases or single words.

10. When the next day arrived, Mr. Govind, the politician, addressed a group which consisted only of his own followers.

    Reduced – Mr. Govind, the politician, addressed only his followers the next day.

11. This small village is inhabited by people who can neither read nor write.

    Reduced – This small village is inhabited by illiterate people.

12. The museum was in a bad state because the authorities had persistently neglected to repair the roof.

    Reduced – The museum was in a bad state due to authorities' persistent neglect.

- Strip circumlocutions to the simple fact.

13. Sohan was introduced to a member of the fairer sex endowed with more than the usual portion of attractive features.

    Reduced – Sohan was introduced to a very pretty woman.

14. They found out that the house possessed another occupant in addition to the presence of themselves.

    Reduced – They discovered that the house had another occupant.

15. The sudden accident necessitated the requisition of the family physician.

    Reduced – The accident made it necessary to call the family doctor.

Whenever you come across a lot of details in the sentence or a paragraph you have to decide deleting unnecessary details and think of what the main point is and which other points support it.

12.5 EXAMPLES

(i) The young girl, dressed in jeans and wearing a cap to protect her hair went up to the window of the burning house, quietly pushed it open, went inside and after floundering through heavy clouds of smoke and burning rubble discovered what she was searching for and came out carrying the charred remains of the precious briefcase.

Note that the above sentence contains 57 words and a lot of details. Stripped of all unnecessary details the sentence can be reduced to: *The girl brought the charred remains of the precious briefcase from the burning house*. (14 words)

(ii) The unfortunate victim of the murderous attack firmly believes, if her statement is to be repeated, that she can identify these men as her attackers and no doubt it is an honest belief on her part. (36 words)

Condensed form -- The victim believes that she can identify her attackers. (9 words)

(iii) Mahatma Gandhi spoke with young men and women, older men and women and also with the middle aged people. (18 words)

Condensed form – Mahatma Gandhi spoke with everyone. (5 words)

(iv) One could travel by bicycle, by scooter, by motor bike, by car, by taxi, by bus, by train; but none is better than walking. (23 words)

Condensed form – Walking is the best mode of travel (7 words)

(v) Her father belittled everything she had been through, making fun of her sufferings and laughing away the problems of hostel life. (21 words)

Condensed form – Her father belittled everything she had been through. (8 words)

Now three more examples are given below; each passage is followed by a suggested heading, and its precis.

Passage I

A man may usually be known by the books he reads as well as the company he keeps; for there is a companionship of books as well as of men and one should always live in the best company whether it be of good books or men. A good book may be among the best of friends. It is the same today, that it always was, and it will never change. It is the most patient and cheerful of companies. It does not turn its back upon us in times of adversity or distress. It always receives us with the same kindness: amusing and instructing us in youth and consoling us in old age.

Title: Importance of Books in Life.

Precis. Books, like friends, determine a man's character. So he should read the best books. A good book is a patient, happy and life-long friend. It cheers up man in his misfortunes, guides him in youth and comforts him in old age.

Passage II

It is said that boys who shine at school do not make the greatest figures when they grow up and come out into the world. The things, in fact, which a boy has to learn in school and on which his success depends, are things which do not require to exercise either of the highest or the most useful faculties of the mind. Memory is the chief faculty called into play in conning over and repeating lessons by rote in grammar, in languages, in geography, arithmetic, etc. so that he who has the most of this technical memory, with the least turn for other things, will make the most forward school boy. The jargons containing the definitions of the parts of speech, the rules for casting up an account, or the inflection of a Sanskrit verb can have no attraction to the tyro of ten years, except as they are imposed as a task upon him his feeling the want of sufficient relish or amusement in other things. A lad with a sickly constitution and not very active mind, who can just retain what is pointed out to him, and has neither sagacity to distinguish nor spirit to enjoy for himself, will generally be at the head of his form. An idler at school, on the other hand, is one who has high health and spirit, who has the free use of his limbs, with all his wits about him, who feels the circulation of his blood, and the motion of his heart, who is ready to laugh and cry in a breath, and who would rather chase a ball or a butterfly, feel open air in the face, look at the fields or the sky, follow a winding path, or enter with eagerness into all the little conflicts and interests of his acquaintances and friends, than doze over a musty spelling-book, repeat barbarous formulae after his master, sit for so many hours pinioned to a writing-desk and receive the reward for the loss of time and pleasure in paltry prize medals or scholarships. There is indeed a degree of stupidity which prevents children from learning the usual lessons, or ever arriving at these puny academic honours. But what passes for stupidity is much oftener a want of interest, of a sufficient motive to fix the attention and force a reluctant application.

Suggested Heading – In Defence of the Idler

Precis. The top-ranking students of schools often do not shine in later life. It is because memory and no exercise of any higher faculty, determines the success of the student. A teenager considers the dull rules of grammar and rote learning of other subjects as an imposition. Naturally a weak boy incapable of physical activities will come first in the class. An idler, on the other hand, enjoys good health and has boisterous spirits. He is witty. He chases butterflies and spends time in the open air. He prefers participating in community life rather than dozing over spelling books and dull formulae for the sake of a medal. It may be true that academically backward students in a class are stupid to a certain extent but often it is lack of interest rather than stupidity.

PASSAGE III

The advance of the age of machinery has not been all gam. In fact, against all that the machine has given us must be set one serious disadvantage- the decline of craftsmanship. In days gone by a furniture maker would use with care and pride the tools which over a period of years, had become almost a part of him and, chair took shape before his eyes. It was the work, not only of his hands but also of his mind and expressed something of himself. No other chair, even one made by his own hands, would be just like that, so it was with all craftsman, everything they made was their own work, the result of their skill in the use of their tools, and they could look on it with pardonable pride.

What is the position today? In the large factories of the machine age, rows of men are engaged in producing not a whole article but only a part of the whole. The individual worker does not even have the satisfaction of feeling that part is the work of his own hands because it is made by a complicated machine. All he has to do is to feed the raw material into the machine, press a lever, and put the finished part on a moving belt, which will convey it to the assembly lines. Thus the modern worker is denied the joy of creation; his work is reduced to monotonous repetition of automatic movements that are carried out almost without the use of his conscious mind.

Yet craftsmanship is not dead. In some country districts there are still people who prefer to make things with their own hands - and they are not old men who have refused to move with the times, but to make beautiful things which have individuality. The fact that art classes in art schools all over the country are full suggests that the urge to create is a deep one and that even the machine age cannot kill it.

Suggested heading: The Decline of Craftsmanship

Precis- One great disadvantage of machine is that it has brought about the decline of craftsmanship. In the past, craftsmen worked with their tools and whatever they made had the mark of their creativity. Besides, they took great pride and delight in whatever they created. In the machine age workers in large factories derive no such happiness. They do mechanical work without paying any attention to what they do. However, there are still some young craftsmen who prefer to make beautiful things even though there is little demand for them. The popularity of art classes indicate that the machine cannot kill the human urge to create.

ASSIGNMENTS

Write a precis of each of the following passages

I

The test of a great book is whether we want to read it only once or more than once. Any really great book we want to read the second time even more than we wanted to read it the first time; and every additional time that we read it, we find new meanings and new beauties in it. A book, that a person of education and good taste does not care to read more than once is very probably not worth much. But we cannot consider the judgement of a single individual infallible. The opinion that makes a book great must be the opinion of many. For even the greatest critics are apt to have certain preferences and prejudices. A man must be many-sided to utter a trustworthy estimate of many books. We may doubt the judgement of the single critic at times. But this is no doubt possible in regard to judgement of generations, even if we cannot perceive anything good in a book which has been admired and praised for hundreds of years. We may be sure that by trying, by studying it carefully, we shall at last be able to feel the reason of this admiration and praise. The best of all libraries for a poor man would be a library entirely composed of such great works only, books which have passed the test of time.

II

We are often told that human misery and crime are the results of ignorance. But ignorance of what? If you mean the ignorance of the physical world around us, ignorance of the laws of nature, I cannot agree that our miseries and crimes come mainly from that. While some may arise from that source, far more and worse are the effects of misusing such knowledge as we have. Much of the scientific knowledge we now possesses is being used in a way which can be described as wicked. To employ our knowledge of chemistry, for example, for the invention of poison gases to be let loose on women and children, is a misuse of knowledge. If we were judged by that alone, we would be stamped as a race of savages. I can see no relationship between the increase of such knowledge and the decrease of misery and crime.

But if we are talking of the ignorance not of the physical world outside us but of the spiritual world within us, then I think we are much nearer the source both of misery and of crime. The foolish or criminal use we make of our knowledge of the outer world of matter largely arises from our ignorance of the inner world of spirit-that is, of ourselves. At the same time we must not forget that moral and spiritual truth is sometimes misused by hypocrites.

I may be told that the cure for the misuse is more knowledge. Again I cannot agree fully. I should expect that the same causes which led to the misuse of the old knowledge would lead to the misuse of the new. All depends on the kind of person to whom the knowledge is imparted, that is, the human quality. The brave and the honest-minded will do his duty when he is told to do it. But the cowardly and the evil-minded will either avoid it or do it wrongly.

There is certainly a relation between morals and scientific progress, but not a fixed relation working at a steady rate in one direction only, either towards good or evil. We cannot say that men's characters improve in proportion as their knowledge increases, nor can we say the opposite. Good or evil to our characters, the increase of knowledge certainly does. But which of these two it does, predominantly depends on the people who get it – that is on ourselves. If we are strong, balanced and self-controlled and we have good will then the odds are that we shall put our knowledge to good use and improve our characters by doing so. But if we are weak, confused and cowardly, if we are treacherous, if we are losing all good human qualities of character – then the odds are that we shall use the new knowledge to make a greater mess of our lives and become a greater nuisance to our fellowmen. There is nothing in any kind of knowledge, to make us absolutely sure that it will be put to a good use. The use that we make of it for good or evil is our own affair.

III

The job scenario today is a paradox. On the one hand you have a surplus of jobs but on the other end, executives are biting their nails due to the fear of job redundancy. Job redundancy is a typical situation which arises in corporations, where a particular job is no longer relevant to the enterprise. Sometimes jobs are made redundant when there is no need for a specialised skill or delineation of role or when the organisation's need of role or when the organisation's needs because of growth or downsizing — requires a more or less qualified person. A lot of activities, today, are occurring around mergers and acquisitions. So what happens then is, some set of jobs overlap with reach other like – HR, some support function areas, at times even excess of sales manpower; that's when some of the functionalities become redundant. Redundancy could also happen as a result of introduction of new technology and change in working styles, for instance, the typical 'personal secretary' has been replaced by the 'executive assistant' phenomenon. Newer ways of working or delivery have made certain profiles redundant. For instance, once railways decided to get away with 'using mugs made of nud' led to huge job redundancy of that genre of labourers.

So what happens when a job gets redundant and how does the company treat its employees whose jobs get redundant? Most of the professional organisations are normally aware of future redundancies. They take it into consideration while training and retaining employees on newer and additional skill sets. However, sometimes employees with less visibility about the future are caught unaware. In a number of joint-ventures and take-overs, the pace of change is so fast that often employees and employers are not able to calculate it well in advance. When skill needed for a particular project is over, employees are kept in the bench and are re-skilled for newer dexterities. However, in smaller organisations, this still hasn't happened on a large scale.

Today in most Indian companies, with functions like payroll, administration, security, etc., being outsourced, related jobs are getting redundant.

So when exit is inevitable, companies give the redundant employees three months of notice and also hire external recruitment agencies to do outplacement for redundant employees.

Well, if the impact on career is directly proportionate to the time it takes for him or her to find another job and if the period between jobs is short, the impact is not much, but if it stretches out, then it can be quite traumatic. A prospective employer will always be influenced by the way the individual has handled redundancy and the reasons for redundancy.

Previous job redundancy will not create a negative impact as long as employees are open to learning and employers value their experience. Normally new employers do understand the past redundancy scenario of a prospective hire and it does not create a negative impact on the employee's profile.

But definitely the new hire needs to convince the new employer why he or she could not get retained and absorbed by the previous employer. At the same time in some senses, it does reflect on the lack of farsightedness of the employee also, as most of the smart employees are always eager to take on role expansions and experience with different roles or functions.

But is India mature enough to handle this? The answer lies in the way our economy is segregated. In the organised sector which is just around 9 per cent, job redundancy is significantly low because the job market is very upbeat and there is a huge demand, hence people can shift careers and can still manage well. However, at unorganised sector, which is about 91 per cent, it's a big challenge.

Again, as employees – we are still not very comfortable and open to move out of our comfort zones. Typically, people below 40 years of age are more open to change and hence redundancies do not hit them hard. However employees in the later age bracket are still very closed to it. Employers are person.

A person's job gets redundant, not because he or she is incompetent, but just because the organisation couldn't offer a role to suit his specific skill sets. So the solution is to be able to scale yourself upto the changing environment, and be perfectly well-equipped to take up any job irrespective of such job redundant scenarios.

IV

What should be the medium through which western 'light' and knowledge could be communicated to the Indian people? There are two ways of making this communication: the one is, by the medium of the languages of those countries; the other is by the medium of English. In general, when foreign teachers proposed to instruct the inhabitants of any country, they have used the vernacular tongue of the people, for a natural and necessary reason, that they could not hope to make any other means of communication intelligible to them. This is not our case in respect of our Eastern dependencies. They are not our own, we have possessed them long; many Englishmen reside among the, natives, and our language is not unknown there and it is practicable to diffuse it more widely. The choice, therefore, of either mode, lies open to us and we are at liberty to consider which is entitled to preference.

The acquisition of a foreign language is, to men of cultivated minds, a matter of no great difficulty. English teachers could, therefore, be sooner qualified to offer instruction in the native languages than the Indians would be prepared to receive it in English. This method hence come into operation more speedily than the other and it would also be attended with the advantage of a more careful selection of the matter of instruction. But it would be fax more confined and less effectual. It may be termed as a species of deciphering. The decipherer is required to unfold, in intelligible words, what has been hidden. Upon every new occasion, he has a similar labour to perform, and the information obtained from him is limited to the single communication then made. All other writings, in the same character still remain, to those who are ignorant of it, unknown. But if they are taught the character itself, they can at once read every writing in which it is used. The employment of the English language thus appears superior in point. And upon this ground, we give a preference to that mode, proposing here that the communication of knowledge shall be made by the medium of the English language.

V

We live in a curious age. We are offered glimpses of a genuine world civilisation slowly emerging: the UN special agencies, organisations like Oxfam and here, and there, as I have seen for myself, remote enterprises, dedicated to healing or education, with international staff as selfless enthusiasts. And such glimpses warm the heart and brighten hope. But along with these are the heat and sounds that suggest that the whole fabric of civilisation, the work of civiliasation, the work of centuries, is rapidly being torn apart. Two official policies clash, and instantly embassies, consulates, centres of information services, are surrounded and then attacked by howling mobs of students, at once defying law, custom, and usage. And that, this may not be merely so many hot-headed lads escaping all control that it may itself be part of government policy, mob antics as additional propaganda to deceive world opinion, makes our situation worse: it is as if we were all compelled to exist now in a sinister circus. No doubt governments have always been dishonest and hypocritical, but now it is beginning to look as if power mania is ready to destroy those long-accepted forms and civilities that make international relations possible. The times may soon come when ambassadors will have to move around in tanks, and embassies and consulates will have to be fortified or abandoned. And perhaps students, on admittance will be given machine-guns and flame-throwers.

There is something else, just as bad, perhaps even worse and evidence of it is amply supplied to us by TV cameras and mikes. What we see in these students faces, illuminated by burning cars and bonfires of books, is not the glow of political enthusiasm but a frenzied delight in destruction. Whatever country or party they may be demonstrating for or against, what really inspires them is an urge towards violent demolition. They do not know and may never know – how to make anything worth having but they need no courses on wrecking and destroying. If degrees were given in window-smashing, car over-turning, furniture firing, they would all have them with honours. They may still be weak in the sciences and the arts, medicine and the law, but they already have firsts in Hooliganism.

VI

Unexpected tragedy is the downside, of this age of opportunity and ambition. It's because an age-old human condition has resurfaced in corporate India. An innocuous condition once considered a state of the mind is, in deadly fashion, eating away at the achievers and strivers of a society that has no time to stop and smell the roses. It is a prehistoric affliction, probably affectiving Adam when he first met

Eve. It is simply a response to a perceived threat or challenge. A wide range of unpleasant sensory or psychological experiences are called 'Stressors': a 300-point drop in the stock market if you are an investor; the whistling of an incoming shell if you are a soldier in Kargil. The adrenaline rush, pounding heart, dry mouth: these are all recognisable signs. Human beings are equipped to deal with stress – if it doesn't happen too often. Your brain's stress response is to secrete messenger hormones to prepare for battle and simultaneously send out more energy and fuel by way of oxygen and glucose. It all helps channel the body's resources for added mental and physical strength or speed. But activate your stress response too often and it can turn chronic. The human body, say experts, was never meant to drag around frustrations, anxieties, overwork and bad thoughts. So chronic stress breaks down the body and makes way for a startling variety of diseases.

VII

Morals are the rules by which a society exhorts (as laws are the rules by which it seeks to compel) its members and associations to behaviour consistent with its order, security and growth. So for sixteen centuries, the jewish enclaves in Christendom maintained their continuity and internal peace by a strict and detailed moral code, almost without help from the state and its laws. A little knowledge of history stresses the variability of moral codes and concludes their necessity.

Moral codes differ because they adjust themselves to historical and environmental conditions. If we divide economic history into three stages – hunting, agriculture, industry- we may expect that the moral code of one stage, will be changed into the next. In the hunting stage a man had to be ready to chase and fight and kill. When he had caught his prey he ate to the cubic capacity of his stomach, being uncertain when he might eat again. Insecurity is the mother of greed, as cruelty is of memory. It was a time when the chance of survival (as now between states) was the ability to kill. Presumably the death rate in men – so often risking their lives in the hunt – was higher than in women. Pugnacity, brutality, greed and sexual readiness were advantages in the struggle for existence. Probably every vice was once a virtue, i.e. a quality making for the survival of the individual, the family, or the group. Man's sins may be the relics of his rise rather than the stigmas of his fall.

We may reasonably assume that when men passed from hunting to agriculture, the new regime demanded new virtues and changed some old virtues into vices. Industriousness became more vital than bravery; regularity and thrift more profitable than violence; peace more victorious than war. Children were economic assets and birth control was made immoral. On the farm the family was the unit of production and paternal authority had a firm economic base. Each normal son matured soon in mind and self-support. So he married early, almost as soon as nature wishes; he did not fret long under the restraints placed upon pre-marital relations by the new order of permanent settlements and homes. For fifteen hundred years this agricultural moral code of continence, early marriage, divorceless monogamy and multiple maternity maintained itself in Christian Europe and its white colonies.

Thereafter the Industrial Revolution changed the economic form and moral superstructure of European and American life. The mechanisation of economic production suggested mechanistic, materialistic philosophies; education removed religious doubts, morality lost more and more of its supernatural supports. The old agricultural moral code began to die.

VIII

The horrors of modern 'pleasure' arise from the fact that every kind of organised distraction tends to become progressively more and more imbecile. There was a time when people indulged themselves with distractions requiring the expense of a certain intellectual effort. In the seventeenth century, for example, royal personages and their countries took a real delight in listening to erudite sermons and academic disputes on points of theology or metaphysics.

Royal personages were not the only people who enjoyed intelligent pleasures. In Elizabethan times every lady and gentleman of ordinary culture could be relied upon to take part in a choral composition on a sacred text. Those who know the enormous complexity and subtlety of sixteenth century music will realise what this means. To indulge in their favourite past time, our ancestors had to exert their minds to an uncommon degree. Even the uneducated vulgar delighted in pleasures requiring the exercise of a certain intelligence, individuality and personal initiative. They listened for example, Othello, King Lear and Hamlet apparently with enjoyment and comprehension. They sang and made much music. And far away in the remote country, the peasants, year by year, went through the traditional rites – the dances of spring and summer, the winter merry making, the ceremonies of harvest appropriate to each successive season. Their pleasures were intelligent and alive, and it was they who, by their own efforts entertained themselves.

We have changed all that. In place of the old pleasures demanding intelligence and initiative, we have vast organisations that provide us with readymade distractions – distractions which demand from pleasure-seekers no personal participation and no intellectual efforts of any sort. A million cinemas bring the same stale nonsense. There have always been fourth rate writers and dramatists; but their works, in the past, quickly died without getting beyond the boundaries of the city or the country in which they appeared. Today the inventions of the scenario-writer go out from Los Angeles across the whole world. Countless audiences soak passively in the tepid bath of nonsense. No mental effort is demanded of them, no participation; they need only sit and keep their eyes open.

Do the democracies want music? In the olden days they would have made it themselves. Now they merely turn on the gramophone. Or if they are a little more up-to-date they adjust their wireless telephone to the right wave length and listen to music. And if they want literature there is the Press. Nominally, it is true, the Press exists to impart information. But its real function is to provide, like the cinema; a distraction which shall occupy them without demanding of it the slightest effort or fatigue of a single thought. This function, it must be admitted, it fulfills with an admirable success. It is possible to go on for years and years, reading two papers every working day and one on Sundays without ever being called upon to think or make any other effort than to move the eyes, not very attentively, down the printed column.

Certain sections of the community still practice athletic sports in which individual participation is demanded. Great numbers of upper and middle classes play golf and tennis in person and if they are sufficiently rich, shoot birds and pursue the fox and ski in the Alps. But the vast mass of community has now come even to sports vicariously, preferring the watching of football to the fatigues and dangers of the actual game.

These effortless pleasures, these readymade distractions that are the same for everyone over the face of the whole Western World, are surely a worse menace to our civilisation than ever the Germans were. The working hours of the day are already, for the great majority of human being occupied in the performance of purely mechanical tasks, in which no mental effort, no individuality, no initiative are required. And now in that hour of leisure, we turn to distractions as mechanically stereotyped and demanding as little intelligence and initiative as does our work. Add such leisure to such work and the sum is a day which it is a blessed relief to come to the end of.

IX

In the height of selfishness men fully appreciate in their own case, the great advantages of a good education, but deny these advantages to women. There is no valid argument by which the exclusion of the female sex from the privilege of education can be defended. It is argued that women have their domestic duties to perform and that if they were educated, they would bury themselves in their books and have little time for attending to the management of their households. Of course, it is possible for women, as it is for men, to neglect necessary work in order to spare more time for reading sensational novels. But women are no more liable to this temptation than men as most women would be able to do their household work all the better for being able to refresh their minds in the intervals of leisure with a little reading. Nay, education would help them in the performance of the narrowest sphere of womanly duty. For, education involves knowledge of the means by which health may be preserved and enables a mother to consult such modern books as will tell her how to rear up her children into healthy men and women and skillfully nurse them and her husband when disease attacks her household. Without education she will not be averse to listen with fatal results to the advice of superstitious quacks who pretend to work wonders by charms and magic.

But according to the higher conception of women's sphere, woman ought to be something more than a household drudge. She ought to be able not merely to nurse her husband in sickness but also to be his companion in health. For this part of her wifely duty, education is necessary, for there cannot be congenial companionship between an educated husband and an uneducated wife who can converse with her husband on no higher subjects than cookery and servants' wages. Also one of a mother's highest duties is the education of her children at the time when their mind is not amenable to instruction. A child's whole future life, to large extent, depends on the teaching it receives in early childhood, and it is needless to say that this first foundation of education cannot be well laid by an ignorant mother. On all these grounds female education is a vital necessity.

X

The whole point of technical advance is that it enables man to manipulate his environment to live in the sort of conditions he wants to live in. So you ask, 'What will man's everyday surrounding be like in forty years' time?' Other animals will get the environment they deserve; man will get the one he wants.

And will man be so different in forty years' time? I do not think so. Healthier, yes; I imagine we shall have mastered the viruses and the problems of cancer in the young; and I am sure we shall know enough to be able to avoid passing on hereditary abnormalities to our children; but I suspect that the illness and hurts of old age will still be with us, because I doubt whether we shall have overcome the necessity of growing old.

And shall we be anymore sensible? No; certainly no. The recorded history of several thousand years shows us that all the logical absurdities of man have always been with us; what we have not outgrown in 4000 years, we shall not outgrow in another forty.

Food is already becoming increasingly hygienic, quick frozen, packaged and pre-packaged and in impregnable plastic containers; increasingly free from all taint of decay – forgetting the fact that many of the flavours which we prize most highly, are due to early stages of decay of one sort or another. Already the production of our organic food is becoming increasingly mechanised. One obvious step remains, and that is to produce all out food-the proteins, carbohydrates, fats, vitamins, roughage, and what-have-you entirely synthetically.

And how do we communicate? We shall still talk to each other. Shall we write? No, I think, not in the way we do today. Even today handwriting is dying out. Typing will last longer, but the time will come when the manual typewriter will in turn become obsolete, and will be relegated to the status of a toy, like a child's printing set. For already computers are beginning to tackle the problem of recognition of ordinary written texts; an already a simple computer exists which will obey verbal instruction. Put these ideas together and you will see that even today we are within sight of the possibility of a machine that will take dictation, and will then automatically print out the dictated text.

Do you find this sort of prospect worrying, depressing, even frightening? I have; envisaged nothing that will not be technically feasible in forty years if we really want it. For it is what we want now that will decide what we get in the future; man, as ever, will make his own environments.

Chapter 13

BUSINESS AND TECHNICAL REPORTS

13.1 DEFINITION

A report is a major form of professional communication. It is used extensively by the government, businesses and industry as well as in professions, such as science, engineering, medicine, etc. It facilitates decision-making and acts as an instrument for nurturing the health of an organisation and promoting its growth. A report is also used for the study of existing procedures and practices as well as for launching new projects and assessing the progress of on-going projects. It is always written to meet a demand or to fulfil a requirement. By its very nature, therefore, report has to convey information and ideas accurately and efficiently. Usefulness, clarity and economy are its primary qualities. A report is not written to express a feeling, to convey an atmosphere or to amuse as some other forms of communication do. A professional writes a report not because he has an impulse to write but because the situation demands it. Among many qualities that a professional should possess, the ability for effective communication is one. The skill of report writing can be acquired by mastering the craft of writing and learning the scientific process of investigation, analysis and presentation.

We may define a professional report as a formal communication written for a specific purpose, conveying authentic information to a well-defined audience in a completely impartial and objective manner, and containing recommendations, if required. All professional reports (business, technical, managerial, etc.,) more or less have basically the same pattern in terms of approach to content and manner of presentation. They can, however, be classified on the basis of their structure and function as shown later in this chapter.

13.2 PREPARATORY STEPS

A report is the result of detailed planning and meticulous execution of the plan. When you are asked to write a report you should first understand the Terms of Reference which would spell out the purpose and scope of the report. Audience determination is the next preparatory step which would help you to give a proper direction to your writing. Very often the collection of data could be required before you draft an outline of the report. There are many ways of collecting the data. The report may simply require you to consult certain documents in your organisation or books and journals in the library. You may need to perform a series of experiments in a lab and record your observations. When you have to collect data from many people, you may have to resort to conducting personal interviews or sending mail questionnaires.

We have already discussed in Chapter 4 how the data collection interview is conducted. Here, let us briefly consider the points you should bear in mind for preparing a **mail questionnaire**. The collection of data from a number of persons is easier through it, especially when the sample population is spread over a wide geographical area. Since additional information and immediate feedback cannot be conveniently obtained when this method is used, one should put in patient effort in drafting the questionnaire.

In framing the questions, keep the following in mind:

- Word the questions in a language easy to understand.
- Make the questions easy to answer. One way is to provide for 'Yes' and 'No' answers. Another way is to ask the respondent to put a tick mark in the appropriate boxes.
- Ask as few questions as possible to obtain the required information.
- Ensure that every question has a definite objective related to the topic of your report.
- Sequence your questions in a logical order.
- Avoid asking questions which may embarrass the respondent. Generally questions on one's personal habits, beliefs, physical defects, etc., fall under this category.

If your questionnaire is long, divide it into parts on the basis of sub-topics your report is going to cover. Get the questionnaire cyclostyled or printed neatly on good quality paper and send it along' with a covering letter. Remember, you are making a demand on a stranger's time for your purpose and so you must draft the letter in as polite a language as possible. Give your respondent a feeling, that you hold him in high esteem and that the information he gives would be of great value to you. Don't forget to enclose a self-addressed stamped envelope for the return of the questionnaire.

A sample list of questions for a personal interview is included in Chapter 4. A sample mail questionnaire along with its forwarding letter is given at the end of this Chapter as Annexure A. The other preliminary steps follow: organisation of data and their analysis, discovery of their significance and conclusions. After this preliminary work is over you should prepare an outline and organise it by using the decimal numbering scheme. An example follows.

A Report on Microcontroller System Design for the Movement of the Telescope.

OUTLINE

1. Introduction
2. Basic System Construction
   2.1 Hardware Designing
   2.2 Address Decoding
   2.3 Software Designing
3. Chips and their Functions
   3.1 Microcontroller Chips
   3.2 Memory Chips
   3.3 I/O Chips
   3.4 Peripheral Chips
4. Circuit Layout
   4.1 Precaution and Testing
   4.2 Handling of Errors
   4.3 Fabricating PCB
5. Microstepping
   5.1 Theory of Microstepping
   5.2 Advantages of Microstepping
   5.3 Implementing Logic Control Circuit
   5.4 Implementing Power Circuit
6. Conclusions

You will notice that topics or sub-topics of equal rank have been placed at the same level and those which are subordinate have been grouped together under a topic or sub-topic. The subordination is shown in two ways, namely, by splitting the number and indenting it.

As you go along you may find that you are not able to follow the outline you prepared at the initial stage. Do not hesitate to revise or modify it, if necessary. An outline merely presents your preliminary thoughts in an organised form.

13.3 TYPES

Very often organisations divide written reports into carefully distinguished categories. Each category is given a name which results ultimately in the creation of a type. Even a quick survey of the different kinds of reports written in an organisation would reveal to you names such as periodic reports, progress reports, interim reports, inspection reports, completion reports, design reports, status reports, experimental reports and so on and so forth. A new member of the organisation is trained when and how to write the different types of reports. When you join an organisation you would soon find your way. Here our purpose is simply to give you an idea of the factors that are relevant for classification of reports and also to discuss the more widely acceptable types.

The purpose, contents, layout and format seem to us to be the main criteria for classification of reports.

Each report has a specific purpose. Sometimes only data has to be presented in an organised form, the purpose being to convey information. On some occasions you may be asked to collect data, analyse and interpret them, the purpose being to take a decision on the basis of your findings. Another purpose may be to record the progress of a project, the result of stock taking, the assessment of the quality of performance of employees, etc. You are likely to find the following three labels for the three purposes mentioned above: informational, interpretive, and routine respectively.

Some organisations make a distinction on the basis of material included in a report. For example; if an interpretive report has a large number of recommendations, it may be termed as recommendatory report.

The 'layout' refers to the structure and presentation of material. Later in this chapter we discuss the structure of a formal written report. In an informational report you are likely to find only the following elements: title page or just the title of the report, introduction, and discussion or description. In the interpretive report you will find some of the other elements also. The structure of routine, memo and letter reports is different from that of the informational and interpretive reports. And so is the presentation. A routine report (also called form report) requires merely filling in a prescribed at required intervals. Annexure B given at the end of this chapter contains a routine report form entitled Project Status Report used by a public limited company; it is self-explanatory.

The last criterion is the format which refers to the size and shape of a report. By their very nature routine, memo and letter reports are smaller in size and different in shape from the other types of formal reports. Annexures C and D give a specimen copy of letter and memo reports respectively.

You will notice that a letter report combines the features of a business letter and a formal report. It frequently displays an informality, generally not found in reports. Its style is positive and personal rather than impersonal and objective as that of a formal report. In structure and format it is exactly like a business letter. But it concentrates on presentation of facts, results, conclusions and recommendations, wherever required. It also contains a number of headings and sub-headings.

A short report may be presented in the form of a memo* which differs both in structure and form from a letter report. Since a memo report is meant only for circulation within the organisation it permits a higher degree of informality. It is also shorn of formal salutation, complimentary close and such other conventions of a business letter report. Because a memo serves as a record of some information, fact or decision, it is put away in a file for future reference. Every organisation usually has a printed letterhead for writing memos. For further information on memo see Chapter 17.

13.4 STRUCTURE

Let us first examine the elements that constitute the structure of informational and interpretive reports. We may define an element as a physical homogeneous part, easily distinguished by its heading, content

---

* A memo has been defined as 'an informal record' or 'an informal written note of a transaction'.

or format. The sequence in which these elements appear in a report are more or less standardised by the prevailing practices in the professional world. The usual sequence is shown below:

(i) Cover
(ii) Title Page
(iii) Acknowledgements
(iv) Table of Contents
(v) Abstract and Summary
(vi) Introduction
(vii) Discussion or Description
(viii) Conclusions
(ix) Recommendations
(x) Appendix
(xi) List of References
(xii) Bibliography
(xiii) Glossary
(xiv) Index

It is customary to call the first five elements as front matter, the next four elements as main body and the last five as back matter. In an informational report there may be no conclusions and recommendation. Similarly, elements such as acknowledgements, appendices, bibliography, glossary may not find a place in your report. In fact, the title page, the introduction and the discussion or the description are the only elements that are found in almost all reports. Whether you should include a particular element in your report would depend upon its usefulness, the terms of reference and the existing practice in your organisation.

A new trend has, however, recently been observed regarding the sequencing of elements. Some managements prefer recommendations and conclusions to be placed immediately after the title page especially in reports written for decision-making. Obviously this is more convenient for the management, which is interested, in knowing what recommendations/conclusions have been arrived at in a report rather than in the details on the basis of which these have been formulated. Often the recommendations/conclusions are circulated as a separate document to the officials who participate in decision-making. Traditionally, this function was supposed to be performed by the abstract. This practice obviously was borrowed from the academic world where the convention is to write the abstract and then present the findings of a piece of investigation or research in the form of a paper or an article.

Let us now briefly look at individual elements.

(i) *Cover*: To protect the manuscript against damage a report is usually bound in a cover. A neat and attractive cover gives a report a professional look. It should contain only essential information, namely, the report number and its classification (e.g. secret) if any, name of the organisation, title of the report, name of the author and the date. The cover is an optional element for a report which has only a few pages.

The specimen of a cover is given below:

Report Number: R14

A REPORT

ON

THE STUDY OF DIGITAL POSITION READOUTS AND MICROPROCESSOR SYSTEMS

BY

VIPUL M. GADRE

SENIOR ENGINEER

NATIONAL HEAVY ELECTRICALS LTD.

HYDERABAD

DECEMBER, 2007

(ii) *Title Page*: It is the first right hand page of the report. In addition to all the information in the cover it contains the following: project or job number, if any, the name and designation of the primary recipient, approvals and distribution list, if necessary. Occasionally one is required to get the report checked and approved by a senior officer before submission and to specify the names of the officers to whom it is to be circulated. These are indicated in the title page under 'approvals' and 'distribution list'. The items should be artistically arranged on the page for balance and symmetry. A specimen follows:

Report Number: R14

A REPORT ON

THE STUDY OF DIGITAL POSITION READOUTS AND MICROPROCESSOR SYSTEMS

PREPARED

FOR

M.Q. KHAN

CHIEF ENGINEER

BY

VIPUL M. GADRE

SENIOR ENGINEER

APPROVED BY

K.L. SHAH

DESIGN ENGINEER

NATIONAL HEAVY ELECTRICALS LTD.

HYDERABAD

DECEMBER, 2007

(iii) *Acknowledgements*: It is necessary to acknowledge any help, assistance or guidance received from different persons or organisations. In doing so you should be sincere and courteous and have variety in your expressions. A few commonly used expressions are given below:

(a) We thank..

(b) We are grateful...

(c) We are indebted ...

(d) We are deeply indebted ...

(e) We must express our gratitude ...

(f) We owe a great deal ...

(g) We are deeply grateful...

(h) We acknowledge our indebtedness ...

(i) We are highly obliged to ...

(j) Thanks are due ...

(k) We are particularly grateful ...

(l) We should like to thank ...

(m) We wish to record our appreciation ...

(n) We must acknowledge our obligation...

(o) We must acknowledge our deep sense of gratitude ...

The reasons for thanking the person or persons are also stated. For example, 'We are grateful to Mr. X for his useful advice', 'We wish to express our appreciation to Mr. Y for reading the first draft of the report'. If there is a preface, acknowledgements may not appear as a separate element but this information may be included in the preface itself. If you have the slightest doubt whether a person would feel embarrassed if his name is mentioned in the acknowledgements, you should secure his permission.

(iv) *Table of Contents*: The main function of the Table of Contents is to help the reader locate specific material in your report. The primary consideration for deciding how detailed it should be is your perception of the reader's needs. The Table is patterned after the final outline of the report. It is an optional element in a short report of about 1500 words but in a long report, say, of 3000 words or more, it is essential to give a Table of Contents. Without it the reader would not be able to get an overall picture of what your report contains.

For proper organisation you should follow the decimal numbering system in listing the topics and sub-topics. Indent the second-order and third-order headings. Generally, sub-headings beyond the third-order are not included in the Table. Number each topic and sub-topic and write the page number on which it appears. The numbering of the elements up to abstract/summary is in small Roman numerals, and that from introduction onwards in Arabic numerals. In preparing the Table leave 4 cm. margin on the left and 3 cm. on the right, top and bottom of the page.

Another point you should keep in mind is the phrasing and grouping of the topics and sub-topics. Ensure that they have parallel grammatical construction. Topics and sub-topics of equal rank should be assigned the same level in the Table. The ideas which can be grouped together should be properly sequenced and placed under the relevant topic or sub-topic. A specimen Table of Contents of a report on Acoustic Steam Leak Detection System is given as follows:

TABLE OF CONTENTS

(v) *Abstract and Summary*: In almost all reports there is a condensation that is termed as an *abstract* or *summary*. Very often these labels are used interchangeably. Discriminating professionals, however, do make a distinction in terms of their contents, function and length.

An abstract is a clear, concise condensation of the purpose and the most important results of the project. It states what the report is all about, what has been accomplished and the significance of the achievement. The emphasis is on the presentation of the idea and not on its explanation. Rhetorical logic is used to organise its contents. It therefore does not include equations, tables and figures. A summary on the other hand is the entire report in a nutshell. It has a beginning, stating why the project was carried out and why the report was written; a middle, highlighting the most important features of the report and an end giving conclusions and recommendations. Thus it contains significant gleanings from the various elements of the report. Normally a summary is characterised by a presentation logic, that is, its contents are presented in the same sequence as they appear in a report. In a summary too, figures do not generally appear; however, equations and tabular data are sometimes included.

The main function of the abstract is to present a qualitative description of the report so that the reader may determine the extent of his interest in it. It is for this purpose that an abstract is self-contained and circulated independently of the report. Abstracts of technical and research papers in a particular area are also published for the same purpose. A few such well-known compilations are *Chemical Abstracts, Physical Abstracts*, etc. A distinction is occasionally made between what is termed as a descriptive abstract and an informative abstract. The former is a sort of prose Table of Contents. An informative abstract concentrates on the presentation of the accomplishment and its importance. You would notice that the descriptive abstract in fact, a summary with respect to its contents. In actual practice it is difficult to classify abstracts; no abstract is wholly informative or descriptive.

Like an abstract, a summary is self-contained and also often circulated independently. By going through it a person can decide whether to go through the whole report or not. Further, it helps the busy reader to form a fairly good idea about the contents of a report.

It is difficult to specify the expected length of an abstract or a summary but usually the former is shorter than the latter. It has been suggested that the length of an abstract should be about 2 per cent of the original whereas that of the summary 5 per cent. In either case, one has to balance between two sets of conflicting variables: brevity vs detail and explanation vs information.

In conclusion we may point out that an abstract is more relevant in the context of a communication by one specialist to another. That is why every technical paper or research paper contains an abstract. The journals which publish such papers require an abstract from every contributor. A report is not necessarily meant to be read by another specialist; hence the abstract loses its importance in the context of reports written in professional organisations. It should, however, continue to remain a compulsory element in a specialist to specialist communication situation, In a vast majority of reports we should be content with a summary which would no less effectively perform the function hitherto associated with the abstract.

How to Condense?

Let us now discuss the steps you should take in condensing the contents of a report into an abstract or a summary: Though the discussion is in the context of reports the steps given below can be used for condensation of any material; only the emphasis, approach and selection and arrangement of contents would differ from one situation to another.

- Pick out and state the central theme.
- Identify the topic sentence in each paragraph. It may be located in the beginning, middle or at the end of the paragraph. In paragraphs which have no topic sentence, identify the idea discussed.
- Examine all the topic sentences or ideas thus identified and try to establish their relationships with the central theme.
- Verbalise the relationships which may be of support, illustration, elucidation, comparison, linkage, etc.

- Write the first draft stating the central theme and explaining if by using the verbalisation of relationships that you have already established.
- Expand the draft or prune it to suit your requirement, but ensure that its self-sufficiency is not lost.

(vi) *Introduction*: The introduction prepares the reader for the content of the report and is a good starting point for one who is not familiar with the subject. In writing an introduction you should, therefore, keep in mind particularly the three basic questions governing all good professional writing – for whom, for what, and why. In specific terms an introduction:

- states the subject and the purpose of the project (investigation, survey, etc.);
- specifies the authorisation;
- gives the background, historical or technical as the case may be;
- describes the basic procedure or methods followed for the collection of data and their sources;
- defines scope* pointing out the limitations or qualifications of the project; and
- indicates the value or importance of the project.

An introduction also sometimes contains a description of the plan of presentation or development and explanation of specialised terms and symbols used if their number is small. Sometimes a report is written in pursuance of a resolution of an organisational unit or in response to a formal executive order. In such cases what a report should contain is clearly defined in what is known as *Terms of Reference*. And then the Terms form the basis for writing the introduction.

(vii) *Discussion or Description*: Except in very short reports, discussion or description itself does not appear as a heading of any section. In long reports, however, there are a number of sections incorporating material under several apt headings and sub-headings.

The function of this element is to discuss or describe the main business of the report. It naturally therefore contains the data in an organised form, often in tables. The analysis of the data which are arranged in a logical order yields results and admits of certain inferences. These are then evaluated and judgements are formed and they ultimately lead to the formulation of conclusions.

Since this part constitutes the bulk of the report almost all illustrations find a place in it. When the data are too numerous or the illustrations too detailed and are likely to impede the flow of discussion or elucidation, they are included in the Appendix. In such a case, only a reference to them is given in this part.

(viii) *Conclusions*: To give a sense of finality and completeness to the discussion or description, it is a common practice to make certain remarks at the end of a piece of writing. These are often referred to as aesthetic conclusions and their function is merely to bring the discussion smoothly to a close, giving the reader a psychological assurance of having come to the end. Such conclusions usually appear in informational reports. Real conclusions are given in interpretive reports and contain the findings or

---

* The scope specifies the range of the subject matter, the detail in which the subject is to be dealt with and the point of view from which it is to be discussed.

results of an investigation arrived at from the discussion in the earlier part. No new material is added at this stage; all conclusions are logically arrived at from what has gone before. They may be in the form of a series of numbered points or in paragraphs. Sometimes at the end of each section of discussion part of a conclusion is reached. Here, then they are simply grouped and presented together. Before giving a final shape you will be well advised to correlate the conclusions with what you promised to do in the introduction.

Conclusions are of great value to a busy executive or a person researching the literature of a subject. In fact, it may be the first part to be read by the busy executive to arrive at a decision. You should therefore check the conclusions carefully before submitting the report.

(ix) *Recommendations*: Recommendations are only given when required. In most cases at the time of authorisation you would be told whether you have to make recommendations or not. If you volunteer to offer them, you may be misunderstood of having assumed responsibility which was not entrusted to you. If you are not clear whether you have to give recommendations or not it is better to seek clarification from the concerned authority.

Recommendations, when given, are clearly derived from the conclusions and indicate future action, application of material, need for further investigation or proposed programme, etc. And these then and not the 'Conclusions' form the basis for decision making. If the number of recommendations is large they may be listed in descending order of their importance. Occasionally they are accompanied by some explanation. In very short reports, conclusions and recommendations are presented together rather than in separate sections.

(x) *Appendix*: Though shoved into the background behind the main body, the appendix is a useful element of the report. It contains the material that needs to be included in the report but it is not an essential and integral part of the main presentation. The appendix relieves the main body from voluminous, detailed information but provides a place for inclusion of material for record purposes or for the sake of those readers who may want or need to read it. The report writer seems to say to the reader: 'I didn't want to interrupt the smooth flow of your thought by bothering you with details and so I have included them in the appendix. They support' my discussion and substantiate my findings. Use them as you wish.'

The appendix should therefore not be treated as a dumping ground for all that cannot find a place in any other part of the report. On the other hand, the material in it should be properly organised and neatly presented; it should not look like a cluttered-up attic. A specific reference to it should be made in the body of the report. If you think that same material included in the appendix is not worth referring to in the main body, it certainly then is not worthy to be put into the report at all.

Each appendix should be a separate unit and should be numbered as Appendix A, Appendix B, etc. The kinds of material that are generally included are as follows: derivations of equations, detailed calculations, copies of exhibits, data sheets, questionnaires used in the investigation, list of questions used for interview, sample of forms, detailed descriptions of equipment or procedure, tables and figures which would not conveniently fit into the body of the report, etc.

(xi) *List of References*: If you have used or quoted in your report matter from any published or unpublished source, you should give credit to the author(s) concerned by citing them in the text and listing them at the end of your report. This list is known as the List of References. The entries in the list with full bibliographical details are made in the alphabetical order or in order of citation in the text. In the latter case, the References are numbered in the text and the entries in the List bear the same numbers. There are several ways of citing a work in the text; the one most commonly used is illustrated below:

... Thus we see that 'language in all its forms and manifestations constitutes the field of the linguist' (Robins 1971: 2) ...

You would notice that the entry simply contains the last part of the name of the author, the year of publication of the work and the relevant page number. When the actual language-used by the author is not cited, but only the idea is borrowed, the page number is not given. This citation would appear in the List of References as follows:

Robins, R.H. 1971, *General Linguistics: An Introductory Survey*. Second Edition. London: Longman Group Ltd.

If the number of references is very small the works may be mentioned at the bottom of the concerned page in the form of footnotes. Attention should be drawn to them by placing a number or a symbol (1 or *) at suitable places in the text. In a footnote the full name of the author(s) is given and the details of notation are separated by commas as shown below:

R.H. Robins, 1971, *General Linguistics: An Introductory Survey*, Second Edition, London: Longman Group Ltd., page 2.

(xii) *Bibliography*: A bibliography is a list of sources consulted. It is serially numbered and the entries in it are made in alphabetical order. The details appear in the same sequence as in the list of references. There is however no reference to a specific page number. Sometimes a bibliography may be annotated or selected. Occasionally a list of works on the same subject suggested for further reading is also termed as bibliography.

Now we give below a few examples of entries as they would appear in the List of References/ Bibliography:

(a) Book with two authors

Clark, W.C. and R.E. Munn. 1987. *Sustainable Development of the Biosphere*. Cambridge: Cambridge University Press (Note: If there are three or more authors, only the name of the first author as shown above is mentioned and the words et al. are added after it.)

(b) An essay/paper/article in an antholpogy

Foster, E.M. 'An Awful Prospect' in *Twentieth Century Prose*. 1965. A.C. Ward. London: Longmans, Green and Co. Ltd.

(c) An article/paper in a journal

Hahn, Cora. "Trial and Error" in *English Teaching Forum*, Volume XXV, Number 3, July 1987, pp. 8-11. Washington.

(d) An unpublished work

Banerji, Meera. 1984. An *Approach to Syllabus Design for English Language Teaching at the Undergraduate Level in India*. Ph.D. Thesis. Unpublished. Pilani: Birla Institute of Technology and Science.

(xii) *Glossary*: A glossary is a list of technical words or terms used by the reporter in a special sense: If the number of such words or terms is small, they may be explained in the introduction or in the footnotes on the pages on which they occur. In the latter case no doubt the train of reader's thoughts would be interrupted but the advantage of this practice is that explanation is provided to him when he is most in need of it. The decision about the inclusion of a glossary in a report would depend on its readership. The sole purpose is to help the reader understand clearly what you say in the report. Obviously, therefore, if the reader belongs to the subject area of the report, you may not include a glossary.

(xiv) *Index*: An index is given only in voluminous reports where a table of contents may not be adequate to help the reader locate a topic or a sub-topic or any other material easily. The entries in the Index are arranged in an alphabetical order and are cross referenced. Against each entry all the page numbers on which some information is available are mentioned. See the index of this book for an example.

(xv) *Other Elements*: There are a few other elements which sometimes appear in a formal report. These are: *frontispiece*, copyright notice, list of illustrations and preface.

In some reports a map, photograph, cartoon or an artistic drawing is included primarily to add interest and to induce the reader to read the report. This is given right at the beginning, facing the title page and is known as *frontispiece*. It is chosen with meticulous care and is always directly related to the subject matter of the report. A frontispiece is a sort of window display that is superimposed on the cover of the report.

Copyright notice is generally given in a report which is published or is likely to be of lasting value or which includes significant material that may be misused. It appears on the backside of the title page. A copyright indicates the legal monopoly on the publication and its distribution. If someone wishes to quote from the copyrighted material, he must obtain permission in writing for quoting any single passage exceeding fifty words. Ideas cannot be copyrighted; only the form in which they are expressed, including their arrangement and sequence are copyrighted.

When the number of illustrations is large, they are listed in order of appearance. The *list of illustrations* contains a reference to the relevant page numbers and is placed immediately after the table of contents.

In very long reports one may include a *Preface*. It introduces the report and specifies any special contribution. It also draws attention to any additional uses to which a report may be put. The preface is written by the author himself, unlike a foreword which is a commendation of the work by an authority or an expert in the subject. Reports, however, rarely have a foreword.

13.5 SAMPLE QUESTIONNAIRE AND REPORTS

ANNEXURE A

Birla Institute of Technology and Science
Pilani 333031

16 December, 2007

Dear

I am conducting a survey on the extent of the use of English in the professional world. And for this purpose I need your help and cooperation.

For collecting the relevant data, I have prepared a questionnaire which is enclosed. It is designed to collect information about the main forms of communication and the purposes for which English is used in the professional organisations. The questionnaire is divided into the following parts:

Part I General Particulars
Part II Present Employment Data
Part III Language Tasks

I would be grateful if you could kindly fill it in and send it in about a month's time from now, say, latest by 15th January 2008. A self-addressed stamped envelope is enclosed for the purpose. All the information supplied by you will be kept strictly confidential and will be used only for this academic work.

I am aware that you have a busy schedule of work but I do hope that you would be able to spare some time to help me in the fulfilment of this task.

Yours faithfully

(Meera Banerji)
Department of Languages

Encl: As above.

Questionnaire No. ______________

Note: Kindly put a tick (√) in the relevant boxes except where asked to indicate your answers otherwise.

PART I

General Particulars

1. Name in full ________________________________
2. Age ____________________
3. Male [ ] Female [ ]

4. Mother Tongue ____.
5. Language spoken at home ____.
6. What language do you generally use for personal correspondence (with members of the family, relatives, friends, etc.)? ____
7. What language do you generally use in written communications for private affairs (communications to different official bodies such as post-office, banks, firms, educational institutions, etc.)?
8. Do you use English in oral interaction for social purposes? Yes [ ] No [ ]

   If YES, approximately how many hours PER DAY do you spend on such interaction? __________.
10. Educational qualifications from the Bachelor's Degree onwards:

Sl. No.	Name of Degree/ Diploma	University/ Board	Year of passing
1.			
2.			
3.			
4.			
5.			

11. Total working experience (in years) ____________
12. Were you taught English language (General/Compulsory English) course(s) as part of your Bachelor's Degree? Yes [ ] No [ ]
13. If YES, did these courses impart adequate proficiency in English? Yes [ ] No [ ]
14. If the English language courses did not impart adequate proficiency, please indicate the areas where you as a student found these courses inadequate. (You may tick more than one box).
    (a) The course(s) did not help me to understand spoken English adequately. [ ]
    (b) The course(s) did not help me to speak fluently. [ ]
    (c) The course(s) did not help me to read proficiently. [ ]
    (d) The course(s) did not help me to write effectively. [ ]
15. Were you taught English literature (fiction, drama, poetry, prose, etc.) as part of your Bachelor's Degree? Yes [ ] No [ ]
16. If YES, how much did your proficiency in using language improve as a result of studying English literature?

Very much	[ ]	Only partially	[ ]
Not at all	[ ]	Not certain	[ ]

17. Which of the following factors were helpful to you in acquiring proficiency in English? If more than one factor was helpful, please write numerals (1, 2, 3, etc.) in decreasing order of their usefulness.
    (a) Use of English as the medium of your education [ ]
    (b) Doing courses in English [ ]
    (c) Self-study [ ]
    (d) Exposure to English through mass media (radio, TV, newspaper, films) [ ]
    (e) Social environment (family, friends' circle, clubs, etc.) [ ]
18. To what extent have the courses in the English language (General/Compulsory English) you did at the university proved helpful in your *professional work*?
    Very much [ ] Only partially [ ]
    Not at all [ ] Not certain [ ]
19. Do you need to improve your proficiency in English even at this stage of your career?
    Yes [ ] No [ ]
20. If YES, please indicate below the main aspects of the use of English in which you need improvement:
    (a) *Oral Communication* (face to face interaction, participation in meetings, oral reporting, making speeches, etc.) [ ]
    (b) *Reading and Comprehension* (reading official documents, professional journals, books, etc.) [ ]
    (c) *Written Communication* (writing letters, reports, notings on files, etc.) [ ]
21. If you need to improve your proficiency in English even at this stage of your career, please indicate the reasons:
    (a) To do your job more efficiently [ ]
    (b) To improve your job prospects [ ]
    (c) To enhance your social prestige [ ]

PART II

Present Employment Data

22. Organisation where employed, at present:
    Name ________________________________
    Location ________________________________
23. Please indicate the category of your organisation *according to its main function.*
    (a) Design/Consultancy [ ]
    (b) Manufacturing/Production [ ]
    (c) Teaching [ ]
    (d) Research [ ]
    (e) Editing and Publication [ ]

(f) Services (such as those provided by insurance companies, banks, Govt. offices, news and transport agencies, etc.) [ ]

(g) Any other. (Please specify) [ ]

24. To which of the following does your organisation belong?

(a) Central Government [ ]

(b) State Government [ ]

(c) Govt. of India undertaking [ ]

(d) State Govt. undertaking [ ]

(e) Autonomous body (Central) [ ]

(f) Autonomous body (State) [ ]

(g) Joint Sector [ ]

(h) Private Sector [ ]

25. Your present official status:

26. Length of service in this position (in years)

27. Total No. of office/duty hours PER DAY:

28. Please indicate below the nature of your main function in the organisation. If you are performing more than one of the following functions, please write numerals (1, 2, 3, etc.) in decreasing order of your involvement.

(a) General administration [ ]

(b) Planning/designing [ ]

(c) Marketing and sales [ ]

(d) Office management [ ]

(e) Consultancy [ ]

(f) Research [ ]

(g) Teaching [ ]

(h) Editing and publishing [ ]

(i) Publicity [ ]

(j) Liaison work and public relations [ ]

(k) Legal advice [ ]

(l) Financial management and auditing [ ]

(m) Imparting pre-service and in-service training [ ]

(n) Labour welfare and personnel management [ ]

(o) Clerical assistance and record keeping [ ]

(p) Purchasing [ ]

(q) Any other (please specify) [ ]

29. What language(s) do you use during office hours for communication in performing your professional duties? (Please indicate below the approximate proportion of time spent on them PER DAY).

Time → Language ↓	More than 75%	51% to 75%	26% to 50%	25% or less
English				
Hindi				
Regional Language (Please name it)				

30. Who are the persons with whom you usually communicate in English in connection with your professional work during office/ duty hours? Please indicate the frequency.

Frequency → Categories of people ↓	Very Frequently	Frequently	Occasionally	Rarely	Never
(a) Superiors in rank					
(b) Colleagues					
(c) Juniors in rank					
(d) Subordinates					
(e) Officials from other organisations					
(f) Government officials					
(g) Students/ trainees					
(h) The Public					
(i) Others (Please specify)					

31. Please indicate the approximate number of hours spent PER DAY during office hours on the following language skills for professional communication in English.

Skills	No. of hours
(a) Speaking (b) Listening (c) Writing (d) Reading	

32. Please write below the approximate number of hours spent by you PER DAY in reading materials in English.

Reading	No. of hours
(a) Official documents (letters, reports, notings on files, etc.) (b) Journals of a professional nature	
(c) Books of a professional nature (d) Journals of a general nature	
(e) Books of a general nature	

33. If you were to communicate for professional purposes entirely in a language other than English, would you be able to function satisfactorily? Yes [ ] No [ ]

PART III
Language Tasks

Listed below are some of the language tasks performed in the professional organisations. Please indicate the frequency of each of these tasks so far as your professional work is concerned.

The Use of Spoken English

Frequency → Language Tasks ↓	Very Frequently	Frequently	Occasionally	Rarely	Never
34. Presenting written material (papers, reports, etc.)					
35. Oral reporting					
36. Making speeches					

Frequency → Language Tasks ↓	Very Frequently	Frequently	Occasionally	Rarely	Never
37. Participating in meetings, seminars, workshops, conferences (presiding, conducting introducing topics/ speakers)					
38. Dictation (letters, memos, instructions, etc.)					
39. Demonstrating, explaining (exhibits, equipment, processes, etc.)					
40. Giving instructions/directions (personally or on the telephone)					
41. Making inquiries or collecting information (personally/on the telephone)					
42. Formal teaching (students/trainees)					
43. Making announcements					
44. Establishing social relations (social talk, greetings, informal invitations/ requests, etc.)					
45. Interviewing (persons for eliciting information, candidates for appointments, etc.)					
46. Negotiating deals; agreements (for sales, liaison with Govt. officers or other commercial/business organisations)					
47. Note-taking					

The Use of Written English

Frequency → / Language Tasks ↓	Very Frequently	Frequently	Occasionally	Rarely	Never
48. Writing reports					
49. Writing letters					
50. Writing memos, orders					
51. Writing notices, circulars, agenda, minutes					
52. Writing technical proposals					
53. Writing handbooks, manuals, regulations					
54. Writing research papers, articles in professional journals					
55. Writing booklets, brochures					
56. Writing press release, news bulletins					
57. Preparing market surveys, financial surveys, questionnaires					
58. Writing formal invitations and requests					
59. Abstracting, summarising, making precis of the correspondence, reports and the published material					
60. Writing short messages (telephone/telex messages/ telegrams)					
61. Writing publicity materials, advertisements (in the newspaper, scripts for radio, TV, etc.)					
62. Editing (house journals, magazines, newspapers, etc.)					
63. Note-making					
64. Filling in forms					
65. Keeping records					

ANNEXURE B

Form for Routine Report
Model Tractors Limited, Bangalore

<table>
<tr><td colspan="10" align="center">PROTECT STATUS REPORT</td></tr>
<tr><td colspan="6">DIVISION

UNIT</td><td colspan="4">PERIOD:

ENDED:</td></tr>
<tr><td rowspan="3">Proj. No</td><td rowspan="3">Location</td><td rowspan="3">Proj. Title</td><td rowspan="3">Approved Project Total Rs.</td><td rowspan="3">Latest Forecast Cost Rs.</td><td rowspan="3">Total Cornmitted to Date Rs.</td><td colspan="3">Expenditure</td><td rowspan="3">Cornpletion Month</td></tr>
<tr><td rowspan="2">Total to Date Rs.</td><td colspan="2">Year to date</td></tr>
<tr><td>Actual Rs.</td><td>Budget Rs.</td></tr>
<tr><td></td><td></td><td></td><td></td><td></td><td></td><td></td><td></td><td></td><td></td></tr>
<tr><td colspan="6">Date of
Submission:</td><td colspan="4">Divisional Head</td></tr>
</table>

ANNEXURE C

Specimen Letter Report

Goenka Automatic Signals Ltd.
Flash Point, Thane Road,
Mumbai - 400056

30 August, 2007

Sri O.P. Gupta
Superintendent Police (Traffic)
Eastern Range
Dorset Lane
Mumbai - 400003

Subject: Crossing Protection at Starway Avenue, Chembur, Bombay

Dear Sri Gupta

Please refer to your letter No. T316-P/20 dated June 12, 2007 in which you asked this company to survey the poor crossing conditions that exist at Starway Avenue and to examine the possibility of our providing visible and audible warning for both Northward and Southward movement of suburban trains.

Results and Recommendations

We have completed the survey and analysed the data collected for the purpose. The results strongly indicate that serious traffic congestion exists and that a warning system should be provided. We recommend that an annunciator system be installed at the Starway Avenue crossing to provide warning in both the directions:

1. Northward on either of the main tracks for approximately 1500 feet.
2. Southward on either of the main tracks for approximately 1800 feet.

Estimate of Cost

Our estimate for installation is as follows:	Rs.
Material	10,300
Freight	1310
Technical Consultancy	1250
Labour	11,527
Contingencies	2148
Total	26,535

Installation Requirements

At present the speed limit in this area is 30 km. per hour. If the contract to install the annunciator system is given to us, we would like the speed limit of train movements over the crossing only reduced to 20 km per hour while the installation is being done. Further, during this period the flagman should be provided with a large stop banner surfaced with retro-reflective sheet material.

Yours sincerely

(R.P. Chopra)

Superintendent, Signals Division

ANNEXURE D

Specimen Memo Report

Hindustan Jute Mills Ltd
Inter-office Memorandum

To: Managing Director

From: Labour Welfare Officer

Ref. TN/37B

30 August, 2007

Subject: Functioning of the Employees' Canteen

Please refer to your Memo No. MD/P/17 dated 16th August, 2007 asking me to examine the complaints against the functioning of the canteen and to suggest measures for improvement, if necessary.

Findings

Interaction with complainants and a few other regular users of the canteen facility, selected at random, has established the following complaints to be genuine:

1. There has been a marked deterioration in the quality of vegetable cutlets, dosa, idli, sambhar, samosa and all varieties of sweets. There are two reasons for it: use of raw materials of inferior quality and laxity in supervision over the quality of finished products.
2. The rates of tea, coffee, cold drinks, and egg and bread preparations have been raised by 25 per cent since 1 July, 2007, this has happened because of (i) acceptance of supply tenders quoting higher rates without recording any reasons; and (ii) showing waste percentage in eggs and bread

(*Continued*)

(Continued)

as 5 per cent since 1 July, 2007 against 3 per cent recorded during the previous three quarters ending on 30 June 2007.

3. The service at the counter and cash collection desk is slow and during peak hours, namely, 11.00 to 11.30 am and 3.30 to 4.00 pm there is a complete breakdown. The causes are: mis-management of supervision at the supply counter and manual totalling of charges.

Recommendations

1. The Advisory Committee of the canteen should be directed to ensure the purchase of good quality material in bulk after an extensive survey of the market. At the same time, steps should be taken to use modern technology in the preservation of both the raw material and the finished products.
2. The prevailing rates in the market justify an increase of only 10 per cent in the price of egg and bread preparations. There is no case at all for a raise in the price of tea, coffee and cold drinks. The prices should therefore be reduced accordingly. With respect to purchases, the canteen manager should be directed to follow the guidelines – strictly in accepting the supply tenders quoting higher rates.
3. To ensure a smooth flow of customers the canteen staff should be better deployed and asked to help the customers pick the desired items. The pace of cash collection can be quickened by using a cash register for totalling the price of individual items,

Zamin Ali

Annexure E

Specimen Formal Report I

A REPORT

ON

AIR POLLUTION CONTROL

Prepared for
The Chief Engineer
Bharat Plastics Limited
Ashoknagar
Kanpur

by
Ashim Saraf
Chemical Engineer

30 September, 2007

bstract

his report describes the existing measures to control air pollution in Bharat Plastics Ltd. and suggests eps for more effective control of the pollution. The suggestions made are likely to prove useful in other, rocess industries also.

Introduction

ir pollution is a major problem in almost all the industries today. It also exists in Bharat Plastics Ltd., shoknagar, Kanpur in the form of heavy dust concentration. Among the various measures taken by e management to solve this problem are the installation of various types of bag filters and provision f ventilation in the affected departments. The purpose of this report is to describe the steps already ken and to suggest ways to control the pollution further.

. *Causes of air pollution*

he pollution of air occurs when in the atmosphere there is more than normal concentration of dust, nd or obnoxious gases. There are certain natural causes for this phenomenon – wind, cyclone, volcanic ruption, forest fire, etc. Among the man-made causes are the concentration of population, poor town lanning, inadequate and inefficient waste management in industries and indiscriminate destruction of cological balance.

ust is the main pollutant in this organisation. It is between 0.2 per cent to 0.25 per cent of the total r pollutants and varies from 10 to 50 micron. Dust is amorphous and insoluble in water but partially oluble in other liquids. It is sticky and has a moisture content of 3 per cent to 4 per cent. Its density 0.3 to 0.4 and specific gravity 1.1 to 1.2. In nature it is hygroscopic, abrasive and corrosive.

. *Departments facing air pollution*

ow air pollution occurs in different departments and the measures taken by them to control it are iscussed below.

.1 *Boiler automatic-I plant*: The boiler of this plant is charged by fuel oil. Smoke is produced from e functioning of the captive generator. The smoke thus generated has a small percentage of carbon ioxide particles and colloidal carbon particulates. The smoke is let out in the atmosphere through a himney of 100 ft., reducing the intensity at the ground level.

.2 *Phenol formaldehyde department*: All the machines in this department, namely, Blender, Sheet utter, Alpiner, Ball Miller, and Roller Machine contribute to the pollution of the air. Dust floats above e machines at about 10 ft. and ultimately gets deposited on the machines.

he pollution of air produced by Blender is controlled by means of two hoods, one at the top and the ther at the bottom provided for dust collection. At the mouth of the Blender there is – a suction pipe to collect the dust particulates. Hoods are provided in the Sheet Cutter, Alpiner and Ball Miller also or the same purpose. However, the Alpiner has in addition 6 balloons made of drill cloth to displace e dust generated in the machine. These balloons are cylindrical and their volume is 83 cu. ft. The mount of pollution is maximum in the Roller machine as hoods are not provided. The phenol ormaldehyde powder is fed into the rollers which makes the dust rise. For safety the workers are provided with heat resistant gloves and masks made of cloth. Plastic masks are not used as they ge clogged with dust, causing difficulty in respiration.

Another measure taken by the Department is the setting up of a pulse-jet bag filter. This sturdil constructed, dust-tight casing contains a number of circular, fabric bags which are mounted on wire mes supported cages. Each cage is fitted with a high efficiency venture which is suspended from a tube plat that separates the dusty and clean sides of the filter. External manifold and solenoid operated diaphrar valves deliver compressed air to header tubes above each row of bags. These valves, which regula the air supply, are controlled by an adjustable solid state timer. There are no moving parts internally Dust-laden air enters the filter through the hopper side. The coarser particles fall out immediately an the finer particles rise with the air stream and accumulate evenly on the outer surface of the filter bag The cleaned air is discharged into the atmosphere. The complete cleaning cycle is carried out in a fractio of a second, allowing the collection operation to continue without interruption. However, the volum of dust in this department is so much that this device has been able to control pollution only partially

3.3. *Urea formaldehyde department*: The main machines in this department are the Kettles (in whic urea formaldehyde is heated) and the Alpiner, Ball Miller and Roller Machine. In this Department to dust is the main pollutant. Its quality is different and it is more hygroscopic in nature. The pollutio is controlled by installing exhaust fans for the circulation of fresh air. These fans force the polluted ai out from the plant into the atmosphere. Further, a ventilation unit containing 12 nets has been installe behind the department to protect it from dust and other contaminants. This unit pumps fresh air throug the ducts specially provided for the purpose. The pollution has been controlled to a great exten However, the problem persists.

3.4 *Melamine formaldehyde department*: In this Department the problem is the same as in the Ure Formaldehyde Department. And here again the same method has been used to control the pollution

4. *Conclusions*

The organisation is aware of the problem of air pollution and conscious of its duty to control it. However the measures it has taken have not been able to control it to the desired extent. Restrictions such a hygroscopic nature of the urea formaldehyde and melamine formaldehyde powders have come in it way. It is because of this reason that the company has not been able to utilise scrubbers and wet dus collectors for controlling pollution. The problem is that the powders when passed into the scrubber, form lumps on getting soaked and settle down in the water. On settling down they form cakes and absorb moisture from the humidifying spray. And it is very difficult to separate the cakes thus formed. Anothe difficulty is that in the Phenol Formaldehyde Department the dust is recovered and reused in the plant And the recovery would not be easy if scrubbers are put to use. This does not mean that there is no scope for further control of air pollution.

5. *Recommendations*

The following measures should be taken to control the air pollution with a view to providing healthie atmosphere to the workers of the factory.

(i) For the control of pollution in Boiler Automatic-I Plant the fuel should be specially treated to reduce carbon dioxide content of the emission. A spray tower should also be installed for the

(ii) In Phenol Formaldehyde Department another pulse-jet bag should be provided to enhance air pollution control. Further, the workers should be provided with masks made of non-permeable cloth.

(iii) In Urea Formaldehyde Department the number of exhaust fans having greater speed and power should be doubled and one more ventilation unit be set up to provide fresh air. The same steps are recommended to control the pollution in Melamine Formaldehyde Department also.

ANNEXURE F

Specimen Formal Report II

A REPORT
ON
A STUDY OF INDUSTRIAL MOTORS

Prepared in Partial Fulfilment of Practice School-1
Course No. BITS: C221

by

Abhimanyu Gopalka
Gaurav Roongta

at

The Hindustan Aluminium Company Ltd.
Renusagar
(A Practice School-1 Station)

BIRLA 1NSTITUTE OF TECHNOLOGY AND SCIENCE,
PILANI
15 JULY, 2007

Acknowledgements

We are deeply indebted to Prof. L.K. Maheshwari, Vice-Chancellor, BITS Pilani and Prof. G. Sunder, Dean, Practice School Division for giving us an opportunity to work at HINDALCO, Renusagar. We express our sincere gratitude to Mr. Jotirmay Bhaumic, Head, Renusagar Power Division of HINDALCO Industries Ltd. and Mr. Sunil Kumar, Head, Technical Training and Management Development Center (TTMDC) for facilitating our work in this organization. We are grateful to Mr. Atul God, Deputy Manager, and Coordinator PS Programme for his encouragement and support. We express our indebtedness to Mr. Shayam Babu Upadhyaya, Assistant Manager and our Guide for training us in essential skills and giving valuable guidance throughout our project. Our thanks our due to Dr. Navin Singh, PS Faculty for giving his whole-hearted support and valuable advice all through the programme. We are thankful to the staff members of TTMDC and the General Electrical Maintenance Department for their whole-hearted cooperation. We are extremely grateful to our family members for their moral support throughout the PS-1 programme.

Abstract

This report describes the working principles, construction and design of industrial motors. It attempts to find out the various reasons for energy losses during motoring operations and suggests ways to improve their efficiency. It deals with power factor, its importance for proper working of motors as well as the methods of improving it. This report also attempts to highlight various tests which are essential for proper maintenance, safety and repair of these electrical devices. The troubleshooting section gives methods of tackling operational hazards effectively.

1. *Introduction*

The report on 'A Study on Industrial Motors' at Renusagar Power Division, HINDALCO Industries Limited, contains concepts through which we try to understand the basic principles, design, and construction of industrial motors, along with some common problems encountered in normal motoring operations. An Industrial motor is a rotatary machine which converts electrical energy into mechanical drive. The motors therefore, are used as prime movers to drive mechanical loads. In this project we have thrown light on the testing, efficiency and troubleshooting aspect of motor and various methods to improve them.

The importance of motors can be seen in every power plant today. In Renusagar, motors have found applications in Aerial Ropeway, pumps, and coal handling plant, cooling tower fans, plant machinery and other prime mover rotation applications. Thus the scope of this project has been as vast as the range of motor applications of motors itself. Various problems such as motor breakdown, voltage and current variations, flux leakages, etc., are encountered and these hamper motoring operations and consequently affect the whole industrial applications. This report also discusses how these problems can be sorted out in a more effective manner.

Even though the project has tried to cover all that has been possible in the context of its topic it has a few limitations in the form of limited hands in terms of practical training for motoring operations and their occasional absence due to repair/servicing. Data have been mainly collected from the richly equipped Training Center Library and the internet.

This work may prove valuable to those who are interested in understanding the basic principles of motoring operations as well as those who are in need of a quick reference for testing, troubleshooting and improving efficiency of industrial motors.

2. *Industrial Motors – An Overview*

Alternating current (a.c.) industrial motors are the most common motors in industrial motion called control system, as well as in powered home appliances. Their simple and rugged design, low maintenance and direct connection to an AC power source are the main advantages of induction motors. Of the various types of industrial motors available in the market, this part discusses the basics of an induction motor, their different types, their characteristics and the selection criteria for different applications and basic control techniques.

The characteristic features of industrial motors are:-

- Simple and rugged design
- Low cost and minimum maintenance
- High reliability and high efficiency
- Self-starting and synchronised ability

2.1 *Basic Operating Principles and Construction*: Like most of the induction motors, an AC induction motor has a fixed outer portion, called the stator and a rotor that spins inside with a carefully engineered air gap. All electrical motors use magnetic field rotation to spin their motors. There are two sets of electromagnets inside a motor. In an a.c. induction motor, one set of electromagnets is formed in the stator because of the a.c. supply. The alternating nature of the supply voltages induces an electromagnetic force (EMF) in the motor as per Lenz's law, thus generating another set of electromagnets. The interaction between the magnetic field of these electromagnets generate twisting force, or torque. As a result, the motor rotates in the direction of the resultant torque.

2.1.1 *Stator*: The stator is made up of several thin laminations of aluminium or cast iron. They are punched and clamped together to form a hollow cylinder with slots. Coils of insulated wires are reinserted into these slots. The stator windings are connected directly to the power source. Internally they are connected in such a way that on applying ac. supply, rotating magnetic field is created.

2.1.2 *Rotor*: The rotor is made up of several thin steel laminations with evenly spaced bars, which are made up of aluminium or copper, along the periphery. In the most popular type of rotor, these bars are connected at ends mechanically or electrically by the use of rings. The rotor consists of a cylindrical laminated core with axially placed parallel slots for constructions. The rotor is mounted on the shaft using bearings in each end; one end of the shaft is normally kept longer than the other for driving the load.

2.2 *Types of a.c. induction motors:* Generally, induction motors are categorised on the number of stator windings. They are:

1. Single-phase Induction Motors
2. Multi-phase Induction Motors

2.2.1 *Single-phase induction motors*: They are induction motors which are least expensive, lowest maintenance type motors. As the name suggests this type of motors has only one stator windings and operates with single-phase power supply. In all single-phase induction motors, the rotor is the squirrel cage type.

2.2.2 *Multi-phase induction motors*: Mostly they are three-phase induction motors which are used for industrial and commercial purposes. The power capabilities and efficiency range from medium to high.

compared to their single phase counterparts. Popular applications of multi-phase induction motors include grinders, lathes, drill presses, pumps, compressors, conveyors, farm equipments and other mechanical duty applications.

3. *Losses in Induction Motors*

Basically, induction motor loses energy by dissipation of heat due to constructional material and motor design. As such, input electrical energy is lost in the form of copper and iron losses.

3.1 *Types of losses*

1. Stator losses
2. Rotor losses
3. Mechanical losses

The stator and mechanical losses can be further sub-divided as iron and copper losses respectively.

3.2 *Factors Affecting the Efficiency of Static Motors*: The efficiency of electrical motors depends on the choice of material used for the core and windings, their physical arrangement and the core and precision with which they are handled and assembled. The factors which effect efficiency are:

- Conductor content (load dependent)
- Magnetic steel (mainly constant)
- Thermal design (mainly load dependent)
- Aerodynamic design (constant)

Manufacture and quality control (constant)

3.3 *Factors causing energy losses in motors*: Factors that lead to losses in motors are increase in iron and copper losses. Increase in iron losses can be caused by:

- Mechanical damage to the core
- Thermal damage to the core
- Electromagnetic changes

Copper loss: stator copper loss is the largest loss in most induction motors. The copper loss varies with the load in proportion to the current square and can be expressed as:

$Pd = R*I^2$

Pd = stator winding - copper loss (w)

R = resistance (ohm)

I = current (amp)

4. *Power Factor of an Induction Motor*

Power factor is the ratio between the KW and KVA drawn by an electrical load where KW is the actual power and the KVA is the apparent load power. It is a measure of how effectively the current is being converted into useful work output and more particularly, it is an indicator of the effect of the load current on the efficiency of the supply system. Power factor = watts/square root (3)* volts*amps.

4.1 *Power factor correction*: One of the methods of power factor correction is capacitive power factor correction, which is applied to circuits, which include induction motors as a means of reducing the inductive component of the current and thereby reducing the losses in the supply. Power factor correction is achieved by the addition of capacitors in parallel to the connected motor circuits and can be applied to the stator, or applied to the switchboard or distribution panel. The resulting capacitive current is the leading current and is used to cancel the lagging inductive current flowing from the supply.

4.2 *Power factor correction principle:* Power factor correction is achieved by the addition of capacitors across the supply to neutralise the inductive component of the current. The power factor correction may be applied by either of the following ways:

4.2.1 *Automatic bank power factor correction (Bulk power factor correction)*: It consists of a number of banks of power factor correction capacitors, each controlled by a contractor, which in turn is controlled by a power factor controller. The power factor controller monitors the supply coming into the switchboard and adds sufficient capacitance to neutralise the inductive component. These controllers are usually set to adjust the power factor 0.9-0.95 lagging.

4.2.2 *Static power factor correction*: Static power factor correction is controlled by a contactor when the motor is started and when it is stopped. With static correction, it is important that the motor is undercorrected rather than over-corrected. It is commonly applied by using the contractor to control both the motor and the capacitors. It is better to use two contractors, one for the motor and one for the capacitors. This determines the magnetizing current of the motor being connected.

5. *Testing of Industrial Motors*

This section will discuss the main causes of electrical failures in motors and how much voltage-testing can help in their early detection.

Most electrical failures are caused by the combination of the voltage spikes that occur at start-up and normal deterioration. The problem often begins with the turn to turn short that eventually goes to the ground. Without high voltage testing many of these problems will go undetected. Before making a logical decision about what kinds of testing should be done on motors to predict the electrical failures, it must be understood what makes these failures occur. It is important to understand the different insulation groups, the aging process of insulation and review typical failure scenarios. Only then will a decision be made about which test is to be made.

5.1 *The Insulation Groups*: The insulation system of a motor consists of ground wall insulation, the phase-to-phase insulation and the turn-to-turn insulation. In a typical induction motor the ground wall insulation is the slot linear paper that protects the insulated copper to ground. The phase-to-phase is often a sheet of insulation. The purpose of this insulation is to protect motors from copper to copper failures.

5.2 *The insulation aging process:* One or more of the following factors can affect the insulation aging process:

1. *Contamination* A. chemical deposit on the windings that causes deterioration of the insulation
2. *Mechanical.* Vibration or movement within the windings of the motor, which wears the insulation system.
3. *Normal thermal aging.* The slow deterioration of the insulation over the windings through normal operations.
4. *Early thermal aging.* Excessive winding temperatures causing premature failure

5.3 *Tests*: This section will highlight the various kinds of tests performed in an induction motor to verify its serviceability.

5.3.1 *Insulation resistance (IR) test:* Developed early in the twentieth century, the insulation resistance test is the oldest and most widely used test for assessing the quality of insulation to ground. On this test, the motor frame is grounded, and the test instrument (Mega ohmmeter) imposes a DC voltage on the motor windings giving the readings through which the serviceability of the motor can be checked.

5.3.2 *Polarisation index test*: This is a ten-minute d.c. test which is performed at a voltage lower then the maximum voltage. A mega ohm reading is taken at one minute and again after 10 minutes to determine the elasticity of the ground insulation. When placed in the electrical field the molecules of the ground insulation should align with that field. If the insulation is aged, hard, and brittle, no polarization can occur. The polarisation index is the ratio of the ten-minute insulation resistance reading divided by the one-minute reading.

5.3.3 *Surge test*: Although surge comparison testing was developed more then 80 years ago, it is the newest of the classic tests performed to determine the winding insulation condition. This test detects turn-to-turn, coil-to-coil, and phase-to-phase insulation defects that cannot be discovered by other methods. Surge comparison testing is premised on the principle that in a stator no winding defects are there and all three phase windings are identical. Each phase is tested against the others like A-B, B-C, and A-C. The test instrument imposes a brief voltage pulses on the phase undergoing the test and reflects ringing pulses on the instrument's oscilloscope screen. If two windings are identical (as they should be) then reflected images are identical and appear as a single trace. This technique is valuable in detecting this shift to the left.

6. *Trouble Shooting of Induction Motors*

The keys to successful motor operation include a total understanding of the application, then choosing the proper type of motor for the application.

This part examines the most mechanically and electrically originated motor problems and their preventive action. Trouble with a motor is like trouble with any rotating machinery. Some problems could be avoided if the application and environment were understood. The reasons of motor failure can be summarized as TEAM stresses, where TEAM stands for

T: Thermal

E: Electrical

A: Ambient

M: Mechanical

6.1 *Types of Troubles*

1. Stator troubles
2. Rotor troubles

Stator troubles: they are the troubles, which we encounter in the stator part of the motor. The common trouble which we encounter here is:

Motor overheating

The possible causes which leads to this trouble are:

- Motor overload
- Ineffective cooling
- Excessive ambience
- Wrong connection
- Supply voltage unbalanced
- Wrong voltage or frequency

Preferred tests are:

- Check load performance data
- Check fan, air flow and temperature of air
- Check connection diagram and nameplate data
- Measure phase-to-phase voltage accurately

Solutions to get rid of this problem:

- Fix problem with load or fit larger motor
- Clean motor, sort out cooling of air temperature and flow
- Sort out connections
- Restore supply to all phases
- Correct voltage or frequency
- Balance voltage supply

6.2 *Rotor troubles*. We encounter rotatary troubles like start failure, motor vibration, etc.

Motor fails to start

Possible causes:

- Fault with supply
- Motor or load locked up
- Wrong connections in control circuits

Preferred tests:

- Check for correct voltage at motor terminals
- Make sure motor and load are free to turn

Solutions:

- Fit new fuses, reset circuit breakers, etc.
- Remove clamps, locks, etc.
- Sort out control circuits

Beside these common troubles there are many other problems which we encounter in a motoring operation. But with proper precautions and correct methodological tests, these troubles can be sorted out.

7. *Conclusions*

Motors play an extremely vital role in the industry. The sheer diversity of motors has given rise to innumerable applications and significantly reduced human efforts. The report discusses different kinds of induction motors, why energy losses occur and what corrective steps can be taken. This is followed by a discussion on different kinds of testing of industrial motors and what troubleshooting measures can be taken to solve the problems of motor failure. It also highlights the scope and applications of industrial motors. It is hoped that this report will serve as a ready reference for those who wish to understand this wonderful invention industrial motor in a better manner.

ASSIGNMENTS

1. The management of the Bharat Cloth Mills, 11 Kasturba Gandhi Marg, New Delhi-110001 finds that its sales have been declining for the last three years. It has appointed a committee to look into this problem and write a report suggesting measures to improve the sales. Assuming that you are the Convener of the Committee write this report which is to be submitted to the General Manager. Invent the necessary details.
2. Assume that you are the Chairman of a Committee appointed by the President of the Employees Union of your company to look into the complaints against the functioning of the canteen on the

premises and suggest measures for improvement. Write a report containing your analysis and recommendations.

3. National Steel Corporation, 41 Nehru Marg, New Delhi-110001 wishes to run a programme for training its engineers (about 90) in report writing. Assuming that, as Director of Training you have been deputed to examine the suitability of running this programme at the Indian Institute of Management, Bangalore during the ensuing summer vacation, write this report for the Personnel Manager of the Corporation. Your report should contain specific information about the availability of staff, facilities for transport, board and lodging, recreation, library, medical facilities, and an estimate of expenditure.

4. India Electronics Limited, 437 Ashokpura, Bharatpur are considering a proposal to establish a television manufacturing factory at Faridabad. Some of the factors that would influence their decision are: manpower, transport, market, climate, construction cost, education, etc. You as a senior electronics engineer have been asked to study the suitability of this town for the establishment of the factory. Write a report for the Managing Director, incorporating the results of your study.

5. Study the following Table showing the number of vehicles produced during 2003-2007, at the manufacturing plant of a company at Gurgaon. Write an informational report indicating the trend of production.

Year	*Car*	*Bus*	*Truck*
2003	3249	1168	210
2004	4201	1020	360
2005	6240	1475	735
2006	2275	1300	610
2007	7315	215	875

6. The Director of Collegiate Education, Rajasthan, Jaipur has been concerned about the poor academic standards and mismanagement of the affairs of B.S. Degree College, Sikar. You as Deputy Director of Education have been asked to enquire into the matter and to submit a report to the Director. Write a report keeping in view the following:

   1. Programmes – BA., B.Sc., & B.Com.
   2. Admissions policy
   3. Number of students 2200
      Number of teachers 40
   4. Quality of teaching
   5. Hostel facilities
   6. Physical facilities such as classroom space, lab-equipment, library, etc.
   7. Facilities for games and sports, etc.

8. State of discipline
9. Role of Students' Union
10. General administration
11. Financial resources.

7. The management of your company proposes to establish a school near the factory site for the benefit of its staff. As Public Relations Officer you have been asked to study its feasibility and submit a report to the Personnel Manager, specially referring to the following: finance, teaching staff, library, games and sports, construction cost, etc. Write this report.
8. Assuming that you are the Regional Representative of the Central Institute of Environmental Studies, New Delhi, write a formal report to the Director of the Institute on the problem of air pollution in an urban area of your region. You should make specific recommendations to minimise air pollution.
9. Bharat Textile Mill, Kanpur manufactures several kinds of cotton and synthetic cloth. For the last five years there has been a gradual decline in profits owing to various causes including fall in sales. As Marketing Manager you have been asked by the Managing Director to investigate into the causes and make suitable recommendations. Write this report.
10. The Government of Bihar had sanctioned Rs. 5 crore for drought relief work for district Hazaribagh in April 2007. This money has been spent on the following:

    (i) Provision of work to landless labourers on afforestation, road construction, digging wells, etc.
    (ii) Free distribution of food grains to the disabled and the aged.
    (iii) Distribution of seeds, fertilisers and fodder at subsidised rates.
    (iv) Supply of free lunch to school, children.
    (v) Supply of drinking water.
    (vi) Supply of essential commodities through fair price shops.
    (vii) Free distribution of medicines.

    As Collector, Hazaribagh, write a report to the Secretary, Home Department, Government of Bihar, Patna containing the details of expenditure and specifying the quantum of work done under various categories mentioned above. Illustrate your answer with suitable graphs, charts, etc., inventing such details as you think necessary for the purpose.
11. The management of Haryana Cotton Mills, Siwani, has announced a new bonus and production-linked incentive scheme. Most of the employees are not satisfied with this scheme. As Personnel Manager you have investigated the causes of dissatisfaction. Now write a memo report to the Managing Director summarising your findings and recommending suitable changes in the scheme.
12. Assume that you have just returned from a conference on sales promotion to which you were deputed by your company. Write a memo to your immediate boss, reporting to him the important matters discussed at the conference and indicating the significance of the conclusions arrived at.
13. A company wishes to modernise its office and accounting procedure and it has written to you for information on a scheme introduced by your company for this purpose. In reply, as Personnel

Manager, write a letter report to your counterpart highlighting the main features of this scheme and describing the steps taken for its successful implementation.

14. The following Table contains data regarding faculty-wise student enrolment during the last three academic years.

Table

Student Enrolment; Faculty-wise

Faculty	*2004-05 Enrolment %*	*2005-06 Enrolment %*	*2006-07 Enrolment %*
Arts	35.6	35.5	35.4
Science	19.6	19.1	18.2
Commerce	16.5	17.1	17.7
Education	3.3	3.2	3.0
Engineering	3.8	4.0	4.1
Medicine	4.5	4.3	4.6
Agriculture	1.2	1.2	1.3
Veterinary Science	4.3	4.3	4.3
Law	5.7	5.8	5.8
Others	5.5	5.5	5.6
Total	100.00	100.00	100.00

As an Education Officer of the University Grants Commission, Bahadur Shah Zafar Marg, New Delhi, write a letter report to the Secretary, Department of Education, Government of India,- Shastri Bhawan, New Delhi, containing your analysis and conclusions about the general trend of student enrolment in the country.

15. As Personnel Manager of Dynamic Tools Manufacturing Co. Ltd., Bombay you have been deputed to investigate the causes of frequent strikes in the company's factory at Nasik and to suggest preventive measures. Write a memo report to the Managing Director incorporating your findings and recommendations.

Chapter 14

STYLE

A report is a verbal structure, and style is the way we select and arrange the elements of structure. So to attain a style that works, we need to know what to select and how to arrange the selected material. In specific terms, a report consists of words, phrases, clauses, and sentences which form paragraphs and the paragraphs constitute the text of a report. The marks of punctuation and graphic aids enhance comprehension and sharpen understanding but these are outside the scope of discussion in this chapter.

We propose to discuss style from a practical point of view – how to attain an effective report writing style – and not to enter into a theoretical discussion of what has already been written, as is done in literature courses. What we say here is applicable with certain modification, to other forms of professional writing also. We cannot of course give you a complete list of do's and don'ts for every writing task but we hope that the discussion which follows would help you write more effectively First, let us look at the importance and features of professional writing.

14.1 IMPORTANCE OF PROFESSIONAL WRITING

Professional writing is an extension of your responsibility. It is hard work, requiring enormous patience and rigorous practice. The ability to communicate effectively is one of the greatest assets anyone can acquire, but the most common and perhaps the greatest communication problem today is that many people are unaware that they lack communicative ability. The organisations also are unable to realise what a heavy price they have to pay because of miscommunication.* Communication inefficiency exercises negative effects on productivity and staff relations, and can result in cancelled orders, strikes, loss of customers, frequent complaints, etc.

---

* If we read what a person has written but fail to understand properly what he means, it is a case of miscommunication.

14.2 FEATURES OF WRITTEN COMMUNICATION

At this stage, it would be helpful to review briefly the main features of written communication. Often a written communication is the only link between the writer and the reader and thus it determines the reader's attitude towards the writer. Once it leaves the writer's hands, for all practical purposes he has no control over it. He cannot clarify or amplify what he has written, neither can he add or delete. Further, in written communication there is no effective substitute for gestures, facial expressions and modulation of voice which make oral communication vibrant.

To be an effective writer, a professional should cultivate certain habits, attitudes and qualities of mind. Let us briefly examine some of the important ones:

- Visualise what you wish to say. If the picture you want to communicate is clear to you, the words would then automatically follow to express it. Remember, clear thinking and clear writing go together. Adequate preparation – organisation of data and their analysis, generalisations based on them, and the plan of writing as manifested in your outline – would certainly help you in attaining clarity of thought.
- Prepare the first draft without caring much for the mechanics of writing. Attention to such details disturbs the flow of thought. The sole concern at this stage should be to present your ideas.
- Stop when you have finished saying what you wanted to say. There is no need to add the so-called concluding sentence. Remember, a professional writes to express and not to impress.
- Revise the draft carefully, this time taking care of all the required details. And have the courage to delete a word, phrase, sentence or paragraph which does not add meaning to the point under discussion.
- Approach the problem with a scientist's objectivity, detachment and passion for truth. This would help you make your writing plain, concise and precise.
- Don't belabour a point unnecessarily, to keep your writing crisp and sharp.

14.3 CHOICE OF WORDS AND PHRASES

Choosing the right words and phrases is the first important step in writing. Words have different meanings in different contexts. Their polysemantic nature makes the task of selection appear to be suitable in the first instance. To perceive their aptness requires a sophisticated sense of language use. Constant concern for the selection of the right word at the right place and an unfailing desire to extract meaning is helpful in attaining an effective style. We give below in the form of 'Do's' and 'Don'ts', a few helpful hints.

We are however not suggesting that the words which we have termed as abstract, long, general or unfamiliar should never be used; in fact they may be the best words in certain contexts. Sometimes their use may be advisable for variety.

Do's

(i) Prefer concrete words to abstract words. A concrete word permits a limited interpretation and conveys a more definite meaning. Its meaning is generally fixed. A few examples are names of persons, number as words, dates, etc., words pointing to one specific person (e.g. I, he, she, etc.). Concrete words tend to be more forceful, direct and exact than their abstract counterparts. Abstract words have a tendency to be general and vague. Look at the use of wards in the original sentences given below and notice how the suggested revision improves communication.

Original Sentence	*Revised Sentence*
(a) Fuel tank deformation was present.	The fuel tank was deformed.
(b) There is adequate access to the site for men and materials.	Men and materials can reach the site easily.
(c) The reason for the popularity of slides is the simplicity of their preparation.	Slides are popular because they are easy to prepare.
(d) Icarus failed because he did not fully understand the phy sical and operational environment of manned flight.	Icarus failed because the waxen wings melted.
(e) Accident frequency depends on the adequacy of roadway visibility.	Accident frequency depends on how well the road can be seen.

Words such as 'nature,' 'condition,' 'character,' 'situation,' 'progress,' 'ideas,' 'excellence' convey abstract meaning and yet we cannot avoid using them. We can make them less abstract by providing a proper context. For example, 'his ideas' is less abstract than 'ideas'. Similarly 'human nature' is less abstract than 'nature'.

(ii) Prefer specific words to general words. The use of specific words makes the writing clearer and immediately creates an image in the mind of the reader. Often specificity and concreteness go together. A few examples are given below:

General	*Specific*
countenance	face
reside	stay
volume	book
employ	use
compensation	pay
activate	start
ramification	branch
conflagration	fire
endeavour	try
demonstrate	show
discontinue	stop

component	part
appellation	name
terminate	end
accentuate	stress
aggregate	total

The above list is only a small sample to show the point we are emphasising.

Let us now see how the replacement of a general word by a specific word given in brackets makes a sentence more effective:

(i) The company has brought out forty *publications* this year (books).

(ii) They have *produced* a book on style. (written)

(iii) She has *developed* a new gas lighter. (designed)

(iv) He has prepared a plan of action after a *critical examination* of all factors. (study)

(v) *Transfer* the liquid into the beaker. (pour)

Modifiers of nouns and verbs tend to be vague and subjective. They generally convey the judgement or the impression of the writer. Beware of them in your writing. Even innocent looking words such as *good, big, small* can bite or embarrass you! An example would suffice. 'The tests indicate that the equipment is good'. This sentence hardly conveys anything. It can be revised thus:

> The performance and fatigue tests indicate that the × 258 coupling will withstand loads 75 per cent above the specified requirements, far beyond the life expectancy of the aircraft.

Another culprit is the *-tion* word formed from a verb:

Phrases	*Verbs*
make an investigation	investigate
have a confrontation	confront
prepare a formulation	formulate
make an application	apply
tender resignation	resign

Now notice how the revised version of the following sentence conveys the meaning more effectively:

> We solicit any recommendations that you wish to make and you may rest assured that any such recommendations will be given our careful consideration as to the utilisation thereof.

Revised version: Please give us your suggestions. We would carefully consider them.

(iii) Prefer plain and familiar words to long and unfamiliar words. Inexperienced writers often believe that pomposity is the hallmark of an effective writer. They are therefore tempted to use long and unfamiliar words instead of plain words, which are short and familiar to the reader. One should not deliberately use words that may compel the reader to consult the dictionary frequently. The use of plain words saves time – the writer's, the typist's and the reader's. The list given below would give you an idea of what we are suggesting.

Long and Unfamiliar	*Plain and Familiar*
effectuate	effect
facilitate	ease
expedite	hurry up
initiate	start
utilisation	use
resource centre	library
articulate	pronounce
viable	practical
metropolis	city
recapitulate	sum up
accentuate	stress
discern	see
appropriate	suitable
optimum	best
endeavour	try
transmit	send
personnel	workers, staff
subsequent to	later, after
purchase	buy
verbose	wordy
commence	begin
dwell	live
envisage	foresee
residence	house

In a speech written for him, President F.D. Roosevelt changed the sentence 'We are endeavouring to construct a more inclusive society' to 'We are going to make a country in which no one is left out'. On another occasion the President replaced 'Terminate the illumination' by 'Turn out the lights'. Both these examples show how plain words make the message more effective.

Unless you are alert, high-flying and fancy words may completely drown your meaning. Notice how in the following example a simple, straightforward message is completely lost. A famous lecturer was asked the formula of success in public speaking.

'Well', he said, in promulgating your esoteric cogitations and articulating superficial, sentimental and psychological observations, beware of platitudinous ponderosity. Let your extemporaneous decantations and unpremeditated expatiations have intelligibility and veracious veracity without rodomontade and thrasonical bombast. Sedulously avoid all polysyllabic profundity, pussillanimous vacuity, pestiferous profanity and similar transgressions. Or to put it a bit differently, he concluded, talk simply, naturally, and above all, don't use big words.

Don'ts

(i) *Avoid cliches*: A cliche is a faded word or a phrase which has lost its effectiveness because of overuse. When it is first coined, it is fresh and vigorous and conveys the meaning vividly. With the passage of time it loses sharpness and ceases to exercise the desired impact.

Very often when you start writing, such words and phrases would come to your mind and if you are not alert, find a place in the text of your report and thus weaken it. Although cliches are not necessarily unsuitable or wrong, their frequent use would tire the discriminating reader. In the beginning you may have some difficulty in recognising cliches. Soon, however, you would discover that phrases such as 'worthwhile areas', 'inter-disciplinary techniques', 'broader fields', the 'long-range view', mean little or merely serve as substitute for real ideas. You may feel tempted to use them only because they readily occur to you. The following extract makes excessive use of cliches. Notice how tiresome it is to read it:

Original extract. He *left no stone unturned* in his efforts to achieve tenure. Finally, *a sadder but a wiser man*, he learned that *in this day and age*, tenured professorships are *few and far between*. His campaign *ground to a halt*, and at subsequent faculty meetings, he was *conspicuous by his absence*. He concluded his farewell to his students with these *words of wisdom,* 'Last but not least, follow this advice: do as I say, not as I do.'

Suggested revision. He tried strenuously to gain tenure. But finally he became aware that few tenured professorships are available. He ceased his efforts and stopped attending faculty meetings. In his farewell to his students, he exhorted them not to follow his career as an example.

Some cliches commonly used are given below:

food for thought, crowning glory, part and parcel, sum and substance, the vast majority, burning question, level best, spare no efforts, overriding considerations, desperate need, discuss threadbare, teeming millions, leave no stone unturned, untiring efforts, eminently satisfactory, kind perusal, favourable consideration, resource personnel, hotbed of politics, explore every avenue, iron hand of the law, day in and day out, awake to one's duty, heart and soul, melting pot, etc.

Here is a caution. There are a few cliches that communicate an idea so clearly that it would be difficult to think of a substitute. The familiar phrases like 'a drop in the ocean', 'wear and tear', 'practice what you preach' are hard to improve upon.

(ii) *Avoid excessive use of jargon*: Webster's Seventh New Collegiate Dictionary defines jargon as 'the technical terminology or characteristic idiom of a special activity or group.' Every group of specialists has developed a set of highly specialised terms; yet these are the very words that cause readers a lot of difficulty. Communication of technical matter in non-technical language is not easy but the ability to do so can be acquired with practice. For report writing it is essential to acquire this ability, for the reader of your report may not be a specialist in the subject. Only an inexperienced writer would think that the use of jargon is the mark of intellectual superiority. If he does not check the habit of using jargon, he would meet the fate of other jargonists. His writing would be weak and unintelligible and tire the reader soon. However, remember that every profession has its jargon and it would be difficult to communicate to fellow professionals without its use. Jargon saves time but this is not the only reason which makes our writing jargon-ridden. Jargon is sometimes used to nourish one's ego and enable a group to speak in terms that impress or mystify the outsider. Its use is also justified on the ground that complex thought cannot be expressed without the use of highly technical language. But the fact is that just as lethargy prompts us to use cliches, false pride impels us to use jargon.

Let your writing be as jargon-free as possible. Try to use words that are more widely understood so that those who do not belong to the specialist group are also able to follow you. Mach-2, for example, is a jargon in aeronautics. But it would be wrong to assume that it is universally understood. If you represent an aircraft company and are trying to impress the shareholders, you may say, 'We are designing a plane to fly at speeds beyond Mach- 2'. Would it not be better if you said instead, 'We are designing a plane to fly over two times the speed of sound?'

Ours is an age of specialisation, which is taking place not only in science and technology, but also in social sciences. Decipher the meaning of the following sentence!

'They ameliorate the stresses of inter-ethnic situations and provide contents of acculturation under relatively permissive conditions.'

The following three general rules will help you in using jargon:

(i) When a word or a phrase from the general vocabulary expresses your thought as well and as precisely as a specialised term, always use the general term.
(ii) Even if the specialised term is more precise and economical than the general term, do not use it unless you are sure that the reader would understand it.
(iii) When you have to use the specialised term repeatedly, define it carefully at its first appearance.

We now give a few examples to show how the meaning becomes clear if the jargon is removed.

Jargon-ridden. The biota exhibited a one hundred per cent mortality response.

Jargon-free. All the plants and animals died.

Jargon-ridden. The responsibility of a person involved in pedagogical pursuits is to impart knowledge to those sent to him for instruction.

Jargon-free. The teacher's job is to instruct students.

Now we give an example that shows how communication completely fails because of the use of jargon.

A plumber discovered that hydrochloric acid was good for cleaning clogged drains. He sent his suggestions to the Bureau of Standards.

'The efficacy of hydrochloric acid,' the Bureau wrote back, 'is indisputable, but the ionic residues are incompatible with metallic permanence.'

The plumber replied, 'Thank you, I thought it was a good idea too.'

Finally someone at the Bureau wrote 'Don't use hydrochloric acid! It corrodes the pipes.'

One more small point. Language is in a state of flux. Among the changes that you would notice all around you is the tendency to form new words with suffixes '-wise', '-ise'. Often these suffixes rob a word of its exact meaning. For example, 'They finalised the contract' may be taken to mean:

(i) They put the contract into its final form.

(ii) They completed the writing of the contract.

(iii) They agreed on the terms of the contract.

(iv) They accepted and signed the contract.

What meaning does the following sentence convey: *We are factoryising our farms. Turning our farms into factories? Setting up factories on farms? Organising farms as though they were factories?*

Look at the challenge '-wise' offers:

- We can do very little about this instrument, resolution-wise.
- These are far enough, atomic number-wise, to produce big changes.
- There are not many things instrumentation-wise a man can do.

Such words foster woolly thinking and vague writing and impede communication. Beware of them.

(iii) *Avoid using foreign words and phrases*: Foreign words and phrases, like jargon, are also often used to impress and mystify the reader or to parade one's scholarship. Some writers believe that their use would make the writing dignified. Thus, instead of 'see above' they use 'vide supra' and for 'the justification for', 'raison d'etre'. To keep your writing simple, use plain English for foreign words and phrases.

In report writing, the use of accepted abbreviations is unavoidable. However, certain abbreviations derived from foreign words and phrases, masked as time-savers such as op.cit., loc. cit., create a lot of confusion, specially if the report has a large number of references. Even though they save the labour of both the author and the printer. They demand extra work from the reader. Abbreviations like, e.g., i.e., vs., viz., am., pm., etc. are well understood and you need not avoid them.

(iv) *Avoid redundancy*: Redundancy is the part cf a message that can be eliminated without loss of information. It may be either the use of unnecessary words or needless repetition of an idea. It has been well said that a sentence should have no unnecessary words, just as a drawing should have no unnecessary lines, and a machine no unnecessary parts. Extra words do not confer extra value to the thought.

To win the race in this highly competitive world we need an alert and agile mind. A ponderous mind breeds, among other things, redundancy in writing. Cut out the unnecessary words from your writing and see how the thought begins to shine clearly. If you prune your language with patience and discernment, your writing would automatically become pointed and sharp. Unfortunately, superfluity is the most common cause of woolliness in expression and yet it is most easily avoidable.

First, let us look at some of the common instances of superfluity. In the phrases given below the superfluous words are italicised; watch out for such expressions in your writing: *basic* fundamentals, refer *back*, consensus of *opinion*, repeated *again*, returned *back*, advance *forward*, *humorous* joke, retreat *backwards*, *detailed* perusal, *fast* speedreaders, alone *by oneself*, true *fact*, in *point of fact*, *close* proximity, *self*-confessed, *absolutely* essential, *actual* experience, at *the* present *time*, *completely* eliminated, few *in number*, *past* history, red in *colour*, until *such time as*, adequate *enough*, collect *together*, *exactly* identical, brief *in duration*, *one* and the same, *make* a mention *of*, *it is* often *the case that*, resume *again*, throughout the *entire* month, *advance* planning, *advance* warning, attached *together*, cooperate *together*, enclosed *herewith*, merge *together*, *mutual* cooperation, state *the point* that, *undertake* a study *of*, *as to* whether, *consequent* results, *duly* noted, *main* essentials, modem methods *of today*, *more* preferable, report *back*, recall *back*.

But the story does not end here. Notice how certain innocent looking words cause redundancy. These words are highlighted in the following sentences.

(i) *Located* at the top of the transformer are the line terminals.

(ii) The preliminary studies required *a total of* 240 man hours.

(iii) During *the month of* July there has been no complaint.

(iv) Total and *complete* protection of all control components is impracticable under all conditions.

(v) I *wish to take this opportunity* to acknowledge the help of my laboratory assistant.

(vi) The parts *which are* in the warehouse can be shipped immediately. Those which are still in process will be ready in three weeks.

Another type of superfluity is the use of roundabout expressions.

In such cases mere deletion does not improve the sentence; rewriting is required as shown in the following examples:

(i) It is not believed that the proposed design will meet all the required specifications based on the previous test experience obtained in the laboratory.

Revised version: Lab tests indicate that the proposed design will not meet all requirements.

(ii) Unemployment decline, which has continued over the past four months, indicates that the recession has bottomed and the upturn in the economy is a fact.

Revised version: The strong reversal of unemployment trends indicates an improvement in the economy.

(iii) It is found empirically that the disintegration of a radioactive element follows a simple decay law which states that the rate of decay is proportional to the amount of the radioactive element present.

Revised version: It is found empirically that the rate of disintegration of a radioactive element is proportional to the amount of the radioactive element present.

Sometimes the change of passive voice into active voice reduces the number of words and also improves the sentence. A few such examples follow:

Passive Voice: The decision was made by the supervisor to call in the workers for overtime.

Active Voice: The supervisor decided to call in the workers for overtime.

Passive Voice: A complaint by Shri T.R. Ghode was voiced to the personnel department.

Active Voice: Shri T.R. Ghode complained to the personnel department.

Passive Voice: The satellites of Mars were discovered by Hall.

Active Voice: Hall discovered the satellites of Mars.

Passive Voice: Oxidation tendency is also accelerated by the presence of metals that act as catalysts.

Active Voice: The presence of metals that act as catalysts also accelerates oxidation.

Passive Voice: Excellent recovery in terms of body weight and long-term survival is afforded to lethally irradiated mice by postirradiation injection of isologous bone marrow.

Active Voice: Lethally irradiated mice make an excellent recovery, in terms of body weight and long-term survival, if after irradiation they receive an injection of isologous bone marrow.

Whenever possible use active voice instead of passive. It is wrong to believe that in professional writing the use of passive voice should be preferred. In fact its use increases the chance of grammatical mistakes, starts long trains of prepositional phrases, fosters round-about expressions and encourages vagueness.

Now let us lead you to a dense forest of words; hunt up the meaning if you can!

> In order for us to understand the details of the history of our attempts to interpret the complicated phenomenon of heat in its evolution from the now extinct caloric concept to the accepted kinetic theory, there are several alternative approaches all of which we must pursue if we are to understand the nature of the phenomenon.

Here is an effort to improve. Examine to what extent the meaning has been recovered:

> Heat is a complicated phenomenon. Physicists have now discarded the idea of a caloric fluid and have generally adopted the kinetic theory. A review of the earlier concepts, however, will help us to understand the nature of heat.

Faraday once wrote: There are three necessary steps in useful research – the first to begin it, the second to end it, and the third to publish it.

Notice how, in the parody that follows, the author's thought is buried:

> Having considered the ultimate and immediately attainable objects which are the focus of rationally directed and effectively integrated scientific effort in the field of original research, it appears philosophically and economically, for the purpose of effective classification, possible to allocate the position under three main divisions, so far as oversimplification is not involved. The first necessity is that of a logically directed inception or coordinated-progress from a state of preliminary consideration to that which may be regarded as an initiation of planned and active

effort along lines previously recognised as possessing potential possibilities of progressive advance. So long as the attack on the problems, visualised as a coordinated whole, yields results which seem commensurate with the expenditure of available resources and effort, without any undue dispersion of effort... Let us stop here; the message is clear.

14.4 SENTENCE STRUCTURE AND LENGTH

The normal order of elements in a statement is subject, verb, object or complement. Each of these may be qualified or modified by adjectives or adverbs. Adjectives generally precede the subject, object or complement they qualify whereas adverbs may be placed anywhere in the sentence. They are movable and their placing determines what they modify. That is why handling adverbs requires greater vigilance. See how the placing of the word 'only' changes the whole meaning of the following sentence:

- Only an experiment can prove this theory.
- An experiment can prove this theory only.
- An experiment can only prove this theory.

Statements can be expanded by the addition of prepositional or adverbial phrases or by further information added by phrases or sentences beginning with coordinating or subordinating conjunctions.

Apart from statements there are other types of sentences such as question: word questions, yes/no questions, commands and exclamations. In your report most of the sentences would be statements. These have been traditionally classified into three types of sentences, namely, simple, compound and complex. A simple sentence consists of one clause. A compound sentence consists of two or more clauses joined together by coordinating conjunctions. A complex sentence contains more than one clause joined together by subordinating conjunctions. Reading comprehension is hampered by too large a proportion of complex or compound sentences. We cannot of course give you a precise figure to indicate this proportion. What you need is to have a sense of proportion, balance and harmony. Other considerations would come in, such as sentence length and variety. If you find in your writing too many compound and complex sentences, you must pause and examine whether their number can be reduced.

Here is an example of how reading can be made easier by simplifying the sentences:

Original Version

The net result of this desire to study the motion and physical characteristics of an unknown body moving through an atmosphere whose properties are vaguely known has been a kind of statistical study of the interaction between the meteor and the medium which fortunately provides sufficient accuracy to give a good, quantitative picture of the thermodynamic structure of the atmosphere, i.e. pressure, density, and the temperature as a function of the height.

Suggested Revision

We cannot describe the precise motion and physical characteristics of an unknown body moving through a vaguely known atmosphere. Therefore, this investigation must depend on a statistical study of the interaction between meteor and medium. Fortunately, the method measures with ample accuracy how the pressure, density and temperature may vary with atmospheric height.

Be careful however not to go to the other extreme of writing only short and simple sentences. If you do so, you may find yourself writing something as follows:

> Ramesh did not do well with the Company at first. Later he managed to succeed very well. Finally he became the Managing Director of the Company.

A complex sentence such as the following would remove the unpleasant jerky effect of the simple sentences:

> Although Ramesh did not do well at first, he was later very successful, finally becoming the Managing Director of the Company.

There are several types of statements which would find a place in your writing. We may classify them on the basis of their functions into the following three categories: *expository* sentences express thoughts in concise, clear and accurate terms; *descriptive* sentences portray things; and *narrative* sentences establish a sequence of events or stages in a process or a procedure. While writing be clear about what function you want your sentence to perform. Let there be no mix-up.

In general, it has been found that short and simple sentences are more effective. They promote easy reading. Long sentences on the other hand, though not necessarily bad, are hard to construct and harder to understand. It is difficult to suggest how long a sentence should be; however generally sentences containing more than 35 words create difficulty. The following two considerations should guide you in determining the length of your sentence: (i) complexity of thought being expressed and (ii) reader's ability to grasp and concentrate. Think of a sentence as a mathematical equation. Extraneous words in a sentence are as confusing as extraneous factors in an equation.

Bear the following points in mind while constructing your sentences:

(i) Don't use a word which does not perform any function. We have given a number of examples in our discussion on redundancy in 14.3.

(ii) Provide the desired emphasis by placing words/phrases in the proper order. Look at the following sentences for change of emphasis.

(a) Overtime went up as a result of the recent strike.

Revised: As a result of the recent strike overtime went up.

(b) Components are soaked here after being washed in cold water.

Revised: After being washed in cold water components are soaked here.

(c) A new product must be experimentally developed to be successful.

Revised: To be successful a new produce must be experimentally developed.

(d) The computer will cost Rs. ten lakh but save Rs. 50,000 annually on administration.

Revised: The computer will save Rs. 50,000 annually on administration and cost only Rs. ten lakhs.

(iii) Avoid monotony by varying the structure and length of your sentences. A piece of writing containing a number of sentences with expressions such as , 'It is observed that ...' 'It is seen that ..:', 'It is found that...', etc., would indeed make the reader yawn with boredom. Among other things variety lends freshness to writing and keeps the interest of the reader alive. One thought can be expressed in a number of ways:

- After collecting the data he wrote the report.
- Having collected the data he wrote the report.
- He collected the data and wrote the report.
- When the data were collected he wrote the report.
- He wrote the report after having collected the data.
- He wrote the report after the collection of data was over.

To attain variety:

- Use judiciously a mixture of simple, compound and complex sentences.
- Place a short sentence in the midst of several long ones.
- Occasionally begin a sentence with a verb or a phrase instead of a subject.

(iv) Read your sentences aloud to discover whether they are too long or too short. And then make the necessary changes. This method would also help you to find out whether there is balance and harmony in what you have written.

14.5 PARAGRAPH STRUCTURE AND LENGTH

A paragraph is a group of closely related sentences that deal with a thought or a division of thought. The thought is usually expressed in a sentence called the **topic sentence**. The other sentences explain, or develop the thought, compare and contrast it with other thoughts, providing details, illustrations or additional information.

The topic sentence may be placed in the beginning, the middle or at the end of a paragraph. Sometimes it does not appear at all and is merely implied. We may classify the other sentences in a paragraph into the following four functional categories:

(i) *Introducers*. They establish the topic focus of the paragraph and often provide a smooth transition from the preceding paragraph.

(ii) *Developers*. They support, develop and clarify the central thought.

(iii) *Modulators*. They provide smooth transition between the sentences of a paragraph whenever there is a shift or change in the tone or viewpoint.

(iv) *Terminators*. They conclude the discussion or summarise the contents of the paragraph, signalling the completion of one aspect or stage of the presentation.

The length of a paragraph depends upon the nature of thought and eye-relief for the reader. If the thought is simple, it would obviously take lesser number of sentences for development. On the other hand, a paragraph dealing with a complex thought would be comparatively longer. Remember that long paragraphs are not easy to read. The reader's attention flags if he has to read a paragraph running into, say, more than a page. He also finds it difficult to keep the central idea in mind if the paragraph is long.

So a skilful writer breaks the text of a report into short paragraphs as far as possible. There are several opportunities to do so. Some of these include the beginning of a different category of facts, the new phase, of a procedure, a fresh point of view, etc. An analysis of professional writing shows that most well-written paragraphs have two to ten sentences.

In writing a report, proposal, letter, etc., it would be advisable for you to follow the established practice of placing the topic sentence first or soon after the transition. You should not keep your reader in suspense about what you are going to say. To check the effectiveness of a paragraph take the following steps:

- Ensure that the location of the topic sentence gives proper emphasis to the thought.
- Examine the transitional devices, if any, to see whether they smoothly lead on to the new thought.
- Check whether all the sentences, deal with the topic under discussion.
- Ensure that all the sentences are properly linked and logically arranged.

14.6 FINAL DRAFT

We close the discussion on style with three ideas which would help you to prepare the final draft.

First, whatever be the form of writing, provide signposts for the reader. Pause and tell him what you have done and what you propose to do. This would enormously help the reader. He would be able to follow the line of thought you are pursuing and prepare himself for what is to follow. The devices that you use for this purpose (a sentence or sometimes even a short paragraph) are like traffic signs along a highway.

Second, view the style of your writing in totality. You may sometimes have to sacrifice one quality for the sake of another. Weigh and consider what serves you best. 'No surrender to words' should be your motto. The primacy of thought must be maintained. In practice you would observe that a good piece of writing contains many qualities and that the removal of only one flaw improves your writing in several ways.

Third, no clear writing is ever achieved without rewriting. Let the process of revision follow this pattern:

- Correct mechanical errors such as wrong punctuation, misspelling, improper capitalisation, etc.
- Bring your writing to the stylistic convention of the form to which it belongs.
- Add, delete or rearrange the material to achieve greater clarity and coherence.

These stages of revision are, however, not mutually exclusive.

14.7 READABILITY FORMULAS

It has been suggested that to find out whether a written communication is effective one should use a readability formula. A number of such formulas have been devised to measure the reading difficulty levels in concrete terms. These are based on the analysis of a wide range of written material. One such formula was devised in 1969 by G.H. McLaughlin* called Smog Index.

This formula is as follows:

Readability Grade = 3 + square root to nearest integer of the number of three syllable words per 30 sentences.

The Smog Grade, significantly enough, is based, on 90-100 per cent comprehension unlike the other formulas** which use 50-75 per cent comprehension levels.

All these formulas suggest that simple and short words and sentences make writing more readable but they do not indicate how one can improve one's writing. Further, there is no clear-cut correlation between readability and the quality of writing. They are therefore of limited use. At best they can help a professional at the time of revision to improve his writing.

ASSIGNMENTS

1. The following extracts have a number of roundabout expressions. Rewrite to make them direct and plain.
   - (i) After the completion of this methodology and protocol, a conference was held.
   - (ii) The initiative and enthusiasm requisite to ultimate success of the programme must perforce come from the employees.
   - (iii) The amplifier has been used continuously, but the reliability of operation that is desired has not been achieved.
   - (iv) It was evident to the research team that when a driver is becoming familiar with a strange automobile, any tendency to collision involvement would seem to be enhanced during an adjustment period.
   - (v) In an effort to consolidate purchases of consumable goods by different departments, the chief buyer should screen all purchase requisitions for the same with a view to reducing the quantity of orders for similar items.
   - (vi) The objectives of this report are: to investigate into the current organisation and existing procedures applied to stores control, to generate recommendations for streamlining and to heighten working productivity.

---

* McLaughlin 'Smog-Grading — A New Readability Formula', *Journal of Reading*, pp. 639-646, May, 1965.

** Rudolph Flesch's Reading Ease Formula discussed in "A New Readability Yardstick", *Journal of Applied Psychology*, Vol. 32(3) pp. 221-233, June, 1948,

E. Dale and J.S. Chale's 'A Formula for Predicting Readability' in *Educational Research Bulletin*, Vol. 27, pp. 11-20, Jan. 21 and, pp. 31-54, Feb. 38, 1948.

Robert Gunning's Fog Index Formula in *The Techniques of Clear Writing*, New York; McGraw Hill, 1952. rev. ed. 1968.

(vii) The preceding chapter has attempted to develop a fundamental conception of exposition as a kind of writing concerned with the orderly communication of ideas in accordance with a preconceived purpose and plan and of a report as a specialised form of exposition in which the use it is to serve determines almost everything – plan, scale and method of treatment, and especially the amount of interpretive comment required.

(viii) A pioneer ecologist pointed out one time that although the earth is 25,000 miles around and weighs billions and trillions of tons, almost all the life-supporting elements are contained in a "skin" or thin layer top soil and vegetation that's less than a hundred feet thick anywhere on earth and, over much of the planet's surface, only a few inches thick, or nonexistent. Yet, this incredibly thin 'skin' of soil supports all the terrestrial plant life which absorbs the sunlight which activates the formation of carbohydrates which feed the animals (including you and me) which convert the carbohydrates into protein which is the basic stuff of animal life (including yours and mine).

(ix) Considerable risks are entailed in building a computer system around instrumentation that is not already invented, manufactured, and well-tested. Much of the grief that has been experienced to date has come from situations in which management decided to install a system that required the use of new types of devices that were almost ready for use – only to find that almost could be a long time in coming.

(x) A proper balance can and must necessarily be established in course of time between the activities of any particular cooperation and that of all our operations together and as I see the picture at the moment no better way or even as good a way has yet been advanced as to ask those members of each organisation who have the same functional relationship to get together and decide for themselves what should be done where coordination is necessary giving such a group the power to deal with the problem where it is felt that the power can be constructively applied.

(xi) In order that the accounts office may achieve quicker settlement of outstanding accounts, and thus maintain more harmonious relationships with suppliers, it would be appreciated if the officials of all departments would henceforth process all their purchase requirements through the purchasing department.

It is known and accepted that this procedure has been followed in most cases; however, owing to the occurrence of certain exceptions, it is hoped that there will be considerable saving of time and avoidance of duplication if all purchase requirements are henceforth processed by the Purchase Department.

(xii) Energy, which makes work possible, is used up every time we move our limbs, or every time the heart beats, or the lungs expand, and this activity continues night and day, maintaining as an added task, the temperature we need to keep warm and alive, and expending in this operation enough equivalent power to bring a large measure of cold water to the boil.

(xiii) If we wish to discover facts we may use our eyes to observe the world around us or use them to search in books for facts and information which have been collected for our benefit for over thousands of years, for the world's knowledge is largely contained in the millions of books in its various libraries, ready for the eager research worker but not prepared to give up that information without some effort on his part, particularly the effort of studying the best ways of extracting that information from the bewildering mass of print.

(xiv) The growing demand for small, efficient motor cars has led to the development of simpler methods of lubrication, transmission, and structure, three factors which have an important bearing on the durability and life-span of the car. The lubrication is increasingly carried out by the owner, who does not wish to wriggle about with a grease gun to deal with twenty or more greasing points, but welcomes the new rubber-cone suspension units which obviate the need to lubricate, and also welcomes the single lubrication unit evolved in some of the front-wheel-drive cars where the sump serves the engine and transmission.

(xv) Safety precautions are essential in a workshop, particularly where apprentices, who are naturally not 'machine-conscious' are working with dangerous machines, such as milling machines or grinders, but the act of putting up warning notices is not sufficient, for the 'old-hands' in the machine shop tend to become careless (familiarity breeds contempt!) and their attitude is communicated to the young people they are teaching.

(xvi) Mr. Gopal tells me that several dealers in the area which you cover are disturbed because their orders are not always filled promptly and they are not notified when these items are out of stock and they don't know when new items are replacing older models of which they wish to be notified, or when such items will soon be released for sale.

2. The following extracts contain redundant expressions. Rewrite to make them concise and precise.

(i) Broadly speaking, this may have the ultimate effect of doubling in numbers the total of bills dispatched outwards in a single day.

(ii) In the main, the majority of the staff are in general agreement with the principal features of the scheme so far as can be judged from the individual replies received to date.

(iii) This knowledge is of peculiar importance in the operation of a system like the one described in this report. This can be realised when attention is directed to the fact that a single error can render such a system worthless.

(iv) Many laboratories here in this country and in other countries abroad are trying to develop techniques for culturing embryos. The goal they are working for is not particularly so much to produce test-tube babies as to understand what factors there are that are involved in control of the gestation process. It is probable this information would help to explain what sometimes goes wrong and in some cases leads to individuals who are born with birth defects. It would also allow researchers to test what effects certain drugs and food additives have on the development of unborn embryos and if they lead eventually to birth defects.

(v) In today's world we hear a lot of things about the generation gap. The age factor is supposedly responsible for the course of recent strained events between parents and children. The young assume that their parents are of a hostile character due to the fact that they are over forty. The parents assume that their children are of an irresponsible character due to the fact that they are under forty.

3. In the following extracts cliches mar the effectiveness of communication. Rewrite to make them simple and effective.

(i) Our universities have today become hot-bed of politics which has become part and parcel of their functioning. We must explore every avenue to remove this evil and use the iron hand of the law to achieve this sacred purpose.

(ii) An extensive evaluation of the field operations department has effectively demonstrated beyond a shadow of doubt that it has mammoth administrative organisation that is grossly out of proportion to the productivity of the department.

(iii) Unfortunately, students seek inappropriate rewards for their endeavours in the pursuit of academic knowledge. They desire high grades because these are indicative of scholastic success. However, they are unaware that they have attained the pinnacle of success if they have acquired a skill. They are unaware that the reward is the knowledge itself and not the academic evaluation.

(iv) Who would believe that the sacred river Ganga venerated all over this country suffers from heavy pollution, so much so that over long areas its water is too polluted for human beings to use it. What an irony indeed! We can however rightly rejoice now that the Central Government has awakened at last from its long slumber and constituted the Ganga Authority which is to cleanse the Ganga of its pollution. The cost of this operation will be huge. It will run into several hundred crores of rupees.

(v) It rained cats and dogs incessantly for several days without any break in this district. As expected, the consequence was that it resulted in extensive damage over large areas to houses all over the district. There was dismay, grief and despair everywhere. The state government did however discharge its duty by coming to the succour of the flood-affected people. In this connection, the Ministries of Industry and Agriculture did yeoman service by doing their level best to help the people in need.

(vi) The engineers and the workers did their level best, roasting themselves in the hot sun, sparing no efforts at all. Their aim overriding everything else was the construction of the museum. Thank God, it was constructed in time and was opened for the public after it was inaugurated by the Chief Minister. Soon it became an object of attraction all over the region. The result was that huge crowds started coming to the museum.

(vii) Two decades ago, food was the burning problem of the teeming millions of this country. The government had to import huge quantities of wheat to the tune of 15 to 20 million tons every year. But now a radical transformation has taken place, thanks to the untiring efforts of our talented and zealous scientists, who left no stone unturned in their efforts to invent hybrid varieties of wheat. India is rightly proud of its brilliant scientists.

(viii) When I passed higher secondary examination, I held the cherished belief that I was a budding genius. My fond parents and my other ardent admirers (members of the weaker sex) agreed. Everything was clear as crystal: the college would be as easy for me as rolling off a log, although not enjoyable. Enjoyment would come later, when I would enter the business world and become a successful captain of industry. And then I came to Delhi and saw the light of day. I am not breezing through. I have found that each and every course is just plain hard work. For all the trials and tribulations of meeting rigid schedules and standards, however, I have also discovered that learning itself can satisfy the inner me and not just the almighty rupee.

4. The meaning is not clear in the following extracts because of redundancy and cliches. Rewrite to make them more easily readable.

(i) The firm was in desperate need of several competent engineers. The General Manager summoned the Chief of the Personnel Department and discussed the problem threadbare, leaving nothing out of the discussion. Two secretaries were also in attendance – one was from the office of the General Manager and the other was secretary to the Personnel Chief. As per protocol, the secretaries kept mum during the whole of the discussion. They however expressed their opinion only when their views were solicited by either of the two dignitaries.

(ii) The monsoon became furiously active in the middle of August after August 13. This is the time of the year when it usually year after year shows virulence. The heavy downpour incessantly day in and day out persisted for a week in northern parts of India. The consequences were what could be expected. All the rivers in the area vied with each other in wreaking havoc on the area by flooding vast tracts of land. The state awoke to its duty, but it was like crying over the spilt milk.

(iii) We know that, if we were to see your face as you read this report, you would be smiling. You would be smiling because your company has managed to do more than just to keep its head above water in this time of recession. You would be smiling because you can expect a dividend of 60 paise per share at the end of the second quarter, which is 10 paise more than your dividend at the end of the first quarter. Although expenses have gone up because of cost-of-living wage increases (84% this year) and higher fuel cost, sales have risen, and this rise, together with higher prices of our products, has enabled us to declare this dividend.

(iv) When the proposal for the new project was mooted, they all without exception gave their acceptance to it. Each one of them fully believed that it would prove a gold mine to them, as they believed that for its profitability the sky was the limit. So none of them bothered to investigate whether the project would be viable or not. However, to their consternation, gradually it dawned upon them that the project was simply a white elephant. Like a giant whale with insatiable hunger, it would simply devour all their resources and would make a mess of their whole industrial venture.

(v) After a long period of rapid expansion and record sales which gave so much pleasure to shareholders in the past, I have the difficult and unenviable task of setting before you a considerable setback in the company's fortunes for the year under review. In the last annual statement I issued, I indicated that sales had levelled off and at the time of the interim dividend announcement I also predicted that, much as I regretted having to make the forecast, profits for the year were likely to be lower than could reasonably be expected. Unhappily, as it turns out from the figures before me, this prediction is not only true but something of an understatement in that there has been a sharper decline in profitability during the last six months than anyone could have foreseen at the time when I made my announcement of the interim dividend.

(vi) It was a small matter. They had the plan to build the building for the museum in three months. The civil engineer who was incharge of the whole operation had not a jot of experience of such a venture. This was his first assignment after he joined the service three weeks ago. It simply did not enter his raw head that he should have an appropriate planning for the building.

Then he was so squeamish and conceited that he thought it below his dignity which had ascended to the seventh sky to consult anybody, say an old veteran civil engineer in his department. Now the first outstanding mistake that he did was that he engaged 500 workers. This number was too large by any calculation. Many of these workers just sat gossiping, some even remained absent without leave and still others obstructed others who wanted to do some work. Actually too many cooks were spoiling the broth. It was after a month and not before wasting half of the resources that our engineer came to realise this mistake.

(vii) Recently the management of Bharat Textiles Mills, Ahmedabad, established brand new machines at their plant. These were imported fresh from Germany and Japan. This happened exclusively owing to the enthusiastic fervour exhibited in the matter by the Production Manager. He staunchly believes in modernisation as the panacea for all industrial ills. He has sojourned for quite sometime in several advanced countries of the world, not excluding Japan and USA. There he has witnessed with his own eyes that technology is developing by leaps and bounds. The inevitable consequence is that a new machine does not last for more than five years. Immediately after it is introduced into operation, practical technologists commence their well-planned work on a new model which represents a distinct improvement upon it. The result is that soon a new and more efficient machine sees the light of day and the old model is kicked out of operation without the least ceremony.

(viii) The Secretary first deliberated with the President in detail on the agenda of the meeting. Then he took into confidence two veteran Directors of the Board who were widely experienced in the affairs of the firm. Feeling himself now on safe ground, he issued the notice for the meeting. The peon who took the notice to various members, however could not come in contact with two of them in spite of his best efforts as they were both out of the town. The Secretary heaved a sigh of great relief for he found both of them as incorrigible nuisance. One would continue to pull the leg of the President through his questions in season and out of season, insinuating that the President was not quite above board. The other would stand up at the fag end of the meeting for no reason on earth and start haranguing the members how the affairs of the firm should be run, throwing in most Don Quixotic counsels for their benefit. The captive audience was bored to death, but there was no escape from the sermons of the Socrates.

Chapter 15

TECHNICAL PROPOSALS

15.1 DEFINITION

IN the highly competitive world of today there is a constant need to review and improve the existing products and services to meet the ever-increasing and complex requirements of the modern society. Progress is not a luxury; it is an absolute necessity of our national life. We need and must have technical proposals containing new and sound ideas to accelerate our advancement. In fact, each design, maintenance or operational problem which we come across should be treated as an opportunity to propose a simpler, more efficient and more economical solution. Every enterprising organisation has therefore a special group of people engaged in what is called research and development (R&D) activities. The main task of this group is to suggest new designs of products that are more economical, technically more sound and more efficient in performance. The suggestions so made are incorporated in the form of a proposal, also called a technical proposal or engineering proposal, or research proposal, depending upon its focus. Another purpose for which a proposal is written is the solution of a technical problem or the performance of a task requiring sophisticated professional skills such as the construction of a power house, the setting up of an atomic reactor, etc. A proposal may, thus, be defined as a written offer to solve a technical problem or to undertake a project of a practical or theoretical nature.

15.2 KEY FACTORS

Every proposal, whatever be its purpose, suggests a particular way of doing a thing, specifies a plan of action and contains an estimated cost of execution. What decides the success of a proposal is whether it is able to persuade the customer and gain his acceptance. Persuasion has been defined as getting someone to do something that you want done because he wants to do it. Every proposal writer should therefore know the factors of persuasion – the factors that can convert a proposal into a project or contract. To persuade the customer you should:

(i) Understand his beliefs and attitudes.
(ii) Meet the anticipated objectives in your presentation.
(iii) Have a fund of goodwill.
(iv) Keep the proposal short and precise.
(v) Let your writing exude zeal.
(vi) Indicate the advantages and possible disadvantages of your proposal.
(vii) Make the terms of your proposal easy for compliance.
(viii) Keep in view the customer's convenience, financial gain and prestige.
(ix) Emphasise distinctive features of your proposal.
(x) Let your proposal look neat and attractive.

Thus you would see that the elements mentioned above do not merely relate to the language of the proposal. In this context the word *persuasion* has acquired a new connotation. So mere use of persuasive language would not win the customer. However, a proposal is more creative than certain other forms of professional writing and hence its style permits informality and personal approach to same extent.

15.3 TYPES

There are two types of proposals, namely solicited and unsolicited, which you may have to write. A solicited proposal is one which is prepared in response to specific invitation or demand. Here is an example. The government has decided that a new electronic system is required in its Silver Arrow aircraft used by Bharat Airlines. It may specify the kind of system it needs and the amount of money it is prepared to spend and then invite reputed electronic companies to submit bids. A proposal written in response to this invitation would be a solicited proposal.

An unsolicited proposal is prepared in the hope that the excellence of the proposed plant would attract the interest of the potential customer or sponsor and convince him that he actually needs the service or product or the plan of work being proposed. Sometimes a proposal of this type is made after a preliminary enquiry. An instance of such a proposal would be, let us say, the submission of a research project on 'Utilisation of Waste Gypsum from Phosphatic Fertiliser Plants – Recovery of Sulphur' by a university professor on his own initiative.

15.4 CONTENTS

Because of the diversity in the nature of a proposal, no firm guidelines regarding its format or style can be given. A number of elements constitute its structure and the overriding consideration to win acceptance makes it more audience-oriented than a formal report. A significant difference between these two forms of technical writing, namely, proposal and report, is that the former is written before the event whereas the latter after the event has taken place. This difference characterises significantly the approach to the two forms.

Very often the contents of a proposal are determined by the request for the proposal. Certain elements, however, are found in every proposal. These are: statement of the problem, immediate background to the problem, benefits to be derived from the solution offered, and feasibility of the solution. A proposal also describes the methods to be used, the facilities available, the schedule for the tasks to be done, and the competence of persons or organisations offering it. These elements are grouped in certain sections, usually sequenced as follows:

I Summary
II Technical Section
III Management Section
IV Cost Estimate

Let us now briefly describe each section mentioned above.

I. *Summary*

The summary is basically the entire proposal in a nutshell. It is likely to be read by more persons in positions of higher authority than any other section of your proposal. Summary is often circulated separately to those responsible for taking a decision on your proposal. A well-written, comprehensive and yet concise summary would persuade the reader to appreciate your idea. Besides the name of the proposed his designation, and the organisation to which he belongs the summary of a proposal should specifically include:

(i) A clear statement of the technical requirement your proposal fulfils.
(ii) An analysis of the problem your proposal solves.
(iii) The method of solution proposed by you.
(iv) A description of the hardware required.
(v) An estimate of the significance of the end-product resulting from the proposal.
(vi) The duration of the planned project.
(vii) A realistic cost-estimate.
(viii) An assurance of the capabilities and experience to execute the project.

Items (i) to (v) are included in the sub-section entitled ‘Proposal Summary’, the remaining three appear separately as specific items.

II. *Technical Section*

This is perhaps the most important section of the proposal, Draft it with great care and accuracy. Since it contains technical details of the area in which you are an expert, clarity of presentation assumes greater importance. The person who is going to read your proposal may not be as knowledgeable as you are in the field.

First, describe the nature of the problem, its background and the work already done in the area. Next, define the task that you propose to perform under the proposed project, clearly giving its scope and limitations. Also Indicate the methodology that you propose to follow and the various phases of results. Lastly, give a plan of action for the utilisation of your achievements.

It may be necessary in some cases to underscore some segment of your proposal which you believe to be unique in design, process or application. State also any major technical problems visualised by you and the solutions offered. Forecast the theoretical, technical or operational advantages that would accrue on the implementation of your proposal. If you are proposing the development of any new components, justify the requirement.

III. *Management Section*

This section should clearly indicate how the proposed task would be compieted. The recipient would obviously be interested in assessing whether you have the ability and talent as well as basic resources to execute the project. In the case of a company, the recipient would like to know whether your organisation has the required business acumen as well as reputation in the industrial community.

If in executing a proposal a number of persons are to be engaged, you should give a brief description of each in the following terms:

- educational qualifications
- professional achievements
- experience in the area of the proposal
- publications in the concerned professional field.

This section also usually contains a description of the existing facilities, e.g. laboratory equipment, plant layout, etc., and the additional facilities required for the proposed work. Ensure that the information you give is directly related to the project and that the manner of utilisation is accurately described.

IV. *Cost Estimate*

In solicited proposals the amount and type of cost data required are given in the request for the proposal: all you have to do is to supply the relevant details. In unsolicited proposals you should carefully include all the items of anticipated expenditure. The estimates should be realistic, accurate and complete. They should also be properly explained and substantiated in detail. Most technical proposals contain the cost analysis of the following items:

- materials
- equipment
- salaries of technical personnel
- salaries and wages of other personnel
- travel
- contingencies
- publications
- outside consultant services.

Practical Hints

Now we give below a few practical hints for preparing a proposal.

(i) Use precise, accurate and definitive description.
(ii) In your style be more personal than is customary in professional writing.
(iii) Avoid sales talk and propaganda material.
(iv) Break the material into clearly defined units by means off headings and sub-headings.
(v) Make it easy to read by getting the proposal neatly typed with short paragraphs and wide margins.
(vi) Let your graphic aids be attractive and functional:
(vii) Ensure that the binding is both durable and convenient.

15.5 FORMAT

The organisations which invite proposals have devised the format for their submission. You have to fill in the required details if you respond to their invitation. At the end of this chapter we are giving a format arrived at after a run-through of some typical proposals. This can also be used with minor modifications for an unsolicited proposal. Sometimes, a proposal which does not have voluminous details may be submitted in the form of a letter. A proposal so submitted essentially contains all the information mentioned earlier, only its presentation acquires a different shape. The structure and sequencing of the elements are the same as those of a business letter, vide Chapter 16.

15.6 EVALUATION

Every proposal is carefully evaluated before it is accepted. The evaluation procedure is usually the same as for making the proposal itself. The three significant aspects of the proposal, namely, the technical content, the management plan and the cost estimate are put to detailed scrutiny by experts in these areas. The assessments on these three aspects are then put together for decision and action. If you are asked to evaluate a proposal, look for evidence of the following:

(i) An understanding of the receiver's problem, requirement, need or interest.
(ii) A sound and feasible technical solution.
(iii) Compliance with the given specifications.
(iv) Clarity of presentation.
(v) Reasonable cost estimate.
(vi) Proper management planning,
(vii) Adequacy of facilities and personnel.
(viii) Realistic performance estimates.
(ix) Practicable schedule of work.

A proposal may be rejected if it does not stand the test of evaluation indicated above. There are however other reasons also for the rejection of a proposal. For example, a sound solicited proposal may be rejected simply because another competitive proposal is found superior to it. Some of the typical reasons for which an unsolicited proposal may be rejected are the following:

- Adequate funds are not available for the execution of the proposal.
- It is not relevant to the accomplishment of immediate objectives.
- The proposed project has low priority.
- The improvement proposed is not significant or is too meagre to justify the overall effort and cost.
- The proposed contribution relates to a system to be phased out of service or to an area becoming obsolete.

PROFORMA FOR THE SUBMISSION OF A TECHNICAL PROPOSAL

(TITLE OF THE PROJECT)

BY

(NAME OF THE PROPOSER)
(DESIGNATION OF THE PROPOSER)

(NAME OF THE ORGANISATION)
(MONTH AND YEAR OF SUBMISSION)

I SUMMARY

1. Project Title: ____________________
2. Name and Designation of the Proposer(s): ____________________
3. Postal address of the Proposer(s): ____________________
4. Name of the Institution/ Organisation in which the Project would be carried out: ____________________
5. (a) Time required for commencement of the project on receipt of approval: ____________________

   (b) Duration of the Project: ____________________
6. Amount of money required (give year-wise breakup): ____________________
7. Proposal Summary (containing technical details in about 200 words): ____________________

II TECHNICAL SECTION

2.1 Introduction
- 2.1.1 State-of-the-art giving background of work done in the area
- 2.1.2 Definition of the problem
- 2.1.3 Objectives
- 2.1.4 Scope and limitations

2.2 Proposed work
- 2.2.1 Technical description
- 2.2.2 Methodology
- 2.2.3 Significance
- 2.2.4 Utilisation of results
- 2.2.5 Plan of action

III MANAGEMENT SECTION

3.1 Schedule of work

3.2 Existing facilities
- 3.2.1 Workshop facilities
- 3.2.2 Water and electricity
- 3.2.3 Laboratory space
- 3.2.4 Air-conditioned room for equipment
- 3.2.5 Telecommunication
- 3.2.6 Administrative and Secretarial support
- 3.2.7 Library facilities
- 3.2.8 Furniture
- 3.2.9 Office equipment
- 3.2.10 Any other

3.3 Additional facilities required
- 3.3.1 Equipment and accessories
- 3.3.2 Materials
- 3.3.3 Any other (Specify)

IV COST ESTIMATE

4.1 Equipment

4.2 Materials

4.3 Salaries and wages

4.4 Travel

4.5 Other costs

ASSIGNMENTS

1. As the Branch Manager of the Punjab National Bank, Siwani you wish to expand the services and facilities on popular demand. These include provision of 50 lockers, 1 teller counter, 3 staff quarters and 1 additional office-room, etc. Invent the necessary details and prepare a proposal to be sent to the Divisional Manager, Rohtak, Haryana.
2. A large public limited company has been spending about rupees seven lakhs per annum on getting its various documents such as routine forms, brochures, reports, proposals, manuals, etc., printed by outside agencies. For greater economy and efficiency it has decided to have its own Publishing Unit to cater to all its printing needs. As Office Manager write a proposal for the creation of this Unit for consideration of the Board of Directors.
3. As the President of the Students' Union of your institution, prepare a proposal for the setting up of a cultural centre on the campus. The proposal is to be written in the form of a letter and submitted to the Dean, Student Welfare Division.
4. The Government of India has recently launched a company to produce personal computers on a large scale. Thirty-two English speaking experts have been deputed during the initial five-year period to aid and train Indians in the production process. To teach Hindi to these foreigners it has been decided to set up an 8-booth language laboratory. As Training Manager of the Company draft a proposal containing all the required details in terms of physical facilities (room, furniture, sound-proofing, air-conditioning, etc.) equipment and staff. The proposal is to be submitted to the Secretary, Department of Company Affairs for approval.
5. As a fresh graduate in engineering you have decided to establish a manufacturing unit in your town. You wish to avail of the liberalised loan facility under the self-employment scheme. Draft a proposal for the manufacture of an item of your choice, seeking loan from the State Industrial Development Finance Corporation, Madras.

Chapter 16

BUSINESS CORRESPONDENCE

16.1 PURPOSE

A business letter is a form of communication written by an authorised person of an organisation.* Like other forms of communication, such as reports, it has a definite purpose. What distinguishes it from them is its structure, layout and form which are well-established by convention and practice.

Some of the purposes for which a business letter is written are as follows: making or answering an enquiry; placing an order; demanding or refusing credit; selling goods and services; making, accepting or refusing a request; making or responding to complaints; etc. Whatever be the purpose, every letter is an ambassador of goodwill. It has to be perceived as your personal emissary and should give the receiver a sensation of an actual meeting.

As a professional you will have to write dozens of letters daily. Remember, even though a letter is a means of contact between two individuals, it establishes a relationship between two organisations. In fact, in writing a letter you perform two functions. One, you attempt to achieve the specific purpose of your organisation and two, you create or cement friendly relationship with another organisation. It would not be difficult to trace examples of embarrassment, anger, or even of a break in the cordial relationship because of a poorly composed letter.

Perhaps no form of professional writing reflects the personality of an individual so vividly as does a letter. Dealing with varied levels of human intellect, experience and different attitudes would demand a number of qualities from you. Writing a successful letter therefore requires:

---

* In government organisations business letters are often termed as official letters. Our discussion is equally applicable to them.

- A deep perception of human nature,
- A clear understanding of the psychology of man,
- A discerning eye to judge the attitude of the respondent, and
- An ability to anticipate the reaction of the receiver.

16.2 STRUCTURE

The structure of a business letter has a number of elements or parts. The following are seven elements that normally appear in every letter: heading, date, inside address, salutation, body, complimentary close and typed signature. Optional elements which appear in some letters are: your reference, our reference, attention, subject, identification marks, enclosure. Let us now briefly discuss each element. In the examples given below we have followed the most common practice of presentation.

16.2.1 Compulsory Elements

(i) *Heading*: The heading includes the name and address of the organisation and sometimes its telephone number and telegraphic address. Many organisations use printed letter-heads for this purpose. The heading is normally printed or typed in the middle of the page just below the top margin as shown below:

Telegrams: EXCEFOOD Telephone: 7481901

EXCELLENT FOOD PRODUCTS LTD.
32, Sardar Patel Road
New Delhi-110006

(ii) *Date*: The date is written or typed flush with the right-hand margin of the letter unless the full block form is used:

21 November, 2007

(iii) *Inside-address*: The inside address contains the full name/designation and business-address of the person to whom the letter is written to, just as it would appear on the envelope. The inside address should be flush with the left-hand margin of the letter:

Shri R.S. Srinivasan
Managing Director
Northern India Dairy Farms
Mehrauli Road
New Delhi 110049

If the person addressed to holds a professional title, then the accepted abbreviation should be used before his name:

Dr. R.S. Srinivasan
Prof. R.S. Srinivasan

In case of ladies, write Smt or Mrs if she is married and Kum or Miss if she is unmarried. Write Ms if you do not know her marital status. Some ladies prefer Ms before their name and if you happen to know that your letter is going to such a lady, prefer Ms to either of the two. When a lady has a professional or academic title, say Ph.D. she may be addressed as:

Dr (Smt) Saral Gupta or
Dr (Mrs) Saral Gupta or
Dr Saral Gupta

When the inside address does not contain the name or the designation of an officer the convention is as follows: In the case of a public limited company the name is written as it is, without any title. In the case of other firms and companies the title Messrs is used if there is a personal element in its name:

Messrs Ramlal and Brothers
10 Netaji Marg, Daryaganj
New Delhi-110002

In Government departments when a letter is addressed to an officer by name, it is called a demi-official letter (DO). It is generally written to draw the personal attention of the concerned officer.

(iv) *Salutation*: The salutation is located two spaces below the last line of the inside address and flush with the left-hand margin. The choice of salutation would depend upon your relationship with the receiver and the form of inside-address.

If you are addressing an organisation (a company, society, association, club, agency) or a post box or a newspaper box number, use 'Dear Sirs'.* However, if you are addressing an officer of the company by designation write 'Dear Sir' or 'Sir'. The former is less formal than the latter. If you are addressing the officer by name you may use any of the following salutations:

Dear Ram Dear Seema	Informal
Dear Shri Gupta Dear Kum Jaiswal Dear Smt Shinde	Formal
My dear Shri Gupta My dear Kum Jaiswal My dear Smt Shinde	Semi-formal

In the above examples the full names of the persons to whom the letters are addressed are as follows:

Shri Ramprasad Gupta
Kumari Seema Jaiswal
Shrimati Shubha Shinde

You will notice that in the informal salutation when the first name of the addressee is written, his or her marital status is irrelevant.

---

* In the USA some organisations use 'Gentlemen' followed by a colon but in India such a practice is rare.

The circulars sent for sales promotion or for collection of data from a large population have salutations such as 'Dear Customer', 'Dear Reader', 'Dear Subscriber', 'Dear Member', 'Dear Friend', etc.

(v) *Body*: The body contains the message of the letter and is generally made up of three parts: (a) an introductory statement specifying the nature of the business or the occasion for writing the letter. If there is any previous correspondence on the subject, it is mentioned soon after this statement; (b) the message that you are conveying along with essential details; (c) the concluding remarks, indicating what action you wish the addressee to take and/or stating your expectations and intentions. Unless the letter is very long, it has no subheadings. The body begins two spaces below the salutation.

(vi) *Complimentary close*: This is a formal, polite way of signalling the end of the letter. It is written four spaces below the body of the letter. The first letter of the first word of a complimentary close is written in capitals and a comma is put at the end of the last word.

The complimentary close is usually a conventional expression corresponding in formality with the salutation as shown below:

	Salutation	*Complimentary close*
(a)	Sir, Dear Sir, Dear Sirs, Dear Madam, Dear Madams,*	Yours faithfully, or Yours truly,
(b)	Dear Ram, Dear Seema, Dear Shri Gupta, Dear Kum Jaiswal, Dear Smt Shinde, My dear Shri Gupta, My dear Kum Jaiswal, My dear Smt Shinde,	Yours sincerely,
(c)	Dear Customer, Dear Reader, Dear Subscriber, Dear Member, Dear Friend, Dear Editor,	Yours sincerely,

You will notice that whenever the salutation contains a nominal element, the complimentary close is 'Yours sincerely', and when there is no such element in the salutation the close is 'Yours faithfully' or 'Yours truly.' Category (c) above is a special category and the intention of the salutation is to draw the

* This is used in addressing an organisation consisting only of women, e.g. Mahila Samaj.

personal attention of the addressee to the message of the letter. Hence the convention of writing 'Yours sincerely' has established itself in such letters.

Some organisations write 'Sincerely' or 'Faithfully' first and put 'yours' later.

(vii) *Typed signature*: Just below the complimentary close the typed signature of the writer of the letter is placed. Six to eight spaces are left to provide enough space for the handwritten signature. The writer's designation or his division or department is positioned on the very next line. It is customary to indicate the marital status if the writer is a woman. If this is not indicated the respondent can use Ms in his reply.

16.2.2 Optional Elements

(i) *Your reference/Our reference*: The office copy of every letter is put away in a file. To ensure that this is properly done an identification number is given in the letter against 'Our Reference'. If you are writing in reply to a letter from some other organisation, write the correspondent's reference number with date against 'Your Reference'. If such a letter does not contain any number you may write 'Nil, dated...' Both these elements appear just above the inside address but below the date line. Two spaces are left between them and the inside address.

(ii) *Attention*: When a letter is addressed to an organisation but is directed to a specific person, his name or designation or both are indicated against this element. It is placed between the inside address and salutation and two spaces are left both above and beneath it. Example:

Mutual Life Insurance Company
22, Sarojini Naidu Marg
Hyderabad-500007

Attention: Shri Ram Prasad

Dear Sirs

(iii) *Subject*: An indication of the subject of the letter may quicken its disposal. It is usually typed and double-spaced between the salutation and the first line of the body of the letter. Sometimes the subject may appear between inside address or attention line, if any, and the salutation. If you are sending the reply of a letter in which the subject is indicated, courtesy demands that you too should specify the same subject. The word 'subject' is followed by a colon and then the matter is indicated. It is like the title of a report indicating the contents.

(iv) *Identification marks*: These are the initials of the typist, and they appear just above the 'Enclosure', if any, but below the line of signature. If the letter has been typed by say, Shri Hoshiyar Singh Kulhari, his identification would be indicated thus:

Yours faithfully

R.K. Sharma

HSK

Enclosure

(v) *Enclosure*: It is typed two spaces below the identification marks and the number of documents enclosed are indicated against it. If the documents attached are important, they are specified, e.g. Demand Draft No. A 32926 dated 20 November, 2007.

We now give the layout of a business letter indicating the position of all the elements,

BHARAT RAYON LIMITED

Heading ⟶ 44, Church Lane Date

Mumbai 400003

30 November, 2007

Your Reference: CW-327 of 21 November
Our Reference: FD-412

Kamala Nehru Charitable Hospital
Park Road ⟵ Inside address
New Delhi 110009
Attention: Shri R. A. Kirke, Administrator

Dear Sirs, ⟵ Salutation

Subject: Donation for Cancer Ward

Body
↓

We have received your appeal for funds for the cancer ward that is being added to your hospital. It would provide a much-needed facility to alleviate the pain and suffering of people who fall prey to this dreaded disease.

We believe that your institution deserves all possible help and we are therefore enclosing a cheque for Rs. 50,000 as our donation.

We wish your venture all success.

Complimentary close ⟶ Yours faithfully,

Typed signature ⟶ R. Jerath

Finance Manager

HSK ⟵ Identification Marks

Enclosure: Cheque No. AB23984

16.3 LAYOUT AND FORM

Since each letter that you write is an ambassador of goodwill, ensure that it has a neat appearance. The paper used should be of good quality and the typewriter should be frequently cleaned so that the marks of the types are clear and bright. If a copy has to be made, the carbon used should be able to give a legible impression.

Your letter should have a picture-frame look; this is possible only if the elements are properly placed and presented. It is advisable to leave a margin of 2.5 cm on the left-hand side and a margin of about 2 cm on the top and bottom of the page and 1 cm on the right-hand side. As far as possible a word should not be broken at the end of the line. If it has to be, make sure that it is done at the end of a, syllable. For example, if 'going' has to be broken, '*ing*' should be taken to the next line and a hyphen placed after *go-* in the previous line. Two spaces should be left between the elements and paragraphs of the body of the letter. In elements consisting of more than one line, single space should be left between the lines.

The envelope should also be neatly typed and it should have the full address of the receiver and the sender. You should establish the practice of the envelope being attached along with the typed letter when it is put up for signature. The envelope is the first thing to be seen by the receiver. Obviously, if it is mutilated, clumsy or dirty, it would create a poor impression.

The following three forms are generally used for writing business letters:

(a) indented form,

(b) block form, and

(c) full block form.

(a) *Indented form.* In typing it each element is indented two to four spaces. The paragraphs of the body of the letter are also indented. Closed punctuation is used in such letters as shown in the specimen below:

NEW BHARAT ENTERPRISES
61, Malabar Road
Jamnagar-361001

5 December, 2007

The Manager,
State Bank of India,
47, Mayoorbagh,
Jamnagar-361001

Dear Sir,

Please refer to your letter No. AL-227 dated 30 November, 2007 conveying your acceptance of our request for a loan of Rs. 1.5 lakhs. The terms and conditions mentioned by you are acceptable to us.

On 12 December, 2007 we shall send our finance officer to sign the deed on our behalf and to collect the draft. We note that he has to carry a Letter of Authority from us.

Yours faithfully,

D.P. Simon
Managing Director

(b) *Block form.* The following elements are aligned with the right hand margin: date, complimentary close, typed signature. Other elements are flush with the left hand margin. The heading is printed or typed in the middle of the page as usual. There is double spacing between the elements and the paragraphs of the body of the letter and single spacing within each element and lines of the paragraph. In it *mixed punctuation* is used. Since most of the elements begin with the left hand margin, the typing of such letters takes less time. The specimen letter given above will be laid out as follows. Note the difference in punctuation.

5 December, 2007

The Manager
State Bank of India
47 Mayoorbagh
Jamnagar-361001

Dear Sir,

Please refer to your letter No. AL-227 dated 30 November, 2007 conveying your acceptance of our request for a loan of Rs. 1.5 lakhs. The terms and conditions mentioned by you are acceptable to us.

On 12 December, 2007 we shall send our finance officer to sign the deed on our behalf and to collect the draft. We note that he has to carry a Letter of Authority from us.

Yours faithfully,

D.P. Simon
Managing Director

(c) *Full Block-form.* In this form all the elements are aligned with the left-hand margin except the heading which is printed. In this form open punctuation is used, i.e. no punctuation mark is used except in the body of the letter. It is more economical in terms of time spent in typing or word processing. That is why the use of this form has become more common. The specimen and examples that follow are in the full block form.

KASLIWAL CONSTRUCTION LIMITED
14A Maharaja Road
Jaipur-302004

5 December 2007

The Chairman
Jaipur Development Authority
Shantipath New Extension
Jaipur-302001

Dear Sir

Please refer to your letter of 2 November, 2007 in which we were informed that a demand draft for Rs. 12.5 lakhs would be sent to us within a fortnight. But so far we have neither received the demand draft nor any information about the cause of delay in its despatch.

We would be grateful if you could kindly get the draft sent at an early date so that the progress of the work is not hampered.

Yours faithfully

Ahmed Khan Baatish
Project Executive

16.4 QUALITIES

Howsoever attractive your letter may be in its layout and appearance, it would not be able to achieve its purpose unless it has an effective style and the right tone. These can be achieved through proper selection of words and phrases and suitable sequencing of sentences and paragraphs. We have already discussed some qualities of professional writing in Chapter 14 on style in the context of report writing. Do keep them in mind.

Here a few practical hints are given to help you write a successful letter.

(i) *Be warm and friendly*: A letter is a personal communication and must therefore follow the tried principle of *I-you communication.* When you write a letter, visualise the person who will read it – his status, background, attitude, etc.

After you have done this analysis, it would be possible for you to form a fairly vivid mental picture of the reader. Draft your letter treating him as your friend. A letter so written would reflect a friendly attitude and exude warmth.

As you know on the receipt of a letter a reader analyses how it would affect him and his organisation and attempts to determine the action on his part. You should therefore ask this question in respect of every letter you write: 'How would I react if I receive this letter?' Remember that self-centredness is one of the chief barriers to successful communication. Self-interest is part of human nature and all of us are basically selfish. You would therefore have to stretch your imagination, and put yourself in a position from where you can see the reader's point of view. There would be considerable variations in the strategy that you adopt to suit the reader's interest. But then this is one of the qualities that you need as a professional. To ensure this quality in your letter give importance to the self-esteem and self-interest of the reader. Address him as an individual and not as if he were a crowd! Look at the following examples which illustrate this point.

Impersonal Approach	*I-you Approach*
(a) The policy requires that the person concerned should fill in and return the enclosed form within a fortnight for processing.	Please fill in the enclosed form and return it within a fortnight so that we may send the cheque to you.
(b) This course will help the readers improve their spoken English.	This course will help you improve your spoken English.
(c) This firm would be glad to demonstrate the working of the new washing machine	We would be glad to demonstrate to you how the new washing machine works.
(d) It is regretted that the goods buyers in time.	We regret that the goods sent by us did not reach the by us did not reach you in time.

(ii) *Be courteous and considerate*. Courtesy costs nothing but wins both friends and business. It makes life pleasant and paves the way for smooth human relationship. Even if you receive a letter whose language is curt or rude, keep your cool. Don't send the reply in anger. Instead send a courteous reply, for after all your aim is to achieve your specific goal and not to take revenge or hurt somebody's feelings. Some of the following phrases are either curt or rude; avoid using them.

We are of the firm view...
We are compelled to refuse ...
We find it hard to accept...
Your statement that ...
Your persistent request ...
You are absolutely wrong in asserting ...

Now look at the following expressions which are likely to make your letter pleasant and courteous.

You will be glad to know ...
Many thanks for...
Thank you very much for ...
We sincerely appreciate ...
It is with regret that we express our inability ...
We are glad to know ...
It is very thoughtful of you to have ...

Be specially considerate when you have to convey bad news to the correspondent – the news that he would not like to hear. Your strategy of communication should be well thought out and it should soften the sting and cushion the blow of an unpleasant message. Be it a credit refusal, job refusal or leave refusal, your letter should be gracious and tactful enough to lessen the disappointment of the reader. One successful way of doing this is to give reasons for saying a 'no' and then conveying the bad news. Look at the following letter, refusing loan to an employee,

> Please refer to your application dated 30 November, 2007 or a loan of Rs. 8000 from the Common Revolving Fund. Please note that it cannot be granted.

This letter is obviously curt and would certainly hurt the concerned employee. It would have been better to give reasons for the refusal and also to inform him when it may be possible to grant him the loan.

Now consider how you would react if you got the following message.

> Your application for the post of Purchase Manager has been rejected.

This message would have become less unpleasant, had it been drafted as follows:

> We have carefully considered your application for the post of Purchase Manager in our Company. We however regret to say that right now we are unable to offer this position to you. However, we have kept your application in our file and if there is another such opportunity, we shall certainly reconsider it. We are grateful to you for the interest you have shown in associating yourself with our Company.

Here is another example.

Rude: You have not mentioned the colour and the size of the dressing gown you wish to buy.

Courteous: We are sending a folder which mentions all the colours and sizes of the dressing gowns we stock. Just put a tick against the one you want and mail it to us in the enclosed postage paid envelope and we shall send the one of your choice.

(iii) *Be specific and positive*. Word your letter in specific language so that it quickly catches the reader's attention and induces in him the right reaction. Specificity helps in creating a proper image of what you say and you can achieve your goal easily. For example, if you say, 'This product is inexpensive,' it would be difficult to understand what you mean by the words 'product' and 'inexpensive'. Instead, say:

> This electric iron carries a guarantee for one year and its price is only Rs. 450.

It would help convey the message to the reader quickly.

A few more examples follow:

(a) *Abstract*: Your remittance will be sent after a short time.
Concrete: Your cheque will be sent within a week.

(b) *Abstract*: Please come for the inspection of your vehicle in the afternoon of 20 December, 2007.

Concrete: Please report at 3.30 pm on 20 December, 2007 for the inspection of your car.

(c) *Abstract*: I hope our response to your communication has reached you.

Concrete: I hope you have received our reply to your letter.

(d) *Abstract*: You will get a substantial discount if you pay promptly.

Concrete: You will get a discount of 20 per cent if you pay by 20 December, 2007.

(e) *Abstrirct*: I am contemplating making a purchase of a new automobile.

Concrete: I am thinking of buying a new car.

Concrete words are easily perceived by the human mind, whereas the abstract ones tend to be general and vague. For example, concrete nouns name objects and things and concrete verbs show action. The use of such nouns and verbs makes the writing vivid and vital. However, you cannot completely avoid the use of abstract words. Examine such words carefully when they find a place in your writing and replace them with concrete or less abstract words.

In business correspondence it is not what you say but how you say it that matters. You should make an all-out effort to organise your message in as pleasant and cheerful a language as possible. One of the ways of doing this is the use of words which create a positive image in the mind of the reader. Remember, even if you have to convey a negative idea, you can do so in a positive way. In fact, the positive idea and the negative idea are the two sides of the same coin. It makes all the difference how you put the coin on the table. Mark how a negative statement is converted into a positive one in the following examples:

(a) *Negative*: These bedcovers are guaranteed not to shrink.

Positive: These bedcovers are guaranteed to keep their shape even after many washings.

(b) *Negative*: You have paid no attention to our complaint.

Positive: Please look into our complaint.

(c) *Negative*: We have not heard from you despite repeated reminders.

Positive: We are eagerly awaiting to hear from you.

(d) Negative: You will never find me uncooperative on the job.

Positive: You will always find me cooperative on the job.

(e) *Negative*: You will never pay high prices at Murugun Department Store because we don't see any need to overcharge you.

Positive: We at Murugun Department Store, always charge the right price.

(f) *Negative*: These dinner sets are not made of inferior material.

Positive: These dinner sets are made of porcelain.

Avoid words and phrases that make your letter seem downcast and pessimistic in its tone. Some such expressions are: helpless, delay, behind schedule, inconvenience, viability, unable to do, etc. Here is an extract from a letter which reflects a pessimistic and negative tone out and out:

> We regret to say we are not able to complete the printing of all the pages of your brochure. In fact, there has been a labour problem and this has caused delay. The result is that we would not be able to supply the brochures on 15 December, 2007 as we had promised. It would take at least ten days more to complete the job. We are sorry for the inconvenience caused.

See the difference that the revised version makes:

> We are glad to report that printing of eight pages of your brochure has been completed. The printing of the remaining twelve pages is likely to take about a fortnight from now as the workers who had gone on a lightning strike have since returned to duty today. We therefore, assure you that we would deliver the brochures latest by 25 December 2007.

(iv) *Be direct and concise*. Professionals are busy people and courtesy requires that messages among them be exchanged efficiently. In addition to keeping in mind the qualities discussed above, come directly to the point and exercise utmost economy in the use of words. This you can do if you clearly know what you want to say. Plan the whole composition of the letter you initiate before you dictate it. In replying to letters, analyse your response or reaction before wrestling with words. Be unaffected, have a natural tone and a straight forward business like attitude.

Directness and conciseness go hand in hand. One way of assuring both is to keep sentences short and to compress your thoughts within as little space as possible. No one likes to read a letter running into several pages unless it carries a special message or deals with an extraordinary situation, demanding voluminous information. Researches show that there is a lot of deadwood and gobbledygook in professional writings. People resort to deadwood as they are too lazy to coin new phrases and use gobbledygook because they need more time to create the right expressions.

Look at the following examples and the suggested revisions:

(a) At the present time the consensus of opinion is that the employee turnover will increase during the month of January. *Suggested revision*: At present the consensus is that the employee turnover will increase in January.

(b) I would like to take this opportunity to say thank you for responding to our request the way you did.

Suggested revision: Thank you for promptly responding to our request.

(c) It will be necessary for you to fill in and complete the enclosed form and return it to us before your request can be considered.

Suggested revision: Please fill in the enclosed form and return it to us so that we may consider your request.

Here is an opening paragraph from a reply letter:

> How delighted I was on receipt of your letter this morning offering me the post of a receptionist in your office at Nariman Point, Bombay. I had been expecting this offer ever since I was interviewed four weeks ago. I really appreciate this thoughtful gesture on your part and with gratitude I accept to work for your Company...

Suggested Revision

Thank you very much for your letter of 15 December, 2007. I am glad to have been offered the past. I shall report for duty on 2 January, 2007 as desired.

You would notice that in the revised version there is a direct approach. The affectation, and the airs that the writer had put on, are removed from it.

One more example:

When I order a product, I want it to arrive in good shape. It passes my comprehension how your packaging department had so much difficulty in providing a proper protection to the tea-set. When I opened the parcel I found all the items broken into several pieces. I have reached the conclusion that I should never place an order with your firm.

Suggested Revision

The tea-set sent by you was not properly packed. Each item was found broken into several pieces. Please send its replacement.

Although the writer did not specify what action he wanted the firm to take, it is obvious that he would be happy to receive a replacement for the broken tea-set. The revised version makes this clear.

A few expressions which are verbose and their suitable substitutes are given below:

Verbose	*Direct and Concise*
As per your instructions	As instructed
Attached herewith	Attached
By reason of the fact that	Because
For the month of December	For December
In compliance with your request	As requested
In early course	Soon
In point of fact	In fact
Should prove of interest to you	Should interest you
This is to thank you	Thank you
Wish to thank	Thank
Wish to acknowledge	Acknowledge
Wish to suggest	Suggest
In the event of	If
In the time of	During
In the matter of	In
For the purpose of	For

The discussion that we have just concluded merely gives a glimpse of key considerations that shape the letters that are effective – letters that either bring about a change in attitude or generate some action.

Try to keep them in mind whenever you have to draft a letter. In practice, however, you will find that in certain situations you have to sacrifice one quality for another. For example, when you have to say 'no' to a request or convey bad news, it may be advisable to sacrifice directness for courtesy. What one needs is a balanced view, a sense of proportion. The real test of the success of a letter is whether it achieves the desired result, hits the target like a missile, howsoever distant it may be. If you have a sense of humour and a cheerful disposition coupled with an optimistic attitude towards life, well and good. These would certainly help you write effective letters. But do remember that the art of letter writing can be cultivated through persistent self-effort. Writing a business letter is a serious business and should be taken as a challenge. Invoking the spirit of Shakespeare, one may say:

Mend your letter a little
Lest it should mar your future
And that of your company too!

16.5 TYPES

Now that we have already analysed the ingredients of successful letter writing, it is time to look at certain basic types of business letters. In the books dealing exclusively with business correspondence a great many types are discussed. Here we shall deal with only those which are more frequently used in the professional world.

16.5.1 Sales Letter

The tone of a sales letter is persuasive. Here are a few guidelines:

- Arrest attention through an attractive opening.
- Arouse interest in your product.
- Present reader benefit information.
- Induce him to take action.
- Close with a clincher sentence.

A *specimen* follows:

Dear Sir

Winter is round the corner. And you must be thinking how to keep your office warm so that the work can go on efficiently. We have an answer to your problem. Keeping in view your needs we have produced room heaters of different capacities. The enclosed pamphlet gives their detailed specifications.

Just fill in the card sent herewith and mail. Our man will then call on you and give a plan for the location of room heaters so that your entire office remains warm and comfortable. This technical advice is provided free. And we may add that each room heater is guaranteed for five years against all manufacturing defects.

If you place your order before 30 November, a special discount of 20 per cent will be given.

Here is a unique opportunity and we trust you would make use of it.

Yours faithfully

Ram Dhige
Sales Manager

Enclosures: Two

16.5.2 Claim Letter

A claim letter (also called complaint letter) is written to get the mistakes made or the wrongs done rectified. A few helpful hints to draft such a letter are given below:

- Explain clearly what has gone wrong, giving data where necessary. For example, if you have received a defective product, mention its model number, the name and address of the shop from where you bought it, a brief description of the defect, etc. Enclose a copy of the cash memo and refer to the previous correspondence, if any.
- Appeal to the company's sense of fair play and to its reputation to motivate prompt action.
- Specify clearly what adjustment you would consider fair.
- Address the letter to a senior officer of the organisation.

A *specimen* follows:

Dear Sir

We bought five Everest refrigerators KL24791 of 165 litres each for our office, from an authorised dealer, Messrs Chagan Das and Company, in November 2008. After about a month all the five refrigerators stopped working. When we brought this to the notice of the dealer he got them checked after several reminders and reported that the compressors had burnt out beyond repair. Since they carry a guarantee of five years, we asked him to replace the compressors. But to this day he has not taken any action despite repeated reminders.

Your company enjoys a good reputation and we were therefore surprised when all the compressors went out of order. Several of our sister organisations had given very good reports about this model and in fact this motivated us to go in for your product.

We believe you would be as prompt in getting the compressors replaced as you had been in supplying them through the local dealer. I trust you would take action quickly and inform us what you propose to do. Copies of the complaint letters and the cash memo are enclosed.

Yours faithfully

Office Manager

Enclosure: As above

16.5.3 Adjustment Letter

When you receive a complaint or a claim letter, keep your cool. Never send the reply in a moment of excitement or anger. Even a short time-gap is enough to restore one to one's usual self. An adjustment letter that you write then would have the desired effect. Keep the following in mind when writing such a letter.

- Convey good news first, the adjustment you are offering or the action you are taking.
- Explain why things went wrong, if the situation warrants.
- Give additional information for the same product or send new sales material about any other product of yours in which the customer might feel interested.
- Close the letter, emphasising the action that you want your customer to take.
- Address your letter to the claimant by name.

A *specimen* adjustment letter in reply to the claim letter given above follows:

Dear Shri

Thank you very much for your letter No. PD/3259, dated 19 December, 2007.

Our Assistant Maintenance Engineer Mr. R.Z. Ansari would call on you at 10 am on Thursday 28 December with five new compressors to replace the ones that have burnt out.

It appears that the compressors were damaged during transit. We have therefore given detailed instructions to our packaging department about safer packaging. We are sorry for the inconvenience caused to you because of the negligence of our authorised dealer in your town.

Incidentally, you would be glad to know that we have started production of minimize (65 litres capacity) refrigerators in seven different colours which could match the decor of an executive's office. The enclosed brochure gives details. Mr. Ansari would be happy to give any further information about them, should you so desire.

We would be grateful if you confirm quickly that you would be available on 28 December. If you have to be away, kindly leave instructions with your secretary to act as a contact for our representative.

With kind regards

Yours sincerely

Sales Manager

16.5.4 Collection Letter

In the world of business many transactions take place on credit and you would came across people who delay the payment despite good intentions. A collection letter is written to persuade them to make the payment. In reminding them about the payment use utmost tact. Remember, your purpose is to get the amount due and also to maintain the business link. People feel irritated when they are reminded to pay. You should not therefore, ask for the payment in a straightforward manner. Here is an *example*,

Dear Sir

As our annual account would be closing on 31 December 2007, we are preparing an income and expenditure statement of the firm. We find that a bill for Rs. 9427.70 is outstanding against your company.

We believe that the bill is being processed and that you would be sending the cheque soon.

We would be grateful if you kindly indicate the date by which we may expect to receive the payment. A self-addressed envelope is enclosed for your convenience.

Yours faithfully

Purchase Manager

16.5.5 Enquiry Letter

A letter of 'enquiry' is written to seek information from other organisations. It may deal with a simple matter such as the availability of a book with a publisher or with a matter of wider dimensions such as the rates of supply for a large number of goods. Each enquiry letter should be drafted keeping the following points in view:

- Indicate the nature of enquiry at the beginning.
- State reasons for the enquiry.
- Clearly state what information you are seeking.
- Close with a statement which would elicit quick response.

A *specimen* is given below.

Dear Sir

We are setting up a branch office of our company at Jaipur. We are interested in furnishing it with good quality furniture.

We understand that you have specialised in producing office furniture. We would like to know whether the following items are readily available and if yes, their rates:

(i) Wooden table for the use of assistants, size 3' x 5'
(ii) Typist's table and chair – standard size.
(iii) Caned office chair with arms – standard size
(iv) Wooden table 4' × 6'
(v) Revolving chair with cushioned seat
(vi) Wooden stool

(*Continued*)

(*Continued*)

(vii) Steel almirah
(viii) File cabinet

Please indicate the terms and conditions of supply. On hearing from you we shall take a decision quickly. Since we want our office to function from the next month, I would be grateful for an early reply.

Yours faithfully

Office Manager

16.5.6 Quotation Letter

A letter sent in reply to an enquiry is called a quotation letter. Be prompt in sending all the required information when you wish to participate in the competition. Remember that the enquiry letter is sent to a number of organisations similar to yours and the responses are examined from several points of view: quality, price, promptness in reply, additional advantages, etc. The information that you give is often included in a sales letter too but there is a difference. A quotation letter is written in response to a specific enquiry. On the other hand, a sales letter may be written unsolicited. Further, sales letter may not give point by point detailed information as is done in the quotation letter.

We now give a sample quotation letter in response to the enquiry letter given in 16.5.5.

Dear Sir

Thank you very much for your letter No .... dated .... We would be glad to supply all the items mentioned by you at short notice as they are readily available in our stock. The rates are as follows:

Sl. No.	*Item*	*Price per item*
(i)	Wooden table 3' × 5'	Rs. 1350.00
(ii)	Typists table and chair (standard size)	Rs. 1700.00
(iii)	Caned office chair with arms (standard size)	Rs. 550.00
(iv)	Wooden table 4' × 5'	Rs. 1850.00
(v)	Revolving chair with cushioned seat	Rs. 4250.00
(vi)	Wooden stool	Rs. 160.00
(vii)	Steel almirah	Rs. 8200.00
(viii)	File cabinet	Rs. 1700.00

Other terms and conditions

(i) Discount @ 10% on an order of Rs. 20,000 and above.
(ii) Packaging free
(iii) Despatch of goods within 15 days of the receipt of order.

I am enclosing a brochure giving details of all the items of furniture that we supply. If you feel interested in any other item, please let us know.

We would be very grateful if you kindly send your firm order. A form for placing an order is enclosed. All that you have to do is to fill in the quantity required.

Yours faithfully

Sales Manager
Enclosure: One

16.5.7 Job Application Letter

A job application letter is like a sales letter; it is written to sell one's services. When you wish to apply for a job, put its requirements against your qualifications and experience. If they match, carefully draft your application letter. Since the amount and variety of information an employer may want to know is great, it cannot be conveniently included in the conventional business letter. It is generally given in the form of a personal data or bio-data sheet or what is sometimes called a resume. A resume contains a brief business or vocational history, emphasising the applicant's educational experience and accomplishments. It is prepared keeping in view the requirements of the job but certainly it does not suppress any vital information or give wrong information. Only, there is a little change in the orientation, the stress or the direction. The covering letter is short and contains a brief introduction to the resume. In preparing the resume give enough information to the employer so that he forms some idea of your suitability for the position for which you are an applicant. The sequence of information usually follows the following pattern:

- Personal details such as date of birth, marital status, address, etc.
- Education beginning from High School Examination to the highest level, calling attention to courses which you feel help you qualify for the job.
- Training, its nature and duration.
- Experience – organisations in which you worked, nature of duties and duration.
- Other accomplishments – prizes and awards won, research papers and books published, etc.
- References – names of usually three persons are given: a senior member of the faculty in the college/ university last attended, the present employer and one other responsible person who is acquainted with you and your work.

The 'references' is an essential element, for it gives the prospective employer an objective assessment of your achievements by reliable persons. If the references contain strong recommendations, your case for the job would get strengthened considerably. These are confidential but courtesy demands that you should inform the concerned persons before including their names in the resume. A letter of reference is also called a letter of 'recommendation', an example of which is given in the Section on 'Social Correspondence'.

Thus the central purpose of an application is to convince the employer that you are the right person for the job and that you would be able to use your special characteristics for the growth of the organisation.

There are two types of application letters: (i) an ordinary business letter containing all the relevant information and (ii) a short covering letter accompanied by a 'resume'. We give below an example of the latter which is more common.

606, Krishna Nagar

Lucknow - 226002

14 January, 2007

The Personnel Manager

National Petroleum Company
80 Netaji Marg

New Delhi-110009

Dear Sir

Your advertisement for an executive engineer in *The Times of India* of 13 January, 1990 interests me because I believe I have the right qualifications and the requisite experience for the job.

After doing B.E. in Chemical Engineering I have worked as an Assistant Engineer in Indian Oil Corporation for about six years. During this period I have gained experience in using modern techniques for increasing the production. The enclosed 'resume' gives all the required details.

I am sure I would be able to make a significant contribution in your forward-looking and expanding organisation. I would therefore be grateful if you give me an opportunity to be interviewed.

Yours faithfully

T. Shankar

End: Resume

RESUME

Personal Details	
Name:	T. Shankar
Date of birth:	15 July, 1981
Marital status:	Married, one son aged two
Nationality:	Indian
Address:	606 Krishna Nagar Lucknow-226002 (UP)

Education

Year	Examination	Division	Institution
1997	High School	I	Govt. Inter College, Lucknow
1999	Intermediate	I	-do-
2004	B. E. (Chemical Engg.)	I	Regional Engineering College, Allahabad

I did Chemical Process Technology, Process Design Decisions and Chemical Process Calculation as part of my B. E. programme which have given me an insight into the oil processing technology.

Training

As a trainee from June 2004 to December 2004 in Indian Oil Corporation I acquired practical experience in oil processing.

Experience

January 2005 to date: Assistant Engineer in Indian Oil Corporation in the scale of Rs. 9000-500 12000-17000. Was responsible for supervising production at Tilchat, Assam.

Awards

Won a Certificate of Merit for record production in 2006.

References

1. Prof. R.N. Bhandari
   Head, Department of Chemical Engineering,
   Regional Engineering College,
   Allahabad
2. Sri B.D. Jaiswal
   Dy. Chief Engineer (Production)
   Tel Bhawan, Sansad Marg
   New Delhi - 110001
3. Sri R.P. Ghosh
   Training Manager
   Indian Oil Corporation, Goswami Raod
   Kolkata - 700056

16.6 BANK AND INSURANCE CORRESPONDENCE

Bank correspondence refers to letters exchanged between

- a bank and its customers,
- a bank's head office and its branches,
- different branches of a bank, and
- different banks.

In respect of style, structure and layout such letters are like other types of business letters; only the subject matter differs. Most banks have now devised printed forms for routine communications. For example, if you want to open an account, all you have to do is to fill in a form obtainable from a bank and submit it to the appropriate authority. Similarly, for several other routine matters such as issue of a cheque book, closure of an account, grant of loan, etc. there is no need to write a letter. Printed forms are available for such transactions. For communication among the branches of a bank or with other banks, ready made printed formats are used. But there may be situations when one has to communicate something for which no forms are available. Obviously, in such situations a business letter has to be written in the manner discussed earlier.

What we have stated above is more or less true of insurance correspondence as well. Like banks, insurance companies provide a specialised type of service. So the language used for transacting business in this area has to be clear and concise and at the same time characterised by legal precision. The slightest ambiguity in composing the message may lead to unintended financial commitment or loss and even attract legal action. No wonder then, the bulk of the correspondence in this field too takes place through printed forms in which carefully thought out, purpose-specific language is used.

We now give below as a sample correspondence exchanged between a customer and a bank and a policy holder and an insurance company respectively.

Ramola Trading Company
44, Tilak Marg
Jaipur-302 019

5 December 2007

The Manager
Bharat National Bank
Bapu Nagar
Jaipur – 302 011

Saving Bank Account No: 6009843786

Dear Sir

Our cheque No.029784 dated 30 November, 2007 for Rs. 20,000 drawn in favour of Amit Electronics has been dishonoured and returned to us with the remarks 'Balance Inadequate'. We are unable to understand the reason for this action. When the cheque was drawn we had Rs.10,530 as credit balance in our account and a cheque for Rs. 25,000 was deposited to your branch on 21 November, 2007 for credit to this account.

I request you to let us know the reasons for dishonoring the cheque and to take suitable steps to prevent such mistakes in future.

Yours faithfully

Hari Dass
Manager

Bharat National Bank
Bapu Nagar
Jaipur 302 011

Reference: SBA/213

Date: 10 December 2007

Mr Hari Dass
Manager
Ramola Trading Company
44 Tilak Nagar
Jaipur – 302 019

Dear Mr. Dass

Please refer to your letter dated 5 December, 2007.

I am sorry we had to dishonor you cheque. But there was no option but to act as we did. The credit for the cheque for Rs. 25,000 deposited by you on 21 November was advised to us only on 2 December. You may be aware that the collection of outstation cheques normally takes about 10 days.

We regret the inconvenience caused to you. However, we would appreciate if you check the balance before drawing a cheque for payments to a party.

Yours faithfully

Azam Khan

Chief Manager

39, Anupam Apartments
Mahatma Gandhi Road
Bangalore-560016

15 November 2007

The Divisional Manager
Long Life Insurance Company

(Continued)

(*Continued*)

33 Mount Road
Chennai – 600002

Policy No. 9984673219-self

Dear Sir

I had to be away from India for six months and so I could not pay two quarterly premiums of Rs. 3,235 due on 15 July and 15 November 2007 and as a result my policy has lapsed. I consulted the local agent. He has advised me to pay the amount of two premiums and a penalty of Rs. 645 in lump sum for the renewal of the policy. Accordingly I am sending herewith Rs. 7115 (Rupees seven thousand one hundred and fifteen only).

I request you to take suitable action for the renewal of my policy. If any further action is required on my part, please let me know.

Yours faithfully

Rachit Kashiwal

End: Cheque No.019372 dated 15.11.2007

Long Life Insurance Company
33 Mount Road
Chennai-600002

Reference: LP/T3798

Date: 25 November 2007

Mr. Rachit Kashiwal
39 Anupam Apartments
Mahatma Gandhi Road
Bangalore – 560016

Dear Mr. Kashiwal

Please refer to your letter dated 15 November, 2007.

The cheque sent by you has been deposited into our account. Soon after it is realised, we shall send you an intimation regarding the renewal of your policy. We hardly need to add that it is in your own interest to avoid any such default in future.

Yours faithfully

S. Ramanujam
Divisional Manager

16.7 SOCIAL CORRESPONDENCE

You would often have to write letters to fulfil social obligations which may not be directly related to your professional work. Nonetheless, writing such letters is essential to maintain smooth and cordial relationship with your counterparts in other organisations and also with employees of your own organisation. Letters of this kind are always addressed by name. Promptness is the key to success in social correspondence.

Some letters of this kind are letters of recommendation, introduction, congratulation, acceptance, regret and condolence. Letters written for bookings in rail, air, and hotels for business visits also fall under this category.

The structure and the style of letters written for social purposes are in general the same as those of a business letter. However, most letters of this type have only the following seven elements: sender's address, date, salutation, body, complimentary close, signature and receiver's address. Their layout is determined by the particular form which is chosen for writing such letters. The style is marked by an air of ease, cordiality and friendship. A few examples follow:

Letter of Recommendation

Dear Shri Reddy

Please refer to your letter No. 315/A-17 dated 16 January, 2007 enquiring about Shri T. Shankar. I believe he is fully qualified to be employed as an executive engineer and I fully support his application. Shri Shankar joined our organisation as a Trainee and later he was appointed as Assistant Engineer. Looking at his initiative, drive and qualities of leadership we soon made him responsible for production at Tilchat. He has gained considerable experience in oil processing technology. He has a high potential for growth and would prove an asset to any organisation.

We would be sorry to lose him but we don't want to stand in his way for a change. I am sure in your fast growing organisation, he would be able to make a valuable contribution.

With kind regards

Yours sincerely

B.D. Jaiswal

Letter of Introduction

My dear Sudhir

This is to introduce to you Shri Atul Gupta, the son of a friend of mine.

Atul, after passing Higher Secondary Examination, from Central Board of Secondary Education, did a 3-year Diploma in Printing Technology from Govt. Printing Institute, Allahabad in the first division. He is sincere, hardworking and ambitious. Being amiable by nature, he can easily get along with people.

He is looking for a suitable opening in an organisation of repute such as yours. I am advising him to see you. I shall feel grateful if you kindly spare some time to grant him an interview. If there is no suitable opening right now, your assessment may prove helpful should an opportunity arise in the near future.

I believe our plan to go to Kathmandu in April still stands. You did not say anything about it in your earlier letter. Do confirm the plan in reply so that I may go ahead with the arrangements.

With warm regards and best wishes

Yours sincerely

Mukund

Letter of Congratulation

Dear Mr Bose

I am very glad to know that you have been promoted as Sales Manager. Please accept my heartiest congratulations.

I wish you many more successes in future.

With kind regards

Yours sincerely

R. Prasad

Reply

Dear Mr. Prasad

Thank you very much for your good wishes. The kind thoughts of friends like you would help me in discharging my duties efficiently in my new position. I hope I would be able to meet the expectations of the new assignment and maintain the high standard of professional excellence established by my predecessors.

With kind regards

Yours sincerely

L.P. Bose

Informal Invitation

Dear Shri Kumar

Could you please give us the pleasure of your company at lunch on Saturday 27 January, 2007, at 1 pm?

We have arranged it at Volga on Clive Road. I have asked a few other common friends to join.

Please do reply or just confirm on the phone your acceptance.

With best wishes

Yours sincerely

Sumant Singh

Acceptance

Dear Shri Singh

Many thanks for your invitation to lunch. I shall be happy to have it with you on 27 January. I look forward to meeting you and other friends.

With best wishes

Yours sincerely

D. Kumar

Regret

Dear Shri Singh

Thank you very much for your invitation to lunch on 27 January. I am afraid I would not be able to make it as I shall be out of town on that date for an important business meeting.

I know I am going to miss the delicious food of Volga and the warmth of your company. I hope I can look forward to some such occasion in future.

With best wishes

Yours sincerely

D. Kumar

Formal Invitation

Shri and Smt. Sumant Singh
request the pleasure of your company at
LUNCH
on Saturday, 27 January, 2007 at 1 p.m.
at Hotel Volga

RSVP

Smt. Singh
Telephone: 618136

Acceptance

Shri and Smt. D. Kumar
accept with great pleasure
Shri and Smt. Sumant Singh's kind invitation
to lunch on 27 January 2007

43 Gupta Marg,
Motinagar
16 January, 2007

Regret

Shri and Smt. D. Kumar
regret that owing to prior engagement
they are unable to accept
Shri and Smt. Sumant Singh's kind invitation
for lunch on 27 January 2007

43 Gupta Marg
Motinagar
16 January, 2007

Letter of Condolence

Dear Smt. Khandelwal

It is with great grief and shock that I learnt about the passing away of your husband. We knew that he had been ailing for some time but none could imagine that he would suddenly leave for his heavenly abode.

My feelings of grief and anguish are shared by my colleagues and all those who knew him. They join me in conveying to you our heartfelt condolences. We pray to God to grant you fortitude to bear the irreparable loss.

I am enclosing a copy of the Condolence Resolution passed by the Employees' Union of the Company.

With kind regards

Yours sincerely

Shantanu Dutta

End: As above

Reply

Dear Shri Dutta

Thank you for your letter conveying your sympathy at the loss of my husband. It gives me some comfort to know that so many of you share my grief and stand by me and my family in this hour of sorrow.

With kind regards

Yours sincerely

(Smt.) Deepa Khandelwal

ASSIGNMENTS

1. As Convenor of the Organising Committee of National Electronics Corporation, Bombay you have been asked to make arrangements for the annual conference of personnel officers based in different parts of India. Draft a letter to be sent to them giving relevant information about the time, date and venue of the conference. Also indicate the arrangements for transport, board and lodging of the officers.
2. Household Goods Co. Ltd. has produced a new food processor Jiffy, and you as Sales Manager have been asked to promote its sale. Draft a letter to be sent to ladies' clubs and hotels in Delhi.
3. Subhash Textile Co. Ltd., Ahmedabad is interested in buying twenty water coolers to be placed in different parts of the office and factory for the use of employees. Write a letter of enquiry to be sent to six firms inviting quotations for the water-coolers.
4. Assuming that you are the Sales Officer of one of the companies producing water-coolers, draft a quotation letter in response to the above enquiry. Invent the necessary details.
5. As Purchase Manager of Subhash Textile Co. Ltd., Ahmedabad place an order for twenty water-coolers with Jindal Refrigeration Corporation, Faridabad, whose quotation was accepted by the management.
6. As Collection Manager of *The Bharat Times*, New Delhi, write a letter to Jain Newspaper Agents, Bikaner against whom a bill for Rs. 1500 has been pending payment for the last one year. Inform them that unless the payment is received within one month, your company may be forced to initiate legal proceedings for collection.
7. (a) Assume that 12 room-heaters out of 50 have been received by your firm in damaged condition from Jupiter Electrical Appliances Co. Ltd., 26 Park Street, Calcutta 700009. As the Manager of your firm write a complaint letter to the supplier, seeking replacement or adjustment for the damaged goods. Invent the necessary details.

   (b) As Sales Manager of Jupiter Company draft a reply offering replacement.
8. Respond to the following advertisements, inventing the necessary details:

   (a) Wanted for a company of reputed group an Estate Manager for disposal of land and building situated near Delhi. Persons having experience of working with reputed builders may only apply. Attractive salary can be offered to the right candidate. Apply in strict confidence to Box 8622, The Times of India, New Delhi 110002.

   (b) A well-established private limited company dealing in foreign trade would like to have a lady secretary with good command over English and a Stenography; knowing French language, extra remuneration. Ladies drawing less than Rs. 2500/- need not apply. Apply within one week. Box No. 8625, *The Times of India*, New Delhi-110002.

   (c) An autonomous Research Institute in Delhi invites applications for the post of Finance Officer in the grade of Rs. 7,000-500-12000 plus allowances at Central Government rates. Other benefits include medical reimbursement, L.T.C., Gratuity, Provident Fund, etc. The candidates below 35 years should have a good Degree in Accounts and Audit and a minimum of 5 years' experience including computerisation of accounts, handling of income-tax matters, preparation of budget proposals, auditing of accounts, etc. Salary negotiable. Applications with name, address for communication, age, educational qualifications, experience, present grade with pay and allowances, salary expected should be sent to Box 133880, *Hindustan Times*, New Delhi-110001 within 15 days of this advertisement.

(d) USHA wishes to recruit young men and women as Commercial Executives in the age group of 20 to 25 years for placement in their corporate office in New Delhi for the following functional areas:

- Marketing Services
- Accounts
- Finance
- Cost Accounts
- Administration/Personnel

Commercial Executives will have the responsibility of providing support services to the concerned functional area, covering maintenance of management information data, writing agendas/minutes of meetings, office maintenance, and co-ordinating with branch offices and other departments.

Applicants should have a good academic/extra-curricular activities record and should have about 3 years and working experience. Local residential accommodation is essential. Gross starting emoluments will be over Rs. 12,500 per month. Contributory provident fund, gratuity, etc., are also provided. Additionally, special allowances are given for capability in computer skills. Please apply within 10 days, indicating the first and second preference of the functional areas listed above, with complete bio-data in an envelope marked P-87/88-6 to Usha International Limited (Personnel Deptt.) Post Box No. 504, New Delhi 110001.

Chapter 17

MEMORANDUM WRITING

17.1 CONTENTS

A memorandum (memo) is the most frequently used form of communication within an organisation. That is why it is also called inter-office memorandum. It is frequently used between persons who work together closely or are acquainted with one another and rarely used for communication with the members of other organisations. A memo is generally brief and to the point, and so the professionals find it a convenient means of communication in all directions: upward, downward and horizontal. It also serves as a record of routine events, requests and points arising out of day-to-day business transactions. Sometimes one may find it easier to communicate with an officer with whom personal contact is to be avoided. Many organisations have printed memo forms on which one can quickly word process or write and transmit a message.

The various types of messages, generally of a routing nature, which are exchanged through this form are: the confirmation of important points discussed on telephone, request for purchase of stationery, furniture, equipment, participation in seminars/conferences, announcement of policy decisions, appointment of officers to key positions, communication of matters relating to staff discipline and office routine, writing short reports, etc.

17.2 TYPES

There are some organisations in which terms such *as confirmation memorandum, request memorandum, purchase memorandum, procedural memorandum*, etc., are used to label different types of memorandums on the basis of their contents and purposes. We would however, prefer to classify them only in two distinct categories, namely, (i) those which are written for transacting the daily business in an organisation and (ii) those which contain short reports. Though the structure of both these categories is the same, in their style there is a difference. The style of the former is informal and direct and is based on the principles of I-you communication. The latter is written in a formal tone and is characterised by objectivity in which accuracy is essential. It contains authentic data, often technical information, conclusions, and recommendations, if required.

17.3 STRUCTURE

The following elements usually constitute the structure of a memo:

(i) Name of the organisation
(ii) Name/designation of the receiver
(iii) Name/designation of the sender
(iv) Reference
(v) Date
(vi) Subject
(vii) Body
(viii) The signature of the sender.

If the copies of the memo are to be sent to the other officers/departments, their names/designations are also indicated at the bottom-left. In the examples that follow we have shown one way of arranging these elements. However, there could be other methods of sequencing them. You should follow the practice prevalent in your organisation. If you find that the approved format misses any essential element. You should get the format amended in the light of information given in this Chapter. A specimen memo report is given in Chapter 13. A sample each of other types is given below.

Apex Electronics Corporation
Interoffice Memorandum

To: All Office Employees

From: Office Manager

Ref: FDs/P19

Date: 7 Oct. 2007

Subject: Dispatch of outgoing mail

Three years ago we had announced a policy that the outgoing mail received after 4.00 pm would be dispatched the same day by the Receipt and Dispatch Section. This was done because the staff had to leave the office at 5.00 pm and they needed one hour to get everything processed and sent to the Post Office.

Since the office now closes at 5.30 pm. You may send the outgoing mail to this Section upto 4.30 pm. As usual urgent letters will be accepted till 5.30 pm and dispatched the same day.

All employees are requested to note this change and cooperate with us in dispatching the outgoing mail promptly.

V. Ram Prasad

Mopatalal Cotton Mills Limited
Interoffice Memorandum

To: Public Relations Manager

From: Labour Welfare Officer Ref : SLR/TS911

Date: 15 Oct. 2007

Subject: Staff Welfare Fund

When I talked to you on the telephone yesterday, you agreed with my suggestion to create a Staff Welfare Fund to extend financial help to the employees and their families in times of prolonged illness or premature death. I have discussed this matter with the Financial Manager and he has endorsed the idea in principle but has suggested that the detailed guidelines should be prepared for the operation of this Fund. If you agree to work out the details we may constitute a three member committee, consisting of the following officers:

Personnel Manager (Convener)

Labour Welfare Officer, and

Budget Officer

D.D. Gupta

Manoharsing Sagar University
Interoffice Memorandum

To: The Registrar

Form: Manager, Printing Press

Ref: COD/101F

Date: 30 Oct., 2007

Subject: Purchase of Three Photocopiers

The Sodhi Photocopiers that we have is no longer adequate to meet all our needs. It is about seven years old and lacks versatility. Moreover, it breaks down frequently and needs major repairs. This year alone we had to spend Rs. 15,000 to keep it in working order. With the addition of four teaching departments and consequent increase in the number of both faculty and students, the volume of work

(Continued)

(Continued)

has gone up considerably. Our estimates show that we now require at least three more photocopiers to cope with the present day demands. We have also studied the features of various types of photocopiers currently available in the market. We recommend the purchase of Copra Xerox, each costing Rs.1,50,000 manufactured by Jackson and Smiths Ltd., Mumbai.

I request you to accord your administrative approval for the purchase of photocopiers.

Iqbal Ahamad

Sitaram Maxwell Ltd.
Interoffice Memorandum

To: Managing Director

From: Sales Manager

Ref: DIT/179

Date: 5 August, 2007

Subject: National Conference on Sales Promotion

As directed, I attended the National Conference held in Chennai on 6 and 27 July 2007 and presented a paper on the strategies for the promotion of sales of washing machines.

There was in-depth discussion on different methods of capturing the market through advertisements on electronics and print media. It was realised that these media did promote the sales. However, to have a competitive edge it is essential to devise and use other ways of reaching the consumer across the country. Some of the suggestions made were as follows: door to door contact with housewives and demonstration at strategic points at different parts of the town, distribution of handbills in regional languages, and hoardings in big towns.

I am enclosing for your perusal the literature containing the details of the suggestions made at the Conference. I, however, believe it would be better to conduct a market survey before devising new methods of promoting the sale of our machines.

T.D. Kashiwal

ASSIGNMENTS

1. As Public Relations Officer of Dynamic Tools Manufacturing Co. Ltd., Mumbai you have been deputed to investigate the causes of frequent strikes in the Company's factory at Nasik and to suggest preventive measures. Write a memo report to the Chairman incorporating your findings and recommendations.
2. Assume that as Assistant Personnel Manager you were deputed by your Company to attend a 3-day Business Communication Workshop organised by the Indian Institute of Management,

Sambhapur. You have now been asked to write a memo to the Personnel Manager, reporting on the various activities of the Workshop in which you participated and indicating the benefits you derived from it. Write this memo, inventing the necessary details.

3. A large number of junior officers of a company have sought permission to improve their educational qualifications through distance learning programs offered by different universities in India. As the Managing Director of this company write a memo to be sent to all employees, spelling out the company's policy in this regard. Also state that the applications already submitted would be examined in the light of this policy and the decision would be communicated to the individuals soon.
4. It has been noticed that a sizeable number of employees take leave on certain occasions such as test cricket, national sports events, etc. This hampers the smooth working of the office and tells upon the efficiency of the organisation. Assuming yourself to be the Personnel Manager, write a memo to the Sectional Heads of the company asking them to take suitable action to prevent mass absenteeism.
5. The General Manager of Jalan Home Appliances Ltd., Kolkata is worried about the non-availability of employees at their desks during duty hours. Draft a memo to be signed by him and circulated to all employees, asking them to follow the office hours strictly and not tc spend more that the allotted time on tea and lunch.
6. As Office Manager of Lalit Industries Ltd, Nagpur, write a memo to the Purchase Officer to procure the following items of furniture for the additional staff recently appointed by the company: 8 office tables, 6 chairs, 3 steel almirahs and 3 file racks. Your memo should refer to the fact that administrative approval for these items have already been obtained. Assume also that a copy of this memo is to be sent to the Finance Manager.
7. The President of Srinivas Textile Mills Ltd., Ahmedabad deputed its Labour Officer to investigate the causes of fire which broke out on 6 December, 2007, in the company's factory located at Navarangpura and to report to him the extent of damage and to suggest preventive measures. Assuming yourself to be the Labour officer, write this report in the form of a memo.
8. Assuming yourself to be the Manager of Sunrise Software Systems, Hyderabad write a memo for circulation to all employees, announcing a change in the working hours and explaining the reasons for doing so.
9. The Ramani Food Products Ltd., Shimla has decided to computerize its accounting procedure. As Finance Manager of this Company write a memo to all the employees of the accounting and audit sections to familiarize themselves with the operation of computers within three months. Tell them that the facilities for training would be available to them from 5 pm to 7 pm on weekdays on the office premises. Also, assure them that because of mcdernization there would be no retrenchment and the surplus staff, if any, would be transferred to other sections or departments.
10. As the Branch Manager of Heavy Electronics Ltd., Ranchi, write a memo to the Purchase Manager informing him that you have bought 3 word-processors, 2 photo copiers and their accessories, costing a total sum of Rs. 6,50,000 and requesting him to arrange for the payment of the bills you are enclosing.

Chapter 18

NOTICE, AGENDA AND MINUTES

FOR every meeting you are asked to hold you will have to issue a notice, draft the agenda, and after the meeting is over, write its minutes. In Chapter 5 we have already discussed how the meetings are organised and conducted. Here we shall briefly discuss how notices, agenda and minutes are written in the professional world.

18.1 NOTICES

Usually every organisation devises rules of procedure for the conduct of meetings. These rules indicate the frequency of meetings of different units and prescribe the notice period for calling a meeting besides indicating the person who has a right to call it and the persons who have a right to attend it. When you are required to call a meeting, send a written notice within the specified time to every member of the group. The notice should mention the name and address of the organisation, and the date on which it is issued apart from mentioning or indicating the day, date, time and venue of the meeting. The business to be transacted should be mentioned in the notice if the number of items is small; otherwise it should be indicated in a separate sheet and enclosed with the notice as annexure.

18.2 AGENDA

Agenda is an official list of items of business to be transacted at a specific meeting. It helps in conducting the meeting in proper order, minimises irrelevant discussion and preserves continuity in the proceedings. Since it is circulated along with the notice, every member knows beforehand the items of discussion and can make up his mind what he wishes to say on a particular issue. The agenda also helps the Chairman to control the members from going off the track and to organise the time to be devoted to individual items.

The items of the agenda are arranged in increasing order of importance and each item bears a number. However, almost every agenda has *confirmation of the minutes of the previous meeting* as the first item and *any other matter with the permission of the Chairman* as the last item. If there is any matter left over from the preceding meeting for enquiry and report, it usually appears as the second item of the agenda. If the meeting is one of a series, each item indicates the number of the meeting as follows:

4.01

4.02

4.03

4.04 and so on.

When the agenda is an annexure to the notice, the following information is repeated:

- Name of the organisation/unit
- Date of circulation
- Day, date, time and venue of meeting
- Signature of the secretary

The following sources might be used for agenda items:

- Minutes of the previous meeting
- Suggestions received from members
- Actions and events since the previous meeting
- Correspondence on the subject

Before finalising the items, get the Chairman's approval.

Standard Items

Certain items appear in almost every annual general meeting of a compan; and also voluntary organisations, such as a club or association. These are given below:

Public Limited Company	*Club or Association*
Director's Report	Chairman's or Secretary's Report
Annual Accounts	Annual Accounts
Auditor's Report	Auditor's Report
Appointment of Auditors	Appointment of Auditors
Declaration of Dividend	Subscriptions
Election of Directors	Election of Office Bearers

However, the sequence of items differs from organisation to organisation. In some the routine matter is placed in the beginning and in some at the end.

18.3 MINUTES

Minutes are the official records of the business transacted at a meeting. Keeping minutes of the meetings of certain organs of public limited companies is a legal requirement but even voluntary organisations find it helpful to record minutes of every meeting. The reason is obvious; minutes act as an aid to memory and provide a basis for decision and action. In fact a run-through of the minutes of a unit or organisation can give a fairly good idea to the reader as to how it has been conducting itself. As the minutes of every meeting are approved by the members at the next meeting and signed by both the secretary and the chairman, they are considered very important records and preserved carefully.

The style of minutes is impersonal, objective and matter-of-fact. The display of emotions, strong feelings and anger has no place in minutes. A cool, concise and accurate account of the main points of discussion, the decisions arrived at, recommendations made and the assignment of tasks to individual members or sub-committees is all that is required to be recorded.

When you are asked to write minutes, take notes bearing these points in mind. The actual writing of minutes can obviously be done only after the meeting is over. You should not hesitate to check or verify a particular point with the chairman or any other member before recording it in the minutes.

Minutes follow the pattern of agenda and bear the same numbers. For each item a heading is given and the discussion/decision on it is recorded. When a resolution comes up for consideration, the names of the proposer and the seconder may be mentioned. In some organisations, however, the practice is only to state whether the resolution was accepted or rejected.

As minutes are self-sufficient records, it is customary to give the following details:

- Name of the organisation/unit
- Day, date, time and venue of the meeting
- Number of the meeting, if in a series
- Names of the chairman and the secretary
- Names of member present
- Names of members absent
- Names of persons who attended the meeting by special invitation, if any
- Record of transactions, item-wise
- Signature of the secretary and the chairman

Practical Hints

Since minutes are not a verbatim transcript of the discussions utmost care should be taken in preparing the notes. A few practical hints are given below:

(i) Summarise as you record what is being said. Use abbreviations, short forms which you can readily decipher later.

(ii) Use agenda as the framework.

(iii) Record the names of the speakers. Though usually omitted from the minutes, they provide a useful reference point.

(iv) Record the names of those present by passing around a list of members for signature.

(v) Use a device to distinguish between the record of decisions and the record of main points.

(vi) Write carefully essential details such as dates, numbers, amounts, quantities and the names of those designated to act.

(vii) If a resolution is moved and a vote taken, make sure to note the name of the proposer, the name of the seconder, the number of members voting 'for' and 'against' and of those abstaining.

(viii) If any matter is raised under the last item of the agenda, state that it is so and give it a suitable heading.

18.4 EXAMPLES

Two examples follow. They show different styles of writing notices, agenda and minutes. The second example which is more formal is used by public limited companies.

Example I

Indian Oil Industries Ltd.
Singhal House
12 Ashok Road
New Delhi 110001

14 February 2006

Staff Welfare Association Executive Committee Meeting

NOTICE

The second meeting of the Executive Committe will be held at 5 p.m., on Wednesday, 28 February, 2006 in Room No. 16, Singhal House. The agenda is given below:

Please make it convenient to attend the meeting.

AGENDA

2.01 Minutes of the previous meeting.

2.02 Cafeteria report.

2.03 Celebration of Holi.

2.04 Raise in subscription.

2.05 Request for donation.

2.06 Grant of study leave.

2.07 Any other matter with the permission of the Chairman.

Gokul Shilpe
Secretary

cc: All Members

MINUTES

Indian Oil Industries Ltd.
Singhal House
12, Ashok Road
New Delhi 110001

Staff Welfare Association

Minutes of the second meeting of the Executive Committee held at 5 pm, on Wednesday, 28 February, 2006 at Singhal House.

Members Present	Shri A.K. Dasgupta (Chairman)
	Shri Y. Nagappa
	Shri Nazir Ahmed
	Miss Clare Thomas
	Shri K.S. Duggal (Treasurer)
	Shri Gokul Shilpe (Secretary)
Members Absent	Shri Ram Bharose

2.01 Minutes of the previous meeting

The minutes of the meeting held on 4 January, 2006 were taken as read, adopted and signed by the Chairman.

2.02 Cafeteria report

The sales report of the Cafeteria was received and approved. The suggestion of the Manager to serve mini meals during lunch time was accepted on a trial basis for three months.

2.03 Celebration of Holi

It was decided to organise an informal get-together and a short entertainment programme at 6 pm on 4 March. A sum of Rs 15,000 was approved for the purpose. The secretary was asked to work out the details.

2.04 Raise in subscription

In view of the rising cost of goods and services a proposal was put forward by Shri Shilpe to raise the annual subscription from Rs 50/- to Rs 75/- from the financial year 2006-07. The proposal evoked mixed reaction and certain modifications were suggested. Ultimately it was decided to raise the subscription to Rs 70 only.

2.05 Request for donation

As it was increasingly becoming difficult to meet the expenditure, from the Association's own resources, a resolution to request the management of the Company for a recurring donation of Rs 20,000/- per annum, moved by the Chair was unanimously adopted.

2.06 Grant of study leave

It was noted that the request of some members for the grant of study leave on full pay to pursue further studies was rejected by the management. A sub-committee consisting of

(i) Shri Gokul Shilpe (Convenor)
(ii) Shri Nazir Ahmed and
(iii) Miss Clare Thomas was asked to discuss the issue with the Personnel Manager and to report the outcome at the next meeting.

As no other matter was raised the meeting ended with a vote of thanks to the Chair.

A.K. Dasgupta
Chairman

Gokul Shilpe
Secretary

Example II

Piramal Steel Corporation Ltd
14 Garden Avenue
Subhash Chandra Marg
Kolkatta 700019

1 March, 2006

NOTICE

Notice is hereby given for the Fifteenth Annual General Body Meeting of the Company to be held at 11 am, on Thursday 15 March, 2006 at Garden Avenue. The agenda is attached.

End: One

R. Chauhan
Secretary

To: All shareholders

Pirmal Steel Corporation Ltd.
Kolkata

AGENDA

15.01 Confirmation of the minutes of the last meeting:
15.02 Directors' Report and Annual Accounts
15.03 Auditors' Report
15.04 Appointment of Auditors
15.05 Declaration of Dividend
15.06 Election of the Directors
15.07 Any other matter with the permission of the Chair.

R. Chauhan
Secretary

MINUTES

Piramal Steel Corporation Ltd.
Kolkata

Minutes of the Fifteenth Annual General Body Meeting of the Company held at 11 am on Thursday 15 March, 2006 at 14 Garden Avenue.

Present: Shri R.C. Chandra	Chairman
Shri P.K. Rungta	
Shri Deepak Narayan	
Shri Kamal Kishore Sharma	Directors
Shri Pawan Kumar	
Shri Ved Prakash Dhillon	

In attendance: Shri R. Chauhan, Secretary
Shri Gulzar Hussain, Solicitor and shareholders as per attendance sheet.

No.	*Subject*	*Minutes*
15.01	Confirmation of the minutes of the last meeting	The minutes of the meeting held on 15 March, 2006 were approved and signed by the Chairman
15.02	Directors' Report and Annual Accounts	The Directors' Report and the Annual Accounts circulated there-with were taken as read. The Chairman reported the progress of the Company and highlighted its achievements besides outlining the next year's development plan. On a motion by Shri R. Diwakar, seconded by Shri T. Varky, the Directors' Report and the Anneal Accounts as audited by the Company's auditors were approved and adopted.
15.03	Auditors' Report	The Auditors' Report which had already been circulated was taken as read and approved. It was noted that the assets of the company had increased by Rupees 87 lakh.
15.04	Appointment of Auditors	On a motion by Shri Pawan Kumar, seconded by Shri Gopal Vyas, it was resolved: 'That Messrs Chopra and Joshi be reappointed as auditors of the Company for the next accounting year at a fee of Rs. 24,500'.
15.05	Declaration of Dividend	The following motion moved by Shri Ram Singh and seconded by Shri Naveen Chandra was adopted: 'That a dividend of Rs. 50 per equity share, subject to deduction of income tax, as recommended by the Board of Directors is approved and will be paid to the shareholders whose names stood on the books of the Company on 1 March 2006'.

15.06	Election of the Directors	Shri A. Ali proposed that the two retiring directors Shri P.K. Rungta and Shri Pawan Kumar be reappointed. The following resolution moved by him and seconded by Shri A.K. Patodia was adopted 'Resolved that Shri P.K. Rungta and Shri Pawan Kumar, being eligible for reelection are hereby reelected as Directors of the Company for a period of two years'.
15.07	Next year's development plan	The suggestion of a shareholder, Shri Ramanand Pandey that the main points of next year's development plan of the Company be printed and circulated to shareholders, was admitted by the Chair and adopted by the general body.

The meeting ended with a vote of thanks to the Chairman.

R.C. Chandra
Chairman

R. Chauhan
Secretary

Date: 17 March, 2006

ASSIGNMENTS

1. Assume that you have been appointed Secretary of a Committee comprising management, staff and workers' representatives, to advise the company to produce a handbook containing information about conditions of service, rules and regulations, fringe benefits and other related matters. The Committee held its first meeting on 16 April, 2006 and discussed the procedures for the collection of information and its organisation for the handbook. Invent the necessary details and draft the agenda and minutes of this meeting.
2. The Executive Committee of Bhiwani Industrial Corporation, Bhiwani, held its fifth meeting on 10 December, 2007 at BIC Headquarters, Bhiwani. The agenda was as follows:
   - 5.01 Minutes of the last meeting.
   - 5.02 Addition of two rooms to the building – one for general stores and the other for office workers.
   - 5.03 Opening a tea stall.
   - 5.04 Appointment of two peons and one treasurer.
   - 5.05 Setting up a paper mill at Bhiwani.
   - 5.06 D.A. to the employees.
   - 5.07 Any other matter with the permission of the Chair.

   As Secretary of the Executive Committee write the minutes of the meeting.
3. Imagine that you are the Secretary in attendance at the seventh annual meeting of the Executive Committee of the Ramgarh Club held at 6 pm on Tuesday, 6 March, 2006. Write the minutes of meeting, assuming the agenda to be as follows:
   - 7.01 Minutes of the previous meeting.
   - 7.02 Chairman's report.

7.03 Appointment of an auditor for the next year.
7.04 Purchase of furniture for the common room.
7.05 Creation of one post of a full-time clerk for the club.
7.06 Increase the the subscription rate.
7.07 Any other matter with the permission of the Chairman.

4. At a meeting of the Executive Committee of the Staff Association of Government Engineering College, Devigarh held at 4 pm, on Friday 23 March, 2006 in Room Number H-39, the following business was transacted: appointment of auditors for the annual accounts, construction of a swimming pool for staff, minutes of the last meeting, establishment of departmental libraries, extra classes for students who failed in the mid-semester examination, any other matter with the permission of the Chairman.

   Assuming that you were the Secretary in attendance, (i) draft a notice to be sent to each member arranging the agenda items properly and (ii) write the minutes.

5. At the tenth meeting of the Board of Directors of Precision Machine Tools Co. Ltd., Jamshedpur the following business was transacted:

   10.01 Minutes of the previous meeting.
   10.02 Tenders for the new premises.
   10.03 Creation of five posts of travelling salesmen.
   10.04 Resignation of the Chief Accountant.
   10.05 Opening branch offices in Nagpur, Hyderabad and Cochin.
   10.06 Any other matter with the permission of the Chairman.

   Assuming that you were the Secretary in attendance, draft the minutes of the meeting.

6. In a TV manufacturing organisation, a meeting has been called to take a decision about an advertising campaign to be launched by the company. A proposal prepared by the Advertising Manager is to be presented for discussion and approval. Assuming that you have been named the Secretary of this meeting, draft a notice and agenda for it. Invent the necessary details.

7. Assume that you have recently taken over as the Secretary of a Public Limited Company. Informal discussion with the senior officers reveals, among other things, that the growth of the organisation has been hampered because of frequent strikes by labourers. After going through your preliminary report, the Chairman has called a meeting of the Board of Directors to discuss the issue in depth and to find a lasting solution to the problem.

   Draft the agenda for this meeting, inventing the necessary details.

Chapter 19

HANDBOOKS AND MANUALS

19.1 HANDBOOKS

PROFESSIONAL organisations usually produce a variety of handbooks* ranging from short, duplicated or photocopied sets of regulations to glossy, multi-coloured reports. These are produced for different types of audience such as office staff, technical personnel, shareholders, etc. Certain handbooks are brought out for general information, e.g. history of the organisation, and certain handbook that are only for the benefit of employees, e.g. sets of rules.

When you are asked to produce a handbook, how should you go about it?

First of all, carefully determine what information you have to convey. Next, analyse its readership, i.e. who the intended readers are. Lastly, decide how best to convey the information. A determination of these three factors would enable you to decide which style of writing is to be used and the technique of presenting the information. In general, every handbook should be easy to read even if the information to be conveyed is complex. For example, when you are asked to convey information about leave, pension, service conditions, etc., avoid legal jargon and complex sentences as far as possible. Often this problem is solved by giving in the handbook only the broadest summary and then referring the reader to another source of information.

The contents are determined by the purpose and readership. For example, when the intention is to inform new employees of the fundamental rules and working conditions of your organisation the handbook may contain the following:

(i) Short introduction by the head of the organisation.

---

* A handbook may be defined as a collection of useful information, combining some of the features of both a dictionary and an encyclopedia.

(ii) Information about the organisation in brief.

(iii) Rules such as attendance, leave, general conduct, health, safety, discipline, etc.

(iv) Benefits such as education, training, entertainment, canteen, D.A., pension, etc.

Remember, whatever be the subject-matter of a handbook, it should be capable of being handled and referred to conveniently. Before you go in for production, find out the number of copies to be produced, the amount of money available and the mode of production (duplicated, photocopied, word processed, printed). Other details to be determined by you are the quality and size of paper, the type of binding and the kind of cover to be used.

19.2 MANUALS

A manual is a concise reference handbook dealing with a particular process, procedure, operation, mechanism, job instruction, etc. It is essentially a how-to-do-it document prepared with meticulous care, containing details of the concerned subject-matter. It explains how a certain thing happens or how a particular job should be done. It thus has an 'if-then' approach to what is being explained.

A manual grows out of the sheer necessity and the concern of an organisation to keep running smoothly and getting jobs done efficiently. It is unique inasmuch as it deals with only one appliance or mechanical device. Typical uses of a manual are:

(i) Instructions to customers on the use of the equipment/ appliance you are supplying.

(ii) Instructions to customers' representatives on how to instruct their own employees on the use of a machine.

(iii) Instructions to management, supporting staff or helping staff on the use of equipment or procedures.

(iv) Instructions to other departments or organisations on how to liaise their operations with yours.

19.2.1 Types

A large organisation may have a number of manuals dealing with different jobs, functions or descriptions. A run through of the kinds of manual used in the professional world, however, indicates that they can be classified into the following three categories:

(i) *Technical Manual*: A technical manual describes an appliance or a mechanical device and contains instructions for installation, operation, maintenance, repair, and overhaul. It may also state how the problems in their working may be solved. A manual of this type in a particular industry is often termed as *Industrial Manual*. When a manual deals only with one of the aspects of a machine, it may be termed as *Operation Manual, Installation Manual*, or *Maintenance/Service Manual* depending upon its contents. In practice, however, a machine has a manual dealing with all these aspects.

(ii) *Laboratory Manual*: This describes how the user of a lab should perform specified experiments and gives information about the concerned equipment, components, devices and testing techniques. It may also contain pre-and post-experiment quiz questions for self-testing. Such manuals are usually written for specific courses in universities or for the conduct of experiments in research laboratories.

(iii) *Procedure Manual*: This deals with established procedures and working practices in an organisation. Generally the contents of such a manual are of a non-technical nature. It may, for example, describe in detail the procedure to be followed for applying for a loan or an advance.

19.2.2 Features

Certain features are common to every manual: sources, parts, and style. It is these which we are going to discuss now.

(a) *Sources*: When you are asked to write a manual, the first problem that you would face would be, where to get the matter from. There are three obvious sources. One, your own personal experience in the area. You would usually be given this task only if you are familiar with the job. Two, others' experience and documents dealing with the subject matter. These may be reports, letters, memos, notes in the files and descriptions by the manufacturers, etc. Three, the internet. You may be able to find through it relevant information on the subject. You should analyse the information that you collect from these sources before you transform the entire data into small units for step-by-step instruction or description. There is another consideration which should guide you, namely, a visualisation of the reader's needs and problems – his education, experience, degree of responsibility, expectations, etc. After the analysis is over, prepare a detailed outline. Organise it on the basis of the reader's need to know what you are saying. Sequencing is as important as the need to visualise all the steps in a particular process. If you miss a single step the entire operation may go wrong just as if you miss a single detail the description may become meaningless. The outline of a manual thus is different from the outline of other forms of writing. Careful thought is required for splitting the information and converting the experience into small but easily understandable instructions or steps.

(b) *Parts*: A manual has the following parts:

(i) *Cover*: Title and type of the manual, name of the organisation, month and year of production.

(ii) *Table of Contents*: It contains the numbers and titles of sections or chapters into which it is divided and the page number on which each item begins.

(iii) *List of Illustrations*: If the number of illustrations is five or more, list them, giving the page number on which each appears.

(iv) *List of Tables*: This list is usually given if the number of tables is five or more. It contains the number, title and page number of each.

(v) *Introduction*: A manual may or may not have this part. It may straight away start with instructions. When an introduction is given, it indicates the purpose and defines the scope of the manual. It also contains the meaning of any abbreviations and symbols used. If it is the second or later edition, a brief reference is given to the changes introduced since its last printing.

(vi) *Description*: It generally appears in a manual which deals with the operation, maintenance or servicing of a piece of equipment. In it a general description of the concerned equipment is given to acquaint the reader with the technical details.

(vii) *Main Body*: In this part, the subject matter properly classified, appears. The headings and the sub-headings are determined by the matter dealt with.

(viii) *Appendices*: This part follows the last section and contains useful details which are considered worthy to be recorded but which do not merit inclusion in the main body.

(ix) *Glossary and Index*: They are the same as already discussed in Chapter 13.

Examples of the Cover and Table of Contents follow:

SERVICE MANUAL
FOR

RECORDAK MAGNAPRINT READER
MODEL PK-4A

MAHAPRABHU INDUSTRIES LTD.
23, Park Street, Second Floor
Kolkatta - 700016
March 2006

TABLE OF CONTENTS

Page Nos.

In the above Table all the items are self-explanatory. Perhaps *warning* needs some explanation. In some technical manuals this goes by two other names, *precaution* or *notice*. Here is an extract from the Operation and Maintenance Manual for Bajaj Chetak Scooter.

> To keep your Bajaj Chetak in perfect running order and not to invalidate the Warranty offered by the company, it is advisable to entrust repairs only to dealers or authorised service stations.
>
> Demand genuine Bajaj Auto spare parts. All Bajaj Auto spare parts are made of the same material, have undergone the same machining operations and inspection as the components of your Bajaj Chetak. This guarantees a long life and normal performance of your machine and your personal safety.

(c) *Style*: We have already discussed in detail the main features of the style of a formal report in Chapter 14. In general, what we have said in that Chapter is applicable to the writing of a manual also. In the latter, however, the focus and the emphasis are different. So here we shall draw your attention to certain special features and emphasise certain points.

In a manual you have to make extensive use of illustrations and give frequent and numerous examples to drive the meaning home. Verbal Instructions are greatly strengthened by graphic representation. Sometimes the latter would be an extension of what is written and sometimes merely an explanation or repetition. You must maintain a suitable correlation between the verbal expression and the graphic language. The language should be plain, concrete and specific. Avoid the use of unnecessary words and jargon. There should be consistency in the use of terminology, abbreviations and symbols. These, if new, should be explained either in the introduction or glossary. The structure of sentences is adapted to the audience of the manual. When you have to give instructions, use the second person imperative and in describing an equipment, for example, use the third person indicative mood. However, remember that accuracy and clarity are the ultimate hallmarks of the style of a manual.

A manual may contain three kinds of expository writing: *persuasive*, as used in sales letters; *instructional*, as in cookery books; and *informative*, as in reports.

Here is an example of persuasive writing from the INTRODUCTION of Bajaj Chetak Manual:

> Now the keys are yours to the new Bajaj Chetak Scooter.
>
> It comes to you from a company that is world famous for its two-wheelers.
>
> Basically, the Chetak has been designed to give you excellent mileage over long and short runs with power to carry two people comfortably.
>
> This Operation and Maintenance Manual gives you necessary information needed to maintain your Scooter, so that you will get the very best out of it for many years to come.

The extract that follows is from a Manual giving instructions for the unpacking of a machine.

> Slit the tape and open the top of the box. Remove the packing cover and the envelope which contains the operations instruction booklet and packing list. Be sure the instruction booklet is kept with the machine.

Now an example from the Operator's Manual for Canon-125, describing one of its features:

> In addition to automatic cassette feed, the NF-125 also accepts paper fed by hand along its manual feed guide. This is extremely convenient when only a few copies of an infrequently used size or type of paper are required.

Before you go in for production, decide on the size of the manual, the number of copies to be produced and the mode of production. While doing so keep the following four important points in mind:

(i) It should be handy as it is frequently referred to.

(ii) It should be easy to revise as frequent changes are made in the process or procedure dealt with.

(iii) It should be kept up-to-date as the users are expected to follow exactly the given instructions.

(iv) It should be cost effective as it may have to be reproduced at short intervals.

ASSIGNMENTS

1. Write a set of instructions for operating an electrical appliance used at your home.
2. Describe in detail the steps that you took in conducting an experiment in the laboratory for the benefit of a new batch of students.
3. Prepare an instructions manual on the registration procedure at your college or university for freshmen.
4. Describe the process of operating a machine on which you have actually worked. This information is to be included in an operation manual.
5. Write a manual describing the in-service training schemes of your organisation and indicating how employees can avail themselves of them. The manual should have separate sections describing the procedure for entry into a particular training scheme.

Chapter 20

RESEARCH PAPERS AND ARTICLES

20.1 RESEARCH PAPERS

EVEN if it is not your profession, you may individually carry out research on your own initiative or as a member of a research project team of your organisation. The results you arrive at would hardly be of any value unless they are made known to others, working, or interested in the same sphere of activity or knowledge. This you can do by presenting your findings in a professional gathering or if you wish to reach a wider audience, by publishing them in a journal. In either case you will have to organise the material (data, analysis, results, etc.) in the form of a research paper.

It is obvious that the knowledge from research should be quickly publicised. There are two reasons for it; one, to avoid wasteful duplication of work and two, to establish the researcher's claim to the priority of discovery. That is why to accord a permanent value to the effort, the results must be published in the form of a research paper. All research journals of repute, as we are aware, control the urge to publish by a rigorous refereeing system and this ensures the originality and quality of contribution.

Research is not the preserve of scientists or an such specialist group of persons; it is, in fact, any systematic investigation towards increasing the sum of knowledge. Sometimes a research work may replicate previous research with a view to testing the reported findings or the relevance of such findings in a different cultural milieu or social setting. It may also be undertaken to follow up new leads to refine or qualify the finding of earlier studies. Research may be based on a careful search of material in journals, books material on the internet and other publications or carefully designed experiments. Whatever be the method of enquiry, every piece of research must make an original contribution to knowledge. The definition of research given in Webster's *Seventh New Collegiate Dictionary* is comprehensive and worth quoting here: 'Investigation or experimentation aimed at the discovery and interpretation of facts, revision of accepted theories or laws in the light of new facts, or practical application of such new or revised theories or laws.'

20.1.1 Definition

We may define a research paper as a documented* prose work, incorporating the results of an organised analysis of a subject. In its style, structure and approach, it closely resembles a formal report. Therefore most of the principles discussed in Chapter 9 are applicable to the writing of a research paper. Similarly, the detailed information given in Part IV of this book is relevant in this context also. However, a research paper in certain respects differs from a formal report. It is written mainly to disseminate knowledge whereas a report is written for decision-making or action. The reading of a research paper is optional but a report must be read by someone. The incentive for a research paper may be the enhancement of one's own professional status, whereas a report is always prompted by a specific need of the organisation.

20.1.2 Characteristics

You are already familiar with the features of a formal report. We give below, if only for the sake of emphasis, four characteristic features of a research paper. You will observe that they are not exclusive to this form of writing; they are given here only to complete this thought process.

(i) A research paper may be written about any subject – social, cultural, scientific, technical, etc., but the treatment is scholarly and is supported by evidence.
(ii) There is a relatively high concentration of certain writing techniques such as definition, classification, interpretation and abstraction or description of a process, procedure or a mechanical device.
(iii) Its formal elements are generally those of a report and the writing is characterised by the use of graphic aids and scientific, technical or specialised vocabulary.
(iv) The emphasis is on the presentation of information accurately and concisely and an attitude of complete impartiality and objectivity is maintained by the writer.

20.1.3 Types

At this stage it might be useful to differentiate various forms of writing that are usually termed as research papers. Let us first make a distinction between what an advanced level student may be required to do as an academic exercise and what a researcher reports as his contribution to knowledge. It cannot, however, be denied that sometimes the contribution of a student may attain a high level of excellence and reach the same status as that of the latter but this is not its primary purpose. A student's paper is sometimes called a *library research paper or a term paper or a theme paper*. There are three preparatory steps in writing such a paper, namely, selecting a subject, locating sources of information and note-

* It indicates that the sources of borrowed material are acknowledged and those consulted in the writing of the paper are listed.

making. Usually such a paper is written under the guidance of an instructor and the student is advised how to go about it. He may also be provided with a preliminary reading list so that he can proceed on the right course and plan his work effectively.

Two other terms, namely, scientific paper and technical paper are often interchangeably used to refer to a research paper. When a distinction is made, it is on the basis of its contents. The former deals with a scientific subject and furthers the theory of a discipline; the latter deals with new ideas, relationships, processes or equipment related to the practice of some technology.

20.1.4 Elements

Although a research paper does not contain all the elements of a formal report, it can be made effective if the matter is broken up into logical sections with suitable headings and sub-headings. Its usual elements which are as follows, are self-explanatory.

- Abstract or Summary
- Introduction
- Materials and Methods
- Experimental Section, Design or Procedure
- Results
- Discussion
- Conclusions
- Acknowledgements
- List of Symbols
- References or Bibliography

There is a large variety in the presentation of matter in a research paper. Every paper does not have all the elements mentioned above. In certain papers results and discussion are combined. In some Notes are combined with References. A paper may also have an Appendix. As in reports, in some research papers the element 'Discussion' does not appear as a heading and the matter relating to this part is broken into a number of sub-headings. A number of journals give detailed instructions about presentation and the contributor has then to follow them.

20.1.5 Evaluation

Occasionally you may be required to evaluate a research paper. We give below some questions that are likely to prove helpful in assessing the merit of a paper.

1. What is the author's purpose? To detail an experiment? To establish a principle? To make an evaluation?
2. Does the writer include all the information that the audience may need to know?
3. Is it at a level of technicality that will be understandable to the audience?
4. Does it have an appropriate structure?

5. Are the central thesis and supporting data integrated into a logical presentation? Can you follow the arguments?
6. Is documentation given in an acceptable form?

20.2 ARTICLES

A *scientific* or *technical article* may deal with subjects similar to those of a research paper, but its approach is different. It is more general and informal and is intended for a wider audience. The article is usually written for a newspaper or a periodical. Some times they are semi-technical in nature, but in either case they try to answer in as plain a style as possible the following questions: 'How does something happen?'; 'Why does it happen?'; 'In what way does it help us?' The emphasis in the articles is on the communication of the human implications of a device, discovery or invention rather than on the details of the process or mechanism used for arriving at the results. For example, a research paper on environmental pollution may explain how it is caused, give the reasons and suggest ways of controlling it in scientific terms. On the other hand, an article on the same subject is likely to emphasise the impact of the pollution on plants, animals and human beings, and the role of the common man in preventing it. In an article there is greater flexibility in the sequencing of material. Formal headings may not appear at all. The author may decide to dramatise or highlight a particular aspect and therefore mention it in the very beginning and then unfold the story. Thus you will notice that an article is a piece of communication which permits greater flexibility in its approach, style and structure.

The samples of a research paper and a technical aslide are given below for illustration.

Sample Research Paper

An Approach to ELT Syllabus Design

Krishna Mohan and Meera Banerji

Abstract

This paper embodies the results of an analysis of ELT syllabi currently in use at the undergraduate level in India and suggests a new approach to syllabus design. The analysis reveals that the design of syllabi does not take into account, either the requirements of the social situation or the principles of curriculum construction. A new approach is, therefore, suggested, on the basis of which, it is claimed, more meaningful and relevant ELT courses can be devised for all the programmes offered by the Indian universities. Such courses would prove effective in imparting, communicative competence, which is the central purpose of language teaching.

Introduction

The syllabus is perhaps the most important referential document of a course. It should, therefore be formulated with great care, keeping in view the specific needs of the learners and the accepted principles of curriculum construction. In India no comprehensive and scientific study of ELT syllabi has so far been made to determine their relevance and effectiveness. The most notable attempt in this direction was the organisation of Zonal Workshops and a National Workshop for Syllabus Reform in English

(UGC 1977). The recommendations made by these Workshops are based on half-baked ideas and much too generalised notions abstracted from experience. There is no attempt to grapple with the main issue, namely, what factors should guide the determination of the nature of the contents and how these should be arrived at.

Role of English

Two studies (Das 1977, Parashar 1979) have corroborated the view that at present, English in India, serves a utilitarian purpose. Its use is maximal in formal domains and competence in using it is essential for success in a profession. We, therefore, went to the actual users to determine the extent and purpose of the use of English in the professional world (Banerji 1984). But before we present the results of this survey, let us look at what the analysis of syllabuses currently in use reveals.

Analysis of Syllabi

In the absence of any guidance from the past a new procedure for analysis has been evolved. In all 346 syllabuses of 79 Universities, relating to B.A., B.Sc., B.Sc., (Ag.), B.Com and B.E. the programmes containing 2564 items were examined Table shows the programme-wise break-up of the syllabuses consulted and the number of items occurring in each.

Table 20.1 General Pattern of Syllabi Programme-wise

Components	*B.A.*		*B.Sc.*		*B.Sc. (Ag.)*		*B.Com.*		*B.E.*	
	Items	*%*	*Items*	*%*	*Items*	*%*	*Items*	*%*	*Items*	*%*
Comprehension	122	14.51	94	13.04	22	11.83	109	16.34	21	14.09
Composition	148	17.60	140	19.42	32	17.20	173	25.94	37	24.84
Grammar and Usage	284	33.77	280	38.83	93	50.00	222	33.28	65	43.63
Lexis	25	02.97	03	00.42	01	00.54	11	01.65	02	01.34
Translation	22	02.61	20	02.77	07	03.76	17	02.55	-	-
Spoken English	07	00.83	05	00.69	03	01.62	04	00.06	06	04.02
Mechanics of Writing	-	-			-	-	01	00.15	01	00.67
Prescribed Texts	233	27.71	179	24.83	28	15.05	130	19.49	17	11.41
Total	841	100	721	100	186	100	667	100	149	100
Total no. syllabi consulted		113		102		22		95		14

As is evident from Table 20.1 'grammar and usage' has the largest share in all the: programmes, indicating a clear trend, showing that the major concern of the courses is to impart grammatical competence. Further, the weightage to the prescribed texts shows a heavy dependence on textbooks for imparting skills. Two language skills, namely, listening and speaking, are relegated to an insignificant place.

The analysis also reveals that a negligible number of universities state the objectives. Even where the objectives are stated, they are vaguely worded or much too generalised and do not provide adequate guidance to the syllabus user. Most of the syllabi are contents-oriented rather than skills-oriented. The texts prescribed include prose passages, poems, one-act plays, drama (usually classics), novels both 'retold' and 'unabridged' and short stories. Scant attention is paid to the central purpose of language teaching, namely, the imparting of communicative competence. In quite a number of cases the components are stated ambiguously. Some of the prescribed texts are stated to be for 'detailed study' and some for 'non-detailed study'. In some syllabuses only the marks allocated to texts are indicated and no further details are given.

Thus we see that the picture that emerges is of utter confusion; no systematic pattern of thought consistent with the requirements of the current social situation and language pedagogy appears to have guided the design of the syllabus of any programme. The syllabus seems to fulfill merely an administrative requirement. It is there because it has to be.

The Needs for English

Now let us turn our attention to the survey of the needs for English in the professional world. For this survey the sample population consisted of 207 subjects belonging to 65 professional organisations located in different parts of India, and engaged in diverse functions such as general administration, planning and designing, marketing and sales, office management, consultancy, research, teaching, editing and publishing, publicity, liaison work and public relations, legal advice, financial management and auditing, imparting pre-service and in-service training, labour welfare and personnel management, clerical assistance and record keeping, purchasing and technical work. The data were collected through a mail questionnaire.

It is discovered that all the 32 language tasks listed in the questionnaire and the related sub-tasks identified by us as relevant for professional purposes are actually performed with varying degrees of frequency as Tables 20.2 & 20.3 reveal:

Table 20.2 Weighted Average of the Use of Spoken English for Professional Purposes

Sl. No.	*Language Tasks*	*Weighted Average*
1.	Presenting written material	70.28
2.	Oral reporting	70.16
3.	Making inquiries	64.25
4.	Giving instructions and directions	62.56
5.	Dictating	61.95
6.	Participating in meetings, seminars, etc.	53.98
7.	Note-taking	44.44

8.	Establishing social relations	43.71
9.	Interviewing	42.51
10.	Negotiating deals, agreements, etc.	41.78
11.	Demonstrating	40.45
12.	Making speeches	37.19
13.	Formal teaching	34.66
14.	Making announcements	24.39

Table 20.3 Weighted Average of the Use of Written English for Professional Purposes

Sl. No.	*Language Tasks*	*Weighted Average*
1.	Writing letters	79.10
2.	Writing reports	76.4
3.	Writing memos, orders	69.80
4.	Keeping records	64.49
5.	Writing notices, circulars, agenda, minutes, etc.	58.57
6.	Filling in forms	56.76
7.	Writing short messages	64.34
8.	Writing technical proposals	52.17
9.	Note-making	50.12
10.	Writing formal invitations	40.45
11	Abstracting and summarizing	38.64
12.	Writing research papers, articles, etc.	32.72
13.	Writing handbooks, manuals	31.88
14.	Writing publicity materials	26.57
15.	Writing booklets/brochures	25.12
16.	Preparing market surveys	23.91
17.	Editing	19.68
18.	Writing press releases	18.23

Inventory of language tasks and sub-tasks

An inventory (vide Appendix) of these tasks and sub-tasks can, therefore, serve as a useful guide for formulating an approach to syllabus design. This inventory is not exhaustive but then selection is inherent in any kind of formal instruction. The term 'language task' is used here to refer to a macro-function, whereas the label 'sub-task' to indicate a micro-function, which is performed by a professional to achieve a specific objective. The relationship of a sub-task to a language task is that of a function to a resultant activity, which may be performed through the spoken or written mode and take different forms of communication.

The list of sub-tasks, like that of language tasks, is not exhaustive. Nor are the sub-tasks unique in relation to a particular language task; there is an inevitable overlap. Hence one sub-task may be realised through the performance of more than one language task. Since our purpose is merely to propose an approach to syllabus design and not to suggest a syllabus, we have not attempted to list the language skills which would be required for the realisation of sub-tasks. Moreover, an undergraduate level student is expected to have acquired sufficient mastery over the linguistic system. Normally, he should need only an ability to manipulate his linguistic resource to meet the communicative demands made of him. It is to be noted that almost all tasks and sub-tasks required for academic purposes find a place in this inventory. Though there is no specific reference to reading, a number of tasks require the exercise of this skill. In fact, the performance of some is entirely dependent upon reading of some kind or the other. Abstracting and summarising, note-making, editing, teaching, demand careful reading on the part of the communicator. There is thus no intention to minimise the importance of reading as a skill in our scheme of things though, without doubt our approach is performance-oriented. The needs of the professions which university graduates enter are not determined by the kind of input but by the nature of expected output. The employer does not look at the past, to what the entrant to his organisation has learnt, but to the future, to what the entrant can do. The university certified claim to proficiency does not impress the employer, he is interested in performance as concretised in day-to-day work. It is significant that out of the total time spent on communication 64.14 per cent is spent on communicating in English, as against 27.22 per cent in Hindi and 8.64 per cent in regional language.

We do not subscribe to the view that the Indian learner needs English for general purposes. The role of English in our society is well-defined and therefore the objectives of ELT are clearly specifiable. In the past, in attempting to do all, we have missed to take care of the specific needs, the most significant aspect of planning a language teaching course. What we are suggesting is a practicable path; how to access the learner's needs, formulate objectives and select content for a syllabus. It is also, by implication, shown how to organise contents and what kind of materials to produce and how to find out whether the objectives are being attained. If a label has to be given to a course based on this approach, it should be termed as English for professional purposes (EPP) rather than English for general purposes (EGP) or General English (GE) as an ELT course in India is generally referred to.

Significance of the suggested approach

Judged in its totality, we have tried to emphasise that ELT, to be effective, must focus on meaning and its organisation and realisation, an issue which has been of perennial concern to people. A properly designed and effectively taught ELT course should be able to unfold the meaning potential of language and provide the learner fresh perspectives on how to manipulate it to fulfil his personal ambitions and at the same time to meet societal aspirations. In L1 acquisition the learner may miss this perception for obvious reasons: no formal instruction is imparted and the mastery is acquired at an age when the analytical ability is not sufficiently developed. It is while Learning L2 that a person for the first time realises the complexity of what language is and diversity of what it can do. The emphasis we are trying to imply is of a sophisticated kind; it regards GE not only as a subject of study but also as an instrument of intellectual development, enrichment of personality, and professional advancement. We have, therefore, no hesitation in claiming that the suggested approach is academically sound as well as socially relevant.

Conclusion

What the suggested approach offers is not a list of isolated and abstract units of meaning. In fact, it is firmly rooted in reality and the specificity attained points to a definite, practicable course of action. It can, therefore, be used for the construction of an ELT syllabus valid for all the programmes at the undergraduate level in Indian universities and also perhaps in the other countries of the Third World where a similar situation exists. The proposal, if implemented, can relieve the university system from the colossal amount of wastage in terms of time, effort and resources in designing the so-called programme-specific, discipline-based syllabi. Further, an ELT course having a syllabus based on this approach will have in-built motivation and yield immediate return on investment in learning. And thus it can reasonably be expected to induce in the academic community a favourable attitude, which is essential for the acceptance of an educational innovation.

Notes

1. A *course* is a unit of instruction in a particular discipline, specifying a syllabus, teaching materials and implying certain techniques of teaching and evaluation.
2. A 'profession' may be defined as an employment that requires advanced education and training and that involves mental rather than manual work.
3. The term 'professional world' has been used here in a sense similar to what Jupp and Hodlin (1975) call 'work situation'.
4. A 'programme' is a set of courses leading to a degree such as M.A., B.Sc., etc.
5. An 'item' is an occurrence of a particular component or a sub-component in a particular syllabus.

Appendix

Inventory of Language Tasks and Sub-tasks

Sl. No.	*Language Tasks*	*Sub-tasks*
	Language tasks (in the order of frequency of performance)	Sub-tasks (in the alphabetical order)
1.	Presenting written material	(The sub-task: required for the written material to be presented)*
2.	Oral reporting	describing, explaining, interpreting, narrating
3.	Making inquiries or collecting information	eliciting information, interviewing, introducing (self-topic), sequencing information
4.	Giving	explaining, ordering, requesting instructions/directions
5.	Dictating	(The sub-tasks required for the matter to be dictated)**
6.	Participating in meetings, seminars, workshops, conferences and other discussion groups,	agreeing, arguing, asking questions, clarifying, concluding, defining, disagreeing, eliciting, information, explaining, formulating decisions, generalising, hypothesising, interjecting, interpreting, intervening, introducing (person, point, topic, idea),

(*Continued*)

(*Continued*)

		obtaining attention, opposing (motion, proposal, resolution), ordering priorities (points of discussion), proposing, responding (to questions), seconding (motions), summarising discussions, supporting (proposals, resolutions), welcoming.
7.	Note-taking	classifying information, evaluating, identifying main points, ordering information, recording information.
8.	Establishing social relations	accepting, acknowledging, bidding farewell, congratulating, consoling, expressing gratitude, expressing, solidarity, greeting, regretting, sympathising, welcoming.
9.	Interviewing	assessing (attitude, temper), eliciting information, recording information, verifying information.
10.	Negotiating deals, agreements	convincing, describing, explaining, highlighting important points, inducing, favourable attitude, ordering priorities (points of discussion), persuading.
11.	Demonstrating	describing, explaining, giving information, illustrating, proving, summarising.
12.	Making speeches	arguing, concluding, convincing, inducing favourable attitude, informing, introducing (idea, person, topic), persuading.
13.	Formal teaching	arguing, demonstrating, explaining, giving information, illustrating, persuading, proving.
14.	Making announcements	obtaining attention, instructing, ordering, requesting, sequencing information.
15.	Writing letters	accepting, acknowledging, advising, agreeing, apologising, appreciating, approving, clarifying, commending, complaining, conceding, condemning, contradicting, declining, denying, describing, disagreeing, disapproving, disclaiming, eliciting information, enquiring, explaining, expressing gratitude, forgiving, granting concession, generating goodwill, giving information, instructing, opposing, ordering, persuading, protesting, reassuring, recommending, refusing, refuting, rejecting, requesting, suggesting, warning.
16.	Writing reports	analysing, classifying, collecting data, comparing, contrasting, describing, defining, differentiating, drawing conclusions, explaining, generalising, implying, inferring, interpreting, justifying, narrating, proposing, quantifying, recommending, suggesting, verifying.
17.	Writing memos, orders	conveying information, eliciting information, explaining, instructing, ordering, persuading, recording facts/decisions, suggesting.

18.	Keeping records	classifying, evaluating and sequencing information.
19.	Writing notices, circulars, agenda, minutes	formulating issues, instructing, ordering, recording decisions, requesting.
20.	Filling in forms	recording information, requesting, sequencing information.
21.	Writing short messages	condensing messages, eliciting information, instructing, requesting.
22.	Writing technical proposals	analysing, defining, convincing, describing, explaining, justifying, persuading, proposing, quantifying, recommending, sequencing information, suggesting.
23.	Note-making	classifying information, recording information, selecting main points.
24.	Writing formal invitations	accepting, acknowledging, expressing gratitude, refusing, regretting, requesting.
25.	Abstracting and summarizing	recording information, selecting main points, sequencing information.
26.	Writing research papers, articles in professional journals	analysing, classifying, collecting data, concluding, defining, drawing conclusions, explaining, hypothesising, generalising, interpreting, introducing, topics and sub-topics, verifying.
27.	Writing handbooks, manuals, regulations	classifying information, describing processes and procedures, giving information, sequencing information.
28.	Writing publicity materials, advertisements	asserting, catching attention, convincing, dramatising aspects, emphasising ideas, highlighting distinctive features, inducing favourable attitude, persuading.
29.	Writing booklets, brochures	acknowledging, defining, exemplifying, explaining, expressing gratitude, organising information, planning information.
30.	Preparing market surveys, financial surveys, questionnaires	analysing, classifying information, collecting data, eliciting information, formulating issues, generalising.
31.	Editing	identifying redundancies, proof-reading, sequencing information.
32.	Writing press releases, news bulletins	explaining, giving information, highlighting main points.

* For example, if a report is to be presented, the concerned sub-tasks would be the ones listed at S. No.16 of the inventory.

** If a letter is dictated, the sub-tasks required would be the same as given for 'writing letters' (S. No.15)

Bibliography

Banerji, Meera, 1984; *An Approach to Syllabus Design for English Language Teaching at the Undergraduate Level in India* Ph.D. Thesis. Pilani: Birla Institute of Technology and Science.

Das, Mahajiteswar, 1977. *The Needs for English in Orissa* An investigation into the English Language requirements and related instructional programmes at the post-secondary level of education. Ph.D. Thesis. Hyderabad: Central Institute of English and Foreign Languages.

Jupp, T.C. and S. Hpdlin. 1975. *Industrial English: An Example of Theory and Practice in Functional Teaching*. London: Heinemann Educational Book Ltd.

Munby, John 1978. *Communicative syllabus Design.* Cambridge: Cambridge University Press.

Parasher, S.Y. 1979. *Certain Aspects of the Functions and Forms of Indian English*: A Sociolinguistic Study. Ph.D. Thesis. Hyderabad: Central Institute of English and Foreign languages.

University Grants Commission 1977. *Syllabus Reform in English*: Reports and Recommendations of Zonal and National Workshops, New Delhi.

Widdowson, H.G. 1978. *Teaching Language as Communication,* London: Oxford University Press.

1979. *Explorations in Applies Linguistics*. London: Oxford University Press

Wilkins, D.A. 1976. *Notional Syllabuses*. Oxford: Oxford University Press

Sample Article

Finger Off the Paper

Maulik Parikh

You can't see it, you can't touch it, but it's everywhere, all around you. It's hyperspace, the fifth dimension...and it's right under your nose. But first, what exactly is a dimension? Think of it as a coordinate. You appear to live in three dimensions because it takes three coordinates, three numbers, to locate you. It could be longitude, latitude and your height above sea level. Or, to find a buried treasure, you might say walk ten steps north, five steps west and dig six feet down. However you do it, three numbers suffice to specify position and that's why the world appears three-dimensional.

It's natural also to think of time as a dimension. As Hermann Minkowski, Einstein's Maths teacher in college, puts it, 'Nobody has ever noticed a place, except at a time, or a time except at a place.' To arrange a get-together with your friends, it's not enough to give them the three spatial coordinates of the location; you also have to say at what time. That's one more number, so chalk up time as the fourth dimension. Actually, there's more to it than that. Imagine the four directions: left-right, back-forth, up-down and past-future. In 1905, Einstein showed that just as what we mean by left and right depends on which way in space we are facing, what we mean by past and future depends on which way in space-time we

---

The research paper has been reproduced from the *Journal of English Language Teaching*, Vol. 39/2, 2003, March- April.

are facing. That may not be obvious but, by uniting space and time, it does justify our inclusion of time as another dimension.

So we have four so far. What about the fifth? Our minds cannot directly visualise more dimensions. But luckily, there's a clever trick we can use to aid our imagination. A fourth dimension of space (that is, a fifth dimension of space-time), sometimes called hyperspace, must appear to us 3D beings much as a third dimension would appear to a 2D creature. To imagine what hyperspace would look like to us, imagine what we look like to a flat amoeba living on a 2D sheet of paper. (This would have to be a most intelligent amoeba, of course.) For example, where is hyperspace? Answer: it's all around us, just as 3D space is all around a 2D piece of paper. Is it different from ordinary space? No, it's just another direction. What would a being from hyperspace be able to do? It would have the god-like ability to reach into your body without going through your skin, in the same way that you can touch the centre of the 2D amoeba without going through its edge; simply by raising your finger off the paper.

Well, that's all fine in the abstract, but does hyperspace really exist? Nobody knows for sure, but for close to a century physicists have seriously contemplated its existence. String theory – our best theory for describing matter, forces, space and time-boldly asserts that there are as many as eleven space-time dimensions! These 11 would include not only our familiar three space and one time but also an additional seven dimensions of space, all waiting to be discovered.

If they're there, the obvious next question is why we haven't seen them yet. There are two possible explanations. One is that hyperspace may have only the tiniest extent. Just as our amoeba might mistakenly think that a piece of paper is purely two-dimensional only because its third dimension-along its thickness is so limited, we might simply have failed to observe that all around us is a thin sliver of hyperspace. The fabric of space-time, like the sheerest of silk chiffons, may have only the most imperceptible thickness in the other dimensions. If this is true, you shouldn't plan to spend your next family holiday visiting hyperspace.

In 1999, physicists Lisa Randall and Raman Sundrum proposed another explanation. Maybe the other dimensions were not so small. Instead, they suggested that the reason we haven't seen them is that we are stuck to our three dimensions. Just as the amoeba is stuck to the paper by the force of gravity, so too we-along with everything else in our familiar universe-might be confined by a force to our familiar dimensions and be prevented from entering the other dimensions that are all around us. Excitingly, this theory can be experimentally tested. This time next year, a giant experiment near Geneva will try to find evidence of hidden dimensions of space. If we find them (a big if), it will be one of the most sensational discoveries in human history.

ASSIGNMENTS

1. Select a research paper from each of the three successive issues of a journal. Analyse these paper to determine the requirements of the journal for structure and layout. Present your survey and analysis in the form of an article.
2. Choose a subject of your interest or specialisation and write two introductory paragraphs, one for a research paper in a journal and the other for an article in a technical periodical.

3. Prepare an outline and a bibliography for the research paper for which you have written the introductory paragraph in response to assignment number two above.
4. Write an article on each of the following topics, after gathering relevant material from newspapers, periodicals, journals, etc. The article is to be published in a periodical of a semi-technical nature. At the end of your article list all the sources you have consulted.
   (i) Water pollution and its control.
   (ii) Use of solar energy in Indian villages.
   (iii) Food for health.
   (iv) Solar cooker.
   (v) Labour productivity and wages in a selected industry.

Chapter 21

ADVERTISING AND JOB DESCRIPTION

21.1 ADVERTISING

MANY organisations use professional agencies for the majority of their advertising needs. You may, however, occasionally be required to design advertisements for your organisation. In this chapter we shall briefly discuss how to prepare them.

Broadly speaking, advertisement (ad) is a form of communication intended to promote the sale of a product or service, to influence public opinion, to advance a particular cause, to gain political support or to elicit some other response desired by the advertiser. It is also used indirectly to enlighten the public at large about new products and services. Here, however, we shall be concerned with commercial advertising, designed to create effective communication between the producer and the consumer. We shall not directly deal with advertisements addressed by the manufacturer to the retailer or those aimed to merely enhance the prestige of the commercial firm. Our main focus will be on the use of language in commercial advertising.

The characteristics of an advertisement are:

- Catching attention
- Stimulating interest
- Arousing desire
- Supplying convincing details
- Motivating action

As you go along you will perceive how different devices are used to incorporate these characteristics in an advertisement.

21.1.1 Media

The media commonly used for advertising are newspapers, magazine radio, television, billboards and direct mail. The choice of the medium depends on the answers to the following questions:

(i) To whom is the advertisement being addressed?
(ii) What are the contents of the message?
(iii) How much money is available for the purpose?

Though the basic principles of advertising are the same, every medium has its own requirements for success in advertising. For example, a television advertisement must be accompanied by effective visuals and appropriate sound effects. Similarly, an advertisement in a magazine must use a harmonious blend of colours and suitable print types besides being presented on good quality paper. In some media the appeal and popularity of film stars, TV stars, sportsmen and models are exploited to make the ad more attractive.

Let us briefly discuss the media, one by one.

(i) *Newspaper*: It is a leading medium for reporting events, disseminating information and for advertising. Through it you can cover a wide area and reach millions of people at a comparatively low cost. A newspaper is sectionalised and usually has a definite page or space for advertisements. It is read by various members of the family and different sections of the society. But remember that a newspaper is read regularly but soon set aside not to be touched again. Further, the quality of the newsprint does not make it suitable for artistic, colourful advertisements. Thus, when you draft an advertisement for a newspaper, you would have to rely mainly on language. You will also have to decide whether you want your advertisement to appear under 'classified advertisements' or 'general display.' The former are small and one column wide. They consist of solid lines of small types, usually of a single typeface. In certain newspapers, however, the first word of the first line is printed in capitals or sometimes in the entire first line boldface types are used. The typography is uniform and they contain no illustrations, no logotypes and no white space. The general display advertisements use varied typefaces and have a more attractive layout. In fact, in most cases layout is the only means of creating a powerful visual impact on the reader. They are scattered and are not grouped together like classified advertisements, Figure 21.1 is an extract from an interesting general display advertisement inviting 'situation vacant' advertisements.

Sometimes advertisements, which look remarkably like news stories, are called *reading notices*. The headline is intended to have some news value or quality. If you decide to insert such an advertisement in a newspaper, do not forget to add the word ad or *advertisement* either on the top or at the end of the notice. Remember also that such advertisements are generally more expensive per line than classified or general display ads.

(ii) *Magazine*: Preparing an ad for a magazine is more or less like that for a newspaper. But here you have an advantage. The paper is of better quality and so you can decide to use colours in your ad. The use of colours obviously makes the ad stand out distinctly, making it more eye-catching and attention-getting. Moreover, you can display the natural colour of the commodity you are advertising. The pictures and photographs can also be made more realistic.

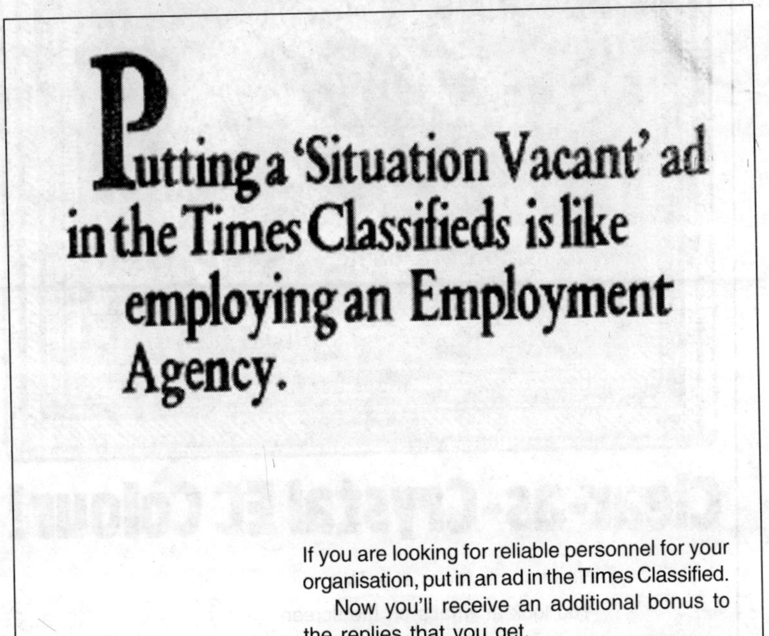

Fig. 21.1 A General Display Ad

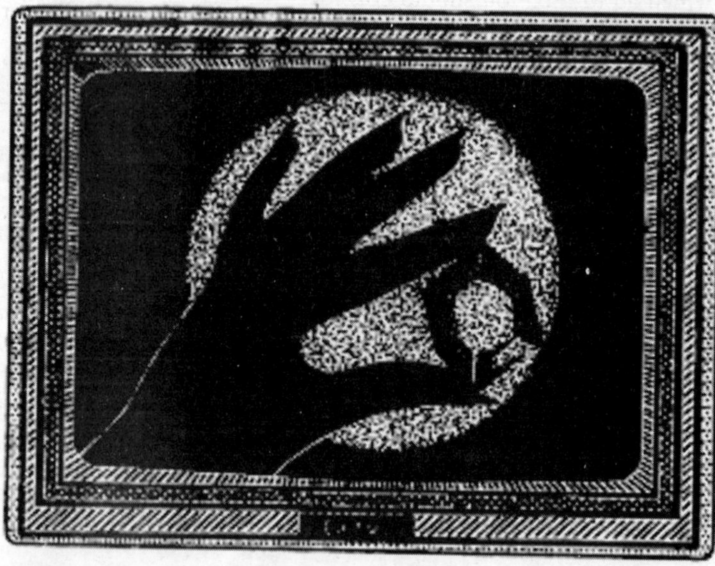

Clear-as-Crystal EC Colour!

No one only looks at a TV.

You look at what's on the screen.

You listen to the sound.

You look at the colours.

You look for quality.

And if you're looking for a good reliable colour TV, then look at the smart new range of EC Colour TVs.

EC Colours TVs are quality controlled to last for years and years.

Have modular design features for instant servicing and maintenance.

Are electronically aged to prevent failures.

EC Colour TVs.

See them and you'll want to take one home tonight

And you can.

Come be dazzled !

ECTV

It's what every TV tries to be

Fig. 21.2 TV Ad in Magazine

In order to decide which ad to use, you should consider two factors, namely, the likely consumers of the product and the readership of the magazine. You should not however overlook the fact that a magazine, unlike a newspaper, is read at greater leisure and the reader may go back to it again and again. On the next page we give an, example of an advertisement for a TV, which appeared in black and white in a magazine.

The picture on the top, a hand holding a piece of crystal, excites the curiosity and the phrase printed just below it in large bold types whets the appetite to go through the ad. The sentences that follow look like a poem. Literary devices such as epigram, alliteration, repetition of words and phrases, etc. are used to drive the message home. And the punch of the ad is contained in the last line: 'It is what every TV tries to be'. Thus you see that the main burden of the message falls on language.

Reading notices appear in magazines also. We now give an example of a reading notice which appeared in *Reader's Digest*:

WHY

Do They Advertise?*

As you read this magazine, you encounter advertisements that talk to you about the merits of a great number of products and services. If you have ever wondered why so much time and effort and money is spent on getting these messages to you, perhaps a ward of explanation might be helpful.

The basic answer is that you are important. No matter how hard the people in a factory work to make a good product, if you, as a possible buyer, don't know that the product exists you're not likely to buy it, are you?

In some way, each product or service you are offered has qualities that none, of its competitors has. It is by building those qualities into his products and then drawing them to your attention that the advertiser hopes to get your business. Again, you are important: You are the final judge. Your decisions spell success or failure for the advertisers.

And the reason the advertisers use *magazines* to tell you their story is that when you are reading a magazine, you really do have time to judge. You read at your own pace. If you want to, you can go back and read the advertisement again. More than anything else, you are being asked to *consider*. That's what magazines do best: provide time for consideration.

Without advertising, the economy would grind to a halt. And after all, we all advertise. You advertise what you are by the way you dress, the way you talk, how you present yourself to others. Thus, the advertisement you see in these pages is simply an extension of how youself behave. Its importance is that, without it, how would you know what is available – and where? And how would you compare qualities or cost?

* Source: Reader's Digest. Vol. 130, No. 777, p. I84, January 1987. Published by RDI Printing Publishing Pvt. Ltd. Orient House Mangalore Street, Ballard Estate Mumbai 400038

(iii) *Radio*: In our country the radio has become a powerful medium both for broadcasting news and for advertisements. The production of a lengthy commercial may require sophisticated professional acumen but the production of a simple and short commercial is within your competence. What you need for such a production is a script, written like a screen play, talented 'voices', recording equipment and a sound-proof room. You may discover a suitable speaker in your own organisation and it would not be, too difficult or too expensive to secure the other requirements. With some thought and discussion it would not be difficult to select appropriate sound effects and music. Usually a slogan, a jingle, or a rhymed couplet extolling the virtues of the product is used for the broadcast. Through this medium you can have an access to all sections of society right from the elite to the peasants arid workers.

(iv) *Television*: Advertising on TV is more illustrative than any other medium, It combines the advantages of colour, sound and language giving a clear visual perception of the object being advertised. Very often an advertisement that you design for a radio broadcast can also be exploited for a TV advertisement. Depending upon the audience you have in mind, you will have to decide whether you want your advertisement to be telecast through the network or regional programme. Another decision would depend upon the amount of money available for the advertisement; remember, advertisements at off-peak times are cheaper than those at the prime time.

(v) *Billboards*: Billboard advertisement is the principal form of out-door advertising. The display is done, sometimes on a wall, but usually a large panel is used for the purpose. It has certain interesting features. Being immobile it can't go to consumers; they must come to it. It takes very little time and reading effort to go through a bill-board advertisement. Since it is displayed at a prominent and strategic point it catches the attention of everybody. An advertisement of this type may use both language and illustrations such as cartoons, pictures, etc. which may at times be coloured. The advertisement material is bold and clear enough to be capable of being read from a distance.

(vi) *Direct Mail*: Another medium of advertisement is the sales letter written directly to the consumer, sometimes even by name. Along with such a letter, which is of high print and display quality, several incentives are offered. It may have, as its enclosures a coloured leaflet, a self-addressed stamped envelope, and may offer special discount and reduced-price coupon. Though this medium is expensive to use, it has the advantage of adopting a personal approach and making the consumer feel as someone special and important. For guidance in writing such a letter consult the discussion on sales letter in Chapter 16.

21.1.2 Language

The language used in every advertisement should be able to catch the attention of the reader and motivate him to take immediate action. Despite the development of sophisticated non-verbal techniques, language still continues to remain a powerful customer-catching tool. To evoke the desired responses advertisements use *word-triggers*. These are used to bring about a close association of a particular quality or state with a particular product. We are persuaded to believe that we are buying success, health, vitality, instant loveliness and tingling freshness when we buy Vimal, Lifebuoy, Glucon-C, Afgan Snow and Limca respectively. And if we wish to invite our neighbour's envy, we should buy an Onida!

The task of creating the language of advertisements is by no means an easy one. You have to stretch your creativity and fantasise your consumer goods. You have an almost unlimited scope for violating the rules and conventions of language to create advertisement literature. You may coin a telling phrase, an epigram or a rhyme to drive your message home. Or if you are a good story-teller weave a fascinating piece of fiction. But ensure that your advertisement does not make a false promise, exaggerate a claim or misinform the customer. This may, in the long run, train the credibility of your organisation, and cut its down its profits. It may even invite legal action. Let an advertisement be succinct as one has to pay dearly for every inch of space or every second of time used.

The language of ads makes an extensive use of lexical and rhetorical devices to convey the message. The potentialities of language are widened and deepened in several ways, the sole aim being to find fresh, interest-provoking methods of conveying meaningful information on the reader's own terms. There is a large variety of linguistic devices used in advertising; It would neither be advisable nor possible to give here a sample of each device. However, a few samples of certain often-used devices are given below just to give a flavour of variety in the language you can use for advertising. These have been selected for their telling effect and are from familiar advertisements in various media mentioned earlier in this Chapter. The examples have been put under eight categories. Four of them, . . . are self-explanatory; the rest are explained in their respective footnotes. As you go along, you will observe that the name of the product is given in the bracket against the example, where the expression does not contain a specific reference to the object being advertised. Metaphors and similes which are often employed for the purpose are not given separately but you will discover them in more than one category. Under category (v) 'Light as mist, soft as spring' and under category (iii) 'A fragrance as pious as gold' are examples of simile. Similarly, 'Go and seek the sun at your nearest Bombay Dyeing stockist now' under category (iii) and 'Satin is the way it feel' in category (v) are examples of metaphors. You will also see that though an example may belong to two categories, to avoid repetition it has been put only under one.

(i) *Coinage of new words*

- Have you goldspotted today?
- Utterly butterly delicious. (butter)
- Limcomaniac. (soft drink)
- Juicedly good. (apple juice)
- Chocolicious. (drinking chocolate)
- Skin-magic. (face cream)
- Ambiqueen. (sarees)
- Tie Q. (ties)
- Trendy prints. (dress material)
- Touch-happy textures. (fabric)
- No icky-plasticky smell. (water jugs)

(ii) *Alliteration**

- Just tasty, tender, tiny garden peas.
- Fragrant as fresh-peeled limefresh as nature itself! Fruity, frothy Lure Lime Shampoo,
- Fashion fabric light as air- depend on climate by Doctaire.
- The suede that's in style to suit all occasions.
- Dashing, debonair and distinctive. (suitings)
- Dancing designs that dazzle. (dress material)
- Puts the crunch into the brunch. (sandwich toastmaker)
- The zing thing. (cold drink)
- Lose weight with taste! (slim-aid)

(iii) *Use of vocabulary in unusual contexts*

- Take years off your feet. (footwear)
- Go and seek your sun at your nearest Bombay Dyeing Stockist now.
- Beautiful skin is something you wear twenty-four hours a day. (face cream)
- Lip service with a difference. (lipstick)
- Today homemakers no longer paint their walls. They create the atmosphere of a thousand pearls. (wall paints)
- If only your finger had bristles. (toothbrush)
- A spark from the SCL Unicorn computer can set your child's mind on fire.
- How do you bite a mosquito? (insecticide)
- A fragrance as precious as gold. (talcum powder)
- Healthy living need not be a tasteless exercise. (saccharin)
- For that dream sleep that you never dreamt of! (mattress)

(iv) *Pun***

- Why not be in Vogue tonight? (thermal blankets)
- I'm a Khaitan fan. (says a film star)
- How Touch Wood protects your beautiful wooden furniture long after polish gives up the fight. (furniture paint)
- We don't want to rub it in but Ralliwell relieves sprains faster than any other balm.
- Your son is sure to rise if fed on pure Sunshine: (butter)

---

* Alliteration is the successive repetition of a particular sound. It is impressed in the reader's memory quickly, thus achieving the first aim of an advertisement.

** It refers to the humorous use of words, suggesting different meanings. Such words may have the same or nearly the same sound but different meanings.

(v) *Parallelism**

- Neighbour's envy, owner's pride. (TV)
- Shave after shave, Crest after shave. (after-shave lotion)
- Satin is the way it feels. Flawless is the way it looks. (foundation cream)
- Colours that command attention. Textures that mean business. (fabric)
- Sealed tight, to remain bright. (electric bulb)
- Light as mist, soft as spring, (fabric)

(vi) *Slogans*

- Hotel Deep – a home away from home
- Britannia – India's best Biscuits.
- Horlicks – the Great Nourisher.
- Amul – The taste of India
- Bajaj bulbs – the ultimate choice.
- Mealmaker – Home maker.

(vii) *Disjunctive grammar***

- For the new dew look Nivea vanishing cream with eucerite.
- His viewpoint? Naturally Kapitan.
- Pretty at a distance. Prettier in close-up in Shreeniwas Florina Sarees.
- The complete name in fashion shoes – Bata Wallanaster.
- Presto – the silk-edge blade tender on skins; ruthless on beards.
- Subscribe to the truth – Newscope

(viii) *Rhyme*

- Old Mother Hubbard
  Went to the cupboard
  To fetch her poor doggie a bone
  Said the pup, I want bread
  With that great Amul spread
  To which very faithful I've grown.
- Breakfast every day with Nescafe
  Any moment of the day, enjoy your
  Cup of Nescafe.

---

* Parallelism is a repetition of phrase or sentence structure. It gives a melodious effect to the message.

** It refers to sentences having incomplete structure, designed to create dramatic effect on the reader.

- Do not cry my child
  I know the world seems strange and new
  But you are safe and in my arms.
  No harm will ever come to you
  (Johnson and Johnson Baby Oil, Soap, etc.)
- Dip, dip, dip
  If you want it stronger
  Dip a little longer
  Dip, dip, dip,
  (tea bags)

In conclusion let us emphasise two points. In drafting an advertisement try to understand the psychology of the target population and use the language that would appeal to it. For example, the advertisement for Thumbs Up loudly proclaims 'Taste the Thunder', thereby suggesting that it is a cold drink meant for bold and adventurous young men and women. The second point relates to the process of composing the message. Writing an advertisement is a group effort, unlike literature which is an individual effort, though both demand imagination and creativity. When you have to write an advertisement, collect a group of persons who have a flair for language. Float an idea and see their reaction. Let the idea be thrown like a ball from one person to another until something clicks to all. In your first effort, try to say something which dramatically highlights the most important quality of the product. For instance, if you have been asked to coin a slogan for a bike, you may propose A lion minus the roar. This phrase emphasises the fact that the scooter is as strong and powerful as a lion but it does not make noise when it runs.

21.2 JOB DESCRIPTION

You may sometimes be asked to draft an advertisement for certain posts in your organisation. You have then to find out in detail the requirements of each post and define the job specifications. These would include the title of the position, accountability, duties and responsibilities, qualifications and experience required, age limit, conditions of service, personal qualities expected and the alary offered. Each post may have its unique requirements but there would be certainly features that are common to all such as the title of the post, qualifications, experience and salary offered.

You are familiar with advertisements appearing in newspapers and periodicals. But if you scan them carefully you might discover that sometimes all the required details are not given. An advertisement of this type may not be able to attract the right kind of applicants for the job and the organisation may suffer.

Here is an example of a job description; it would give you an idea of how to prepare a specification of this kind.

Title: Manager, Public Relations, National Electronics Limited

Accountable to: Managing Director

Duties and Responsibilities

- Projecting the image of the Company at various levels, both external and internal.
- Maintaining relations with the press, Government-owned media, opinion leaders, local communities and public in general.
- Organising exhibitions, preparing audio-visuals and other presentations.
- Editing and running the House Magazine.
- Organising and co-ordinating advertisement campaigns and publication of Annual Reports, product literatures, brochures, etc.
- Co-ordinating in-house publicity for Quality Drive, Safety Campaign, Suggestion Scheme, etc.
- Formulating, processing and maintaining P.R. Budgets.

Qualifications and Experience

- Master's Degree in Arts/Commerce with Postgraduate Degree/ Diploma in Public Relations/ Journalism/Mass Communication from a recognised university/institute.
- At least 10 years' experience of which a minimum of 5 years should be as Head of the Public Relations Department of a professionally managed company.

Personal Qualities

- Pleasing and outgoing personality with a flair for public relations.
- Knowledge of communication techniques and processes.
- Excellent command over English.
- Ability to work under pressure.

Salary: Commensurate with qualifications/experience.

Age Limit: Not more than 35 years.

Conditions of Service

39 hours week: 14 days holiday; gratuity; contributory provident fund; leave travel allowance, free medical aid; bonus.

At times the policy of your organisation may not permit you to give all the above mentioned details in the advertisements. You should then abstract essential details after actually preparing a description as shown in the example given above.

ASSIGNMENTS

1. Comment on the following advertisements, stating the category to which they belong and giving reasons for your views:
   (a) Everyday is a wedding day when you wrap yourself in Kalpana. (sarees)
   (b) Unveiling beauty is our business. (dress material)

(c) You can bask in the confidence we sell. (suitings)

(d) Have a plastic surgeon
In your own home...
Wrinkles disappear in a jiffy
At the youthful touch of Glorine.
(face cream)

2. Draft advertisements for the following products, to be published in a popular weekly magazine. Your advertisement should belong to the category mentioned against the product.

	Product	*Category*
(i)	Scooter	alliteration
(ii)	Nail polish	rhyme
(iii)	Baby food	pun
(iv)	Colour television	slogan
(v)	Electric toaster	parallelism
(vi)	Dress material	disjunctive grammar
(vii)	Toilet soap	coinage of new words

3. Assume that your organisation has decided to advertise its new washing machine on television. Write a script for a short presentation for being telecast. Invent the necessary details such as the number of characters, their age, the physical setting, etc.

4. Draft advertisements for the following posts – to be published in a leading daily newspaper:
   (a) Production supervisor in a publishing company.
   (b) Senior mechanical engineer in a chemical industry.
   (c) Accounts Officer in a state electricity board.
   (d) Personnel manager in a public limited company manufacturing synthetic fabric.
   (e) Scientist C in a national institute of electronics engineering research.

Chapter 22

GRAPHIC AIDS

YOU will often have to work with a mass of statistics and a complexity of ideas when you write a formal piece of communication such as a report, a technical proposal, etc. Many a time you would find that you can use graphic aids to make your communication easy to understand. In fact, these aids have become a sort of vocabulary for the professional.

22.1 USES

Graphic aids are mainly used to:

- Communicate more effectively and accurately.
- Make description, explanation and comparison more vivid and eye-catching.
- Clarify and supplement the verbal analysis.
- Reinforce and support verbal communication.
- Enable the writer to present information in an organised way.
- Present a large number of details in less space and with greater precision.

You should however never permit a graphic aid to compete with your verbal presentation. And don't be tempted to use an aid solely for dramatic or aesthetic effects. Each aid must present some significant information relevant to the content.

There are several types of aids which a professional uses. Before we discuss them, we would like to give a few general rules which are applicable to all aids.

(i) Give an aid when it is the best way to communicate information.

(ii) Each aid must be neat, accurate and self-contained.

(iii) The content of an aid should be closely related to the text.

(iv) An aid should be explained in the text howsoever briefly and placed as close to the first reference as possible.

(v) The size of an aid should be such that on reproduction it remains clearly legible.

(vi) Each table and figure should be numbered and captioned. Usually the number in consecutive Roman numerals and the caption of the Table are given on the top, e.g. Table I, Table II, etc. The number and the caption of the figures are given in Arabic numerals, e.g. Fig. 1, Fig. 2. etc. at the bottom.

22.2 TYPES

We may classify graphic aids into the following two types:

(i) Tables: dependent and independent.

(ii) Figures: graphs, charts, drawings, photographs and maps.

22.2.1 Tables

A *dependent table* is a part of the text, a sort of continuation of the text. It does not have any number or tide and for identification it depends on the text. It may have a maximum of three or four columns and runs over eight to ten lines. Often such a table completes a sentence and its beginning is usually marked by a colon. An example is given below.

The number of employees who have not opted for the pension scheme in different departments is:

Marketing 21

Finance 12

Production 17

Human Resource 24

An *independent table* is separated noticeably from the text. It is self-contained, i.e. it bears a number, a title, and if necessary, a legend. Usually such a table consists of two or more columns of numeric data or derived statistics. When the data are in the form of words, it is called *a phrase table*. A table has a number of rows and columns. A row runs horizontally across the page and columns run vertically. The first column is called *subhead* under which a number of items are listed; the other columns are called *boxheads*. All columns are of equal size and the data are recorded in the centre of the concerned column. The absence of data in a particular column is shown by a dash. Any additional information is given as footnote to the table and the unit of measurement is indicated either in the title or separately in the right hand corner at the top of the table.

In preparing a table, bear the following points in mind:

(i) Plan the data you wish to present in the form of tables.

(ii) Choose the best position for placing a table. If your table is short, try to place it soon after the first reference in the text, slightly above the centre of the page. If the table is long and runs into several pages, place it after the text. Indicate its continuity by writing 'continued' at the bottom of the page. If a table is referred to several times throughout your written communication, include it as an appendix.

(iii) Present the data in a clear and precise manner, keeping in mind the purpose of the table.

(iv) Keep the size of the table suitable to the format of your communication. Let it not be too small or too large. It should not look either overcrowded or too spacious. To give the table a neat appearance you may use standard or self-explanatory abbreviations.

(v) Arrange the data logically. In the first column give an independent variable such as time and in the other columns dependent variables. Write the items in the stubhead in the order of their importance.

An example each of the two types of an independent table is given below.

Table 22.1 Number of Sets Produced

Year	Unit I	Unit II	Unit III	Unit IV
2002	140	160	166	150
2003	160	168	189	160
2004	187	189	200	180
2005	201	205	2011	200
2006	240	200	240	220
2007	275	190	300	240

Table 22.2 Schedule for Engineers' Day Celebration 2006

<table>
<tr><th>Date →
Time
↓</th><th>16 September</th><th>17 September</th><th>18 September</th></tr>
<tr><td>10.00</td><td>Inauguration
(Central Hall)</td><td>Invited Lecture
(Room 49)</td><td rowspan="2">Paper
Presentation
(Rooms 42
and 43)</td></tr>
<tr><td>11.00</td><td>Key-note address
(Central Hall)</td><td>Paper Presentation
(Room 42)</td></tr>
<tr><td>12.00</td><td>Exhibition
(Electronics Lab)</td><td>Exhibition
(Electronics Lab)</td><td>Invited Lecture
(Room 49)</td></tr>
<tr><td>13.00</td><td></td><td></td><td></td></tr>
<tr><td>14.00</td><td></td><td></td><td></td></tr>
<tr><td>15.00</td><td rowspan="2">Paper
Presentation
(Rooms 42 and 43)</td><td rowspan="2">Seminar
(Room 49)</td><td rowspan="2">Exhibition
(Electronics
Lab.)</td></tr>
<tr><td>16.00</td></tr>
</table>

17.00			
18.00			Concluding Session (Central Hall)
19.00			
20.00	Film		
21.00	(Engineering Theatre)	Films (Engineering Theatre)	
22.00			

22.2.2 Figures

Figures are useful in the following two ways: as visuals to summarise the text and to present the details left out in the discussion. We may classify the figures broadly into graphs, charts and pictures. Graphs and charts can present symbolically and pictorially the data recorded in tables. The presentation in the former can be more easily grasped.

The presentation of data in a table is more accurate than in a graph or a chart. However, the latter also show round totals, trends, directions, distributions and comparisons more vividly.

Graphs

There are several types of graphs. Let us discuss them one by one.

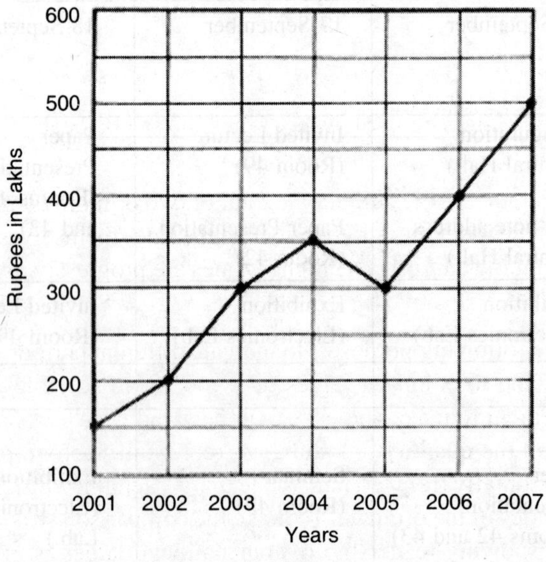

Fig. 22.1 Rectilinear Graph Showing Capital Growth of Bharat National Bank

(i) *Rectilinear graph*: It is used for depicting the trends of progress over a period of time. It is useful when the time factor continuously varies. Figure 22.1 given below shows the growth of deposits in Bharat National Bank during 1981-87.

(ii) *Multiple line graph*: This graph is used to present data of related units and has more than one index line. The lines should be clearly identifiable. Ideally such a graph should not have more than four index lines. An example is given below in Fig. 22.2.

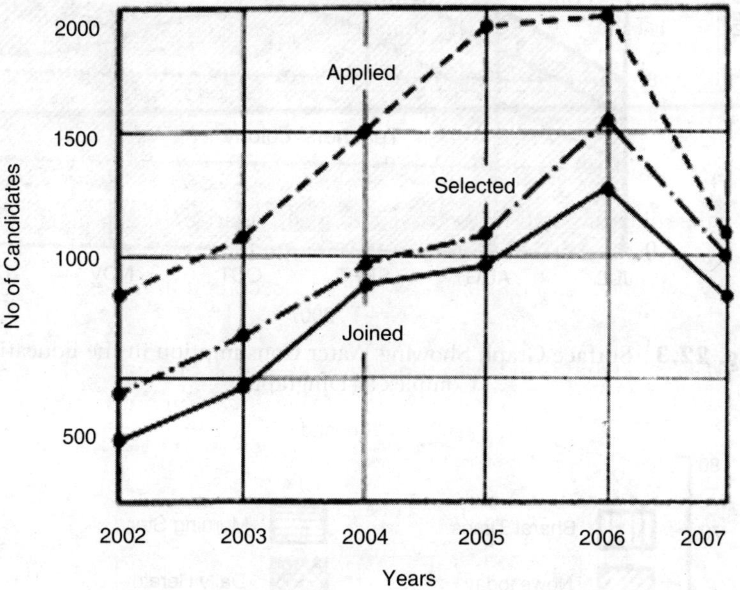

Fig. 22.2 Multiple Line Graph Showing Admissions to B.Sc. (Hons.) Physics in a University

(iii) *Surface graph*: It is used to indicate the cumulative total of two or more components. The emphasis is on showing the area between the index lines rather than on the lines themselves. The zones are shaded or crosshatched, the lowest being the darkest. The higher zones are progressively made lighter in shade. An example is given in Fig. 22.3.

(iv) *Bar graph*: It is used for the following purposes: to indicate different periods or quantity of different items during the same period, and to compare values of two or more variables. This type of graph is widely used as it is both convenient to make and easy to understand. The bars have the same width but varying lengths depending upon the quantity or value they represent. Such graphs may be prepared in three ways: bars extending horizontally from left hand scale, bars extending vertically from bottom scale, and bars extending from both sides of the ordinate. To make the comparison striking, the bars are shaded differently. A specimen graph showing readership of four national dailies is given in Fig. 22.4.

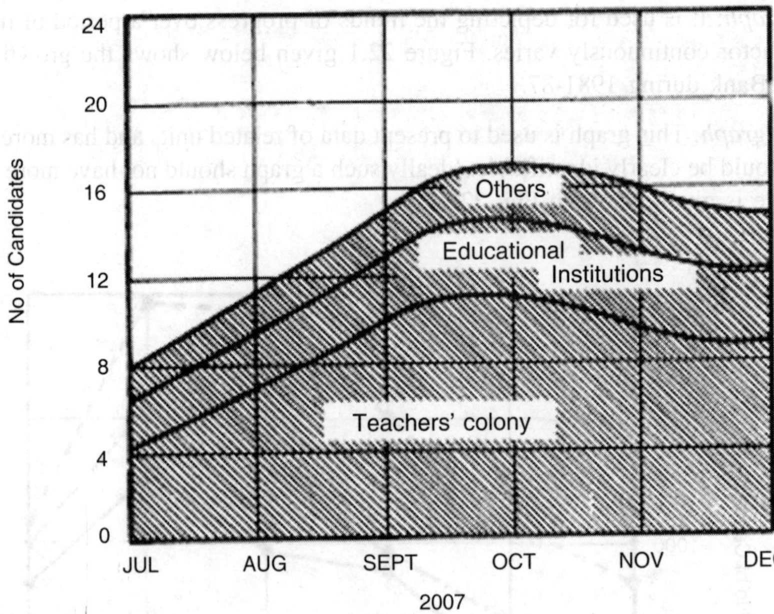

Fig. 22.3 Surface Graph Showing Water Consumption in the Educational Complex at Dingrapur

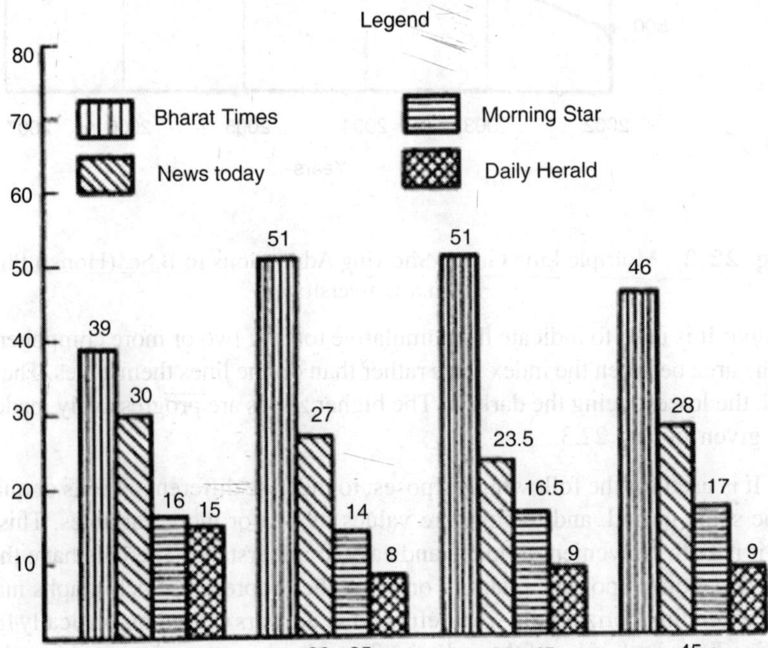

Fig. 22.4 Bar Graph Showing Readership of Four National Dailies

(v) *Pie graph*: It is a hundred per cent graph used to display data in terms of relative percentage. It is marked off by slices, each slice showing a proportion of the whole unit and hence shaded differently. This graph is in the form of a circle. However, the same data can be presented in the form of a semicircle or square using the technique of presentation of a pie graph. An example is given in Fig. 22.5.

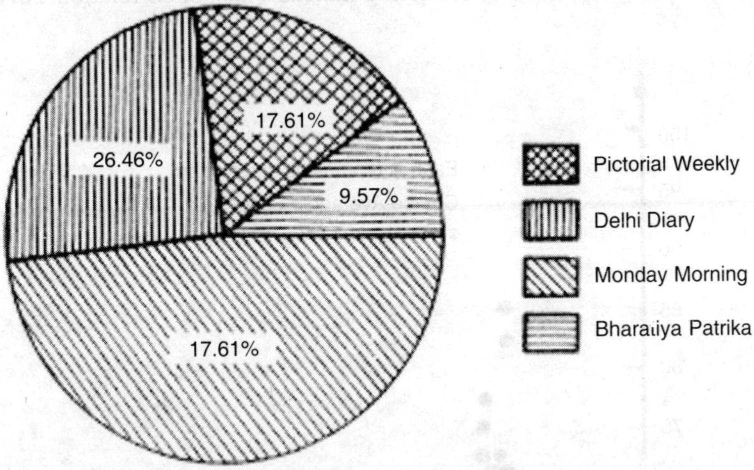

Fig. 22.5 Pie Graph Showing the Percentage Readership of Four Magazines

(vi) *Semi-log graph*: It has linear scale on one axis, usually the x-axis, and the logarithmic scale on the other. Usually this type of graph is used when the range of one variable as compared to another is very

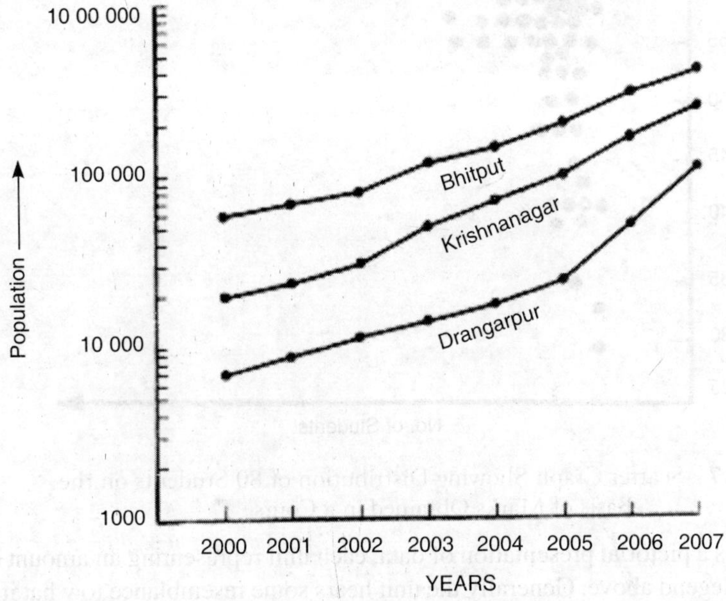

Fig. 22.6 Semi-log Graph Showing Population Growth in Three Cities During 2000-07

large. The rate of change indicated by the graph can predict the future trend also. In Fig. 22.6 the population has been shown on the logarithmic scale vertically whereas years have been shown on a linear scale horizontally.

(vii) *Scatter graph*: In this graph dote or other marks are plotted to display the agreement of two variables, one on each axis. The absence of clustering indicates lack of correlation. An example is given in Fig. 22.7.

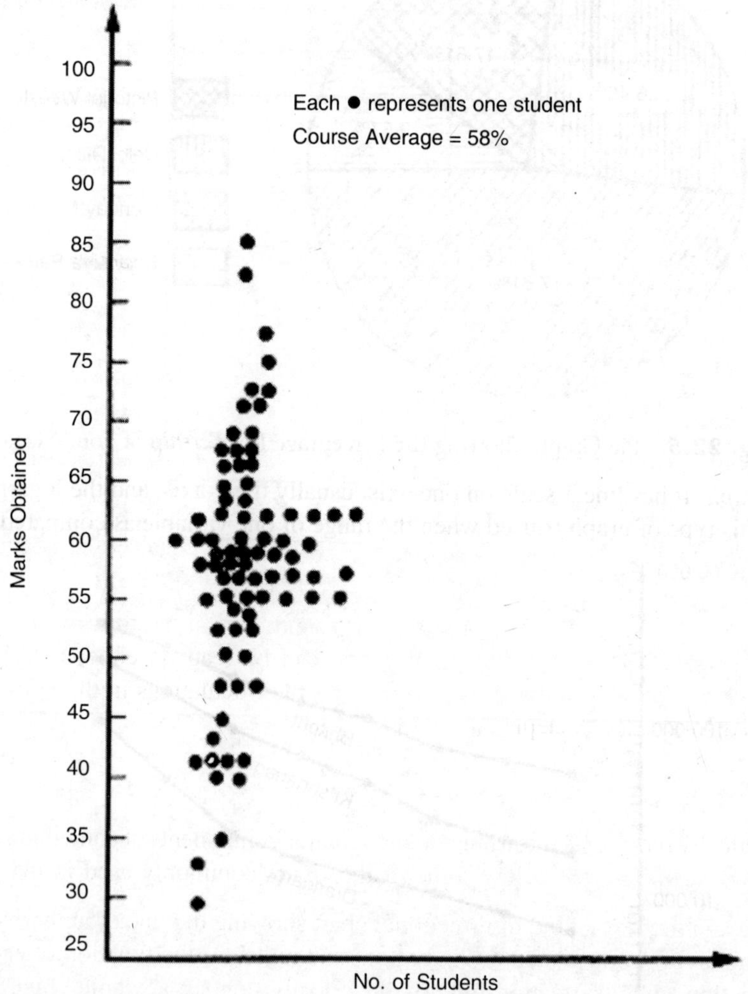

Fig. 22.7 Scatter Graph Showing Distribution of 80 Students on the Basis of Marks Obtained in a Course

(viii) *Pictorial graph*: It is a pictorial presentation of data, each unit representing an amount or quantity, which is specified in the legend above. Generally the unit hears some resemblance to what it represents. An example is given in Fig. 22.8.

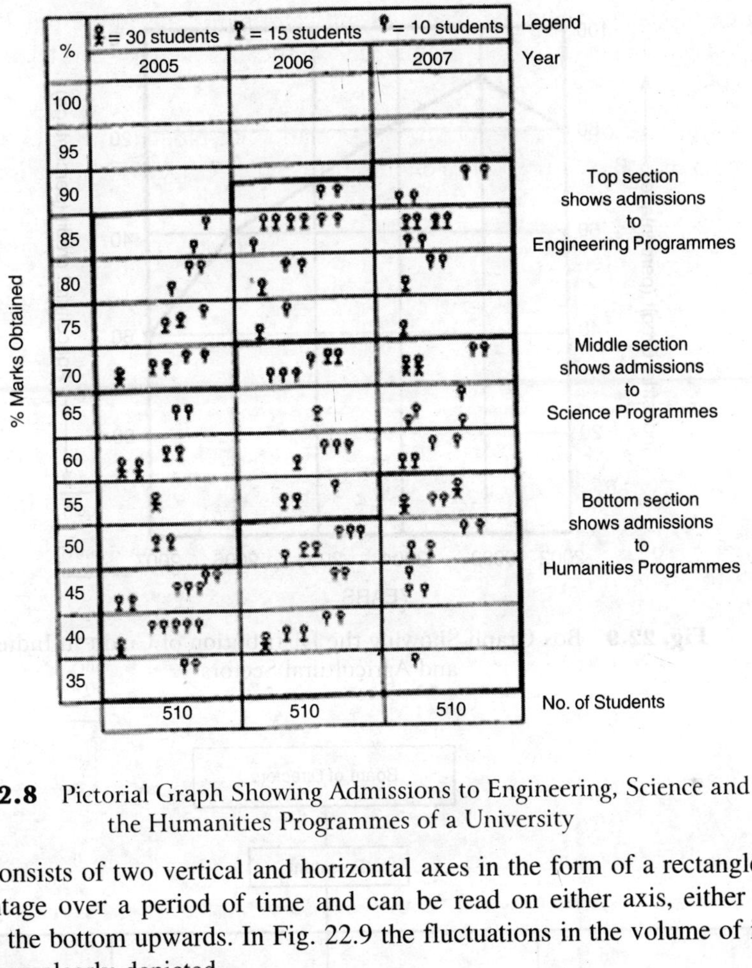

Fig. 22.8 Pictorial Graph Showing Admissions to Engineering, Science and the Humanities Programmes of a University

(ix) *Box graph*: It consists of two vertical and horizontal axes in the form of a rectangle. The data is presented in percentage over a period of time and can be read on either axis, either from the top downwards or from the bottom upwards. In Fig. 22.9 the fluctuations in the volume of industrial and agricultural credits are clearly depicted.

Charts

A chart symbolically represents the arrangement of major components of something or sequence of steps in a process. We shall describe below some of the charts commonly used in the professional world.

(i) *Organisation chart*: It is a kind of directional chart showing the line of authority in an organisation. It shows the hierarchy from the top to the bottom and indicates the function of each department, sub-division or section and its relationship to the organisation as a whole. Figure 22.10 shows the administrative structure of a public limited company up to the level of manager. Further sub-divisions can be shown like-wise.

(ii) *Flow chart*: A flow chart depicts the various steps taken to complete a process. The symbols indicating the steps are placed in blocks connected by straight lines and the direction is marked by arrows. The production process of steel ingots is shown in Fig. 22.11.

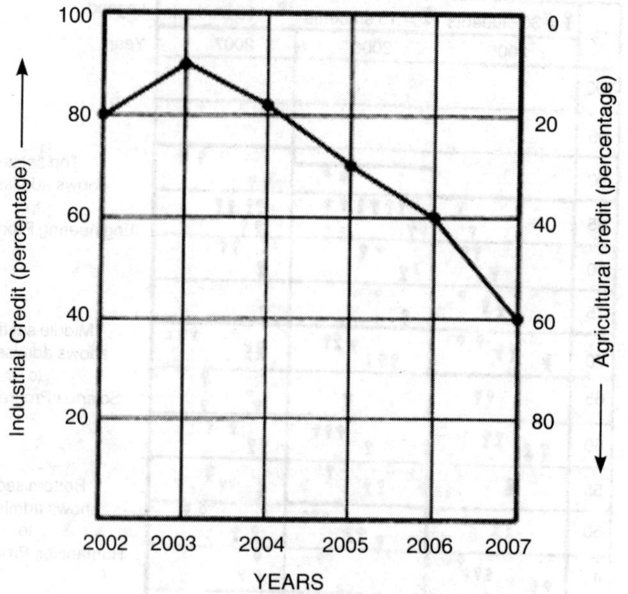

Fig. 22.9 Box Graph Showing the Distribution of Credit in Industrial and Agricultural Sectors

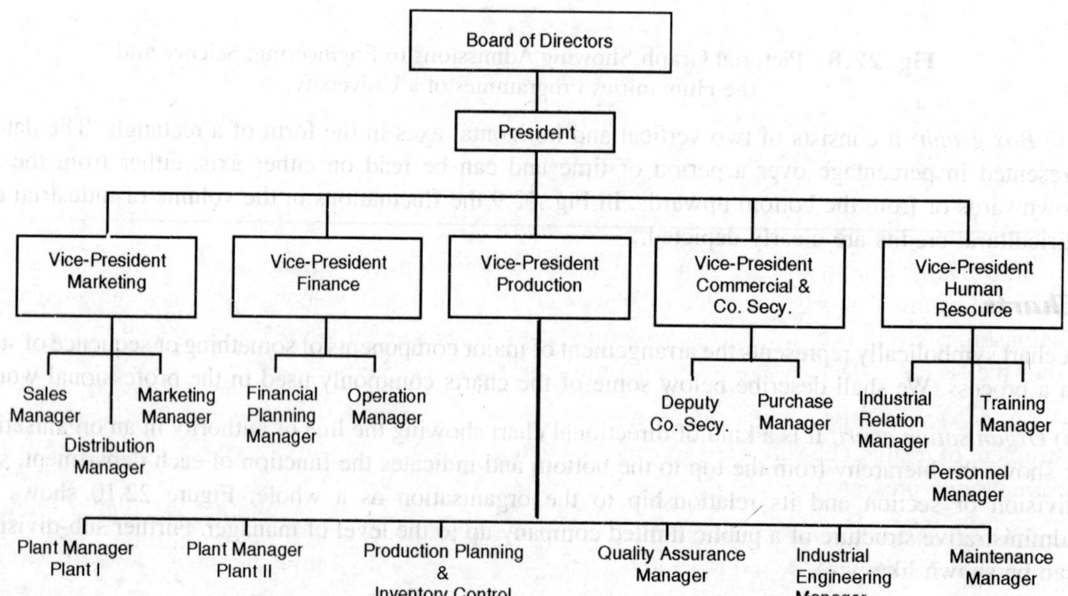

Fig. 22.10 Organisation Chart Showing the Administrative Structure of a Public Limited Company

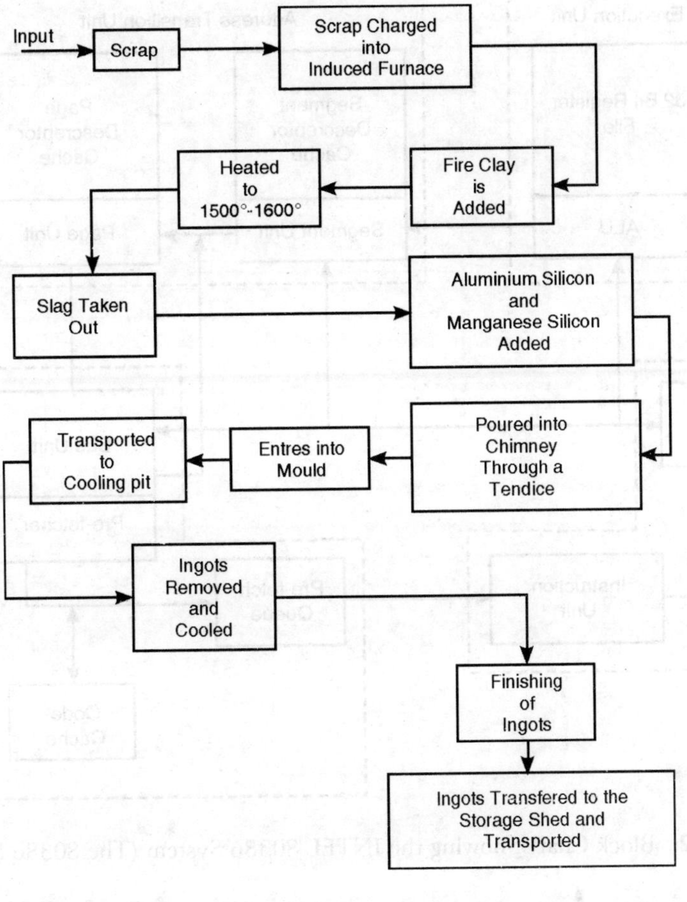

Fig. 22.11 Flow Chart Showing the Production Process of Steel Ingots

(iii) *Block chart*: The major elements or components of a complex structure or system, especially of a technical nature, can be represented in a block chart. Each block symbolises a major element and the relationship of all the constituents is shown by arrows and straight lines. The specimen in Fig. 22.12 shows the INTEL 80386 system of a microprocessor.

(iv) *Control chart*: It is plotted to indicate variation in the quality from the standard and is used as an instrument of quality control of the goods manufactured by the company. Figure 22.13 shows how this information is presented.

(v) *Trilinear chart*: It is used to study the properties, chemical compounds or alloys of three metals or a compound mixture of any three variable elements. It is in the form of an equilateral triangle whose altitude represents 100 per cent of each of the constituents. Figure 22.14 shows the tensile strength of copper-zinc-tin alloy.

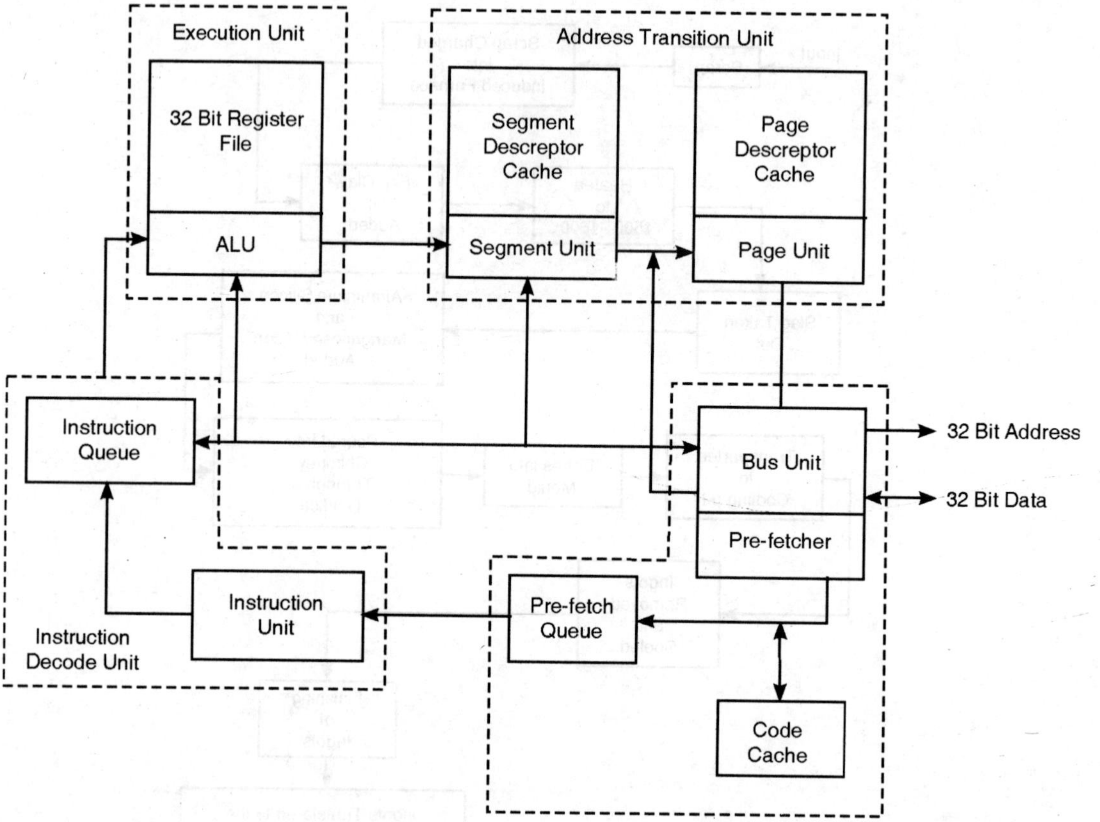

Fig. 22.12 Block Chart Showing the INTEL 80386 System (The 80386 Microprocessor)

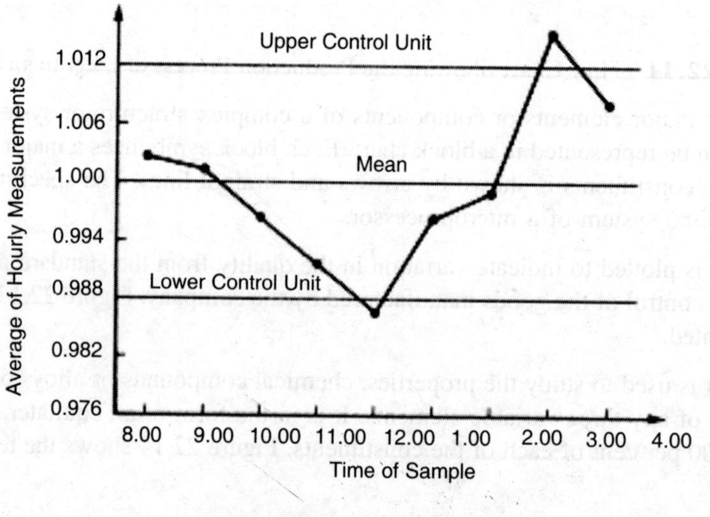

Fig. 22.13 Control Chart

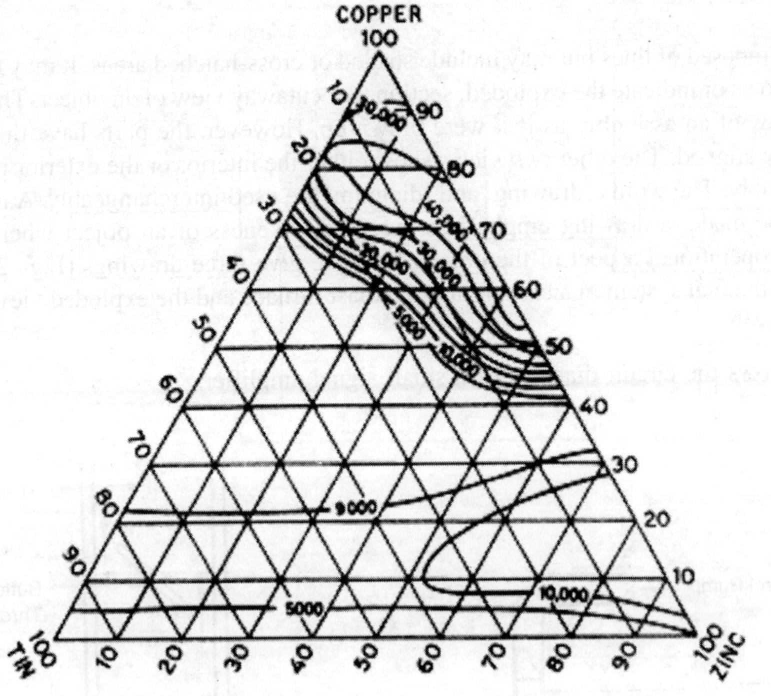

Fig. 22.14 Trilinear Chart Showing the Final Tensile Strength of Copper-Zinc-Tin Allay

(vi) *Strata chart*: It presents the quantity of different objects acquired for a definite purpose. In appearance the representation of quantities looks like a layer. In Fig. 22.15 for example, the three layers indicate the purchase of lead, tin and copper for manufacturing purposes.

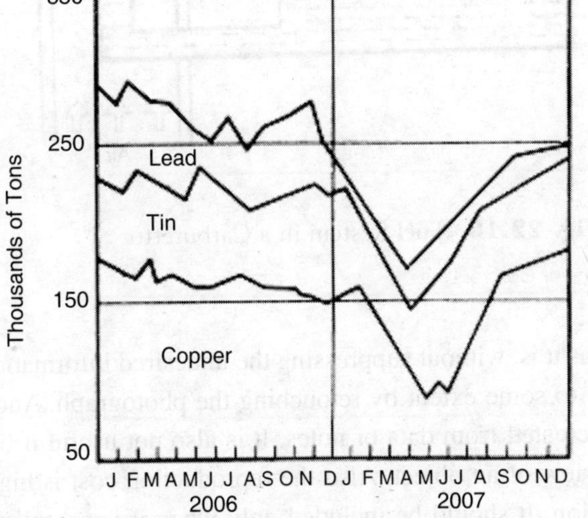

Fig. 22.15 Strata Chart Showing the Purchase of Lead, Tin and Copper

Drawings

A drawing is composed of lines but may include shaded or cross-hatched areas. It may represent objects as they appear to us or indicate the exploded, sectional or cutaway view of an object. The exploded view presents the view of an assembly as if it were blown up. However, the parts have the same sequence and are properly aligned. The other two views show either the interior or the exterior parts of a device, system or assembly. The words 'drawing' and 'diagram' are used interchangeably. A minor distinction may however be made, a drawing emphasises the visual likeness of an object whereas the diagram emphasises the operational aspect of the object. Here we give three drawings (Figs 22.16, 22.17 and 22.18) showing the fuel system in a carburettor, the blast furnace and the exploded view of a wall roller support respectively.

Figure 22.19 shows the circuit diagram of a small signal amplifier.

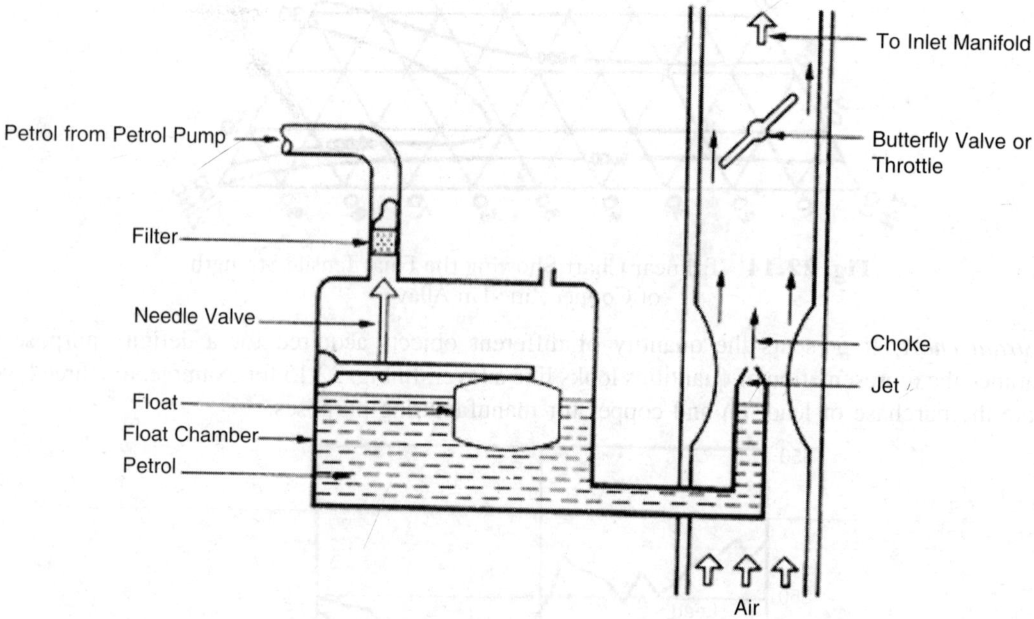

Fig. 22.16 Fuel System in a Carburettor

Photographs

A photograph shows the object as it is, without suppressing the undesired information, if any. However, this weakness can be overcome to some extent by retouching the photograph. Another limitation of a photograph is that it cannot be created from data or notes. It is also not useful if one wants to present an interior view or an all side view of an object. Also the reproduction cost is high. It is therefore of limited use in written presentation. It should be included only when it is essential.

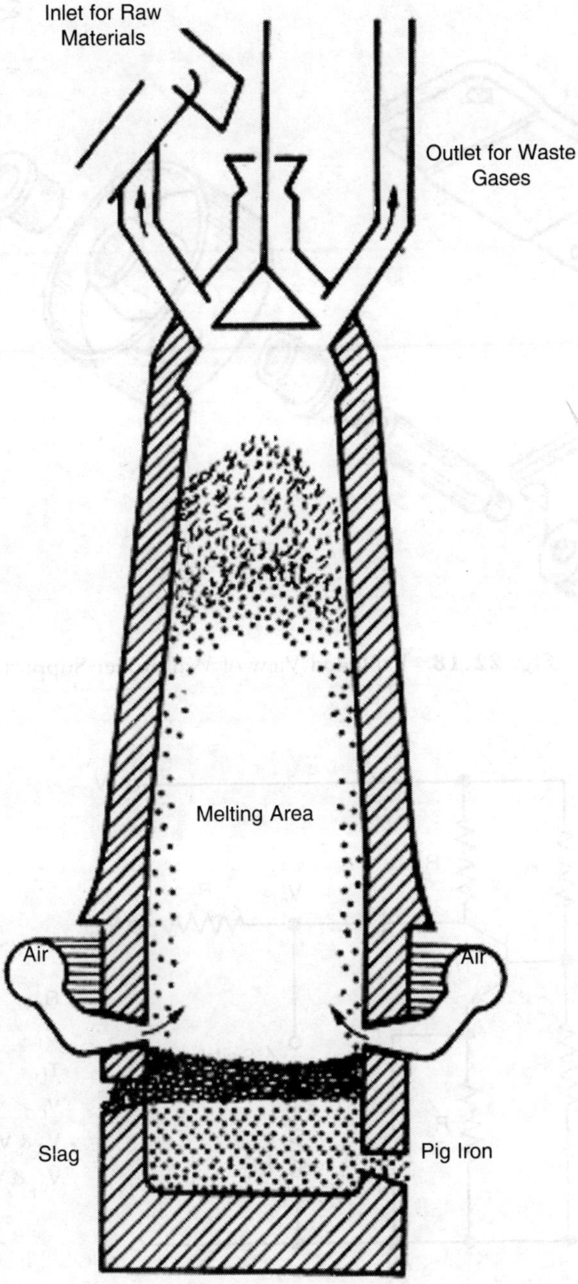

Fig. 22.17 Blast Furnace

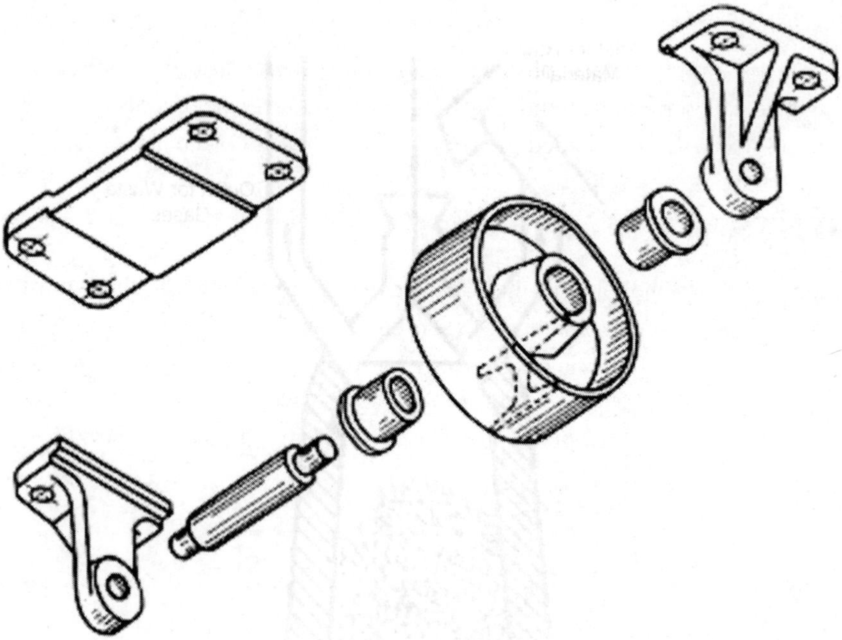

Fig. 22.18 Exploded View of Wall Roller Support

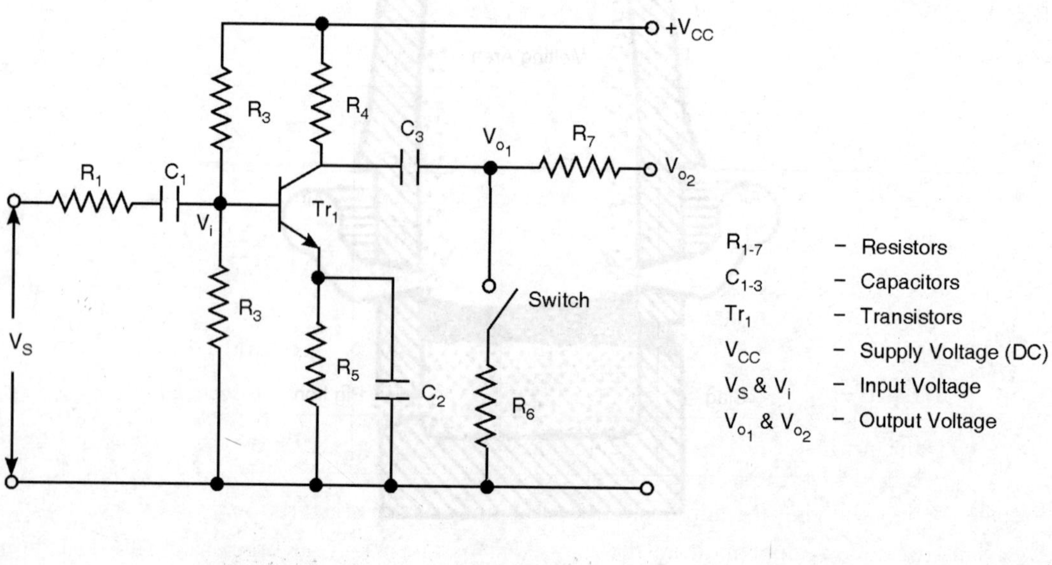

Fig. 22.19 Circuit Diagram of a Small Signal Amplifier

Maps

A map indicates the location of places, physical features or geographical distribution of units, etc. It obviously contains the data on which attention is to be focussed. All other details are omitted. The data can be plotted in the form of dots, shaded areas or symbols of the objects presented.

ASSIGNMENTS

1. Present the data given in the table in this Chapter in a graph which you think most suitable.
2. Prepare a drawing giving the exploded view of a piece of equipment with which you are familiar.
3. Draw a pictorial graph showing the growth of deposits in the National Bank and Universal Bank during the years 2004-5, 2005-6 and 2006-7. Invent the necessary details.
4. The following is the age-wise readership of *Sunday Morning*, a pictorial weekly.

Age Group	*Readership (in %)*
26 - 35	33
36 - 45	17
46 - 55	22
56 - 65	28

   Present the above data in the form of
   (a) a pie graph and
   (b) a bar graph.
5. Devise at least two graphic aids to present the data tabulated below:
   Incidence of fires in textile manufacturing factories in a country.

Years → Causes ↓	2006	2007	2007
Short circuiting	84	61	52
Smoking	50	45	62
Debris/Scrap burning	22	31	29
Unknown	05	09	06
TOTAL	161	146	149
Damage (in Rs.)	2,46,000	2,29,000	2,08,000

6. Prepare a chart showing the administrative structure of your organisation.
7. By means of a flow chart indicate the various steps taken in your organisation to deal with a communication received from outside.

PART FOUR

Mechanics of Manuscript Preparation

Chapter 23

EDITING AND PROOFREADING

IN the section on Final Draft in Chapter 14, we have briefly described the process of revision. The same process is followed in editing too. There are, however, a few differences:

- Revision is a process of going through one's own writing with a view to improving its quality and ensuring that it is free from mistakes of grammar, usage and punctuation. Editing refers to a process of going through somebody else's writing.
- While revising, the author may change emphasis or even modify his viewpoint or approach to the matter. The editor has no right to make any such changes.
- Large-scale changes are the preserve of the author, not the editor. If a major flaw, gap or inconsistency is noticed in a manuscript (MSS), the editor usually returns it to the author for revision and correction.

Editing is followed by copy editing, which we will discuss in detail in Chapter 24. After copyediting, the MS is sent for typesetting – to get page proofs, which are then proofread by the Production or Editorial department. After ensuring that the final proofs are error-free, they are sent to the author for approval. The author goes through the final copy to satisfy himself that it is proper and complete in all respects. He then sends it back to the publisher for final production. The following diagram shows the various stages of production.

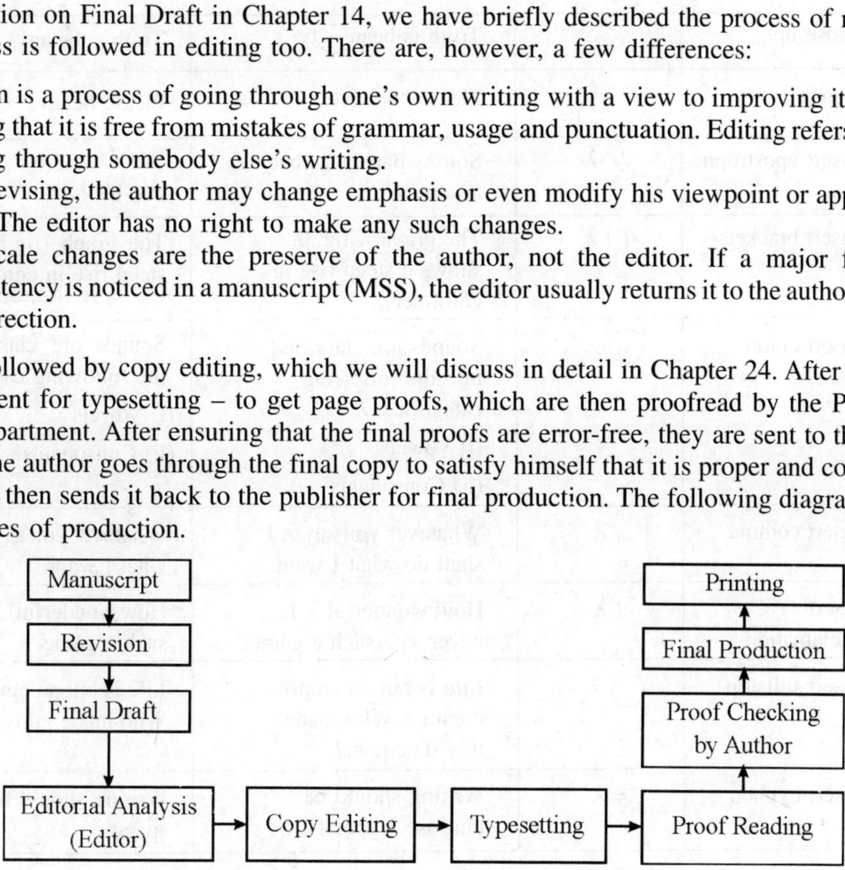

To indicate the corrections to be incorporated at every stage certain standard proofreading symbols are used. A list of symbols commonly used for this purpose is given below.

Proofreading Symbols

S. No.	*Meaning*	*Symbol*	*Examples*	
			Before Correction	*After Correction*
1.	Align	‖	‖ Plastics are of two types natural and synthetic	Plastics are of two types, natural and synthetic.
2.	Begin new para.	¶	Do not make exagge-rated claims. λ In fact, before applying analyse job requirements.	Do not make exaggerated claims. In fact, before applying analyse job requirements.
3.	Change the font or its size.	w.f.	Hard work always pays.	Hard work always pavs.
4.	Close up.	⁀	Truth is beau⁀ty.	Truth is beauty.
5.	Delete	δ	Pleasɇ behave.	Please behave.
6.	Insert apostrophe	∨’ λ	Somλs paper has been accepted.	Som's paper has been accepted.
7.	Insert brackets	[ ] λ	The graph λ fig.3λ shows a steep rise in enrolment.	The graph (fig.3) shows a steep rise in enrolment.
8.	Insert colon	(:) λ	Sounds are classified into the following categories. λ (i) Vowels (ii) Consonants	Sounds are classified into the following categories: (i) Vowels (ii) Consonants
9.	Insert comma	, λ	Whatever you say λ I shall do what I want.	Whatever you say, I shall do what I want.
10.	Insert exclamation	! λ	How wonderful λ I never saw such a game.	How wonderful! I never saw such a game
11.	Insert fullstop	(.) λ	Life is but an empty dream λ Who made this statement?	Life is but an empty dream. Who made this statement?
12.	Insert hyphen	= λ	Writing should be purpose λ specific.	Writing should be purpose-specific.

13.	Insert question	? λ	Where do you work λ	Where do you work?
14.	Insert quotation	❛❛ ❜❜ λ	Explain the statement, λ Truth is Beauty λ in about 50 words.	Explain the statement, "Truth is Beauty" in about about 50 words.
15.	Insert semicolon	; λ	Brave men never die λ they are immortal.	Brave men never die; they are immortal.
16.	Insert word or phrase	a λ	Man is λ social animal.	Man is a social animal.
17.	Lower to proper position	⎺⎺_	DEMOCRACY Democracy may be defined as the government of the people.	DEMOCRACY Democracy may be defined as the government of the people.
18.	Move as indicated	∽	The main of this (aim) course is to impart communication skills.	The main aim of this course is to impart communication skills.
19.	Move this to the right	⌐	Man has been using language for thousands of years.	Man has been using language for thousands of years.
20.	Move this to the left	⌐	It has been rightly said that time and tide wait for none.	It has been rightly said that time and tide wait for none.
21.	Put in capitals	Caps	Ramesh has joined the faculty of (bits)	Ramesh has joined the faculty of BITS.
22.	Put in lowercase	lc	Hari has come Back from Delhi.	Hari has come back from Delhi.
23.	Put in small capitals	Caps/ small	(FINAL draft)	FINAL DRAFT
24.	Raise to proper position.	_⌐	SEASONS There are three seansons-winter, summer and rainy.	SEASONS There are three seansons-winter, summer and rainy.
25.	Replace the letter	e/	A meeting will be høld tomorrow to discuss the issue.	A meeting will be held tomorrow to discuss the issue.

(*Continued*)

(*Continued*)

26.	Replace the word	attend/	All members must ~~albsent~~ the meeting.	All members must attend the meeting.
27.	Run together	Run on	What is the author talking about? Read carefully and you will find that the passage is about symbols.	What is the author talking about? Read carefully and you will find that the passage is about symbols.
28.	Set the matter in normal type.	Rom/	Raise your VOICE	Raise your voice.
29.	Set in bold face type	bf	What is meant was import not export	What is meant was **import**, not export
30.	Set the matter as it was.	Stet	Greed ~~leads~~ to grief.	Greed leads to grief.
31.	Spell out	sp	The pole is only 9ft long.	The pole is only nine feet long.

Chapter 24

COPY EDITING

YOU may occasionally be asked to copy edit a document intended for publication. You have then to look at the manuscript (Ms) from the publisher's point of view. If you pay meticulous attention to details at this stage, you would be saving time later when you have to read the proofs. Remember, those who handle the manuscript in the press are strangers and may not be familiar with your requirements. So you will have to provide detailed instructions.

Copy editing demands a close scrutiny of the style of presentation. Apart from examining the language used, you would have to ensure that the accepted rules and conventions of the mechanics of Ms preparation have been followed. In Parts Two and Three we have already indicated in detail the kind of language to be used for individual forms of communication and also shown what format is to be followed in each. The practical hints given therein would help you edit the written matter. In the Chapters that follow we have provided practical guidance in spelling words and using punctuation, capitals, abbreviations and numerals. Here we shall discuss briefly what you should do to ensure the printing of the Ms in the required format and style.

Some instructions to the printer relate to the size of the printed document and the quality of paper for the text and the cover that you want to use. The paper is bought by the ream (500 sheets) and the weight of paper is based upon the weight of a ream in the standard size. For example, the standard size sheets for a 5½" × 8½" book pages are 23" × 36". The final decision is taken after examining the samples of both the text paper and the cover paper. You have also to give instructions while handing over the Ms to the printer about the type of binding. For publications having a small number of pages, side wiring may be done, stapling of pages on the left margin and gluing of the cover to the first and last pages. If the number of pages is large, say forty or more, they are first properly sewed and glued to the cover supported by a piece of cloth. If pages are of different sizes or shapes, one may go in for mechanical binding or for ring binders. The latter however, though adjustable, are expensive. The best method would be to prepare a layout drawing, showing the exact size, proportions and the placement of the material, both verbal and graphic, on the proposed cover and pages of the document to be printed. If you decide to include a frontispiece and a blurb*, instruct the printer about their design and also provide the material to be printed in the beginning itself.

The second set of instructions is given on the Ms itself. These are briefly mentioned below:

(i) *Choice of typefaces*: Write in the margin the size of the typefaces of headings and sub-headings to be used. Indicate the matter that has to be set in capitals, italics or bold face. Draw three lines below the matter which is to be set in capitals, one line below the matter to be set in italics and write in the margin b.f. for the matter to be set in bold face. The use of capitals is discussed in Chapter 28. The following categories of words and phrases are usually printed in italics:

- Names of books, reports, journals, manuals, etc.
- Foreign words and phrases, not yet completely anglicised.
- Words, letters and figures referred to as such.
- Words and phrases requiring special emphasis.

The matter which you want to be made distinct from the rest should be in bold face. Usually these would be certain headings or sub-headings or rules, definitions and other significant statements. You should, however, take care not to overload the page with bold faced matter as this would mar the grace of your presentation.

(ii) *Numbering*: Check the numbering of pages, headings, sub-headings, figures and tables. The pages from the Introduction onwards are in Arabic numerals and may be given in the middle of the top or the bottom of the page. On the top odd numbers may be given on the right hand side and the even numbers on the left hand side. For the matter before the introduction small Roman numerals are used. Use decimal system in numbering the headings and sub-headings but don't go beyond three degrees as shown below:

1.
    1.1
    1.2
        1.2.1
        1.2.2

In Chapter 23 we have already indicated how to number figures and tables.

(iii) *Spacing and margin*: Give a clear indication of the space to be occupied by the printed matter and the margin to be left on all the four sides of the page. On a book page whose size is 5½" × 8½" the printed matter is approximately 4" × 7". The rest of the space is left blank. This print area of 4" × 7" is inclusive of the page number and running head.

(iv) *Indentation*: Examine carefully whether there is proper indentation within the text and also in bibliography, list of references, appendices, etc. If some matter is not indented, show where it should be done by using the appropriate proof-reading symbols.

---

* It is a publisher's commendatory description of the contents of a printed document usually on the outside of the back cover or jacket. The blurb may also include information about the author.

Sometimes you may not be clear about the intention of the author in using a particular technique of presentation. You should then query the author and writing (?) in the margin.

Above all, ensure that there is uniformity in all aspects of presentation. Remember, copy editing is a skill and can be acquired through patience and sustained practice. You have to develop a sharp eye for locating departures from the accepted norm and need the ability to keep in mind the picture of the entire composition.

Chapter 25

WORDS OFTEN CONFUSED

YOU often come across two or three words which are spelled differently, have different meaning but have almost the same pronunciation e.g. tell, tail, tale. Then there are words with the same pronunciation but different meaning and spelling, e.g. cease and seize. There are many words that are sometimes just confused with others like *elicit* and *illicit*. We give below a short list of such words:

1. **Accede** (agree): My friend **acceded** to my proposal.

   Exceed (surpass, to be greater). Write a precis of the following passage not exceeding 200 words.

2. **Accept (take)**: His father **accepted** the apologies of his employee.

   Except (leaving out): He announced that every boy **except** his son would compete in the contest.

3. **Access** (approach, reach): All the citizens of a free country should have an **access** to the courts of law.

   Excess (additional, immoderation, more than). These **excesses** committed by the troops when they occupied the capital will never be forgotten.

4. **Adapt** (suit, accommodate to). Rekha should **adapt** herself to the new situation she finds herself in.

   Adept (expert, skilful). My daughter is **adept** in cooking.

   Adopt (take somebody into one's family, take an idea, a custom etc.) I like your methods of teaching and will **adopt** them in my school.

5. **Addition** (putting something more). Would you like to have curd in **addition to** the other dishes?

   Edition (form in which a book is published at one time, (2 total number of copies of a book, newspaper etc. issued from the same types.) He bought a cheaper **edition** of the novel.

6. **Affect** (to pretend, to have influence or effect on). I was too much **affected** (by the sad news) to answer.

   Effect (as a verb refers to accomplish or carry into practice). He **effected** the cure through his hard work.

7. **All together** (at the same time, in the same time). The whole family went to the temple **all together**.

   Altogether (entirely, wholly). It is **altogether** out of question.

8. **Allusion** (refer to, speak or write of indirectly). His friend's death made him very sad; don't **allude** to it when you meet him.

   Illusion (the seeing of something that does not really exist). He cherishes the **illusion** (likes to believe that) that everyone admires him.

9. **Alter** (change in character) Meena's suit is too large and needs to be **altered**.

   Altar (raised platform for offerings in temples or churches). After the examination Sohan lit ten candles at the **altar.**

10. **Alternate** (coming by turns). He **alternated** kindness by severity.

    Alternative (of two things that may be had). Is there no **alternative to** what you propose?

11. **Amiable** (good tempered, easy and pleasant to talk to). I was to make myself amiable to the guests.

    Amicable (friendly). Everyone should live together **amicably** in the society.

12. **Antagonise** (make an enemy). His anti-social activities antagonised his neighbours.

    Alienate (to estrange, turn away friendship etc.). She **alienated** all her friends due to her funny ideas.

13. **Antic** (odd, strange, grotesque movement, attitude meant to amuse). The antics of the clown in the circus made us all laugh.

    Antique (old fashioned, ancient). My mother is very fond of collecting antique furniture.

14. **Apposite** (proper, suitable for the purpose or occasion) He made a number of arguments apposite to the case.

    Opposite (standing in front or contrary). His brother built a house opposite the local club.

15. **Assay** (test of the fineness, purity of quality of precious metals). Mr. Lal called an expert to make an **assay** of the ore.

    Essay (a piece of composition). This **essay** lacks coherence.

16. **Assent** (agree, concurrence). Lilavati gave her **assent** to the proposal.

    Ascent (going up) The **ascent** to this high mountain is not easy.

17. **Bale** (package of goods). Please send us four **bales** of cotton.

    Bail (sum of money demanded by a law court as security). The accused forfeited his **bail** when he did not pay the full amount.

18. **Beneficial** (useful). Fresh air and good food are **beneficial** to health.
Beneficent (kind, doing good). The **beneficent** man gave the worker a large amount of money.
19. **Berth** (a sleeping place in a train). Please reserve a first class **berth** for me in the Prayag Raj Express.
Birth (coming to life). Sheila gave **birth** to a girl child.
20. **Bridal** (of marriage). The mother-in-law expects a lot of bridal presents from the bride's parents.
Bridle (part of the horse's harness). The horse trainer bridled the dangerous wild horse.
21. **Calendar** (list of the days, weeks and months of a particular year). He looked at the **calendar** to find out when there was the second Sunday.
Calendar (machine for pressing and smoothing cloth and paper). They bought a new **calendar** for their textile mill.
22. **Canvas** (a kind of rough cloth). School children wear **canvas** shoes for their games.
Canvass (go from person to person to ask for votes). He is **canvassing** for his party candidate.
23. **Career** (profession). Mr. Singh was very successful in his legal **career**.
Carrier (person or company which carries goods, support for luggage in bicycles.) The goods train is the biggest carrier of goods.
24. **Casual** (happening by chance, informal, unmethodical). He earns his living as a casual labourer.
Causal (of cause and effect). There is no **causal** connection between the lunar eclipse and price rise.
25. **Censer** (a vessel in which incense is burnt). Put the incense in the **censer**.
Censor (an official with authority to examine letters, books, plays, films, etc.) During Indo-China war all our letters were **censored**.
Censure (criticise unfavourably). I read a review containing unfair **censures** of the new novel.
26. **Cession** (to yield or give up. It is the noun form of the verb *cede*). The political leaders had to agreed to the **cession** of a large piece of land to China.
Session (the time when educational institutions, courts or public body sits). These days the new **session** starts in schools in April.
27. **Childlike** (qualities like innocence, sweetness, etc. in children worth possessing). Everyone was vastly impressed by the young girl's **childlike** innocence.
Childish (qualities which are silly, foolish and not admired). I am ashamed of my brother's **childish** arguments.
28. **Cite** (quote). She **cited** many examples to prove that she was hardworking.
Site (place where something was or is to be) He is looking for a good **site** to build a school.
Sight (view, scene). I have lost **sight** of Smita.
29. **Complacent** (over-pleased). People living in the village are often **complacent** with their fate.
Complaisant (polite, obliging). He is always ready to help others due to his complaisant nature.

30. Complement (that which completes). I have two books which are complementary to each other.

Compliment (admiration, approval). I received a book from the publisher with a note 'With the **compliments** of the publisher.

31. Confident (feeling or showing confidence). She feels **confident** of passing the examination.

Confidant (a person trusted with secrets or private affairs). Mr. Kishore is his friend's **confidant**.

32. Conscious (aware). His brother is very **conscious** of his short height.

Conscientious (dutiful, sincere, careful). The new secretary was very **conscientious**

Consensus (common agreement of opinion, etc.). There was no **consensus** of opinion that there should be a partition.

34. Contagious (of disease spreading by touch; figuratively spreading easily by example). Scarlet fever is **contagious**. His enthusiasm is highly contagious.

Infectious (infecting with disease esp. through germs; influencing others likely to spread to others). Typhoid is an **infectious** disease. We all like him for his **infectious** humour.

35. Corroborate (to confirm or establish a statement or belief) All the witnesses **corroborated** Mr. Singh's statement.

Collaborate (work together with one or more in writing or in art). He was requested to **collaborate** on a novel with a friend.

36. Credible (believable). The incident described in the novel was not **credible**.

Credulous (someone too ready to believe). Uneducated persons are often **credulous.**

37. Curtsy (bending knee to show respect) The young girls were taught to make a **curtsy** to the Queen.

Courtesy (good and polite manners) This radio program is presented by **courtesy** of Red Label Brooke Bond Tea.

38. Defy (resist openly). The teenagers of today often **defy** rules and regulations.

Deify (worship as God). A few fans of popular actors **deify** them.

39. Deprecate (to feel and express disapproval of). The manager **deprecates** the changing of rules.

Depreciate (become less in value). The purchasing power of money has **depreciated** since he bought his saving certificates.

40. Descent (going down, ancestry, handing down titles, property, etc. sudden attack). The land slopes to the sea by a gradual **descent**. She traces her descent from an old Rajput family. The terrorists made many descents upon the people living in the valley.

Dissent (as a noun expressing disagreement; as a verb have a different opinion.) They strongly **dissent** from what their leader said. Most of the club members expressed their strong **dissent**.

41. Desert (a waste part of land as noun; to forsake as verb). Name the biggest desert in the world. Venna's friends deserted her when she lost her property.

Desserts (something which a person deserves)' The police officer beat the thief and he got his just **desserts**.

Dessert (sweet-dish or fruits served after dinner). We like the ice-cream served to us as dessert.

42. **Device** (a plan as noun). Modern technology has given many **devices** to man to help him.

Devise (to plan, to think out). The young men **devised** a scheme to make more money.

43. **Discrete** (discontinuous, separate). These two are discrete entities.

Discreet (judicious, prudent). The newly elected leader is very **discreet** in all statements he makes.

44. **Disease** (illness). Cancer is used to be an incurable **disease**.

Decease (death) Due to his father's **decease** he could not go abroad for higher studies.

45. **Draught** (the amount of water or liquid a person drinks at a time). My brother suffering from high fever wanted to drink a **draught** of water.

Drought (lack of rain). Many parts of Rajasthan are drought-prone.

Draft (initial sketch). He finished writing the first **draft** of his report.

46. **Egotist** (one who talks about himself, is selfish and conceited). No one likes to befriend an egotist.

Egoist (one who believes that sell-interest is most important). Rohan, an **egoist**, believes that his actions are guided by the desire to benefit himself.

47. **Elicit** (draw out). He **elicited** the necessary information from the young student.

Illicit (unlawful, forbidden) The sale of opium is **illicit.**

48. **Eligible** (fit to be chosen). Sundari is the most **eligible** candidate for the general secretary.

Illegible (impossible to read). His handwriting is **illegible**.

49. **Elusive** (tending to escape). The police caught the most **elusive** thief at last.

Illusive (deceptive) Many travelers in the deserts have lost their lives in the **illusive** search of an oasis.

50. **Emigrant** (one who leaves his country for another country). They are **emigrants** from Bangladesh.

Immigrant (one who comes into a country from another). Usually, an **immigrant** in Sough Africa enjoys the same rights and privileges as other South Africans.

51. **Eminent** (distinguished). Mother Teresa was an **eminent** social worker.

Imminent (near at hand). With his careless and irregular habits he is in **imminent** danger of losing his job.

52. **Enable** (make able, give authority or means to do something). The end of the strike **enabled** the authorities to resume normal work.

Unable (not able to). The student was down with fever and was **unable** to complete his assignment.

53. **Envious** (feel jealous) He was **envious** of his neighbour's popularity.

Enviable (arousing envy). They are in an **enviable** position at present.

54. **Eruption** (outbreak of a volcano). There were sudden **eruptions** of ashes and lava from the silent volcano.
Irruption (sudden and violent entry). The **irruption** of the Chinese army destroyed the Sino-Indian brotherhood.

55. **Fain** (happily). She would **fain** see her friend again.
Fein (to pretend) When Ramesh is criticized severely by his friends, he **feins** deafness.

56. **Fair** (lovely, just). My son wants to marry a **fair** maiden. This shop charges fair prices.
Fare (money charged for bus, train, taxi, etc. journey; food; progress). The taxi driver had only one fare that day. My mother served a simple **fare** to the guests. Hostel life has **fared** well with him.

57. **Farther** (relating to distance). We can not go any **farther** with out a long rest.
Further (in addition, besides, moreover). The library will be closed until further notice. She told that her purse was lost, and **further**, there was no hope of its being found.

58. **Felicity** (happiness or contentment). A sinner can not enjoy real **felicity**.
Facility (aids, circumstances which make learning or doing things easily). This school provides ample **facilities** for all-round development of students.

59. **Feminine** (of, like, suitable to women). Needlework is a **feminine** hobby.
Effeminate (womanish, unmanly). No one really likes a man who is **effeminate**.

60. **Fiance** (man who is engaged). Sunita introduced her **fiance** to her friends.
Fiancee (woman who is betrothed) Sunil gave a diamond ring to his **fiancee**.

61. **Forceful** (of a person, argument, etc. full of force.) The leader's **forceful** arguments convinced the public.
Forcible (using force). The dacoit made a **forcible** entry into my neighbor's house.

62. **Gild** (to have a thin covering of gold). The bride refused to wear **gilded** jewellery.
Guild (association or society of men of a particular profession). During the Middle Ages members of a **guild** helped one another for furthering their common interest.

63. **Hail** (frozen rain drops, blows greeting. It **hailed** during the morning. Blows **hailed** down her back. Cheerful voices hailed the distinguished visitors as they entered the hall.
Hale (healthy). The patient is quite **hale** and hearty.

64. **Hoard** (carefully stored, saved money, food or treasure objects). The black marketeer **hoarded** grains when there was a plentiful supply of these in the market.
Horde (nomads; multitude). A gipsy **horde** passed by our car. Suddenly a **horde** of locusts descended on the wheat field.

65. **Identical** (When two things or persons are absolutely similar). She gifted two **identical** sarees to her sisters.
Synonymous (words which have almost similar meaning but are not exactly the same). The word 'exalt' is **synonymous** with high and elevated.

66. Imperial (relating to the king or kingdom). Is Mr. Logan a member of the **Imperial** Council?

Imperious (naughty). Sona, the Chess Champion, is known all over the state of Rajasthan for her **imperious** manners.

67. Incite (stir up, rouse). The remarks of the speaker **incited** the public to take up arms.

Insight (power of seeing with the mind). People of experience develop **insight** into human character.

68. Indite (put into words, compose). The teacher asked her students to **indite** a speech.

Indict (legal) accuse one for riot, etc.). Mr. Lakra was **indicted** for spending party funds.

69. Industrial (relating to industry). Kanpur is an **industrial** city.

Industrious (hardworking). Everyone likes an **industrious** worker.

70. Informant (one who gives information). The government gave the **informant** of this news a cash prize of thousand rupees.

Informer (one who informs against another). The distiller of illicit liquor killed the **informer**.

71. Ingenious (skilful). Her ingenious methods of teaching young children impressed us all.

Ingenuous (artless, plain, innocent). The ingenuous remarks of the child surprised the judge.

72. Innumerable (uncountable). There are **innumerable** starts is the sky.

Enumerable (Countable, mention one by one). She **enumerated** all the factors responsible for air pollution.

73. Intolerable (unbearable). The student's mischief was **intolerable**.

Intolerant (not tolerant, narrow-minded persons.) Mr. Khosla is **intolerant** of opposition.

74. Invidious (likely to cause ill feeling because of injustice). When the overseer made **invidious** distinctions among the workers, they were very angry.

Insidious (doing secretly, crafty). An **insidious** enemy crossed the western border of India.

75. Jealous (feeling ill-will or fear because of possible loss). He was **jealous** of his friend's increasing popularity.

Zealous (enthusiastic). The new employee was **zealous** to please his employer.

76. Later (more late in time). My friend went out **later** than I did.

Latter (contrasted with 'former', recent). Of these two leaders, the former is dead but the **latter** is still alive. The latter half of the year was full of problems.

77. Loose (free, not held or tied up, make free). This dog is too dangerous to be left **loose**. Wine loosed his tongue.

Lose (lost, disappear). The ship and all the crew were **lost**.

78. Luxuriant (strong growth, abundant). Mr. Yadav took many photographs of the **luxuriant** vegetation of Suderbans.

Luxurious (very comfortable with luxuries). The rich people get used to live in **luxurious** surroundings.

79. **Maize** (grain plant, also called Indian corn). In the rainy season roasted **maize** tastes good.

    Maze (labyrinth). The old house has a number of **mazes**.

80. **Marshal** (officer of the highest rank; arrange in proper order). Mr. K. P. Luthra was the Air-Vice **Marshal** of the Indian Air Force. As the report was very important, Mr. Dev had to **marshall** all the facts laboriously.

    Martial (associated with war) During the emergency, the President put the country under **martial** law.

    Marital (of a husband; of marriage) All the husbands are expected to fulfil **marital** obligations.

81. **Minor** (underage; lesser). Our law gives special protection to **minors** and women.

    Miner (Worker in the mine). The lives of the **miners** are not always safe.

82. **Moat** (deep, wide ditch filled with water around a castle). He got a castle built, he got a **moat** around it.

    Mote (a dust particle). We can see **motes** dancing in a sunbeam.

83. **Momentary** (lasting for a moment). He had a **momentary** loss of memory when he stood at the witness box.

    Momentous (very important). Mr. Shekhawat will never forget the **momentous** occasion when he had been awarded the President's medal.

84. **Monetary** (of money). It is wise not to think of **monetary** motives all the time.

    Monitory (to give advice or warn). We must listen to our elders' **monitory** counsel carefully.

85. **Moral** (relating to the principles of right and wrong). Parents should inculcate a **moral** sense in their children to enable them to distinguish between right and wrong.

    Morale (state of discipline and spirit in an army, a nation, etc.) The film stars went to Kargil to boost the **morale** of the army posted there.

86. **Necessities** (something urgently needed) People work hard to get the **necessities** of life like food and shelter.

    Necessaries (those things which can not be done without or escaped from.) Is war one of the **necessaries** of modern civilisation?

87. **Novice** (a beginner who is still learning, not skilled). She is still a **novice** and not a nun yet.

    Amateur (one who paints, performs music, plays, etc. for the love of it, not money). Harish is an **amateur** photographer.

88. **Ordinance** (authoritative direction, decree). In order to prevent any unpleasant incident, the Delhi administration passed a few **ordinances** on the eve of the Republic Day.

    Ordnance (mounted guns, canons). My father worked in an **ordnance** factory for twenty years.

89. **Peal** (a loud sound of thunder or bells). I got up in the morning when I heard **peals** of bells.
Peel (to remove the skin of fruits or vegetables). The little girl **peeled** the orange and ate it.

90. **Persecute** (harass, worry). The daughter-in-law was **persecuted** by her mother-in-law for not having brought any dowry.
Prosecute (institute legal proceeding, pursue). Gopal was **prosecuted** on the charge of encroachment of government land.
The boy prosecuted his studies despite illness.

91. **Perspicuity** (the quality or state of having mental vision or clarity). The interviewer was impressed by the candidate's **perspicuity**.
Perspicacity (clear sightedness, discernment). The young man was blessed with **perspicacity**.

92. **Practice** (noun) **Practice** makes a man perfect.
Practise (verb). I was asked to **practise** what I preached.

93. **Precede** (go before). The leader **preceded** the other party members.
Proceed (to go on). After the meeting he **proceeded** with his office work.

94. **Prescribe** (impose authoritatively). The doctor **prescribed** anti-biotics for his patient.
Proscribe (banish, ban). The government **proscribed** all kinds of meetings and demonstrations.

95. **Prophecy** (noun, prediction). The **prophecy** of the science-fiction writers has come true.
Prophesy (verb, to foretell). It was **prophesied** that the inflation rate would drop.

96. **Raise** (to lift up). Bhola **raised** many objections in the meeting.
Raze (to destroy). The huts were **razed** to the ground.

97. **Recourse** (turn to for help, seek help from). It is not advisable for you to have **recourse** to moneylenders.
Resource (wealth, supply of goods, raw materials etc.) We must exploit our natural **resources** with great care.

98. **Revenge** (as noun: retaliation). The leader of the gang of dacoits wanted to take **revenge** on the new gang in his area.
Avenge (always a verb; to punish justifiably). The young boy finally **avenged** his father's death upon the murderer.

99. **Reverend** (worthy of reverence). Mohini is a **reverend** woman for she cleared the misunderstanding completely.
Reverent (respectful). Don't speak ill of Gadhiji; your attitude should be **reverent** towards him.

100. **Righteous** (just, upright). He is famous for his **righteous** action.
Riotous (lawless, tumultuous). We had seen **riotous** crowds during partition days in 1947.

101. **Roll** (to run over). Don't **roll** the log towards the river.
Role (part). The mother has an important **role** in her children's life.

102. Route (course). There are several **routes** from here to Jaipur.

Rout (flight). The enemy soldiers were put to **rout**.

Root (underground part of a plant). All plants have **roots**.

103. Sensible (having good sense). The young boy was very **sensible**.

Sensitive (quick to receive impression). Her delicate constitution was very **sensitive** to extremes of weather.

104. Sensual (given to the pleasures of the senses only). **Sensual** inclinations hinder intellectual and spiritual advancement.

Sensuous (relating to the senses). As some poets are romantic they have **sensuous** thoughts.

105. Serge (a kind of woolen cloth). He wore a suit made of serge.

Surge (move like waves). The waves of the ocean **surged** violently in the moonlit night.

106. Siege (surrounding encamped attacking force to make them surrender). The king surrendered when his fort was under **siege** for a fortnight.

Seige (a flock of herons). The bird watches sighted a **seige** of herons.

107. Sooth (truth, fortune teller). My mother said to me, '**Sooth** to say, you are a born leader'

Soothe (make a person quiet or calm). The doctor gave me a **soothing** lotion for my skin.

108. Sore (painful). The changing season causes sore throat to may people.

Soar (to fly high). The swallow soared up in the sky.

109. Spacious (having more space, roomy). This flat has **spacious** rooms.

Specious (apparently true or right but not actually so). You cannot fool me with **specious** arguments that you are not interested.

110. Stationary (not moving or changing). The train collided with the **stationary** engine of the goods train.

Stationery (writing materials like paper, pencils, etc.) The office buys all its **stationery** from this shop.

111. Statue (an image carved in stone). We have a **statue** of Mahatma Gandhi in our library.

Statute (a written law). There are many **statutes** which govern India.

112. Suit (a set of clothes; an action in a law court). My sister got two salwar **suits** stitched. The old lady was forced to file a suit in the court.

Suite (a set of rooms in a hotel). The bride's father booked a bridal **suite** for his daughter.

113. Tamper (meddle with). Sohan **tampered** with the seal of lock put by the Police Inspector.

Temper (state or condition of the mind). No one likes to talk with a person who is in a bad **temper**.

114. Temporal (earthly). A spiritual man does not care for **temporal** matters.

Temporary (transitory, short lived) His brother has been appointed to a **temporary** post.

115. Tenor (general meaning, drift). He knew enough French to get the **tenor** of what was being said.

Tenure (period or time of, condition of). The **tenure** of office of the Prime Minister in India is five years.

116. Toe (a part of the foot). Don't tread upon somebody's **toes**.

Tow (flax, hemp, etc. for making rope; pull along by a rope or chain) He **towed** a damaged boat to the shore.

117. Umpire (referee). We expect a better game of cricket with the appointment of the third **umpire**.

Empire (dominion). The fall of the Gupta **Empire** was predicted by the sages.

118. Vacation (holiday). All of us enjoy a **vacation** after a spell of hard work.

Vocation (person's trade or profession; special aptitude; feeling that one is called to do a certain kind of work.) He took up a job in **vocational** guidance. She has little **vocation** for teaching. According to Florence Nightingale nursing is a noble **vocation**.

119. Vain (having no real value or useless; proud). He tried to reform his younger brother but in **vain**. No one appreciates Mr. Tilak's vain display of riches.

Vein (blood vessel). Blood flows in our **veins**.

120. Vale (valley). He went to Kashmir to enjoy the beauty of the **vales** there.

Wail (cry or complain in a loud, shrill voice) The young mother was **wailing** for her lost child.

121. Vane (weather-cock). There is a **vane** on top of the tower.

Wane (to decrease). During the days preceding Diwali the moon **wanes**.

122. Veracity (truthfulness). One cannot question the **veracity** of his statement.

Voracity (greediness). One day her **voracity** of gold would make her suffer a great deal.

123. Vigorous (strong, powerful). He pursues his goals with **vigorous** discipline.

Rigorous (harsh, severe). The serial killer was sentenced to **rigorous** imprisonment for life.

124. Virtuous (chaste, righteous). Everyone should respect a **virtuous** man.

Virtual (being in fact, acting as). Sri Somnath is the **virtual** head of the business.

125. Waive (forego). The manager **waived** the age-limit for the post of the Technical Advisor.

Wave (move to and fro, up down; of seas). The signalman **waved** the flag. He heard the **waves** strike against the shore.

126. Weather (climate). We went out shopping in the fine **weather**.

Whether (if). Tell me **whether** he would send the parcel or not.

127. Whither (where). No one knows **whither** she went after she left her house.

Wither-(become dry, faded or dead). As days passed without any news of her husband, her hopes **withered**.

128. Wilful (headstrong, obstinate). The teacher could not reform the **willful** boy.

Willing (desirous). He is **willing** to work hard.

129. Wreck (ruin or destruction). The sailor retrieved some food and supplies from the wrecked ship.

Wreak (to give expression to, to give effect to). She wreaked havoc upon all those who had harassed her.

130. Yarn (story, thread). The beggar spun a **yarn** about his misfortunes. Please bring the some yarn so that I could knit a cardigan.

Yearn (long for a thing). Having lived outside India for years, he **yearned** to return home.

131. Yolk (the yellow part of an egg). Many heart patients are advised not to eat the **yolk** of the egg.

Yoke (shaped piece of wood placed across the necks of the oxen, servitude). He threw off the **yoke** and refused to obey any rules and regulations.

Chapter 26

Common Errors

A few errors often made in the use of articles, nouns, pronouns, adjectives, verbs, infinitives, gerunds, participles and prepositions are listed below for reference.

I. Articles

	Incorrect	*Correct*
1.	Sun gives us light and life.	The sun gives us light and life.
2.	The sinner was condemned to the hell.	The sinner was condemned to hell.
3.	This man is second Tilak	This man is a second Tilak.
4.	Ashwani is M.P.	Ashwani is an MP.
5.	Suhana is a virtuous and a beautiful girl.	Suhana is a virtuous and beautiful girl.
6.	More a greedy man gets, more he wants.	The more a greedy man gets, the more he wants.
7.	Pupil should obey his/her teacher.	A pupil should obey his/her teacher.
8.	It takes two to make the quarrel.	It takes two to make a quarrel.
9.	Latter suggestion is more objectionable.	The latter suggestion is more objectionable.
10.	It is written in Gita that God incarnates	It is written in the Gita that God incarnates
11.	Himalayas lies to the north of India.	The Himalayas lies to the north of India.
12.	Does the tourist wish to travel by the water or by the land?	Does the tourist wish to travel by water or by land?
13.	She is an university professor.	She is a university professor.

	Incorrect	Correct
14.	Rohan has been suffering from fever for last six days.	Rohan has been suffering from fever for the last six days.
15.	The iron is a ordinary kind of metal.	Iron is an ordinary kind of metal
16.	The judge had both the civil and criminal jurisdiction.	The judge had both the civil and the criminal jurisdiction.
17.	Darkest cloud has silver lining.	The darkest cloud has silver lining.
18.	It is the moral duty of a man to help a poor.	It is the moral duty of a man to help the poor.
19.	Honesty is a best policy.	Honesty is the best policy.
20.	He is interested in learning the French and the English languages.	He is interested in learning the French and English languages.

2. Noun/Noun Phrases

	Incorrect	Correct
21.	The family has received no informations.	The family has received no information.
22.	The students packed their luggages.	The students packed their luggage.
23.	Junior Section boys wear half-pants.	Junior Section boys wear shorts.
24.	Romen saw a theatre.	Romen saw a play.
25.	There is no place in this compartment.	There is no room in this compartment.
26.	His brother got a bad companionship.	His brother got into bad companionship.
27.	We brought all our furnitures from the old house	We brought all our furniture from the old house.
28.	There are many news published in The Times of India.	There are many items of news published in The Times of India.
29.	Switzerland in very famous for its beautiful sceneries.	Switzerland in very famous for its beautiful scenery.
30.	This is not her book. It is somebody's else.	This is not her book. It is somebody else's.
31.	Have you read Goldsmith and Cowper's poems?	Have you read Goldsmith's and Cowper's poems?
32.	My son has learnt the alphabets.	My son has learnt the alphabet.
33.	He was determined to fight to the bitterest end for justice's sake.	He was determined to fight to the bitterest end for the sake of justice.

34.	I have <u>a ten-rupees note</u> which is torn.	I have <u>a ten-rubee note</u> which is torn.
35.	She has six <u>brother-in-laws</u>.	She has six <u>brothers-in-laws</u>.
36.	The only fault they find is one which this author shares <u>with many Indian writers</u>.	The only fault they find is one which this author shares <u>with many other Indian authors</u>.
37.	The more we consider, the less we are disposed to agree to your views,	The more we consider your views, the less we are disposed to agree to them.
38.	<u>Debu's</u>, the grocer's business is flourishing.	<u>Debu</u>, the grocer's business is flourishing.
39.	His <u>daughter's-in-law</u> brother is studying in school.	His <u>daughter-in-law's</u> brother is studying in school.
40.	Munna Bhai has failed in this, but he will appear in the next <u>examination</u>.	Munna Bhai has failed in <u>this examination</u>, but he will appear in the next.
41.	The <u>drainage and sanitary system</u> of this town is not good.	The <u>drainage and sanitation</u> of this town is not good.

3. Pronouns

42.	Sohan and you have read Plato's writings, <u>who</u> was a disciple of Socrates.	Sohan and you have read the writings of <u>Plato, who</u> was a disciple of Socrates.
43.	He has <u>resigned to his</u> fate.	He has <u>resigned himself to his</u> fate.
44.	Mr. Saxena invested all his money in cotton <u>business, and which has</u> left him penniless.	Mr. Saxena invested all his money in cotton <u>business, which has</u> left him penniless.
45.	It is I <u>who is</u> to blame.	It is I <u>who am</u> to blame.
46.	My younger brother is taller <u>than me</u>.	My younger brother is taller <u>than I(am)</u>.
47.	Sagar loves you more <u>than him</u>.	Sagar loves you more <u>than he</u> (loves you).
48.	Rakesh made a statement about <u>a man who</u> he said he met in Calcutta and who was a journalist from China,	Rakesh made a statement about <u>a man whom</u> he said he met in Calcutta and who was a journalist from China.
49.	Two boys <u>absented from</u> school.	Two boys <u>absented themselves from</u> school.
50.	Please <u>avail these</u> unique facilities.	Please <u>avail yourself of these</u> unique facilities.
51.	Many persons, <u>who we know</u>, are hypocrites,	Many persons, <u>whom we know</u>, are hypocrites.

	Incorrect	Correct
52.	Let you and I solve this question.	Let you and me solve this question.
53.	There is no period in ancient or modern history so interesting as the Renaissance	There is no period in ancient or modern history so interesting as that of Renaissance.
54.	It is the dowry system, not the individual which I condemn.	It is the dowry system which I condemn, not the individual.
55.	One should not boast of his own merits.	One should not boast of one's own merits.
56.	A cunning man can do anythine what he likes.	A cunning man can do anything that he likes.
57.	Deepak took my leave.	Deepak took leave of me.
58.	Your problem is greater than that of mine.	Your problem is greater than mine.
59.	Man can not get all what he wants.	Man can not get all that he wants.
60.	Here is a pupil whose mind works fast but his actions are slow.	Here is a pupil whose mind works fast but whose actions are slow.
61.	Neither Monali nor her friends succeeded in her attempts.	Neither Monali nor her friends succeeded in their attempts.

4. Adjectives

	Incorrect	Correct
62.	This is a worst example of dishonesty that I have ever come across.	This is the worst example of dishonesty that I have ever come across.
63.	The Kutub Minar is a worth-seeing monument.	The Kutub Minar is a monument worth-seeing.
64.	We often find the kind of things.	We often find things of this kind.
65.	Shyam is more intelligent student of the class.	Shyam is a very intelligent student of the class.
66.	She is superior than me.	She is superior to me.
67.	My friend prefers apples than grapes.	My friend prefers apples to grapes.
68.	Sameer is the smartest of all other boys in the class.	Sameer is the smartest of all boys in the class.
69.	She has the best voice of any musician.	She has a better voice than any other musician.
70.	This is a most interesting play written by Shaw.	This is the most interesting play written by Shaw.
71.	Will you please lend me any money?	Will you please lend me some money?

72.	He will buy any vegetables from the market.	He will buy some vegetables from the market.
73.	These kind of oranges are not very sweet.	Oranges of this kind are not very sweet.
74.	My brother only is responsible.	My brother alone is responsible.
75.	Ramesh is a cunning and a rubbish man.	Ramesh is a cunning and roguish man.
76.	The whole Punjab rose in protest against Emergency Rule.	The whole of Punjab rose in protest against Emergency Rule.
77.	He is a most perfect gentleman.	He is a perfect gentleman.
78.	She is elder than me.	She is older than me.
79.	Surendra missed a most golden opportunity.	Surendra missed a golden opportunity.
80.	No less than hundred persons were killed in the railway accident.	At least hundred persons were killed in the railway accident.
81.	Mahesh was present on both days.	Mahesh was present on both the days.

5. Verbs

82.	Nishant, the painter and scholar are dead.	Nishant, the painter and scholar, is dead.
83.	The peace and order of society were not promoted by the Zamindari System.	The peace and order of society was not promoted by the Zamindari System.
84.	Bread and butter are the staple food of many families.	Bread and butter is the staple food of many families.
85.	The committee is divided in their opinion about nuclear policy.	The committee are divided in their opinion about nuclear policy.
86.	The army do not present a smart appearance.	The army does not present a smart appearance.
87.	Ten miles are a long distance for me.	The miles is a long distance for me.
88.	My friend said, 'The wages of sin are death.'	Many friend said, 'The wages of sin is' death.'
89.	Many students find that mathematics are a very dull subject.	Many students find that mathematics is a very dull subject.
90.	Physics are now taught in ninth class also.	Physics is now taught in ninth class also.
91.	Silver, as well as gold have risen in price.	Silver, as well as gold, has risen in price.

	Incorrect	Correct
92.	Your father, and not your mother were present.	Your father, and not your mother was present.
93.	The shop with all its furniture, curtains and fittings were sold.	The shop with all its furniture, curtains and fittings was sold.
94.	The teacher together with her pupils have gone to the museum.	The teacher together with her pupils has gone to the museum.
95.	Either you or Ramesh are in the wrong.	Either you or Ramesh is in the wrong.
96.	Each one of these students have their school diaries.	Each one of these students has their school diaries.
97.	Every man and woman were killed in the war.	Every man and woman was killed in the war.
98.	A rise in rents and wages has been found to go together.	A rise in rents and a rise in wages have been found to go together.
99.	He asked me how did I solve the problem.	He asked me how I solved the problem.
100.	Ram has been ill for a week when the doctor visited him.	Ram had been ill for a week when the doctor visited him.
101.	Mona told me that she saw the film last week.	Mona told me that she had seen the film last week.
102.	I should be glad if you will come in the morning.	I should be glad if you would come in the morning.
103.	No sooner he had reached the station than the train left.	No sooner had he reached the station than the train left.
104.	Neither Radha writes nor she phones.	Neither does Radha write nor does she phone.
105.	Sohan has returned from Jaipur yesterday.	Sohan returned from Jaipur yesterday.
106.	The man whom you met yesterday, his brother has died.	The brother of the man whom you met yesterday has died.
107.	When I went there I found the tiger was disappeared.	When I went there I found that the tiger had disappeared.
108.	When he will go to Rohtak, he will see her.	When he goes to Rohtak, he will see her.
109.	Saroj said that she saw him last year.	Saroj said that she had seen him last year.
110.	He said to him to go.	He asked him to go.

111.	She has given the examination.	She has taken the examination.
112.	All day Kasturi was putting on a sweater.	All day Kasturi was wearing a sweater.
113.	Keep this on the table.	Put this on the table.
114.	People respected him at the airport.	People showed him respect at the airport.
115.	The ship was drowned	The ship sank.
116.	Always fair out a written composition.	Always make a fair copy of a written composition.
117.	The maid filled water in the bucket.	The maid filled the bucket with water.
118.	My friend's leg has been operated.	My friend had an operation on his leg.
119.	I thought how it was made.	I wondered how it was made.
120.	He asked to Shyam why your father is angry.	He asked Shyam why his father was angry.
121.	They asked had we taken our dinner.	They asked if we had taken our dinner.

6. Infinitives, Gerunds and Participles

122.	You should aim to please other.	You should aim at pleasing others.
123.	Somnath is confident to secure the first prize.	Somnath is confident of securing the first prize.
124.	Hoping for an early reply yours truly.	Hoping for an early reply, I remain, yours truly.
125.	Anjali intended to have gone there on Sunday.	Anjali intended to go there on Sunday.
126.	He will not go to the market unless he has to.	Unless he is forced to go to the market, he will not go there.
127.	My teachers helped me to progress and to prosper.	My teachers helped me to progress and prosper.
128.	It lies in his power to succeed or fail.	It lies in his power to succeed or to fail.
129.	Dinesh has no pen to write.	Dinesh has no pen to write with.
130.	Mukul seems to enjoy his stay in Delhi.	Mukul seems to have enjoyed his stay in Delhi.

	Incorrect	Correct
131.	Flower gathering delighted the little girl.	The gathering of flowers delighted the little girl.
132.	He helped her in the supplying of her needs and in realising her dreams.	He helped her in the supplying of her needs and the realising of her dreams.
133.	Stop to write.	Stop writing.
134.	My father dislikes my friend coming so late.	My father dislikes my friend's coming so late.
135.	Please forgive me being rude.	Please forgive me for being rude.
136.	Kindly excuse them being late.	Kindly excuse them for being late.
137.	These girls have a great desire for being educated.	These girls have a great desire to be educated.
138.	Returning home the other night the moon went behind a cloud.	Returning home the other night I saw the moon go behind a cloud.
139.	Sitting on the fence a scorpion bit me.	While I was sitting on the fence, a scorpion bit me.
140.	Harish sailed for England on Monday arriving there on Sunday.	Harish sailed for England on Monday and arrived there on Sunday.
141.	Monali persisted to do her needlework.	Monali persisted in doing her needlework.
142.	Being a sunny day, I washed all the bedsheets.	It being a sunny day, I washed all the bedsheets.
143.	Hearing that there was a vacancy, an application was sent by me.	I sent an application hearing that there was a vacancy.
144.	She can avail of this.	She can avail herself of this.
145.	One kind of grain was only allowed to be grown.	One kind of grain was allowed to be grown.
146.	Misfortunes when faced bravely and manly become less troublesome.	Misfortunes when faced bravely manfully become less troublesome
147.	Pradeep does not know to swim.	Pradeep does not know how to swim.
148.	The baby has soundly slept.	The baby has slept soundly.
149.	Naresh is too wise to do it.	Naresh is wise enough not to do it.
150.	My brother is enough strong to walk ten miles at a stretch.	My brother is strong enough to walk ten miles at a stretch.

151. This problem is much irritating.	This problem is very irritating.
152. He never remembers having met this man.	He does not remember ever having met this man.
153. Quite a crowd of people had gathered there.	A large number of people had gathered there.
154. We could not find her nowhere.	We could not find her anywhere.
155. It is nothing else than vanity.	It is nothing else but vanity.
156. She is so fat.	She is very fat.
157. The students have carried out faithfully his orders.	The students have faithfully carried out his orders.
158. Neha *has been not suffering* from fever.	Neha *has not been suffering* from fever.
159. *Seldom she comes* to my hotel.	*She seldom comes* to my hotel.
160. Pooja came *quicker than* I expected.	Pooja came *sooner than* I expected.
161. She *never remembers* to have seen a more exciting film.	She *remembers never to have* seen a more exciting film.
162. I found in him a suppressed and *seldom anger*.	I found in him a suppressed and *unusual anger*.
163. *Mohit was fortunately not absent* at that time.	*Fortunately Mohit was not absent* at that time.
164. Sania defeated her opponent *at lengths*.	*At length* Sania defeated her opponent.

7. Conjunctions

165. The student wrote, 'To err is human *and* to forgive divine.'	The student wrote, 'To err is human *but* to forgive divine'
166. Karamchand is very generous *but* gives alms to the homeless.	Karamchand is very generous *and* gives alms to the homeless.
167. Both Sudesh *as well as* her sister were invited for the function.	Both Sudesh *and* her sister were invited for the function.
168. *Though* Harsh is a hard working student but he did not get a first division.	Though Harsh is a hard working student, he *did not* get a first division.
169. *Neither* he helps his old father by money nor by any other means.	He helps his old father *neither by money* nor by any other means.

170. She is *either manager, proprietress* or both.	She is either manager or proprietress or both.
171. This biscuit is *as good*, if not *better than that*.	This biscuit is *as good as, if not better than that*.
172. Ram *is not only* tall.*but* well-built.	Ram is *not only* tall *but also* well built.
173. Nita *not only* broke her pencil *but also* her pencil box.	Nita *broke not only* her pencil but also her pencil box.
174. As I have a cold today, *so* I cannot go to office.	*As* I have a cold today, I cannot go to office.
175. *Hardly* had I corrected one set of papers *than* another set arrived.	*Hardly* had I corrected one set of papers, *when* another set arrived.
176. *No sooner* had Mr. Sharma finished his song but the boys began clapping.	*No sooner* had Mr. Sharma finished his song than the boys began clapping.
177. Murali *defined* genius *to be* an infinite capacity for taking pains.	Murali *defined* genius *as an* infinite capacity for taking pains.
178. *When* you do not trust me, I must keep quiet.	*Since* you do not trust me, I must keep quiet.
179. *Unless* Sita does *not practice* hard, she will not pass in the practical examination.	*Unless* Sita practices hard., she will not pass in the practical examination.
180. *Because* he misbehaved in the class, *therefore* the teacher punished him.	*Because* he misbehaved in the class, the teacher punished him.
181. Sonu will *either* give his brother a pen *or* some money.	Sonu will give his brother *either* a pen or some money.
182. This is the *reason I do* not eat in hotels.	This is the *reason why I* do not eat in hotels.
183. This painting does not *have either* harmony of colour or of design.	This painting does not have harmony *either of colour or of design*

8. Prepositions

184. The little child fell *in* the open gutter.	The little child *fell into* the open gutter.
185. Flowers grow *into* the gardens.	Flowers grow *in* the gardens.
186. Ritu does not devote much time for her duties.	Ritu does not devote much time *to* her duties.

187.	You should not listen *the advice* of a false friend.	You should not *listen to the advice* of a false friend.
188.	Send this parcel *on* this address.	Send this parcel *to* this address.
189.	The policeman fined fifty rupees *on* him.	The policeman fined fifty rupees *to* him.
190.	Shilpa wrote the answer *by* a fountain pen.	Shilpa wrote the answer *with* a fountain pen.
191.	Sanjay closely resembles *to* his brother in facial features.	Sanjay closely *resembles his* brother in facial features.
192.	I have not heard from my son *from a long time*.	I have not heard from my son *for* a long time.
193.	The officer dispensed the peon's services.	The officer dispensed *with* the peon's services.
194.	Both leaders *signed* to the agreement.	Both leaders *signed* the agreement.
195.	The prisoner was honourably *acquitted from* the charge.	The prisoner was honourably *acquitted of* the charge.
196.	He does not have any *influence* upon his children.	He does not have any *influence* on his children.
197.	The first Unit Test will *commence from* Friday.	The First-Unit Tests will *commence on* Friday.
198.	He is *enamoured of* the new actress.	He is *enamoured with* the new actress.
199.	Deepa is not *capable for such* mean acts.	Deepa is not *capable of* such mean acts.
200.	You must *apologise for* the teacher for your misbehaviour.	You must *apologise to* your teacher for your misbehaviour.
201.	Christmas *corresponds with* Deepawali.	Chirstmas *corresponds to* Deepawali.
202.	Manjit is *superior than* his brother in studies.	Majit is *superior to* his brother in studies.
203.	My father *suggested me* to read aloud the lesson.	My father *suggested to* me to read the lesson loudly.
204.	My friend rented a bigger house *to live*.	My friend rented a bigger house *to live in*.
205.	This Englishman has *married with* lady.	This Englishman has *married an* Indian an Indian lady.
206.	There was a football match between India *against* Germany.	There was a football match *between* India and Germany.
207.	His mother cannot *approve her* conduct.	His mother cannot *approve of her* conduct.

208	You should not *part with your friends* in any circumstances.	You should not *part from your friends* in any circumstances,
209.	The spirit of adventure *pervades through* all these stories,	The spirit of adventure *pervades all* these stories.
210.	Never be *neglectful to* those who have shown you kindness.	Never be *neglectful of* those who have shown you kindness.
211.	Open you English Reader *in* on page eight.	Open your English Reader *at* page eight.
212.	My son's teacher is greatly *displeased* at him.	My son's teacher is greatly *displeased with* him.
213.	Write an *equivalent word to* this.	Write an *equivalent word for* this.
214.	Sumit *prevailed on* all difficulties.	Sumit *prevailed over* all difficulties.

Chapter 27

Words Commonly Misspelt

We have a mental image of words and their spelling. Very often we spell words by sheer force of habit. Sometimes, when in doubt, by writing the concerned words we can recollect their correct spelling.

English spelling is not as queer or as difficult as it is made out to be. In fact, there are a number of rules for spelling words. But it may be more convenient to keep a good dictionary handy for consultation than to remember all such rules. A few which can be easily memorised are given below. Following the rules is a list of words which you are likely to use in your writing frequently.

Spelling Rules

(i) The silent *e* occurring at the end is dropped in words when a suffix beginning with a vowel is added to them.

behave	behaviour	fertile	fertility
admire	admirable	arrive	arriving

Exceptions: seeing, agreeing, guaranteeing, saleable.

(ii) The silent *e* is retained in words ending in *-ce* and *-ge* when a suffix other than that beginning with *-e* or *-i* is added to them.

conduce	conducive	service	serviceable
charge	charging	courage	courageous

(iii) In a monosyllabic word, ending in a consonant and preceded by a single vowel letter, the consonant is doubled if a suffix beginning with a vowel letter is added to it.

cut	cutting	big	bigger
win	winner	hot	hottest

(iv) Rule (iii) applies also in multisyllabic words provided they are stressed on the last syllable.

permit	permitted	begin	beginning
control	controlled	occur	occurred

(v) If a word ends in two consonants or one consonant preceded by two vowel letters the consonant does not double before any suffix.

gold	golden	feed	feeding
wait	waiter	wood	wooden

(vi) A monosyllabic word containing one vowel letter does not end with the following single consonants: *-s*, *-f*, *-l*, *-z*.

hiss, staff, bull, buzz

(vii) A monosyllabic word with one vowel letter does not end in *-c* but requires *-ck*.

pick, back, chick, luck

(viii) A monosyllabic word containing two vowel letters does not end in *-ck* but requires *-k* alone.

freak, look, leak, speak

(ix) A monosyllabic word containing one vowel letter does not end in a single *-l* whereas a monosyllabic word containing two vowel letters never ends in *-ll*.

spill, tall, peal, stool

Exception: pal

Developing Communication Skills

(x) In a multisyllabic word ending in one vowel letter and *l*, the *l* is doubled if a suffix beginning with a vowel is added to it

repel	repellant	travel	traveller
marvel	marvellous	pedal	pedalled

(xi) If the final *y* of a word is preceded by a consonant, the *y* changes to *i* before all suffixes except *-ing*.

supply	supplies	study	studies
multiply	multiplies	dry	dries

(xii) The final *y* of a word, if preceded by a vowel, remains unchanged before any suffix.

convey	conveyed	destroy	destroying
buy	buyer	enjoy	enjoys

(xiii) The letter *i* occurs before *e* except after *c*, or when pronounced like a as in 'neighbour' and 'weigh'

conceive, receive; achieve, believe

Exceptions include: leisure, forfeit, either, seize, species

(xiv) The letter *q* is followed by *u* in whatever position it occurs in a word.
quote, square, earthquake, squeeze

LIST OF WORDS

A

abbreviate	align	absence	all right
absorption	already	acceptable	all-round
accelerator	allegiance	accessible	allergic
accessories	amateur	accidentally	antecedent
accommodate	antedate	accomplish	antenna
accumulate	aperture	accustom	apparatus
achievement	appropriate	achievable	approval
acquaint	approximate	acquaintance	ascend
acquitted	attendance	acquiesce	auditorium
admissible	auxiliary	advisable	awkward
affiliate	aggravate		

B

beginning	bottleneck	believing	boundaries
beneficial	brilliance	benefit	bureau
bilateral	bureaucracy	bimetallic	by-product blueprint

C

cafeteria	commitment	calendar	committed
calibre	committee	camouflage	comparative
cancellation	competitive	carburettor	complementary
career	complimentary	catalogue	concede
category	conceivable	cautious	conciliate
changeable	convenience	characteristic	conscientious
chauffeur	consensus	chosen	controversy
cipher	convenient	circuit	corollary
clientele	corroborate	co-efficient	courteous
colossal		column	
combustible			

D

deceive	dictionary	decision	dilapidated
deductible	discrepancy	de-energise, de-energize	dissipate

deferred	dissolve	deficient	dubious
deficit	dye-stuff	desirable	
depreciation			

E

economise, economize	equipped	effervescence	equitable
efficiency	equivalent	eligible	erroneous
eliminate	exaggerate	elliptical	exchangeable
embarrass	exhaustible	enforceable	exhilarated
enroll	existence	enthusiastic	exorbitant
envelope	expansion		

F

fascinate	forecast	feasible	forgo
flammable	fulfil	forcible	fuselage
forfeit			

G

gasoline	grammar	genealogy	guarantee
grievance			

H

haemorrhage	hindrance	harass	homogeneous
haulage	humorous	height	hygiene
heterogeneous			

I

illegible	inoculate	illiterate	insistence
imaginary	installation	impromptu	instantaneous
inadvertently	insulator	inaugurate	intercede
inconvenience	interchangeable	incredible	interest
indelible	irresistible	indispensable	irretrievable
inflammable			

J

jeopardise, jeopardize	judicious	judgement, judgment	justifiable

K

kaleidoscope	knowledgeable	kernel	

L

laboratory
leisure
liaison
license
logarithm
luxuriant
laborious
liable
liquefy
longevity

M

maintenance
manoeuvre
margarine
mediocre
merchandise
miscellaneous
moccasin
monopolise,
moratorium
mosaic
multispeed
munificence
manageable
monopolize
massacre
mercantile
mileage
misspell
moisture
mortgage
multi-cylinder
multivoltage
myriad

N

naive
nauseous
necessary
nickel
nozzle
nutrient
naptha
nautical
negligible
noticeable
numerator

O

obsession
occasionally
omission
overrule
obsolete
occurred
outrageous
oxidise, oxidize

P

pageant
parallel
pavilion
peffnissible
persistence
persuasion
placeable
precedent
preponderance
privilege
promissory
pamphlet
paralyse, paralyze
pedestal
perseverance
personnel
plausible
preferred
prevalent
proficient
pronunciation

Q

questionnaire
quota
quorum
quotient

R

rarely
recede
receivable
reciprocal
reducible
referred
reimbursement
reminiscence
remittance
ranonslrate
replaceable
restaurant
reticent
rhythm
rebuttal
receipt
recipient
reconcile
redundant
regrettable
reiterate
remission
remnant
removable
requisition
resuscitation
revocable
runway rejuvenate

S

saccharin	silhouette	sacrilegious	simultaneous
safety	soliloquy	salutary	soluble
salvage	sophomore	sandwich	sponsor
sanitary	spurious	saturate	squeeze
scarcity	subsidiary	schedule	substantiate
seize	suffrage	separately	superintendent
sententious	supersede	serviceable	supplementary siege

T

tangible	transferred	transcribe	treasurer
transferable	tyranny		

U

ultraviolet	uncontrollable	unanimous	unilateral
unbelievable	until unconscious		

V

vacuum	vicious	valuable	voltmeter
ventilation	volume	versatile	voluminous vicinity

W

warranted	wholly	water-resistant	wrought

Y

Yardstick	yeast

Chapter 28

PUNCTUATION AND CAPITALISATION

28.1 PUNCTUATION

PUNCTUATION marks are like pauses in speech. They act as a guide to the structure of sentences and help us understand their meaning. However, if a sentence requires too many punctuation marks to make the meaning clear, it would be better to restructure it. The modern tendency is to use only such punctuation marks as are necessary to communicate the meaning. Thus punctuation is not a crutch for the writer, it is an aid to the reader.

We give below a few commonly used punctuation marks.

(i) End Punctuation Marks

(a) *A full stop* is used to indicate the following:

End of a declarative or an imperative sentence or indirect question.

Examples:

- The report has been submitted.
- Please wait for sometime more.
- Mr. Joshi asked me whether I would be able to prepare the minutes by Monday morning

For abbreviations. Examples:

- B.E., M.Sc. (Tech), Ph.D.
- Dr., Prof., Mr., Capt.

- I.I.T., C.S.I.R., N.C.E.R.T.
- Indication of ellipsis (three stops are used and if the omission is at the end of a sentence, three stops plus any other punctuation mark). Examples:
- Wherever light or heat is wanted... we are likely to find electricity at work.
- The chances of the moon and the earth coming exactly in a straight line are small. Even if they do, the eclipse can be observed only in certain parts....

(b) *A question mark* is used at the end of a direct question or to express doubt or uncertainty.

- How many proposals have been received?
- Have you informed all the members about today's meeting?
- Did they agree to sign the contract?
- The National Steel Corporation was established in 1951?
- Have two copies of the report been prepared?

(c) An *exclamation mark* is used at the end of a statement expressing a strong feeling.

- Mr. Gulati worked throughout the night to meet the deadline – what grit and devotion!
- The brochure has already come from the press – what a pleasant surprise!

(ii) The Comma

The comma represents the shortest pause and has a variety of uses. The modern tendency is to avoid using it except where either the fluency, of expression or the communication of meaning is likely to suffer if it is not used. Here we shall indicate the types of expressions in which the cola aia is commonly used.

The comma is used to separate the following:

(a) Three or more words of the same parts of speech.

- Mr. Gupta, Mr. Simon, and Miss Joyti were specially invited to the meeting.

(b) Pairs of words of the same class or rank.

- By night or day, asleep or awake, he keeps on thinking about the heavy loss suffered by his firm.

(c) The words addressing a person or persons.

- Sir, 1 am ready to do the job.
- Gentlemen, we should all work together to complete this new project in time.

(d) An interjection from the rest of the sentence.

- Oh, I didn't know you were coming to preside.

(e) Nouns or pronouns and phrases which are in apposition.

- Mahatma Gandhi, the Father of the Nation, lived and died for the poor and the oppressed.

(f) Certain words and phrases such as *that is, namely, for example, in fact, however*, etc.

- Only one member, namely, Mr. Sen was absent at the meeting.

- All important documents (for example, reports, technical proposals) should be preserved carefully.
- In fact, wherever light or heat is wanted, we are likely to find electricity at work.

(g) An absolute phrase from the rest of the sentence.

- The seminar being over, they all left for lunch.

(h) Independent parts or clauses of a compound sentence.

- He came, he saw, he conquered.

(i) A quotation from the rest of the sentence.

- The Manager said, 'I wish you good luck.'

(j) Titles, parts of dates and addresses in sentences.

- The memo report is to be submitted to Mr. Arun Lal, Personnel Manager.
- The panel discussion will take place on 27 October, 1989.
- Please send this proposal to Mrs. Geeta Dhawan, Executive Assistant to the President, Rajasthan Cotton Mills, Civil Lines, Ajmer.

(k) In figures to separate thousands, lakhs, crores.

- Rs. 98,321
- Rs. 14,98,321
- Rs. 5,14,98,321

(iii) The Semicolon

The semicolon symbolises a longer pause than does a comma. Its use can be helpful in avoiding a monotonous succession of short declarative sentences.

It is used to separate:

(a) Parallel expressions where a distinct pause is desired.

- Do not let us speak of darker days; let us rather speak of brighter days.

(b) Main clauses of a sentence not joined by a coordinating conjunction.

- Mr. Ghose will be out of town on Monday; you may come to see him on Tuesday.

(c) Clauses of a sentence joined by conjunctive adverbs such as however, therefore, hence, accordingly, furthermore, moreover, nevertheless, thus.

- The diagram is clearly drawn; therefore, there is no need to describe it in detail.
- The survey confirms the need for a new plant; however, right now no funds are available for its establishment.
- The engine was badly damaged; nevertheless, the plane safely landed.

(d) Sentence elements already internally punctuated by commas.

- The company has factories in Patna, Nagpur, Kolkata and Chennai; warehouses in Lucknow and Hyderabad; and sales offices in 14 States of India.

(iv) *The Colon*

The colon is a formal mark of anticipation. It is used to introduce a list or a long quotation and to amplify or explain a previous statement. It is customary to use a capital letter when the matter that follows consists of complete sentences and a small letter when what follows the colon is part of the same sentence.

- A report writer must possess many qualities: common sense, discernment, scientific attitude and communicative Competence.
- Here is a quotation from the Chairman's Report: 'The two basic factors that contributed to increased profits are the introduction of a new strategy for marketing and the implementation of new measures for quality control.'
- Please send the following items of stationery:

Pencils	-	2 dozen
White paper	-	2 reams
File covers	-	16
Refills (Red)	-	3 dozen
Refills (Blue)	-	5 dozen

- In drafting a letter you should bear in mind two points: the expectations of the recipient and the objective you wish to achieve.

(v) *The Apostrophe*

The apostrophe performs the following functions.

(a) It shows possession.

- The Manager's duties.
- The Supervisors' responsibilities.
- Jones's office.
- Everybody's concern

(b) It indicates the omission of letters or figures.

- The year '88.
- Doesn't, isn't, it's.

(c) It forms the plurals of figures, letters, and words referred to as words.

- Don't let your 7's look like 9's.
- Cross your t's properly.
- There are too many if s and but's in your report.

  Remember, the apostrophe is not used with personal pronouns.
- The decision is theirs (not their's).
- The book is probably hers (not her's).
- Yours faithfully (not your's).

Note further that its indicates possession whereas it's means it is.

(vi) Quotation Marks

Quotation marks are used by a writer to mark off the actual words spoken or written by somebody else. Single quotation marks are used for the following purposes.

(a) To enclose a quotation within a quotation.

- Prof. Dubey remarked: "A good example of antithesis is, 'The child is the father of man'. If you ponder deeply, you will discover a profound truth in this statement."

(b) To enclose words used in a special sense or words referred to as words.

- Some people think that French is a'sweet' language.
- The words 'nice' and 'fine' are often misused in formal writing.

(c) To enclose titles of stories, poems, chapters, or sections of books.

- Have you read 'The Party and After' published in the *Pictorial Weekly in India* dated 9 Oct. 1989?
- In this year's syllabus 'Ode to a Skylark' is not prescribed.
- Chapter 4, 'Participative Management,' has not yet been written.

Some writers use double quotation marks in (b) and (c) above.

Remember the following two points when you use quotation marks. If a direct quotation consists of more than one paragraph or a stanza, put a quotation mark at the beginning of each paragraph or stanza but at the end of only the last paragraph or stanza. Secondly, commas and full stops are placed inside the quotation marks whereas a question mark, the semicolon or colon and the exclamation marks are put inside if they belong to the quoted part and outside if they do not belong to the quoted part.

(vii) The Hyphen

The hyphen is used to hyphenate the following.

(a) Compound numbers from twenty-one to ninety-nine.

- Forty-four employees.
- One hundred and twenty-nine members.

(b) Words that form a single name

- Commander-in-chief.
- Secretary-treasurer.
- Instructor-in-charge.

(c) Words forming a compound adjective

- A well-considered plan.
- A second-rate mechanic.

(d) Words that occur at the end of a line and that have to be split.

- The liberty of the individual is guaranteed by the Constitution. (The splitting is done at the end of a syllable.)

(viii) *The Dash*

The dash is used for the following purposes.

(a) To indicate abrupt or sudden break or change in thought or structure of a sentence.

- A few months ago – I think it was in March – we bought a lot of furniture.

(b) To give special emphasis to a word or a phrase.

- Mail the order form in the self-addressed envelope – now.

(c) To set off an explanatory or appositive expression.

- Over the last ten years the rate of inflation has been constantly increasing – from 3.5 per cent in 1978 to the present 10 per cent – and it might increase further if effective steps to control it are not taken.

(ix) *Brackets*

Brackets are used to enclose interpolations, explanatory remarks, and supplied omissions added to a quotation by the person who is quoting.

- This is not the first time that they (the workers) have gheraoed the new manager.
- Addressing the members the Union Secretary remarked: 'Let's wait for some time more. He (Executive President) has promised to look into the master and convey his decision within three days.'
- Santayana says, 'Religion lay on him (Dickens) like the weight of the atmosphere.'

28.2 CAPITALISATION

Like punctuation, capitalisation makes writing easy to read and understand. Professional writing requires greater use of capitals than does informal or journalistic writing. Remember the general rule: Capitalise when there is a definite reason for it or when the convention demands it. Capitals are used in the following cases.

(a) First word of every sentence, every independent group of words, and every line of poetry.

- Be like a sandalwood tree that perfumes the very axe that cuts it.
- The second report? Not yet.
- We look before and after And pine for what is not.

(b) Proper names of persons, organisations, things, places, races and religions, days, months, periods, designations, and derivatives of proper names.

- Persons: Arun Ghule, Sits Gopalan.
- Organisations: Life Insurance Corporation of India, Hindustan Machine Tools Co. Ltd.
- Things: Vijayanta Tank, Shaheed Express, Sagar Samrat.
- Places: Delhi, Italy, Teen Murti Marg, Latin America.
- Races and Religions: Negro, Aryan, Hindu.

- Days: Monday, Tuesday, Friday.
- Months: January, March, April.
- Periods: The Mughal, The Gandhian Era, The Elizabethan Age.
- Designations: Prime Minister, Police Commissioner, Accountant General.
- Derivatives of proper names: Indian, American, Chinese.

(c) Title of respect when it precedes a name.

- Reverend John Smith, President Truman, Captain Gupta, Queen Victoria, Emperor Jahangir, Padma Vibhushan Shri G.D. Birla.

(d) A name that describes a following numeral.

- Room 31, Order 207, Article 22.

(e) All the words in the titles or headings of a book, report, paper, etc., except articles, prepositions and conjunctions having less than four or five letters.

- *Aspects of Applied Linguistics.*
- *Writing Laboratory for Beginning Students of Russian.*
- *The Illustrated Weekly of India.*
- *A Handbook of Business and Social Correspondence.*

Chapter 29

ABBREVIATIONS AND NUMERALS

29.1 ABBREVIATIONS

AN abbreviation is the short form of a word or a phrase. Its use is common in professional writing as it saves the time of both the writer and the reader. Certain abbreviations are commonly used as they are widely understood. You should not hesitate to use such abbreviations in your writing. However, if you are uncertain about the intelligibility of an abbreviation, use the full form and within brackets indicate its abbreviated form. Thereafter you may use only the abbreviated form.

Remember the following guiding principles in the use of abbreviations:

- Be consistent in their use.
- Omit the full stops from abbreviations whenever the omission would not lead to misunderstanding.
- Do not space the letters in such abbreviations as UNESCO, DNA.
- Write the abbreviation in capitals if the full form is capitalised.
- Where the same abbreviation is used both for singular and plural, ensure that the verb agrees with the quantity indicated, e.g. ' 1 ft. is' '5 ft. are'.
- Do not begin a sentence with an abbreviated form of quantity or measurement unless it follows numerals.

Now we give a classified list of certain abbreviations which you may have to use in your day to day work.

Full form	Abbreviated form	Full form	Abbreviated form
(i) Title before names			
Kumari	Kum	Srimati	Smt.
Mister	Mr.	Mistress	Mrs.

(Continued)

(Continued)

	Doctor	Dr.	Captain	Capt.
	Professor	Prof.	Messieurs	Messrs.
(ii)	Degree after names			
	Doctor of Philosophy	Ph.D.	Doctor of Medicine	M.D.
	Bachelor of Engineering	B.E.	Master of Arts	M.A.
(iii)	Days			
	Sunday	Sun.	Monday	Mon.
	Tuesday	Tues.	Wednesday	Wed.
	Thursday	Thurs.	Friday	Fri.
	Saturday	Sat.		
(iv)	Months			
	January	Jan.	February	Feb.
	August	Aug.	September	Sept.
	October	Oct.	November	Nov.
	December	Dec.		

Note: March, April, May, June and July are not abbreviated.

(v) Measurements

Many units of measurement are abbreviated and these abbreviations are universally accepted. Usually a small unit such as 'acre', 'mile' is not shortened. It is customary to abbreviate a unit when a figure precedes it. Examples:

17 lb. but seventeen pounds

11 kms. but eleven kilometres.

A few commonly used abbreviations of the units of measurement are given below:

Full form	*Abbreviated form*	*Full form*	*Abbreviated form*
	LENGTH		
millimetre	mm	centimetre	cm
decimetre	dm	METRE	m
dekametre	dkm	hectometre	hm
kilometre	km		
	CAPACITY		
millilitre	ml	centilitre	cl
decilitre	dl	LITRE	1
dekalitre	dk 1	hectolitre	hl
kilolitre	kl		

WEIGHT			
milligram	mg	centigram	cg
decigram	dg	GRAM	g
dekagram	dkg	hectogram	hg
kilogram	kg		

(vi) Miscellaneous

Full form	*Abbreviated form*
Alternating current	a.c.
Account	acc.
Anno Domini (Lat.) in the year of our Lord; after the birth of Jesus Christ	AD.
Advertisement	ad.
Ante meridiem (Lat.) before noon	a.m.
Before (the birth of Jesus) Christ	B.C.
Centigrade	C., Cent.
Cash to be paid on delivery	C. O. D.
Creditor	Cr.
Direct current	d.c.
Dozen	doz.
Dram	dr.
Errors and omissions excepted	E. & O.E.
Editor, edited by	ed.
Exempli gratis (Lat.) for example	e.g.
Et cetera (Lat.) and other things and so on	etc.
Fahrenheit	F., Fahr.
Free on board (commercial use)	f.o.b.
Fellow of the Royal Society	F.R.S.
Foot, feet	ft.
Gallon (s)	gal.
Honorary; The Honourable	Hon.
Horse power; hire purchase	h.p.
Hour(s)	hr(s).
Ibidem (Lat.) in the same place	ibid.
Incharge of	ic.
Id est (Lat.) that is	i.e.

(Continued)

(Continued)

Inch (es)	in.
Intelligence Quotient	LQ.
Italic (type)	it., ital.
Kilowatt	Kw.
Libra (Lat.) pounds in weight	lb.
Miscellaneous	misc.
Manuscript (s)	Ms., Mss
Nota bene (Lat.) note carefully	N.B.
Nimine Contradicente (Lat.) unanimously, with no one raising an objection	nem. con.
All correct, agreed	O.K.
Operecitato (Lat.) in the work cited	op. cit.
Ounce	oz.
Per Annum	p.a.
Per Procurationem (Lat.) by proxy	per pro.
Post meridiem (Lat.) afternoon	p.m.
Pages	pp.
Pro tempore (Lat.) for the time	pro tern.
Respondez S'il vous plait (Fr.) please reply	R.S.V.P.
Videlicet (Lat.) namely	viz.
Water closet	w.c.
Yard	yd.

29.2 NUMERALS

We give below a few rules based on commonly accepted practice in writing numerals.

(i) Use figures for exact numbers for ten and above and words for numbers below ten.
11 months
seven days

(ii) If in the same sentence or passage, several numbers occur, some of which are above ten and some below ten, use figures for all. 9 chairs, 20 tables and 46 desks

(iii) If a numeral appears in the beginning of a sentence, spell it out even if it is ten or more. You may recast the sentence, if necessary, to avoid beginning it with a numeral.
Thirty-six members were present at the meeting. At the meeting 36 members were present. One-third of a metre.

(iv) Use figures in writing dates, addresses and the time of day.

4 Oct., 1988

168 Vidya Vihar

5.45 pm

(v) Use numerals to number objects in a list.

Page 34

Chapter 21

Column 2

Fig. 17

File No. S-C/97

(vi) To indicate the sums of money in a column, use numerals..

Rs.	P
2.	45
13.	50
325.	25
341.	20

(vii) Write in figures the exact quantities indicated in units of measurement.

12%

120 km

40 watt

3 mg

50 kl

4 kHz

(viii) Express in words either the first or the shorter number when one number is immediately followed by another.

fifty 40 watt bulbs

6 four-engine aeroplanes

(ix) Place a zero before the decimal point in writing numbers with no integer.

0.48

0.0032

(x) Put a double zero after the decimal point if some of the numbers in a table have a fraction,

3,420.07

366.00

1,10,003.29

(xi) Use a comma to demarcate units in figures having four or more digits.

9,200

43,127

8,72,462

APPENDICES

Appendix–A

FUNDAMENTALS OF SPEECH

If you drive a car, it is advisable to have an elementary knowledge of how it runs. Similarly, understanding of the basic concepts of English speech can prove helpful in using it for oral communication. The concepts considered significant from this point of view are briefly explained below.

A.1 PHONEME

The English alphabet has 26 letters and these are used to represent 44 sounds of the language. To refer to a sound we use the technical word *phoneme*, which may be defined as the smallest segment of speech that distinguishes one word from another. For example, if we replace 'm' in 'man' by 'f', we get a different word, that is 'fan'. To represent each of the 44 sounds graphically a unique phonetic symbol is used. Phonetic symbols are also called IPA symbols, because these have been devised by the International Phonetic Association – a body of experts and scholars that meets periodically to alter, delete or add to the list of existing symbols, which represent the sounds of all major languages of the world. So, if you are familiar with all IPA symbols, you can speak any major language provided it is written in phonetic script, without, of course, understanding its meaning.

It is customary to write a phonetic symbol between two oblique lines. This is done to distinguish it from a letter. For example, 'b' refers to the letter whereas /b/ represents the sound.

The sounds of English are classified as follows:

The sounds can be further subdivided on the basis of place and manner of articulation but it is not necessary to do so in the present context. All vowels are voiced but out of 24 consonants, 9 are unvoiced, i.e. in their production, vocal cords do not vibrate and audibility is obtained by friction at some place in the mouth at the time of releasing air.

Now we give a complete list of English sounds together with a few words in which they occur for exemplification.

Table I Pure Vowels (12)

Sl. No	*Symbol*	*Words*
1.	/i:/	seat, breeze, grieve, keep
2.	/i/	sit, built, knit, tilt
3.	/e/	set, quest, head, went
4.	/æ/	sat, glad, had, land
5.	/a:/	glass, dance, mark, past
6.	/ɔ/	shop, box, clock, boss
7.	/ɔ:/	door, court, four, lawn
8.	/u/	book, pull, good, should
9.	/u:/	soon, soup, true, shoe
10.	/^/	sun, son, cut, won
11.	/∂:/	pearl, shirt, heard, work
12.	/∂/	again, mother, stir, account

Table II Diphthongs (8)

Sl. No	*Symbol*	*Words*
13.	/ei/	day, clay, wait, great
14.	/∂u/	go, no, blow, know
15.	/ai/	glide, bright, site, bride
16.	/au/	cow, bout, house, browse
17.	/ɔi/	boy, boil, voice, point
18.	/i∂/	deer, tier, mere, clear
19.	/Σ∂/	share, their, there, careful
20.	/u∂/	tour, fluent, sure, poor

Table III Voiced Consonants (15)

Sl. No	*Symbol*	*Words*
1.	/b/	book, best, blast, bulb
2.	/d/	read, double, radar, glad
3.	/g/	guest, game, begin, flag
4.	/dʒ/	just, change, adjust, engine
5.	/v/	love, van, vim, vigour
6.	/∂/	breathe, they, leather, those
7.	/z/	zoom, zigzag, freeze, please
8.	/ʒ/	leisure, enclosure, measure, pleasure
9.	/m/	mother, most, remember, same
10.	/n/	nose, knows, fan, gone
11.	/η/	song, king, thank, sink,
12.	/l/	feel, leaf, pulp, glad
13.	/w/	were, wise, question, adequate
14.	/j/	university, young, yesterday, tune
15.	/r/	race, crisp, generate, rest

Table IV Unvoiced Consonants (9)

Sl. No	*Symbol*	*Words*
16.	/p/	pen, oppose, gap, painting
17.	/t/	taste, attend, clutter, plot
18.	/k/	k[illegible], acquire, clap, school
19.	/tf/	cha[illegible], reach, watched, juncture
20.	/f/	fan[illegible]y, full, craft, puff
21.	/θ/	thr[illegible]ng, think, mouth, earth
22.	/s/	sa[illegible]e, seek, best, rests
23.	/s/	s[illegible]ame, sure, cash, shave
24.	/h/	[illegible]ome, hastle, behind, here

A.2 SYLLABLE

A syllable is a unit into which a word is divided. It contains a vowel sound and may have one or more consonants before or after it. In fact, the vowel sound forms the nucleus of a syllable. We may represent the structure of a syllable as follows:

$$(C_n) + V + (C_n)$$

In this formula, C_n indicates an indefinite number of consonant sounds, v stands for a vowel sound, and brackets indicate that a consonant sound is not a compulsory constituent of a syllable.

A few examples are given below:

	Word	*structure*	*Word*	*structure*
(i) Monosyllabic:	eye	v	go	cv
	no	vc	glad	ccvc
	strain	cccvc	crisp	ccvcc
(ii) Disyllabic:	ago	v/cv	wanted	cvcc/vc
	almost	vc/cvcc	salute	cv/cvc
	inform	vc/cvc		
(iii) Polysyllabic:	production	cv/cvc/cvc	gentlemanly	cvcc/cvc/cv
	deployment	cv/ccv/cvcc	probably	cv/cvc/cv
	examination	cv/cv/cv/cv/cvc		

The oblique lines in (ii) and (iii) above indicate the division of words into syllables.

There is a very small number of words in which a syllable does not have a vowel sound. For example, in the following words the second syllable has no vowel sound: *little, bottom button*. Such words are said to have a syllabic ending. In pronouncing them care has to be taken to avoid inserting a vowel sound where it does not occur.

A.3 WORD STRESS

If a word is disyllabic or polysyllabic, one of the syllables is stressed, that is, it is spoken with stronger voice. Where required, the stress is graphically shown as follows: a'go, 'industry, pro'duction, 'management.

In the above words - *go, in-, -duc -, man* - are stressed. The place where a word would take stress is fixed and one has to learn to pronounce individual words. There are a few rules of stressing words but a large body of English vocabulary is outside their ambit. The stressed syllables occur at regular intervals of time and contribute a great deal to the rhythm of speech. The unstressed syllables occurring between two stressed syllables tend to become weak and hence often shortened in spoken form.

A.4 SENTENCE STRESS

All the words in a sentence are rarely of equal importance. Those which are, are spoken with greater force (stressed) than those which are not (unstressed). In the following sentence '*The manager* has *called* a *meeting* to *discuss* the *problem* of *absenteeism*.' The words in italics are the main carriers of significant meaning and hence are stressed. In speaking what we stated while discussing word stress should not be forgotten. The stress should fall on the right syllables of these words. However, unlike word stress, sentence stress is variable. The stress pattern changes according to what the speaker considers more significant in the context of his speech. For example, in the following sentence, meaning and emphasis change if we shift stress from one word to another.

- *Swami* has won the first prize in the debate. (not Hari)
- Swami has won the *first* prize in the debate. (not second)
- Swami has won the first prize in the *debate*. (not in poetry competition)

For effective speaking it is important to be conscious of this aspect. Communication may suffer if stress is not put on the right syllable of the right word. There are certain classes of words which generally take stress and certain classes which do not. Both are listed below.

Words which take stress	*Words which do not take stress*
• nouns	• articles
• adjectives	• prepositions
• main verbs	• auxiliary verbs
• adverbs	• personal pronouns
• interrogative	• conjunctions
• negative markers	
• demonstratives	
• numerals	
• interjections	

A.5 INTONATION

A rise and fall in the voice in speaking is called intonation. A spoken sentence not only conveys the meaning but also the mood and attitude of the speaker. Intonation therefore plays a crucial role in oral communication. English has a number of intonation patterns but the basic ones are:

- Tone I or Falling Tone
- Tone II or Rising Tone

In the former, the pitch of the voice falls at the end and in the latter it rises. This fall or rise usually takes place at the last stressed syllable in the sentence.

Generally the following types of sentences are spoken with Tone I

(i) Statements

- The proposal has been accepted.
- The ability to speak effectively is an important quality for success in a profession.

(ii) Commands

- Come here.
- Close the windows.

(iii) Questions with question words

- When will the presentation begin?
- How many books did you buy last month?

(iv) Question tag, if an extension of statement

- You have done the assignment, haven't you?
- The management has not yet announced a raise in D.A., has it?

(v) Choice questions

- Would you like to have tea or coffee?
- Do you want to watch TV or just listen to music?

(vi) Exclamations

- How beautiful!
- Well done!

TONE II

(i) Yes/No questions

- Has the boss gone for a meeting?
- Was the seminar held as scheduled?

(ii) Requests or apologies

- Pass the salt, please.
- I'm so sorry.

(iii) Question tags if real questions.

- You have completed the task well in time, haven't you?
- He can be approached easily, can't he?

(iv) Incomplete statements

- Before he comes here...
- I was trying to say ...

(v) Protests

- You could have invited me as well.
- Shyam never said so.

(vi) Statement meant to be a question.

- I hope you are young enough to attend the forthcoming conference?
- You are leaving for London tomorrow?

In general, the falling tone indicates certainty and business-like objectivity whereas rising tone signals courtesy, politeness, doubts protests, etc. Thus it tends to be subjective in nature. The use of the right intonation pattern is both context-specific and purpose-specific and needs utmost attention and care for the desired impact.

A.6 PAUSE

When a person speaks, he has to pause after every few words, say, two to five. It is physically impossible to continue to speak without a pause even for a short time of two to three minutes. Normally in one breath four to five words can be spoken. So the number of pauses depends upon the length of the breath. Musicians are trained to control their breath and can therefore produce a sound longer in a continuous stream if required in the singing of a *raga*. In speech too, proper control of breath is necessary and so also the control over pauses in order to create an impact on the listeners. At some places short pauses would do and at some long pauses are required. In reading aloud it becomes easier to do so because of the punctuation marks, which act as speed breakers. The comma and dash, for example, indicate a short pause whereas semicolon, colon, and full stop signal a long pause.

It must be realised that pause is one of the elements that contributes to the rhythm of speech and facilitates the communication of meaning. If the pause is not at the right place, meaning may be affected. Look at the following pair of sentences.

- The stout major's/wife inaugurated the fancy show.
- The stout/major's wife inaugurated the fancy show.

In the first case the major is stout and in the second the pause suggests that the major's wife is stout. The latter utterance can be embarrassing because calling a lady 'stout' is not complimentary.

Appendix-B

Basics of Grammar

B.1 UNITS OF GRAMMAR

THERE are five basic units of grammar. These are listed below in order of their rank; that is, from lower to higher rank:

- morpheme
- word
- phrase
- clause
- sentence

Each unit is meaningful, whatever be its rank.

Morpheme

Being the smallest unit, it cannot be split further. For example, 'looked' has two morphemes, namely, 'look' and '-ed'. If either of these is split, we would get letters of the alphabet which in themselves are not meaningful. In this example '-ed' is meaningful because it conveys the motion of 'pastness'. Had it been meaningless, there would have been no difference between the meanings of 'looked' and 'look'. However, it is true that '-ed' conveys meaning when it is affixed to a verb. That is why whereas 'look' is a *free morpheme*, '-ed' is a *dependent morpheme*. When affixed to a verb, it changes the form from present to past. Often, therefore, 'ed' is used as a symbol to represent the past morpheme. Thus we can say: sit +-ed = sat, stand +-ed = *stood*, go +-ed = *went*, catch + -ed = *caught* and so on.

There are in fact, six forms of the verb, three finite and three non-finite as shown below:

Sl. No.	*Symbol*	*Morpheme*	*Description*	*Example*
(i)	V^{o}	-	present plural	go
(ii)	V^{S}	-es	present singular	goes
(iii)	V^{d}	-ed	past	went
(iv)	V^{g}	-ing	present participle	going
(v)	V^{n}	-en	past participle	gone
(vi)	V^{t}	-	infinite	to go

The first three are finite forms i.e. they can occur independently in a sentence. The last three are non-finite forms, i.e. they cannot occur independently and need an auxiliary verb to find a place in the sentence. For example, we can say 'Shyam goes for a walk daily' but we cannot construct a sentence like 'He going to Delhi tomorrow'.

What we have stated above applies to main verbs. The auxiliary verbs (listed below) do not behave in a similar manner. Their number is fixed and some of them function as main verbs in certain circumstances. First let us look at the classified list of auxiliary verbs:

Modals	*Perfective*	*Be*	*Do*	*Miscellaneous*
will	has	is	does	need
would	have	are	did	dare
shall	had	am	done	used to
should		was	doing	ought to
can	having	were	to do	
could	to have	being		
may		to be		
might				
must				

Out of the above list the auxiliary verbs belonging to three categories, namely, perfectives, Be and Do can occur independently just like main verbs. Look at the example given below:

(i) Ram *has* done the assignment. (auxiliary ve.b)

(ii) Ram *has* three brothers. (main verb)

(iii) I *am* going to Delhi tomorrow. (auxiliary verb)

(iv) I *am* fine. (main verb)

(v) He *does* not like being given detailed instructions. (auxiliary verb)

(vi) Hari *does* his part well. (main verb)

It is to be noted that Do category verbs have six forms like the main verbs. In addition they act as auxiliary in three types of sentences:

- What do you want from me? (interrogative)
- The Indian team did not perform well in the last Test-Series against Australia. (negative)
- I do like mangoes. (emphatic)

Further, in the list given above the last two forms in categories perfective, Be and Do, are non-finite forms. Perfective *has* no past participle form whereas Be has eight forms, an additional form each in present and past forms. Because of this complexity in the functioning of auxiliary verbs, some grammarians call them Anomalous Finites.

Let us now see how morphemes change the meaning of the other three main classes of words, namely, noun, adjective and adverb. A few examples are given below to show these changes.

(a) From noun to adjective

Verb	*Dependent Morpheme*	*Adjective*
child	-ish	childish
fool	-ish	foolish
beauty	-ful	beautiful
need	-ful	needful
tradition	-al	traditional
season	-al	seasonal
worth	-y	worthy
greed	-y	greedy

(b) From verb to noun

Verb	*Dependent Morpheme*	*Noun*
reduce	-tion	reduction
examine	-tion	examination
pay	-ment	payment
fulfil	-ment	fulfillment
grow	-th	growth
hate	-red	hatred
injure	-y	injury
mix	-ture	mixture

(c) From adjective to noun

Adjective	*Dependent Morpheme*	*Noun*
good	-ness	goodness
high	-t	height
clear	-ity	clarity
sane	-ity	sanity
wide	-th	width
warm	-th	warmth
false	-hood	falsehood

(d) From adjective to adverb

Adjective	*Dependent Morpheme*	*Adverb*
quick	-ly	quickly
soft	-ly	softly
clear	-ly	clearly
clever	-ly	cleverly
gentle	-ly	gently
anger	-ly	angrily
early	-er	earlier
late	-er	later

Note: A large number of adjectives can be converted into adverbs by the addition of -ly. In all the examples given above, a morpheme has been added at the end of the word. Such a morpheme is called *suffix*. The dependent morpheme which is added in the beginning of the word is called a *prefix*. A few examples are given below for illustration.

Word	*Prefix*	*Changed Form*
proper	im-	improper
legal	ii-	illegal
stabilise	de-	destabilise
appropriate	in-	inappropriate
finite	non-	nonfinite
responsible	ir-	irresponsible
allow	dis-	disallow
kind	un-	unkind
understand	mis-	misunderstand

Certain morphemes are neither prefixes nor suffixes. The change that they cause is internal, sometimes completely changing the base itself. A few examples follow:

Word	*Morpheme*	*Changed Form*
Thesis	Plural	Theses
Man	Plural	Men
Woman	Plural	Women
Go	Past	Went
Stand	Past	Stood
Eat	Past	Ate

Word

In the chapter on Style, words have been discussed from the usage point of view. Here we shall look at them as a grammatical unit.

We have noted earlier that a free morpheme can occur independently in a sentence. That is why it enjoys the status of a word, which is also defined as 'a minimum free form'. It consists of two or more letters of the alphabet, arranged in a meaningful sequence with space on either side. There are however three single-letter words, namely, A, I and 0.

A word is the basic unit of meaning; hence it has a sentence potential. In certain circumstances we may utter single-word sentences such as 'Today' 'Definitely', 'Move', etc.

Every word refers to or denotes something. But all words are not of a similar nature. Certain words create a clear image in our mind, e.g., *house, boy, computer*. Such words have a greater potential of occurring in isolation as sentence. Then there are words which create a hazy image of the meaning they convey, e.g., *progress, democracy, excellence, honesty.* Words of this type require a specific context of situation for communication of meaning. There are some words which do not form any image, e.g., *to, the, if.* These words cannot occur independently as a sentence. They convey meaning only by virtue of the position they occupy in the structure of a sentence.

Words may be divided into the following three categories in terms of their structure:

- Simple
- Compound
- Complex

A simple word (also called the first form, stem, or base) consists of one free morpheme, e.g., *write, speak, play, think, eat.*

A compound word consists of two or more free morphemes, e.g. *gentlemen, landlady, whatsoever, bathroom, breakfast, football sweetheart, teaspoon, moonlight, go-as-you-please.*

A complex word consists of two or morphemes, out of which, at least one is dependent as shown in the following examples.

Word	*Morphemes*	*Structure*
assignment	assign + ment	base + suffix
gentlemanliness	gentle + man + li + ness	base + base + suffix + suffix
dehospitalisation	de + hospital + ise + ation	prefix + base + suffix + suffix

Another way of looking at words is in terms of their function. On this basis the words have traditionally been divided into the following well-known classes: *noun, adjective, verb, adverb, pronoun, article, preposition, conjunction and interjection*. In general, the first five classes change their forms according to the function they perform and the meaning they convey and hence are called *variable words*. The last four do not change their form in similar situations and hence they are termed as *invariable words*. We would not go into further details such as characteristics and functions of various classes of words, 'Part of speech' or 'word classes' finds a place in almost all grammar syllabuses. And so it can be assumed that the readers are familiar with these aspects of words.

Phrase

A phrase is a unit higher than a word. It consists of a group of words which are closely knit together grammatically and function as a block in the structure of a sentence. In each phrase there is a main word called head; other constituent words govern, modify or qualify the head. There are however, many sentences which have a single-word phrase. In the sentence 'Man is a social animal' *man* is a free morpheme, a word as well as a phrase. Same is the case with *is*. The third part of the sentence, 'a social animal' is a phrase consisting of three words. In grammatical hierarchy, by definition a sentence consists of one or more than one phrase; a phrase consists of one or more than one word; and a word has one or more than one morpheme. So if a person says yes' in reply to a question, 'Are you going home?' *yes* is conceptually a morpheme, a word, a phrase and a sentence at the same time. The discussion on clause and sentence given later would further clarify these concepts. Here, let us look at the phrase more closely.

There are four types of phrase in English:

- Nominal Phrase (NP)
- Verbal Phrase (VP)
- Prepositional Phrase (Prep P)
- Adverbial Phrase (Adv P)

Two examples of each are given below:

Phrase	*Type*	*Head Word*
(i) My neighbour next door	NP	NEIGHBOUR
(ii) Hari's brother	NP	BROTHER

(Continued)

(Continued)

(iii) has been written	VP	WRITTEN
(iv) must have been done	VP	DONE
(v) in the office	Prep P	OFFICE
(vi) at the desk	Prep P	DESK
(vii) very slowly	Adv P	SLOWLY
(viii) how often	Adv P	OFTEN

In (i)'neighbour' is modified by 'my' and qualified by 'next door'. In (ii), (iii), (iv) and (viii) the head words are modified by word(s) preceding them. In (v) and (vi) the head words are governed and modified by prepositions 'in' and 'at' and by article 'the' respectively. Now let us examine the patterning of each type of phrase one by one.

Nominal Phrase

NP occurs as a subject, object or complement in a sentence:

- *All the projects* were completed in time. (Subject)
- Hari published *four research papers* last year. (object)
- All agree that Ritik is *a good player.* (complement)

A pronoun functions like a noun and so an NP may consist of a pronoun as well:

- *He* has returned the book to the library. (subject)
- Salim never permits *her* to go out at night all by herself. (object)
- The pleasure is entirely *mine*. (complement)

Verbal Phrase

A VP is the verbal element in a sentence. It expresses 'action' or 'being' in a sentence:

- Dheer *pushed* the ball into the goal with amazing speed.
- Within minutes Mathai *was* fast asleep.

If a VP has a finite form of a verb in it, it is called a finite Verbal Phrase (FVP). If not, it is termed as a Non-Finite Verbal Phrase (N-F VP). Usually an FVP occurs in a statement after the subject and before the object/complement, if any:

The manager has called a meeting to discuss the issue.

The arrangement of the constituents of a FVP is changed in certain types of interrogative and negative sentences:

- *Has* the manager *called* a meeting to discuss the issue?
- The manager *has* not *called* a meeting to discuss the issue.

The structural position of N-FVP is not fixed in a sentence.
Having gone there I had no option but to join the party.

Prepositional Phrase

A Prep P consists of a preposition and a nominal element (noun or pronoun) which is governed by it:

- in the field
- on the topic
- through the tunnel
- over a cup of tea
- from her
- with me

To identify a Prep P care has to be taken to see that words which look like prepositions also act like adverbial particles. It is essential to do so because some prepositions act like adverbials in certain constructions:

- worked *in*
- *over* there
- *on* time
- move *on*
- run *about*
- arrived soon *after*
- come *before*

Adverbial Phrase

An adverbial phrase (Adv P) functions like an adverb and mainly indicates manner (thus), place (there) and time (then). To the first category belong adverbs ending in -ly, most of which are formed from an adjective base, e.g. *slowly, quickly, properly, ultimately, adversely*, etc. In the second category fall words like, *here, away, out, yonder*, etc. Time indicators words such as *today, again, recently, yesterday, all night, now, daily*, etc. belong to the third category.

Most Adv P consist of a single word or two or three words and are moveable:

- Ramu was promoted as a manager *two years ago.*
- *Two years ago*, Ramu was promoted as a manager.
- Ramu was promoted *two years ago* as a manager.
- *Now* Chandra is going to join a management institute.
- Chandra is *now* going to join a management institute.
- Chandra is going to join a management institute *now*

However, a change in the position of an Adv P may alter the emphasis or the focus of communication; so the positioning of an Adv P in a sentence is determined by the nuances of meaning that a speaker -writer intends to convey.

Clause

The next unit higher in rank is clause. It has all the properties of a sentence but it does not occur independently. In other words, a clause forms part of a sentence; it is a sentence within a sentence. We shall look at sentence in some detail later. Here let us examine clause briefly. We may define it as a group of words, having a finite verbal phrase (FVP) and occurring as part of a sentence. So the number of clauses in a sentence would depend upon the number of FVP it has. Look at the following sentences.

After giving her instructions the manager asked Sheelu to leave his chamber

In this sentence there are three verbal elements, namely, *giving*, *asked*, and *to leave*. Out of these only one, 'asked' is a FVP. So the sentence is monoclausal.

Now examine the following sentence:

The principal went to the assembly and made an important announcement.

This sentence has two clauses because it has two FVP's. Likewise the following sentence has three clauses:

He *came*, he *saw*, he *conquered*.

The clauses are classified as follows on the basis of the function they perform:

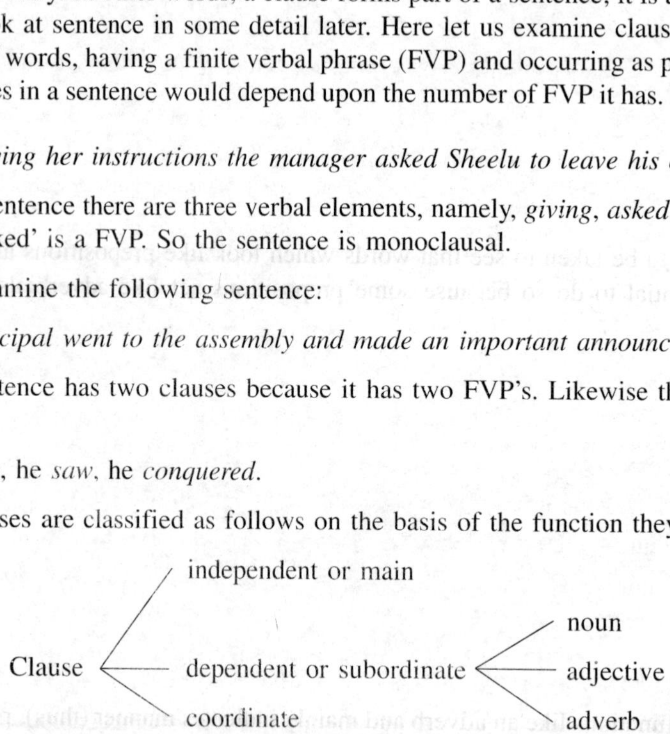

Noun Clause

It functions like a noun and occupies the same position as an NP in the structure of a sentence.

(a) Subject:

(i) *All the heroic deeds he has done* would be written in history with golden letters.

(ii) *Why the train has left before time* is a mystery.

(iii) *When the marketing Manager will resume duty* is uncertain.

(b) *Object of a transitive verb:*

(i) Tell me *what he has done to deserve such sever punishment.*

(ii) The visitor wanted to know from the technician *how the machine worked.*

(iii) Nitin explained satisfactorily *why he had to leave office suddenly.*

(c) Object of a preposition:

(i) Listen to *what the doctor is saying.*

(ii) The gathering was not impressed by *what the speaker suggested.*

(iii) You have to take interest in *what is discussed in class.*

(d) Complement

(i) His next request will be *that he should be rewarded for completing the project before time.*

(ii) My fear is *that he will not be able to solve the problem within the given time.*

(iii) In making this remark Sohan's intention was *that he should be left alone for sometime.*

(e) *Apposition to a noun or pronoun*:

(i) It is rumored that *the meeting of the Review Committee will again be postponed.*

(ii) Salma gave the explanation *that the delay in completing the assignment was owing to her ill health.*

(iii) It is rather unfortunate *that you missed the First Division by just one mark.*

Adjective Clause

An adjective clause performs the function of an adjective and so it qualifies a noun or pronoun in the main clause. A few examples are given below:

(i) This is the book *that I was looking for.*

(ii) The time *when the train would arrive* has not yet been announced.

(iii) Give me some interesting novel *which I may read during my journey to Delhi.*

(iv) The man *who won the first prize in the National Essay Competition is my* next door neighbour.

(v) Sing a song *which she likes.*

Adverb Clause

An adverb clause performs the function of an adverb and so it modifies a verb, an adjectives or adverb in the main clause. There are nine main types of adverb clause. An example of each is given below:

(i) *When you have completed this assignment*, you may leave the class. (time)

(ii) You can keep your suitcase *wherever you like*. (place)

(iii) You must go for a walk daily *so that you may keep fit*. (purpose)

(iv) *Since you have worked on this project*, you are the best person to explain it. (cause)

(v) *Unless you work hard*, you will not be able to obtain a good grade in Mathematics. (condition)

(vi) The presenter spoke so slowly *that many in the audience began to yawn with boredom.* (result)

(vii) Shyam is older *than he looks.* (comparison)

(viii) *Although the students were hungry* they marched sprightly. (concession)

(ix) *Even if it rains*, we shall come to your son's birthday party. (supposition)

Coordinate Clause

A coordinate clause is capable of occurring on its own and so its status is the same as that of the main clause. It is joined to the main clause by a coordinating conjunction. If the subject of the main clause and that of the coordinate clause is the same, it is generally not repeated as shown in the following example:

Keshu came home late last night *and quietly went to his room.*

A few examples using main types of coordiante conjunction are given below:

(i) Geet Saxena can *neither* speak properly *nor* can he write effectively. (copulative)
(ii) Sheetal is a sincere worker *but* he is rather slow (adversative)
(iii) Either Nition is very clever *or* he is too busy to behave like this (alternative)
(iv) Geeta is suffering from cold, *and* would not be able to engage the class today. (illative)

Sentence

In the chapter on Style we have discussed *sentence* briefly, in a different context. Here we shall go into details to make the discussion complete and self-contained.

When a person uses language, he does not go on speaking without a pause. After every group of a few words there is a pause. It is true that pauses occur between phrases also but if the pause is relatively longer and is preceded by a complete intonation pattern, it is indicative of the end of a sentence. So a **spoken sentence** may be defined as a segment of speech uttered with a complete intonation pattern and preceded and followed by a pause.

In writing, punctuation marks are used to indicate the boundary of a sentence. Thus we may define a **written sentence** as a word or group of words written between two end punctuation marks, namely, full stop, question mark and exclamation mark. Sometimes a colon also indicates the sentence boundary. An additional identification mark is that the first letter of the first word of a sentence is written in capitals.

The importance of pauses in speech and punctuation marks in writing can best be realised by speaking continuously without a pause for a short period of time and writing material without any punctuation mark. The speaker-writer would soon get tired and at the same time cause loss of interest in the listener-reader. Thus both physical and semantic constraints compel us to divide our linguistic communication into sentences.

By definition a sentence could thus be a word or phrase as shown below:

Ia When do we have to submit the project report?
Ib Tomorrow.
IIc Have you sent the proposal to the finance division?
IId Yes.
IIIe When did you come back from Mumbai?
IIIf Last night.
IVg How would you travel upto Delhi?
IVh By taxi.

The sentences b, d, f and h do not have a FVP and hence such sentences are sometimes called truncated or shortened sentences. Most sentences used for informal writing have a FVP as an essential constituent. But in informal situation and conversation, the use of truncated sentences is common. Such sentences make complete sense like full length sentences. The logic is that if one word would communicate the same meaning as, say, five words, there is no point in using the longer version. For illustration let us stretch the truncated sentences given above by adding a FVP.

- We have to submit it tomorrow.
- Yes, I have.
- I came last night.
- I would travel by taxi.

To sum up, sentence is the highest grammatical unit. A clause when independent attains he status of a sentence provided it occurs between two end punctuation marks. So do words and phrases if they have the contextual potential to be stretched to full length sentences by the addition of a FVP, and other phrases, if required. A full-length sentence is a group of words which contains a FVP.

Types of Sentences

Sentences can be classified

(a) according to their structure; and

(b) according to their function.

According to their structure they are classified into three categories, namely, *simple*, *compound*, and *complex*. A simple sentence consists of one independent clause. A compound sentence has two or more clauses, out of which one is the main clause and the rest are coordinate clause(s). A complex sentence contains two or more clauses, out of which at least one clause is a subordinate or dependent clause. In the discussion on clauses, a number of examples of each type have already been given.

According to their function, sentence are divided into the categories mentioned below. Two examples of each type are also given.

(i) Statements (also called Declarative or Assertive)

(a) Affirmative

- The seminar on 'Environmental Pollution" will be held at 3 p.m. today.
- Our college has won the first prize in the state level science quiz.

(b) Negative

- The meeting will not be held tomorrow owing to unavoidable circumstances.
- With this speed he will never be able to achieve the goal.

(ii) Interrogative

(a) Question-word questions

- Why has the seminar been postponed?
- How may research papers were presented at the conference?

(b) Yes/ No questions

- Has everybody submitted the project report?
- Is there any point in asking Suresh to join the discussion at this stage?

(c) Question-tag questions

- They have already left for Delhi, haven't they?
- Shyamal is going to join Info Hardware Systems, isn't he?

(iii) Imperative

(a) Command

- Keep quiet.
- Stand at ease.

(b) Request

- Please ask him to return my book tomorrow.
- Pass the salt, please.

(c) Entreaty

- May God help Nitin to accomplish this difficult task.
- Be considerate and do something for him to tide over the crisis.

(iv) Exclamatory

- How wonderful!
- What a shot!

As the examples given above show, the names of each type clearly indicate their functions.

However, a few points regarding this scheme of classification are worth mentioning.

(i) To the statement category also belong, what are termed by some grammarians as emphatic sentences, e.g. 'He does like speaking on such an occasion.'

(ii) Occasionally a statement is made to function like a question. This is done in writing by putting a question mark (instead of a full stop) at the end of the statement. In speech, such a statement is spoken with a rising tone (see Appendix A). Similarly, the question-tag question functions like an interrogative if the question tag is spoken with a rising tone.

(iii) Sometimes an interrogative sentence is used more like a powerful statement than a real question:

Is that the reason or disappointment?

It is also used to attract attention or to emphasise and/or dramatise apoint:

What are the conclusions reached?

Such questions are called *rhetorical questions.*

(iv) All requests are not imperative in form. There are several other ways of making a request. A few examples are given below:

- Do you mind returning may book tomorrow?
- Would you please return my book tomorrow?
- Return my book tomorrow, will you?

As we stated in the beginning, sentence constitutes the upper limit of grammatical analysis. But communication does not always coterminate with a sentence. It mostly goes beyond and sentences are grouped into paragraphs and paragraphs into texts by lexical and semantic links. What a paragraph is and how it is developed has been discussed in the chapter on Style. The character of a text can be best understood by viewing the highest unit of meaning that is communicated through language. **Each text is completed, self-contained and has an independent entity**. A novel, an essay, a poem, a report are some of the examples of a text.

B.2 DIRECT AND INDIRECT SPEECH

There are two ways of reporting what a person says:

(i) Hari said to me, 'The manager wants to see you tomorrow at 10 am'

(ii) Hari told me that the manager wanted to see me the next day at 10 am.

In the first sentence the exact words spoken by Hari have been quoted. This is called Direct Speech. In the second sentence the same information has been transmitted but without quoting the exact words used by Hari. This is called Indirect Speech. A number of changes have been made in converting the Direct Speech into Indirect Speech:

- The comma after 'me' and the quotation mark have been removed.
- A conjunction, 'that' has been used to connect the main clause with the subordinate clause.
- The present tense of the verb 'wants' has been changed to past tense wanted.
- 'You' in the subordinate clause has been changed to 'me'.
- 'Tomorrow' has been replaced by 'the next day'.

Indirect speech is used when we have to tell somebody else what we heard and the context of situation does not require the exact reproduction of words we heard. The main clause is usually followed by one clause or two or more clauses in a sentence. The verb in the main clause is called *reporting verb* and the verb(s) in other clause(s) is called reported verb(s). The tense of the reporting verb determines the tense of the reported verb. The changes are made in accordance with the rules of sequence of tenses. If the tense of the reporting verb is present or future, the tense of the reported verb does not change:

(i) • Hari says to Sita, 'I have not borrowed your book.'
- Hari tells Sita that he has not borrowed her book.

(ii) • Hari will again say to Sita, 'It is better to download the material from the computer.'
- Hari will again advise Sita that it is better to download the material from the computer.'

If the tense of the reporting verb is past, the tense of the reported verb changes as follows:

(i) *From simple present to simple past.*

- Som said to his host, 'I take breakfast at 8 a.m'.
- Som told his host that he took his breakfast at 8 am.

(ii) *From present continuous to past continuous.*

- Nitin said to Mini, 'I am reading a very informative book on yoga'.
- Nitin told Mini that he was reading a very informative book on yoga.

(iii) *From present perfect to past perfect*

- Som said to Simi, 'I have passed on you message to Ramu'.
- Som told Simi that he had passed on her message to Ramu.

(iv) *From present perfect continuous to past perfect continuous.*

- Simi said to her husband, 'Bunty has been playing tennis since 5 p.m'.
- Simi told her husband that Bunty had been playing tennis since 5 p.m.

(v) *From simple past to past perfect.*

- Neel said to Sam, 'Ramu went home without taking leave'.
- Neel informed Sam that Ramu had gone home without taking leave.

(vi) *From past continuous to past perfect continuous.*

- Nahar said to his mother, 'Monty was sleeping in the class'
- Nahar told his mother that Monty had been sleeping in the class.

(vii) *In past perfect and past perfect continuous tenses no change is made.*

- Som said to Shyam, 'Hanif had presented his case very effectively'.
- Som informed Shyam that Hanif had presented his case very effectively.
- Abdul told John that Som had been going to Maths class regularly.

(viii) *No change in the tense of the reported verb takes place if a scientific fact or a universal truth is stated.*

- The teacher said, 'Reproduction is a natural process'.
- The teacher remarked that reproduction is a natural process.
- Renu said, 'Necessity is the mother of invention'.
- Renu said that necessity is the mother of invention.

The changes in the pronoun are made, keeping in mind who is speaking to whom and the noun to which the pronoun refers to. An example is given below:

- Nitin said to Sunita, 'Your research proposal has been accepted'.
- Nitin told Sunita that her research proposal had been accepted.
- Nitin said to Sunita, 'My research proposal has been accepted'.
- Nitin told Sunita that his research proposal had been accepted.

Certain indicators of *direction*, *time* and *place* are also changed in indirect speech. A few examples are given as follows.

Direct Speech	*Indirect Speech*
This	That
These	Those
Here	There
Now	Then
Ago	Before
Today	That day
Yesterday	The day before
Tomorrow	The next day
Last night	The night before
Last week, month, year, etc.	The previous week, month, year, etc.
Next week, month, year, etc.	The following week, month, year, etc.

What we have discussed so far applies mainly to one type of sentence, namely, statement. Let us now look at the changes that take place in other types of sentences.

Interrogative Sentences

(i) When a question-word question is reported, the subordinate clause is preceded by words such as *asked, enquired,* etc. and the interrogative form is changed into a statement:

- The teacher said to Rama, 'When are you going to submit the project report?'
- The teacher asked Rama when he was going to submit the project report. (Indirect)
- The officer said to me, 'Where do you live?'
- The office asked me where I lived. (Indirect)

(ii) In reporting a Yes/No question the clauses are connected by *whether* or *if* and the question form is changed into a statement form.

- The teacher said to Hari, 'Is your younger brother also a student of this college?'
- The teacher asked Hari whether his younger brother also was a student of that college. (indirect)

Imperative Sentences

The reporting verb is replaced by an appropriate verb such as *ordered, requested, asked, warned, urged, advised,* etc. and the imperative form is changed into infinite form:

- The officer said to cadets, 'Stand at ease.'
- The officer ordered the cadets to stand at ease. (Indirect)
- Nitin said to me, 'Pass the sugar pot, please'

- Nitin requested me to pass the sugar pot. (indirect)
- The speaker said to the audience, 'Be quiet and listen to what I am going to say now.'
- The speaker urged the audience to be quiet and to listen to what he was going to say then. (indirect)

Exclamatory Sentences

In reporting such sentences the reporting verb is replaced by a verb that reflects the strong feeling or emotion expressed in the exclamation. The mark of exclamation is removed and phrases such as *with grief, with regret with joy, with wonder*, etc. are used in indirect speech. Two examples are given below.

(i) They shouted, 'Hurrah! India has won the match!'

- They exclaimed with joy that India had won the match. (Indirect)

(ii) Sita said, 'I have lost everything!'

- Sita sadly stated that she had lost everything. (Indirect).

B.3 SEQUENCE OF TENSES

We have already given some rules of sequence of tenses while discussing the change of Direct into Indirect Speech. But there are a few more rules which one needs to know in this context:

(i) When the verb in the main clause is in the present or future tense, the verb in the subordinate adverbial clause of purpose is always in the present tense.

- Shyamal eats plenty of green vegetables and fresh fruit so that he may keep good health.
- Arpit will teach Mathematics to Shilpa so that she may score more marks in the Annual Examination.

(ii) If the verb in the main clause is in the past tense and the subordinate clause begins with 'than', then the tense of the latter would depend upon the meaning intended to be conveyed.

- He valued his friendship with Govind more than he values mine.
- Govind worked longer than Hari does.
- I used to meet him more frequently than I did during last month.
- Som's attitude towards Sam was more positive than it was towards me.

(iii) If the subordinate clause is introduced by *as if* or *as though*, it is in the past tense.

- Hamif behaved in the party as if he was drunk.
- Sohan reacted violently to the remarks of Sally as though somebody had beaten him.

(iv) A subordinate clause beginning with lest always takes *should* in its verbal phrase, whatever be the tense of the verb in the main clause.

- Get lost lest the boss should come.
- Rachit spoke in whispers lest Shimpi should be disturbed.
- I shall go now lest I should be misunderstood.

B.4 ACTIVE AND PASSIVE VOICE

Active voice is used when the focus is on the doer or the agent, i.e. the subject. In the passive voice the thing acted upon is focused and the agent is relegated to a secondary place or not mentioned at all.

- Her bag was stolen from the bus.
- The students were given intense training in spoken English.

In the above sentences the agents, that is, the person who stole the bag and the person who imparted the training are not mentioned. There are certain fields of activity or knowledge in which 'what is done' is more important than 'who does it', e.g., science and management. So in the discourses relating to these fields there is a preponderance of passive constructions:

- Quasi-stars *were discovered* in 1963 as a result of an effort to overcome the shortcomings of radio telescopes.
- In the digital computers the numbers to be manipulated are represented by sequences of light which *are first recorded* in suitable code and then converted into positive and negative impulses.
- The Dearness Allowance of all employees *was raised* from 90 per cent to 95 per cent with effect from 16 December 2007.
- The proposal to acquire Sonaar Communications Limited *would be taken up* in the next meeting of the Board of Directors.

There are, however, situations in which the agent is mentioned in the passive voice also. A few examples are given below:

(i) • Rohit has composed this interesting poem.
  • This interesting poem has been composed by Rohit. (Passive)

(ii) • Rohtas received me with utmost courtesy.
  • I was received by Rohtas with utmost courtesy. (Passive)

(iii) • Ali will return my Mathematics book tomorrow.
  • My Mathematics book will be returned by Ali tomorrow. (Passive)

(iv) • The teacher has not yet evaluated the answer books.
  • The answer books have not yet been evaluated by the teacher. (Passive)

When a sentence in active voice is changed into passive voice, two important changes take place:

(a) The object is shifted to the position of the subject and the subject to the position of an object and is governed by the preposition *by*.
(b) Only sentences having a transitive verb, which can take object, can be transformed into passive as shown above. The most crucial change takes place in the verbal phrase as shown below:

Tense	*Active*	*Passive*
• Simple present singular	gives	is given
• Simple present plural	give	are given
• Present continuous	is/are giving	is/are being given
• Present perfect	has/have given	has/have been given
• Simple past	gave	was/were given
• Past continuous	was/were giving	was/were being given
• Past perfect	had given	had been given
• Simple future	will give	will be given
• Future continuous	will be giving	will be being given
• Future perfect	will have given	will have been given

INDEX